Tears, Fire, and Blood

Tears, Fire, and Blood

The United States and the Decolonization of Africa

JAMES H. MERIWETHER

The University of North Carolina Press Chapel Hill

Set in Charis by Westchester Publishing Services
Manufactured in the United States of America

The University of North Carolina Press has been a member of the Green Press Initiative since 2003.

Library of Congress Cataloging-in-Publication Data
Names: Meriwether, James Hunter, 1963– author.
Title: Tears, fire, and blood : the United States and the decolonization of Africa / James H. Meriwether.
Description: Chapel Hill : University of North Carolina Press, [2021] | Includes bibliographical references and index.
Identifiers: LCCN 2020056897 | ISBN 9781469664217 (cloth) | ISBN 9781469664224 (paperback) | ISBN 9781469664231 (ebook)
Subjects: LCSH: Decolonization—Africa—History—20th century. | United States—Foreign relations—Africa. | Africa—Foreign relations—United States.
Classification: LCC DT30.5 .M4553 2021 | DDC 327.730609045—dc23
LC record available at https://lccn.loc.gov/2020056897

For

H

Contents

Maps

Acknowledgments

The opportunity to thank those who have made one's work possible is a true joy, and in this case the support of friends and colleagues deserves profound appreciation. I have been enriched by these relationships and can only hope that my gratitude has been expressed somewhat adequately along the way.

There is an essential and proper starting point: Chuck Grench, that most wonderful of editors. Hearing the news that Chuck was closing the chapter on his time at the University of North Carolina (UNC) Press, retiring, I suspected he did not fully understand the importance of his handwritten note in my office, the one that kept me on task even when the demands of building a new university occupied so much time. Yet as he did since the beginning, Chuck shepherded this manuscript along until it was ready to hand off. I cannot thank him enough for the encouragement he never failed to provide and the understated grace with which he did so. I am also enormously grateful to Debbie Gershenowitz, Dylan White, and the rest of the good people at UNC Press who made the transition seamless.

I do not believe any person could ask for a more thoughtful and generous set of readers than Tim Borstelmann and Nicholas Grant. From surgeons to athletes to academics, there are those who transcend, and I have been deeply fortunate that these two shared part of themselves. The same sentiment holds true for a set of colleagues who have gone out of their way to read, discuss, or encourage parts of the manuscript. I owe all of them deep gratitude, in particular Carol Anderson, Abou Bamba, Andy DeRoche, Phil Muehlenbeck, and Bill Worger, as well as Nema Blyden, Mary Dudziak, Frank Gerits, Jason Parker, Joe Parrott, Brenda Gayle Plummer, Robert Trent Vinson, Ron Williams, and Carl Watts. Putting aside their own work to elevate others, these colleagues embody the spirit that infuses our profession. Any errors are mine alone. Similar thanks go to two others who raised crucial questions: Jim Campbell and Fred Logevall. I've also been fortunate to have shared time with a set of academic and personal lodestars, and thank particularly Jeanne Harrie, who, at a pivotal moment, answered my call yet again, and Bruce Schulman, who will always deserve my gratitude. The list of debts grows long and extends to the archivists too numerous to mention, and I have no doubt I will discover—and deeply regret—the person I have failed to mention.

I have been incredibly fortunate to have been able to twice benefit from the Fulbright Foreign Scholarship Board and spend a year teaching and researching at the University of Zimbabwe and then another year at the University of Nairobi. The people who opened their doors and hearts are too extensive to list, but particular thanks go to Ken Manungo, Mary Mwiandi, and Ephraim Wahome. I have also benefited from sharing parts of this work at the German Historical Institute in Washington and at the American Political History Conference at Clare College.

Several years ago I came to California State University Channel Islands to help build the newest campus of the nation's largest public university system. While there has been a lot of heavy lifting, the task has been made joyful by sharing it with colleagues who inspire me to never set down my tools: Frank Barajas, Rainer Buschmann, Marie Francois, Nian-Sheng Huang, Hanni Jalil, Robin Mitchell, Lance Nolde, Julia Ornelas-Higdon, and Jackie Reynoso, along with colleagues from across the hall and across the campus. I also thank the university for a sabbatical that helped advance the project.

I am blessed with a wonderful extended family, all of whom have lifted me up with their good cheer and encouragement. Each deserves a shout-out, but one particularly goes to my sister Peggy, who has taken on the unrequited task of clarifying thoughts, muddy prose, and garbled syntax with an unrivaled generosity and gentleness. All who read further should thank her for smoothing the road ahead; any remaining bumps are mine. Many thanks to my parents—Mom, no longer with us physically but in enduring spirit, and Dad, here in both—and the retreat they provided when the manuscript needed particular attention. Finally, and most importantly, is my appreciation for those nearest and dearest for their unyielding love and support throughout.

Tears, Fire, and Blood

Introduction

Ours is a continent in revolution against oppression. . . . Our continent has been carved up by the great powers; alien governments have been forced upon the African people by military conquest and by economic domination; strivings for nationhood and national dignity have been beaten down by force. . . . [But now] our people everywhere from north to south of the continent are reclaiming their land, their right to participate in government, their dignity as men, their nationhood. Thus, in the turmoil of revolution, the basis for peace and brotherhood in Africa is being restored by the resurrection of national sovereignty and independence, of equality and the dignity of man.

—Albert Lutuli, Nobel lecture, 1961

Everything that makes man's lives worthwhile—family, work, education, a place to rear one's children and a place to rest one's head—all this depends on the decisions of government; all can be swept away by a government which does not heed the demands of its people, and I mean all of its people. Therefore, the essential humanity of man can be protected and preserved only where the government must answer—not just to the wealthy; not just to those of a particular religion, not just to those of a particular race; but to all of the people.

—Robert F. Kennedy, Day of Affirmation Address, June 1966

Fighting for survival as the Axis powers threatened its island home and far-flung empire, Great Britain, the world's leading colonial power, desperately recruited manpower from its African colonies. Need was everywhere in this world war, and the Europeans sent men who joined the King's African Rifles to stop the Japanese advance in Asia. Tramping through war zones thousands of miles from their homes, these Africans served as vital forces against the spread of totalitarianism. When their service ended, heroic returning soldiers, having fought in faraway lands in the name of freedom and democracy, brought with them newfound hope of winning greater freedoms in their homeland.

Onyanga, a veteran who had been born as the Scramble for Africa established the British East Africa protectorate, returned to Kenya to find that, despite his service in the war, opportunities for Africans remained severely limited. The reality was mirrored elsewhere throughout the continent; little seemed to have changed for African veterans or their families. While he struggled to support his family, his eldest son applied to several universities in the United States with the encouragement and financial support of two American women working in Kenya. Access to a liberal arts education in Kenya was not open to African students, no matter how strong their credentials. In a curious turn, one of America's own former overseas possessions, annexed after local ruler Queen Liliuokalani was deposed, had recently been admitted as the fiftieth state. It accepted the young Kenyan—its first African student—at its flagship university. Traveling over ten thousand miles to the University of Hawai'i, he met a fellow student, married her, and fathered a child. Soon thereafter, he left his wife and son behind for graduate studies at Harvard and then returned alone to Kenya, which in his absence had gained independence. He threw himself into the task of building the nation as a government economist.[1]

As his American son grew up, he too became inspired by the fight against white supremacy in Africa, becoming politically active in the anti-apartheid movement while at university. He later recalled, "As the months passed and I found myself drawn into a larger role—contacting representatives of the African National Congress to speak on campus, drafting letters to the faculty . . . arguing strategy—I noticed that people had begun to listen to my opinions. It was a discovery that made me hungry for words. Not words to hide behind but words that carry a message, support an idea."[2] The young man scraped together the money to fly to Kenya in search of family and identity, though he was too late to see his father or grandfather, both of whom lived to witness the independence of their country but died before the scion's visit.

Two decades later, the American son returned again, this time aboard Air Force One as president of the United States and leader of the most powerful nation in the world. Proclaiming himself a Kenyan American, Barack Obama stood before thousands, speaking of his family history and the "arch of progress" in the story "from foreign rule to independence." He reflected on the need for all people to understand where they come from, but counseled, "We also have to remember why these lessons are important. We know a history so that we can learn from it."[3]

Three generations of a family: a grandfather born into a colonized Africa, a father nation-building in a decolonizing continent, a son arriving as president of the United States. In less than three generations, Kenya moved from Onyanga Obama fighting in world wars for Europeans who had taken Africa to further white hegemony to President Barack Obama walking the same ground on a liberated continent. This family saga is now a familiar one, but the story of the important intertwining of the United States and Africa during this remarkable period is not. The pages that follow examine that relationship in the era of decolonization, when a continent cast off European rule during the extraordinary half century from Haile Selassie's triumphant return to Addis Ababa in May 1941, to Namibia's securement of independence in March 1990 and the last vestige of white minority rule crumbling with the collapse of apartheid in South Africa and Nelson Mandela's election as president in 1994.

"Choose between Portugal and South Africa . . . and the Rest of Africa"

When Onyanga Obama returned to Kenya from the fighting in Asia, he arrived on a continent almost entirely under European colonial rule. From the rubble of the failed League of Nations and World War II, the group of fifty-one countries that joined to form a new United Nations had only four members able to enter as independent states in Africa: Egypt, Ethiopia, Liberia, and South Africa. During the next half century, almost fifty African nations gained independence, creating a defining chapter in the ongoing struggle to reverse a half millennium of expanding white supremacy, colonial rule, and exploitation. While the nineteenth century saw the imperial appropriation of vast chunks of the world, the twentieth century saw the people taking back power and control.[4] These African nations took their place among the pantheon of independent states, joining others around the world to cast off colonial rule in the most significant political and social movement of modern history.

During this transformational era, Africa stood at the crossroads of many defining features of the twentieth century: colonization and decolonization, white supremacy and the global Black freedom struggle, race and identity, the Cold War, economic exploitation and development, elemental questions of human rights. Africa brought together grassroots, transnational, multiethnic movements, perhaps most notably the worldwide anti-apartheid movement. The emergence of a liberated Third World and the rise of the Global South created enduring changes in world affairs that extend beyond the often more focused on rival of the time, the Cold War.[5] Decolonization fundamentally reshaped the world in which we live and the lives of the majority of the world's population.

As colonial empires in Africa were challenged and confronted collapse, the United States found itself pulled toward diametrically opposite poles: waxing African anticolonial nationalists seeking majority rule and support for independence, and European anticommunist allies wanting to maintain their continuing (white) rule and waning control. This was a different bipolarity than the commonly understood postwar United States–Soviet Union, East–West bipolarity. This rival bipolar world, between white rule and majority rule, also demanded engagement and decisions that affected the lives of millions.

Early on, arguments in Washington that there should be no "premature independence" for African nations provided a guiding approach, reflecting two prevalent postwar views in the nation's capital: the Cold War–enhanced standpoint that European allies were the priority, and the racially based opinion that Africans were not "ready" to run their own nations. On Eleanor Roosevelt's program *Prospects of Mankind*, nationalist leader and future president of Tanzania Julius Nyerere offered his perspective on the matter during a 1960 episode revealingly titled "Africa: Revolution in Haste": "If you come into my house and steal my jacket, don't then ask me whether I am ready for my jacket. The jacket was mine and you had no right at all to steal it from me. . . . You have no right at all to ask me whether I was ready for my jacket." Nyerere would point out elsewhere that the signers of the U.S. Constitution "were the same average age as we—and [now they] say we are too young!"[6]

Yet in Washington, views of African independence all too often were informed by the deep-seated racial prejudices of officials who had grown up in a Jim Crow America. In 1950, American consul Donald Lamm, a career Foreign Service Officer posted in Mozambique, wrote to George McGhee, the assistant secretary of state for Near Eastern, South Asian, and African affairs, to assure McGhee that "the native population does not present any problem from a political point of view." Lamm provided his reasoning: with no political organizing and widespread illiteracy and censorship, the people "accept the complete and autocratic rule of the white minority as the natural order of things."[7] Soon thereafter, McGhee spoke publicly and forcefully that "immediate independence" was not the cure for all colonial problems: "The United States government has always maintained that premature independence for primitive, uneducated peoples can do them more harm than good and subject them to exploitation by indigenous leaders, unrestrained by the civil standards that come with widespread education, that can be just as ruthless as that of aliens."[8]

A potent mix of Cold War anticommunism and racial prejudices fueled arguments that Africans were not "ready" and that the result would harm "national security." McGhee's successor, Henry Byroade, declared that "premature independence can be dangerous, retrogressive, and destructive." Byroade defended slow evolution toward independence over immediate change. Surveying reasons why "premature independence" served neither the interests of the West nor those of colonized peoples themselves, Byroade justified the continuing colonial presence in Africa, declaring that "serious observers of the African scene agree that the European governments are making substantial contributions to the evolution of these peoples."[9]

"The natural order of things," "primitive, uneducated peoples," "substantial contributions to the evolution of these peoples," and so it went, the racialized paternalism extending to the highest officials. Hailed as the father of a new African policy that called for greater attention to the continent, Vice President Richard Nixon argued during National Security Council meetings that it was naive to hope that Africa would be democratic, so perhaps developing military strongmen would offset communist development of labor unions. Nixon shared with the room not only his skepticism that democracy could develop and flourish in Africa but also his judgment that some people in Africa had been "out of the trees" for only about fifty years. It got worse from there. Director of the Bureau of the Budget Maurice Stans, recently returned from a trip to the Belgian Congo, chimed in that many Africans "still belonged in the trees."[10]

The power of such racist thinking in Washington helped produce the tortured formulation of the "middle path" by U.S. officials. Pioneering historian Thomas Noer led the way in pointing to the middle path that officials spoke of as early as the Truman administration. The "middle path" reflected the language of the officials at the time, a chimeric path that seemingly provided a way to navigate competing desires and pressures. The approach sought to develop long-term relations with prospective majority-ruled African states via expressions of support for eventual independence while backing short-term interests and stable alliances with European partners who wanted to maintain their colonial rule.[11] Scholars continue to use the language and concept for analyzing the era, and we are overdue for addressing the premises involved, language used, and implications for policy and action in Africa.[12]

In reality, Washington typically backed white minority rule, for there was no actual "middle" path. With limited exceptions, Washington supported its European allies; and as happened elsewhere around the world, Washington generally chose a go-slow approach and the known comfort of the status quo, which reinforced continuing white supremacy in Africa. In the day to day assessing and reassessing of American policy on decolonization in Africa, those in Washington felt greatest concern for and comfort in preserving the strength and control of its Cold War European allies and acted accordingly, even as some sought stronger support for democratic self-determination. In many ways, this choice was reflected domestically by those resistant to unwinding pervasive patterns of white control and racial inequities in America.

As the Cold War progressed, national security concerns, economic interests, and deep-rooted prejudices repeatedly outweighed historical and ideological impulses for promoting freedom and majority rule throughout Africa. As issues of African independence became more prominent in the post–World War II landscape, most Americans—and particularly those in Washington—were much more concerned with stopping communism and winning the Cold War. Existential national security seemed at stake. The choice not to press harder for swift decolonization may have been seen as necessary and pragmatic, a strategy to minimize disruptions while encouraging gradual change; the effect, though, regularly countenanced conditions that impeded the path to racial equality and majority rule.

Even during the Kennedy administration, when the United States seemed more attuned to African anticolonial nationalism, historian and presidential adviser Arthur Schlesinger Jr. warned that Africans wanted the United States to "choose between Portugal and South Africa, on the one hand, and the rest of Africa, on the other." Schlesinger articulated with eloquence that history and justice were on the side of the Africans, then unequivocally advised that the United States must "evade that choice."[13] Schlesinger's advice spoke to the American dilemma, and revealed that at heart, Washington would evade doing all it could to end white supremacy in Africa, mirroring the same predispositions in America.

Only occasionally and with much effort did Washington move toward any illusive middle, let alone the pole of concrete support for African independence. Even into the 1980s, with the world turned against the last holdout of white supremacy in Africa, President Ronald Reagan vetoed comprehensive economic sanctions against South Africa. Looking at the long arc of this particular half century, the general pattern for Washington of the fears of undoing the status quo in a dynamic Cold War world and the security of white allies in control led to choices that prolonged decolonization and even caused some of those struggling for freedom to turn toward communist bloc nations they saw as more supportive. African nationalists inevitably sought more than anticolonialism in words; from their perspective, there was no "middle path" and no "neutral" pole: they would push white rule out of Africa, with or without the United States on their side.

Indeed, Africans typically felt less concern about joining or validating a side in the Cold War than with ending colonialism and gaining meaningful independence. Self-determination and self-rule, economic development and combating poverty, racial equality and equity: these were paramount issues. Cold War geopolitical rivalries, like continental politics, regional tensions, and internal disputes, were a complicating element to navigate in pursuit of the larger objective. For people in Africa and the rest of the colonized world, there was clarity in this intertwined relationship: the primary process, decolonization, being influenced by an outside, secondary element, the Cold War.

In contrast, the Cold War was the main event for most Americans. The tangled relationship of other global issues, such as decolonization, were to be dealt with as part of that construct, reflecting other asymmetries in the relationship across the Atlantic, from economic wealth to political power. Yet in important ways in the United States—and the Soviet Union—decolonization brought questions as to how newly independent nations would fit into their competing visions for humankind. Would these areas join one bloc or the other? Would they follow a liberal capitalist path or a Marxist socialist one? The answers were significant in toting up numbers and resources for one side or the other in the Cold War. They also held deeper meaning, in the words of historian Robert McMahon, "about the proper path toward development and modernity—indeed, about the very direction of history." A decolonizing world could validate one of those directions.[14]

"What Matters More Than . . . All Other Votes"

As scholars increasingly look to the "global Cold War" as more than a United States–Soviet Union, East–West binary, they have started to recast the "periphery" as fundamental to our understanding.[15] The use of the term "periphery" itself, of course, reflects an essential issue: a Eurocentric "core" worldview and framing that dominated the views and opinions of most U.S. and European officials of the era, and much of the writing on twentieth-century Western history. Much like the Mercator projection map, the framing arrogates for the Global North a larger projection, diminishing alternative networks of connections among countries in the world. Nevertheless, it seems a truism that for many during this era, Africa was not a high priority. For most Americans, be it the broad general public or highly placed government officials, residing in small town Main Street or 1600 Pennsylvania Avenue, there was a tendency to think of Africa as remote and its issues as a secondary concern. Americans perceived twentieth-century Africa's role as peripheral—economically, politically, culturally—and U.S. officials generally held a Eurocentric orientation that influenced the shape of their engagement with the African continent and its peoples.

The book that follows does not try to upend this characterization. Rather, it explores the ways in which America's perceptions and prioritizations shaped its policies and actions at the time. By defining Africa as less important, upholding national ideals there seemed less necessary. Support for the democratic principle of one person, one vote, could be more easily argued away in a Third World setting than when a First World imperative was at stake. Yet as Lyndon Johnson could attest, lower priority does not necessarily equate to less importance; events on the "periphery" in places like Vietnam can and do assert their significance in unanticipated ways.

Such places often took center stage when hot spots flared, be it Vietnam in Southeast Asia or the Congo in Africa, and scholars tend to focus on those events. Partially as a consequence, our understanding of enduring relationships and engagement remains underdeveloped, and Africa remains marginalized in work done to internationalize twentieth-century and Cold War history. The circular result, of course, is that we are less aware of that historical engagement.[16] Other striking international episodes and currents push into the background explorations of the unfolding relationship between America and Africa. Even scholars engaged with the Africa-U.S. relationship sometimes take a reticent position, noting that relations with Africa were on a back burner, or some similar imagery.[17] This tendency helps perpetuate myths of "no interest" as well as an emphasis on crisis, and the broader attention drawn by crisis in turn builds on insidious notions of Africa as a "crisis" continent riddled with problems. We are overdue addressing more comprehensively the relationship between the United States and Africa, filling in ellipses of understanding.

Fifty African nations gained independence in fifty years, a revolution covering one-fifth of the world's land, with reverberations back to governments and societies of Europe and America. Yet the engagement of the United States with that story remains generally unknown. These events certainly are subsumed in Western historical memories of the contemporaneous Cold War. But there were officials in Washington and people across America deeply engaged with decolonization. The reality was a world in which people and events continually pushed and prodded for a response, compelled action or often reaction, on the part of officials. And the relationship across the Atlantic held great meaning throughout.

For centuries, the United States has pushed itself into Africa. The devastating effects of the enslavement and forced removal of millions of Africans to become the builders of societies in the New World can never be overestimated. Early connections to the nineteenth-century exploration and colonization of the continent existed from at least the embarkation of Henry Morton Stanley, whose initial foray into Africa was funded by the *New York Herald*. The United States soon thereafter sent observers to the Berlin Conference and became the first country to recognize King Leopold II's rapacious sovereignty over the Congo.

In superficial ways, the United States' role during the years of colonization appears to have defined the U.S. posture toward the continent for ensuing generations: observing European powers acting as they would and following their lead. Yet the United States did not play such a passive role, particularly as a colonized Africa moved toward independence after World War II. Emerging from the war as the world's most powerful and influential nation, the ways that the United States did or did not engage Africa had meaning for the people living there. No country had more power—politically, economically, militarily, arguably even morally—to help or hinder change. As South African foreign minister Eric Louw highlighted to the U.S. ambassador in 1958, "I wish to be frank. A specific and strong resolution against South Africa voted for by a majority of nations in [the] U.N. does not matter so much as one might expect. What matters more than . . . all other votes put together is [the position] of [the] U.S. in view of its predominant position of leadership in [the] Western world."[18]

As the world's leading power during the era of decolonization and as the undisputed post–World War II leader of the Western alliance, the United States had the potential to be a part of virtually any aspect of the postwar world. How much support would Africans see from the ostensible leader of the free world in their pursuit of freedom from colonial and white minority rule? It could pursue strongly anticolonial policies and could even promote internationalizing processes of decolonization through the UN. Or it could support the colonial powers and continued white rule, forgoing anticolonial positions for other priorities. Washington's actions would influence the pace, path, and priority of decolonization in Africa.

Importantly, influences in America's relationship with Africa flowed in both directions. Sometimes in subtly nuanced ways and other times in thunderous claps, for five hundred years the ties between North America and Africa have shaped societies in both. A decolonizing Africa helped propel the Black freedom struggle in the United States and around the world, thereby advancing discussion of fundamental human rights. It forced the nation to confront the realities of diversity abroad in ways that intertwined with the fight over how to do so at home. In this manner, African liberation movements and American civil rights activists informed the thinking of key leaders. Their influence on Jimmy Carter's views, for example, affected not only his approach to civil rights but also how he chose to address Rhodesia and its play for international recognition as a white minority-dominated state. The transnational social and political connections of the global freedom struggle tried, as former ambassador to Tanzania Charles Stith notes, to push "American policy in the direction of human rights" and, in so doing, to advance "a more progressive agenda for U.S. foreign relations with non-Western countries."[19]

In confronting colonialism in Africa, people in the United States wrestled with their own national ideals and priorities. The struggle over which principles to follow and which ideals to promote abroad helped define what they meant at home. The relationship with Africa propelled Americans to grapple with ideas of freedom and equality—and their commitment to those ideals—in the most human of dimensions: from slavery and the slave trade to the struggle against white supremacy in the civil rights and decolonization era. The relationship drew out national and ideological dilemmas: principles of self-determination ran up against fears of potential communist gains; democratic ideals of one person, one vote, crashed into concerns about weakening western alliances and anticommunist friends. Did support of freedom include the freedom to choose other paths and allies? Would Washington follow a liberal internationalism, believing that cooperation and the soft power of the U.S. political and economic model was sufficient to persuade other countries to choose it? Or would the United States follow the lead of advocates who worried that other countries would be too fragile, or fall prey to the siren song of alternate, even communist, paths? In a fraught world, was it best to rely on hard power, reliable allies, and strongmen rulers, even if that conflicted with democratic ideals? As AFL-CIO head

George Meany put it to President Jimmy Carter, would the nation choose policies with "a single standard: what actions by the United States will effectively promote the prospects of democratic majority rule?" Yet even then, how and who would determine what constituted the effective promotion of democracy? And as the nation struggled to confront its own racial inequalities and prejudices, how would it handle similar issues abroad?[20]

In making these choices, the United States had the advantage of never having been a colonial power in Africa. It was philosophically supportive of liberal democracy and the rule of law, with these values enshrined in texts going back to the Declaration of Independence and the Constitution. It had a set of ideals and principles that taught its young schoolchildren to be on the side of "liberty and justice for all." In the words of Abraham Lincoln in his Gettysburg Address, it was a nation "conceived in liberty, and dedicated to the principle that all men are created equal." Julius Nyerere turned to these ideals when discussing Africa and democracy, choosing as a fundamental building block Lincoln's "Government of the People, by the People, for the People" as he built his case for African forms of democracy.[21]

Yet in an Africa seeking self-determination and equality, Washington found it hard to carry high Lady Liberty's burning torch. Those who pressed for greater application of American ideals faced heavy resistance. When Senator Theodore Green (D-RI) argued in 1952 that the sympathy of the American people should be with those seeking self-government, Secretary of State Dean Acheson cautioned Green that the United States needed to be careful about what it did in the short run, even in terms of saying too much about U.S. sympathies.[22] Acheson later bewailed "purists who would have no dealings with any but the fairest of the democratic states, going from state to state with political litmus paper testing them for true-blue democracy."[23] The record shows that with limited exceptions, seen particularly in the Kennedy, Johnson, and Carter presidencies, anticolonial nationalists would receive little assistance.

Over the arc of the second half of the twentieth century, the relationship of the United States with Africa posed what to many seemed conflicting choices: stable relations with long-standing allies or opposition to racial injustice; the desire for proven anticommunist governments versus democratic principles of majority rule; the comfort of shorter term economic and strategic certainties against longer term calculations of interests. Washington commonly pursued the former, even as people across the nation tried to push it toward the latter. Liberal democratic ideas of anticolonialism and self-determination were consistently contradicted by perceived national security concerns, challenged by economic interests, and undermined by racist perceptions of African abilities. As Africa continually compelled America to wrestle with fundamental principles, wide gaps often yawned between professed ideals and concrete actions.

The common misperception that the United States had no policy—or its partner, no interest—in Africa reflects a limited understanding of the relationship, as well as a missed opportunity to explore the broader meanings of the engagement.[24] Moreover, the "no policy" misperception subtly reinforces and perpetuates centuries of Eurocentric hierarchies that have defined Africa as unimportant, without a significant historical past or a meaningful contemporary present. While not always at the forefront of people's agendas or the daily news, an Africa struggling to cast off colonialism and embark on an independent future muscled its way into the conversation. In 1960, for instance, which came to be known as the Year of Africa, the continent was on the rise, with dozens of nations rapidly achieving independence. World dynamics—with an expanding nonaligned movement altering voting power in the UN—faced potentially seismic shifts. Both major-party U.S. presidential candidates projected themselves as vitally engaged with the broader world, and Africa was repeatedly on their lips. Other places, in hindsight perhaps most conspicuously Vietnam, were barely mentioned. During the final three months of the campaign, John F. Kennedy referred to Africa an eye-opening 167 times in speeches and statements, more than twice as often as he mentioned Asia.[25] Africa was on the minds of people and voters, perhaps especially Black voters in a tight election. This book builds on recent efforts by scholars to debunk the view that the United States had no interest in and was largely uninvolved with the colonization and decolonization of Africa.[26] Even in the decade following World War II, when colonial empires still held sway in Africa and U.S. attention seemed primarily focused on East-West Cold War concerns, the United States "was no mere passive observer of events."[27]

To the contrary, U.S. government officials, American business and religious groups, civil rights and humanitarian organizations, and a dizzying array of individuals played vital and underappreciated roles throughout the "long hundred years" from the Scramble for Africa to eventual independence, north to south and west to east. In examining some of the many people and organizations involved in the engagement, a particular focus will be on African Americans and their ongoing relationship with the continent, building on the growing and valuable work on twentieth-century connections between those of African descent and Africa, and the important literature on race, the Black freedom struggle, and the Cold War.[28] Tightly woven twentieth century links with Europe, close and intimate connections to Latin America, commercial and strategic interests in Asia, and complex and fraught ties to the Middle East have all had deep significance, and the same holds true for the enduring and significant relationship with Africa.

"Africa Has a Single Common Purpose and a Single Goal"

Analyzing the broader contours of the role of the United States and its relationship with Africa as independence swept the continent, the pages that follow examine connections and policies during the remarkable period of Africa's liberation, from World War II to the early 1990s. The book is less concerned with finer-grained analysis of the different views and positions held by specific bureaucratic agencies, nongovernmental organizations, and concerned individuals than with the essential approach to an Africa seeking freedom. It similarly avoids focus on back-and-forth exchanges between Washington officials and their counterparts in European capitals, acknowledging that much can be written on behind-the-scenes North-North dialogue, but instead letting relations with European allies infuse the narrative without commanding it. In taking a longer arc and a continental lens, less common in writings on Africa simply because of the scale involved, this book leaves ample room for further scholarship offering rich, finely honed studies focused on specific times or places.

The task of analyzing the broader contours is not small. Encompassing 20 percent of the earth's land, extending five thousand miles from the shores of the Mediterranean to the confluence of the Atlantic and Indian Oceans, Africa could fit all of the United States, Europe, and China within its borders. With more than fifty countries, the continent is characterized by a vast variety of languages, cultures, and peoples, belying any effort to think of it as a single entity. No one relationship, no individual story, reveals the continent. While that is no different from Asia or Europe, Africa remains most likely to be generalized and stereotyped by those in other parts of the world. This tendency goes at least as far back as the era of the slave trade, and continued into and through the twentieth century. For many around the world, Africa exists in unvariegated stereotypes.

Similarly, writings and thinking about Africa in the United States have often framed it as a single entity: Africa. For some, Africa is an ancestral home to which they feel a powerful connection, one that may not depend on any more specific location. Others simply do not disaggregate this highly varied and complex continent. But while Africa often has been imagined as a monolithic entity, there was and is no monolithic Africa. This book seeks to disarm tendencies to lump all of Africa together while considering historical actors who often did just that. The words of Albert Lutuli offer guidance in navigating an Africa imagined as a whole and the clear fact that there was no one homogeneous continent: "Though I speak of Africa as a single entity, it is divided many ways by race, language, history, and custom; by political, economic, and ethnic frontiers. But in truth, despite these multiple divisions, Africa has a single common purpose and a single goal—the achievement of its own independence."[29] The book strives for a balance, then, to disaggregate while using some broad brushstrokes, realizing that both Africa and the United States are complicated and diverse.

The story of America's involvement in the decolonization of Africa holds tremendous variation and complexity. With a half dozen European empires arbitrarily creating boundaries and borders, Africa divides into over fifty nations, each of which contains enormous differences and diversity within them. Every nation has its own independence story, not all of which can be told in these pages. Instead, the chapters reflect the historical unfolding: in the earlier stages, as dozens of nations cast off colonial rule in a few brief years, the sweep left an underprepared Washington addressing the rapid changes in a broad and more aggregated fashion; as events continued to unfold, and as the chapters progress, fewer nations sought independence, yet the efforts became more protracted and the United States even more intricately involved.

Scholars continue to find new ways to examine the dynamic process of decolonization, the worldwide efforts to roll back white supremacy, and the international history of the twentieth century. The circumstances surrounding anticolonial movements and their growing global force were shifted dramatically by World War II, in particular initial defeats of Western powers by the Japanese. The removal of European rulers from Asia offered evidence of the fragile basis of European control in the region, and when Japan was defeated, anticolonial nationalists from Burma to Vietnam to Indonesia sought independence. India, too, was on the march. British, Dutch, and French efforts to reclaim empires swiftly led to protracted liberation wars across Southeast Asia. The United States would play an early role in Asia, charting a potential path in its response to the Dutch in Indonesia. Over the course of the immediate post–World War II years, Washington evolved its position, shifting from supplying the Dutch with military and economic aid that allowed them to pursue reestablishing control to instead using economic pressure to help push the Dutch to de-escalate the war with Indonesian insurgents and ultimately agree to Indonesian independence.[30] Washington would not, however, walk that path exceedingly often, even as that first wave of decolonization in Asia would soon be followed by a second wave in Africa.

Decolonization was more than simply a course of action "whereby colonial powers transferred institutional and legal control over their territories and dependencies to indigenously based, formally sovereign nation-states."[31] Decolonization was a process as well as a point in time; the transfer of power was but one part of confronting legacies of empire politically, economically, socially, intellectually, and culturally.[32] This study concentrates on the period up to the transfer of power and the debates over how to handle that possibility, by and large leaving the story of nation-building and postcolonial Africa for a further study. At the same time, the paths and legacies of liberation struggles in countries that moved more swiftly to majority rule influenced opinions and approaches toward nations still seeking independence, and these inform the narrative.

In some ways, this work has a foot in older traditions of nation-states and policymakers, and in newer currents of transnational history beyond these actors. Notwithstanding concerns about overprivileging the role of the state, during the era of decolonization a profoundly essential effort of people throughout Africa, in fact around the world, was to cast off colonial rule and assume power in an independent nation. In doing so, "colonized peoples renounced imperialism and sought to escape from it in considerably less fixed ways than a Cold War framework would suggest," notes historian Mark Philip Bradley. "The Cold War, therefore, tends to obscure the significance of transnational postcolonial visions in the Global South that imagined a world apart from the bipolar system and from the imperial order."[33] The very thing anticolonial movements sought was control over their own state, and the choices and destiny that could then follow. And while those choices are not the subject of this work, Kwame Nkrumah, Léopold Sédar Senghor, and other anticolonial nationalists did not see the nation-state as being a defined stasis. Nkrumah imagined new political and economic links creating a United States of Africa, and when Ghana became a republic in 1960, at his insistence "it included a clause that conferred on the parliament 'the power to provide for the surrender of the whole or any part of the sovereignty of Ghana' once a United States of Africa was formed." Guinea and Mali followed Ghana's lead. The postcolonial world had pan-African possibilities overcoming the nation-state. But first Africans had to control their own nations. As Adom Getachew notes, "Those committed today to internationalism tend to see nationalist claims as insular, exclusionary, and frequently violent. But the age of decolonization reminds us that nationalism was also a vehicle for demanding democracy and international equality."[34]

Two further notes: First, South Africa, with its long history of extensive European settlement, complicates and arguably stands outside the era of decolonization. As Zambian president Kenneth Kaunda told U.S. secretary of state Henry Kissinger, "South Africa itself is an independent African state which is not a colonial power, and we accept that fact. We do not accept apartheid, however, and we support those who are struggling to change apartheid."[35] While there were differences in the South African case regarding historical backdrop and political status, this work views South Africa as part of the totality of European colonization and white supremacy in Africa. In related ways, the long struggle for independence in Namibia was made knottier by the League of Nations mandate for South West Africa given to South Africa. That mandate meant that the post–World War II white minority rule that the peoples of Namibia were fighting against was not based in Europe but rather next door, in South Africa. Yet the struggle in these places stands as part of the story of the struggle against white supremacy in Africa writ large.

A second note regards Arab North Africa. Links across the Sahara span thousands of years, and decolonization in North Africa, especially Algeria, had meaning south of the Sahara, as did diplomatic outreach and a small amount of material support for freedom struggles, given a human face by the images of Nelson Mandela receiving military training in Algeria. On the other hand, long-standing historical and historiographical trends tend to create a demarcation between North Africa and the continent south of the Sahara. Ties of religion, politics, and economies made Egypt, Libya, Algeria, Tunisia, and Morocco seem more connected to Middle Eastern politics than to sub-Saharan African affairs. Contemporary discussions generally connected the tier of states north of the Sahara to the Middle East more than to sub-Saharan Africa. Although it is not the principal emphasis, this book situates North Africa as part of the broader effort to end European rule in Africa.

Historic Connections: Africa and America

Spanning hundreds of years, ties across the Atlantic long preceded the formation of the United States and, with the exceptions of Egypt and Ethiopia, the current states in Africa. From the days of its active role in the slave trade, to the founding of Liberia, to the exploration of Africa and its subsequent colonization, the United States has had enduring connections to Africa. Over the centuries, private citizens, religious groups, public officials, and business interests have shaped, influenced, and fought over the contours of that relationship. As historian Odd Arne Westad reminds us, it is "wrong to see American Third World policies as a kind of afterthought to US foreign affairs, as some historians have done. Africa was at the heart of the new republic's policies both at home and abroad during the first hundred years of its existence. . . . It was through battles over the institution of slavery that much of American foreign policy ideology took shape and the form of liberty that the United States was to stand for in the twentieth century was defined."[36]

Slavery and Slave Trading

With the opening of the New World to European exploration, conquest, and settlement, there quickly followed an ever-increasing demand for labor. Slavery quickly took root across the Caribbean and spread onto the mainland of the Americas, and in August 1619, the struggling British settlements in North America started buying enslaved Africans. As the slave trade grew, staggeringly huge numbers of men, women, and children in bondage ended up throughout the New World, the largest numbers in Brazil and the Caribbean, while a relatively smaller but significant number of enslaved Africans were forced into chattel slavery in North America. The growing colonies reshaped traditional English law in order to expand and bolster the use of slavery throughout the thirteen British colonies.

Americans did not simply exploit Africans and their descendants for labor; they also actively participated in the slave trade itself. Each of the leading ports of the American colonies—New York, Boston, Newport, Providence, and Charleston—were heavily involved with the slave trade. That two of those ports were in Rhode Island offers one simple indicator that while the southern colonies imported the largest proportion of slaves, New England had its own enormous investment in the slave trade and slavery as well. Indeed, Rhode Island headquartered most of America's slave-trading fleet, with more than 60 percent of slave voyages from North America originating from this one small territory.[37]

By the time of the American Revolution, well over a half million Africans and their descendants resided in the newly independent United States. Most were in bondage, although some had gained their freedom. As the Declaration of Independence proclaimed that "all men are created equal," Thomas Jefferson and others wrestled with the implications of that declaration. By 1776, revolutionary rhetoric had led some to conclude that freedom for slaves was necessary to live up to those ideals. When a group of Black men petitioned in June 1774 to end slavery in Massachusetts, it prompted Abigail Adams to write to her husband, future president John Adams, that "it always appeared a most iniquitous scheme to me. Fight ourselves for what we are daily robbing and plundering from those who have as good a right [to] freedom as we have."

Others saw it differently. While the American Revolution helped put some northern states on the path toward ending slavery, with a few minor shrugs southern states continued to import enslaved Africans by the tens of thousands. At the time of the new nation's first census in 1790, roughly 750,000 people of African descent lived in the United States, over 90 percent in bondage. As the century drew to a close, hundreds of thousands of Africans were still being torn from their homes, clapped into chains, and carried across the Atlantic.

At the same time, efforts in Britain and the United States to end the slave trade slowly gained ground. In March 1807, the U.S. Congress passed legislation stating that it would "not be lawful to import or bring into the United States or the territories thereof from any foreign kingdom, place, or country any negro, mulatto, or person of colour with the intent to hold, sell, or dispose of such . . . as a slave, to be held to service or labour."[38] While moral or ethical considerations motivated some opponents of the slave trade, others backed the legislation to gain financially, as cutting off importation of slaves increased the value of slaves for existing owners and boosted the internal slave market. As of January 1808, importation of enslaved Africans was illegal, but slavery and the internal slave trade inexorably, horrifically expanded.

That the United States was being built by enslaved hands would force a reckoning with its stated ideals that all are created equal, with "unalienable rights" of life, liberty, and the pursuit of happiness. From its founding forward, the nation would continue to debate the meaning of freedom and equality in the shadow of its original sin.

ACS, Liberia, and Missionaries

As a delegation of white Americans worked in 1787 on drafting what would become the U.S. Constitution, a group of Black Americans led by Prince Hall, grand master of African Masonic Lodge No. 459 in Massachusetts, petitioned the state legislature for financial support regarding a plan "to return to Africa, our native country . . . where we shall live among our equals, and be more comfortable and happy, than we can be in our present situation."[39] The petition marked an early organized moment in efforts to find better circumstances in Africa than in the newly independent United States, in this case by men barred from joining existing white fraternal organizations who had persevered to create their own separate institution. Although the effort came to naught, others carried forward the idea of African emigration, and as early as 1815 the sea captain and entrepreneur Paul Cuffe aided thirty-eight émigrés in their voyage to Sierra Leone.

Supporters of efforts to return those of African descent to Africa existed among white Americans, too. In December 1816, the American Society for Colonizing the Free People of Color in the United States was established and shortly thereafter renamed the American Colonization Society (ACS). It soon became the primary vehicle for efforts to repatriate Africans and their descendants, its endeavors supported by President James Monroe and other high officials. After Lieutenant Robert Stockton of the U.S. Navy helped persuade local African ruler King Peter to sign a treaty while pointing a gun at his head, ACS colonists arrived at Cape Mesurado to establish a permanent settlement on the west coast of Africa, not far from the spot where the United States still has its embassy in Liberia. Establishing Monrovia as its headquarters, the colonists aggressively expanded during the 1820s but faced a terrible toll in terms of basic survival.

The motives of the ACS quickly became suspect among the broader African American community. Backers of the ACS seemed too strongly in favor of removing free Blacks, not ending slavery itself. Misgivings about its motives caused many African Americans to turn away from ACS endeavors, though given the intense discrimination they faced in the United States and their interest in building a new life, some continued to voluntarily emigrate in the years that followed. The growing, indispensable population of Africans and their descendants in America would continue to build the nation culturally, materially, and spiritually, helping create the integral fabric of a nation that too often sought to relegate them to the margins.[40]

Of those who went to Liberia, some carried with them a missionary zeal to bring Christianity. Like many, the minister Jehudi Ashmun, who had traveled to Liberia in 1822 as official representative of the U.S. government while quickly assuming an essential governing role in the small colony, not only believed in the endeavor to build Liberia but also believed he had a calling to uplift Africa, spreading Christianity, commerce, and Western civilization. He was situated within a broad evangelical movement in nineteenth-century American Protestantism, with individuals and church organizations sponsoring numerous missionaries to Africa.

African Americans played a particularly active and important part. Some saw a special role in redeeming Africa, an idea dating back to at least the late eighteenth century and the rise of the fortunate fall doctrine. While the doctrine has several variations, it encompassed "the belief that slavery, although a terrible affliction on the African people, would become, through the workings of divine providence, a blessing in the fullness of time."[41] The explicit reasoning faded over time, but the idea that African Americans would play a vital role in uplifting Africa remained powerful through the nineteenth and into the twentieth century. Alexander Crummell, an Episcopalian priest, served in Liberia for twenty years beginning in 1853; with the dawning era of colonialism, missionaries of all creeds and colors would find new opportunities in Africa.

With the ACS in financial straits and the United States unwilling to assume a colony in Africa, Americo-Liberians declared independence in 1847. Joseph Jenkins Roberts, who had come from Virginia, was elected as the first president of an independent Liberia. The new nation continued to receive emigrants, with influxes at times spiking in response to conditions in America, as when segregation and lynchings inflicted their gruesome toll in the late 1800s. During that time, Liberia's close relationship with the United States helped prevent it from being colonized by Europeans during the Scramble for Africa.[42]

Commerce, Exploration, and Colonialism

Before the legal importation of slaves ended in 1808, and continuing up to the Civil War, the United States developed broad trade contacts with Africa. U.S. traders worked along thousands of miles of African shores to secure palm oil in West Africa for its varied uses in homes and industries, gum copal in East Africa as an ingredient in fine lacquers and varnishes, and dyewood and ivory across the continent. Both private businesspeople and government officials were involved. Seeking to develop trade links, in 1837—before the Scramble for Africa had fully begun and the Civil War had disrupted overseas trade connections—the United States was the first country to establish a consulate in Zanzibar. The U.S. naval squadron sent to help suppress the slave trade also worked to open markets, and Commodore Matthew C. Perry honed his skills in opening ports and trade in Africa well before arriving in Japan. By the end of the Civil War, however, the European presence in Africa was rapidly advancing while the United States was focused more on Reconstruction and its own internal industrial expansion.[43]

Still, Americans kept a thriving interest in Africa. In the early hours of 21 March 1871, Henry Morton Stanley embarked from Dar es Salaam to find the "lost" missionary and explorer David Livingstone. Born in Wales to an unmarried mother, Stanley had spent his childhood shuttling between relatives and the workhouse. When he turned eighteen, he crossed the Atlantic to try his fortune in the United States. Like many before and since, he reinvented himself upon arrival. He changed his name from John Rowlands to Henry Morton Stanley, after a merchant who befriended him. He fought in the Civil War, first in the Confederate army; after being captured at the battle of Shiloh, he ended up joining the Union army and then the navy. By the time the war ended, Stanley was heading West to seek his fortune. There he encountered firsthand racial conflict and white imperialism as settlers sought to wrest control of the continent from Native Americans, foreshadowing his time in Africa, and found that he had a taste for journalism, travel, and adventure.[44]

Stanley's foray into Africa to find Livingstone, funded by the *New York Herald* newspaper, came in the dawning era of the European exploration and colonization of Africa. Driving hard into the interior, after eight months Stanley found his man and his scoop. Even more, he secured his reputation as an intrepid explorer of Africa. Subsequent expeditions led him across the continent, down the Congo River, and out its mouth to the Atlantic Ocean. His unparalleled knowledge of the region and willingness to push himself and his team to the limits of endurance made Stanley a prize catch for the ambitious Leopold II, king of Belgium. He signed Stanley to a five-year personal services contract, hoping to open the heart of Africa to his desires.

Seeking support for his claims in Africa, Leopold II helped engineer the Berlin Conference of 1884–85, which set the ground rules for the Scramble for Africa. The conference itself formalized a process already set in motion. The United States sent observers, who found little to object to. To the contrary, even before the Berlin meetings, President Chester A. Arthur's administration had recognized Leopold's claims in the Congo, the first country to do so, helping prompt the Berlin Conference itself. The United States' participation at the conference marked a significant advance in the country's growing political involvement beyond the Western Hemisphere.

Acquiescing to the Scramble for Africa helped establish an initial pattern of largely supporting European actions on the continent. The colonizing of Africa also fit well with white Americans' romance with social Darwinism, revealing deeply rooted racist impulses that drove the relationship with Africa as much as national interest or ideology. A broad faith in Western civilization meant that late nineteenth-century Americans did not generally oppose the colonial push in Africa, just as most did not oppose contemporaneous U.S. expansion into Native American lands. Many Americans believed in the "civilizing" mission of the Europeans, particularly when done by the British.[45] In time, even Bishop Henry McNeal Turner, who spoke with pride about his African heritage and in admiration of particular characteristics he saw in Africans, believed contemporary Africa had fallen and needed to be raised. "The heathen Africans, to my certain knowledge," declared Turner, "eagerly yearn for that civilization which they believe will elevate them and make them a potential for good."[46] Historian Kevin Gaines connects support for the imperialist "civilizing mission" with the domestic racial uplift strategy of the late nineteenth century, with U.S. racial conditions so utterly despairing that some Black elites felt need to include themselves as agents of civilization and progress as a way to defend themselves against racial stereotypes, topple racial barriers, and regain citizenship rights. For broader America, awash in negative images of Africans, European colonialism seemed a positive force, except when it overly interfered with American trade and commerce.[47]

League of Nations, Liberia, and Ethiopia

Although some voices raised concerns about European actions, most famously in the Congo amid the horrors of Leopold II's reign, even the atrocities in the Congo did not bring about a robust debate on colonial rule by Europeans. It simply led to a change in European control, from Leopold II to the Belgian government. There was little questioning of colonialism in Africa, even in the aftermath of the Great War. In January 1918, President Woodrow Wilson, seeking a "just and secure peace," outlined his Fourteen Points to Congress. Five of the points dealt with general principles, eight

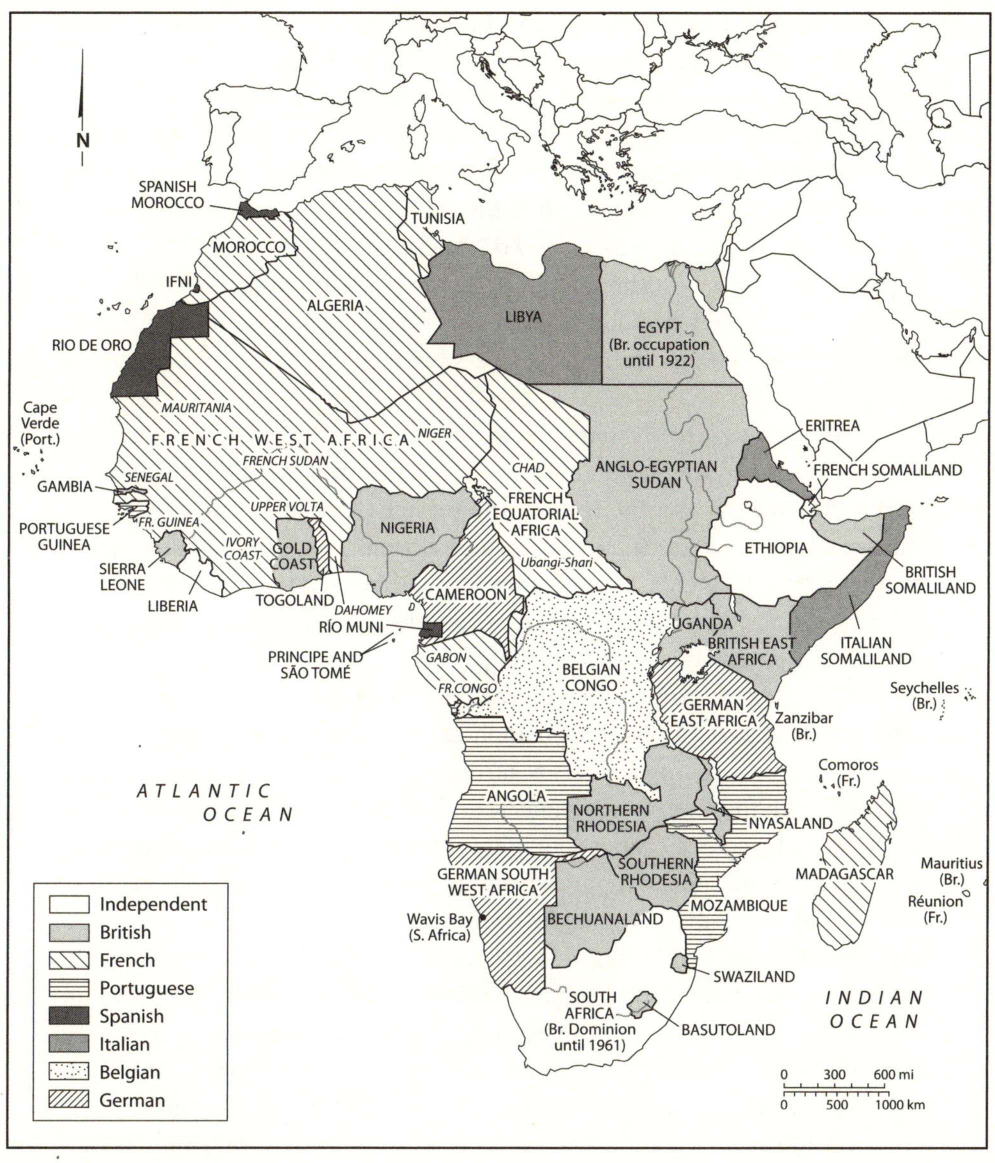

Africa, January 1914

more addressed territorial issues in Europe, and the last proposed what would become the League of Nations. The fifth point spoke directly to colonialism: "A free, open-minded, and absolutely impartial adjustment of all colonial claims, based upon a strict observance of the principle that in determining all such questions of sovereignty the interests of the populations concerned must have equal weight with the equitable claims of the government whose title is to be determined." Those colonized should have their interests considered—although not necessarily their voices heard—by the great powers as they decided what to do with Germany's colonies. African interests would be determined by others because no Africans would be in the room.

As Wilson and other leaders met at Versailles, W. E. B. Du Bois simultaneously convened the first Pan-African Congress in Paris. The congress in part addressed African interests in the former German colonies, with Du Bois speaking of "political rights for the civilized" and "development of autonomous governments along the lines of native customs with the object of inaugurating gradually an Africa for the Africans." Immediate self-determination was not yet on the table.[48]

The European victors divided up vanquished Germany's African colonies, albeit under League of Nations mandates. The United States sought commerce and trade, ceding matters regarding sovereignty in Africa to the Europeans, with the exception of Liberia and Ethiopia. As the world came out of the war, the cost of rubber soon plunged. Great Britain, looking to boost prices, restricted rubber supplies from its possessions. Seeking alternative sources of cheap rubber, U.S. industrialist Harvey Firestone turned to Liberia, where the United States held the most influence in Africa and which was struggling mightily to keep itself afloat and independent. Extensive financial problems in Liberia had already prompted a commission from the United States to investigate political and economic conditions. Financial reorganization and loans, at the cost of increased U.S. and European control over Liberian affairs, had nevertheless failed to provide financial stability. In 1926, faced with critical economic problems and enormous pressure from the United States, Liberia agreed to a one-million-acre concession for the Firestone Tire and Rubber Company. As part of the arrangement, the Liberian government agreed to supply laborers under a "contract system" in return for a $5 million loan from a subsidiary of Firestone. None of the terms were advantageous to Liberia.[49]

Questions over Liberian sovereignty took an even more ominous turn with the worldwide economic depression, the plummeting price of rubber (dropping from over $1.40 per pound in 1925 to less than $.16 per pound in 1930), and the exposure of the forced labor systems at work in the country. Most notoriously, stories of the taking and sending of young male laborers to work the cocoa fields in Fernando Po led the League of Nations in 1929 to establish an International Commission of Inquiry into the Existence of Slavery and Forced Labor in the Republic of Liberia. The commission's damaging report, along with exposés such as George Schuyler's *Slaves Today: A Story of Liberia*, forced the resignations of President Charles King and Vice President Allen Yancey. Liberia remained independent, yet by the 1930s it had become a virtual client state of America.[50]

On the other side of the continent in East Africa, one of the last pieces of independent Africa remained. Ethiopia's long and glorious history had been enhanced at the Battle of Adwa in 1896, when it fended off Italy's effort to invade and colonize. Nevertheless, and indeed partly because of that humiliating defeat, Italian dictator Benito Mussolini pursued grand designs to take Ethiopia. In 1935 he launched what would be the last formal European effort to colonize in Africa. Emperor Haile Selassie traveled to Geneva to personally appeal for help from the League of Nations. The organization, based on collective security, turned a deaf ear, as did the United States. By May 1936, Italian troops walked the streets of Addis Ababa, at least for the moment.

At the time, no one could know that Mussolini's invasion would hasten the collapse of the League of Nations and the advent of the deadliest war in human history. Nor could it be known the extent to which the colonial powers in Africa would weaken, or that at war's end the United States would be poised as the world's new superpower, with an interest in everything that happened around the globe, just as the era of African decolonization began.

1 No Premature Independence, 1941–1951

> The delegates to the Fifth Pan-African Congress believe in peace. How could it be otherwise when for centuries the African peoples have been victims of violence and slavery? Yet if the Western world is still determined to rule mankind by force, then Africans, as a last resort, may have to appeal to force in the effort to achieve Freedom, even if force destroys them and the world. . . . We will fight in every way we can for freedom, democracy, and social betterment.
>
> —Manchester Fifth Pan-African Congress, 1945

> The breaking up of the colonial systems and the gradual withdrawing of the colonial powers from these areas has faced the US itself with the problem of filling the gap left by their withdrawal. The US stand on the colonial issue and economic nationalism will have a major effect on the attitudes of these colonial and former colonial areas.
>
> —CIA, September 1948

As 1941 dawned, maps of Africa showed a continent almost devoid of independent territory, and even those areas did not appear to have unfettered sovereignty. Liberia, although independent since 1847, was ruled by a tiny Americo-Liberian elite and remained strongly under the influence of the United States. Egypt, independent since 1922, still had British military forces and political influence, even after the 1936 Anglo-Egyptian Treaty formally ended British occupation. South Africa, unified and self-governing since 1910, was under white minority rule and nominally still under the British monarchy. Mostly the map showed vast European colonial empires, including an Italian East Africa that included an occupied Ethiopia. Yet the transformation of Africa was already underway. Within months the map changed, restoring Ethiopia as Emperor Haile Selassie triumphantly returned to Addis Ababa after a five-year absence. Within fifty years, European empires would be wiped entirely from the map of Africa.

Broad historical currents were creating conditions for sweeping change. By the time the United States entered World War II later that year, Winston Churchill and Franklin D. Roosevelt had already had conversations about the place of colonies in a postwar world. As the war ended, discussions about the future of colonial areas took on added immediacy in the context of a rapidly changing world. By then, the United States had moved into a dominant position, and colonial empires had become highly vulnerable to change. Of course Washington could not single-handedly determine their fates, but the vulnerability of its European allies gave America profound leverage.

That very vulnerability, however, made exercising leverage a risk in a world where communism seemed to be on the march. American interests in pursuing new markets and commercial opportunities clashed with arguments that European allies needed African colonies in their own postwar rebuilding efforts. Ideals of self-determination collided with seemingly safe harbors of European rule. The Truman administration chose what seemed the more secure route: to support European allies in their efforts to maintain their empires. The decision did not come without dissent and division, but it came, despite historic threads of anticolonialism and ideological commitments to freedom and democracy. Fear of communism was a prominent factor in the decision to support allies and their quest to keep their colonies. But domestic considerations, including prevailing racial views that Africans were better off under white rule weighed heavily. Indeed, the international intertwining of anticommunism and white supremacy became pronounced. Policymakers in Washington believed the continent was highly stable under the rule of European allies, with the State Department determining as late as 1948 that there was "no need" for a formal position on all of French West Africa, for example, "since neither international nor local political developments pose serious problems in the area."[1] Europeans seemingly were in Africa to stay for the time being.

While U.S. officials sought to shore up allies in Europe against the threat they increasingly perceived from the Soviet Union, colonialism not communism was the issue at hand for Africans. Nationalism and the push to end colonial rule was on the rise, with the Manchester Pan-African Congress in 1945 bringing voices from Africa and the diaspora together in a foundational moment of this growing movement. Condemning colonial economic exploitation and seeking steps toward political self-determination, the delegates' "Challenge to the Colonial Powers" declared their belief in peace as well as their willingness to wage war. Kwame Nkrumah, speaking at a session chaired by W. E. B. Du Bois, indicted imperialism and called for strong and vigorous action to end it.[2] At the same time, on the continent soldiers returning from the war carried with them perspectives for change. "Perhaps most important, I had become conscious of myself as a Kenya African, one among millions whose destinies were still in the hands of foreigners, yet also one who could see the need and the possibility of changing that situation," recalled Waruhiu Itote, whose nom de guerre for the Kenya Land and Freedom Army became General China.[3]

Africans such as Nkrumah and Itote pursued various paths toward the goal of independence. By the end of 1951, an imprisoned Nkrumah had been elected leader of government business in the Gold Coast (Ghana), and Itote had moved toward insurgency. Libya had become the first postwar state in Africa to gain independence. U.S. officials worked to define Washington's position. Pulled toward politically and financially supporting European allies and colonial powers but still verbally supporting eventual independence for African nations, U.S. officials embarked on a so-called middle path. But it was becoming a bipolar world, and Washington was drawn to the pole of continuing white rule, even as some in America, particularly African Americans, advocated greater support for African independence.

"The People of Ethiopia Are Freed"

When Ralph Ellison's protagonist in *Invisible Man* happened on a Harlem rent eviction, he found himself cataloging the minimal possessions of the elderly couple being cast out: "knocking bones" used to accompany music at country dances, an old folded lace fan, pots of green plants, lapsed life insurance policies, a picture of Marcus Garvey. Among these tattered remnants was an Ethiopian flag.[4] While fascist dictator Benito Mussolini and his Italian compatriots prepared to invade one of the last independent states in Africa, many in the United States—from President Roosevelt in the White House to Harlemites struggling to stay in their tiny walk-up apartments—turned their attention to Ethiopia's fate. Much was at stake, as a member of Woodrow Wilson's cherished League of Nations blatantly and belligerently threatened another.

Mussolini conjured up a number of reasons to invade Ethiopia. His desire to re-create the glories of the Roman past led him to seek lands to conquer for an Italian empire. He also sought to reverse Italy's shattering defeat at Adwa in 1896, when Ethiopian emperor Menelik II repulsed the Italian imperialists, inflicting severe losses and securing Ethiopia's independence. Mussolini used bitter memories of the battle as a rallying point for a fresh attempt at conquering Ethiopia. A handful of imaginary slights, a border controversy, and shopworn appeals to Ethiopia needing "civilizing forces"

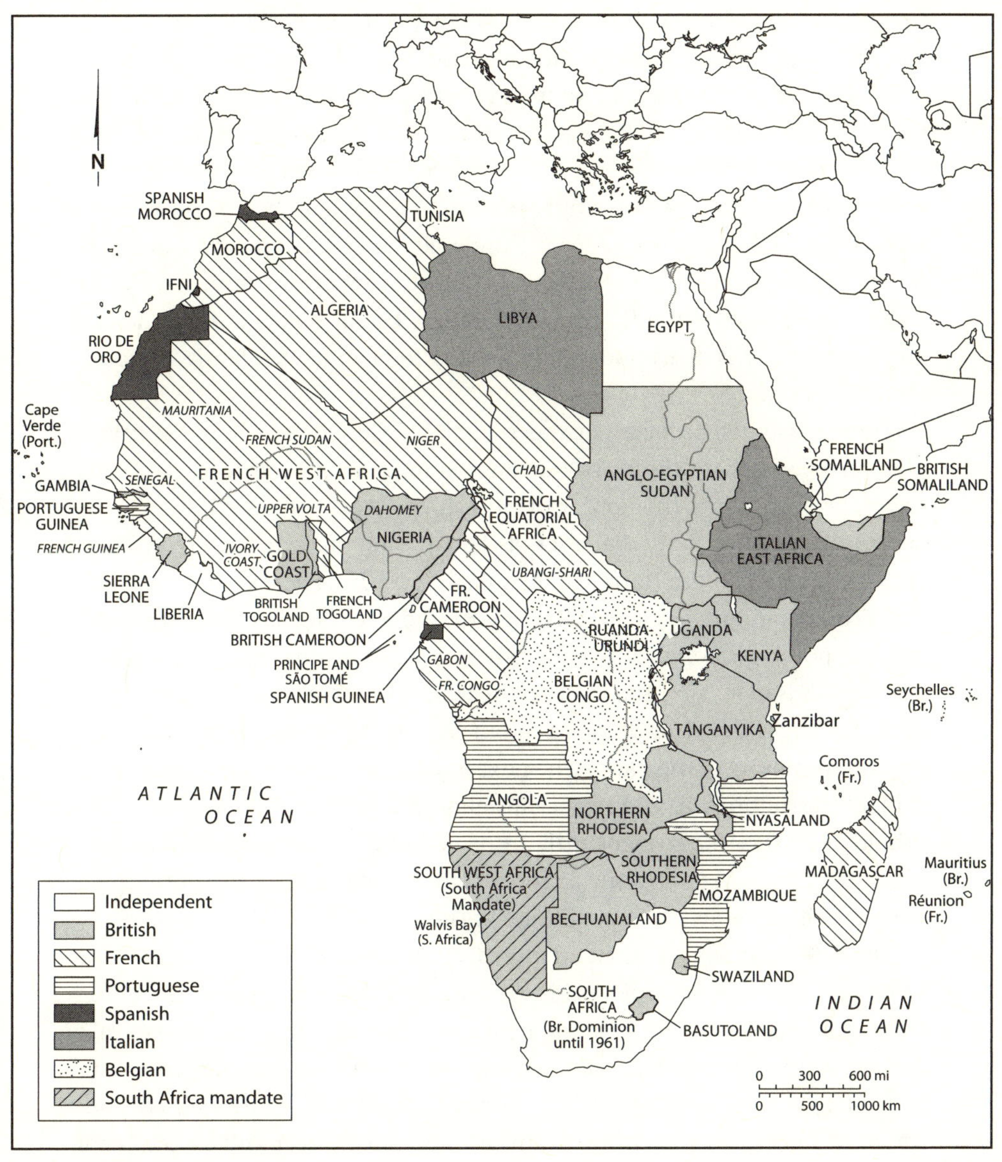

Africa, January 1941

furnished Mussolini with the basis for invasion. In early October 1935, Italian troops poured across Ethiopia's borders.

Wishing to avoid war and knowing that he was at a military disadvantage, Ethiopia's emperor Haile Selassie turned to the League of Nations and its doctrine of collective security. But the league's limited response actually hindered Ethiopia. The seemingly neutral and noble policy of refusing to sell arms to warring nations hurt the underequipped Ethiopia far more than it harmed the Italian war machine. Additional sanctions imposed by the league on Italy were mainly cosmetic, largely because they did not include an embargo of the one import Italy needed to keep its mechanized troops on the move: oil.

There existed little basis to expect official U.S. intervention in the Ethiopian crisis, and from the start Washington made every effort to avoid any entanglement. When the border dispute at the Wal Wal oasis initiated the crisis in December 1934, the chief of the Division of Near Eastern Affairs, under which the State Department subsumed Africa at the time, warned that Ethiopia might invoke the Kellogg-Briand Pact. Signatories of the pact pledged not to go to war with each other. If Selassie took this step, Wallace Murray advised leaving the issue to the league and making "every effort to avoid having the matter dumped in our lap on the score that we were the original initiators of the Pact." The next day, Secretary of State Cordell Hull cabled instructions to the American chargé d'affaires in Ethiopia: "You should keep the Department fully informed of developments and scrupulously refrain from taking any action which would encourage the Ethiopian government to request the mediation of the United States."[5]

The American domestic mood increased the obstacles. Notwithstanding some supporters of Ethiopia, primarily among Black Americans, the nation was determinedly isolationist and neutralist. Indeed, fears that Mussolini's actions were a prelude to another world war contributed to the Neutrality Acts of 1935 and 1936. Roosevelt himself may have wanted embargoes imposed in order to keep Mussolini at bay, but he recognized that that sentiment in America worked against active measures to halt Italian aggression.[6]

Ethiopia also found little support among the European powers in the League of Nations. In March 1935, Hitler shocked France and Britain when he openly repudiated the disarmament clauses of the Versailles Treaty by revealing the existence of a German air force and plans to build a half-million-man army. Fearful of the growing German threat, the two powers did not want to alienate Italy and drive Mussolini closer to Hitler, and their concerns ensured that the league would not take forceful action against Mussolini.

No Western government encouraged efforts on behalf of Ethiopia, though organizations and individuals tried to rally support. In March 1935, for instance, the NAACP (National Association for the Advancement of Colored People) called on Secretary of State Hull to ensure that the United States would do everything possible to support the remaining independent states in Africa. A follow-up letter asked Hull to tell Italy that America "does not look with favor" upon its attempt to plunder Ethiopia, and to remind Italy and Ethiopia of their commitments under the Kellogg-Briand Pact.[7] The NAACP's 1935 Annual Conference, held in late June, adopted a resolution unequivocally condemning Italian aggression in Ethiopia and vigorously urging the president and the Department of State to voice publicly their disapproval of the Italian government's actions. On 3 July 1935, the NAACP sent telegrams expressing its concerns to Roosevelt and Hull.[8]

Yet the State Department did all it could to avoid any role in the dispute. When W. Perry George, the chargé d'affaires in Ethiopia, informed Washington that Selassie summoned him to the palace and asked how to secure Italy's observance of the Kellogg-Briand Pact, the State Department counseled George yet again to point Selassie to the League of Nations.[9] As the Roosevelt administration received plain warning that Italy intended to attack, it continued to temporize. In the critical weeks before Italy's invasion, Hull insisted that Selassie's government await the outcome of the League of Nations' efforts before some other peace machinery "be projected into the situation." The Roosevelt administration argued that any effort it made to mediate "might interfere with the efforts of the League," and reiterated this stance up to the start of the war.[10]

Once hostilities began, however, the State Department unapologetically altered its stance. Having pressed Selassie to delay any invocation of the Kellogg-Briand Pact, Hull now argued that the most opportune time to invoke the pact had passed—it should have been done before the outbreak of hostilities. He noted that the pact contained no provision for signatories to act when a country broke its commitment, and cautioned that any action using the pact as a basis might "seriously interfere with the League's program." Of course, there was no such program.[11]

The Italian invasion met with stiff Ethiopian resistance, and Mussolini worried that his expected easy victory faced catastrophic defeat. He ordered his generals to use "any means" to ensure victory. Marshal Rodolfo Graziani requested "maximum liberty" to rain "asphyxiating gas" on the "barbarous hordes." After dropping barrels of lethal gas proved too localized, the Italians fitted their planes with crop duster–like equipment to spray the mustard gas onto the Ethiopians, as if exterminating locusts.[12]

Invaded, gassed, and driven back, Selassie ultimately fled Addis Ababa into exile in London. His presence there created no small discomfort as the British government sought to work with Rome to keep Italy from allying with Germany. But keeping Selassie on hand provided a useful backup when that strategy collapsed in utter failure.[13]

In 1940, Selassie learned that Britain planned to restore his government. Ethiopian fighters and British troops soon combined to drive the Italians from Ethiopia. Selassie entered the country from Sudan, joined in the fighting, and triumphantly entered Addis Ababa on 5 May 1941, carefully timed to coincide with the fifth anniversary of the Italian occupation of his capital. With a biblical allusion, Selassie proclaimed, "Today is a day in which Ethiopia is stretching forth her hands to God in joy and thankfulness and revealing her happiness to her children." Noting the day as one "on which the people of Ethiopia are freed from the oppressive foreign yoke," Selassie struck a chord for African aspirations of freedom and independence. Selassie's agreement with Britain confirmed Ethiopia's sovereignty but gave Britain authority over territory in the Ogaden, the railroad, currency, and trade. In the ensuing years, the Ethiopian government pushed to remove these onerous elements, as well as to press its claim to Eritrea.[14]

The United States quickly restored relations with Selassie's government and, seeking a Western-friendly ally in control of the strategic coast along the Red Sea, backed Ethiopia's claims to Eritrea. As historian Brenda Gayle Plummer notes, however, Washington's interest in self-determination and opposition to colonial domination came "rather late in the history of aggression against Ethiopia." Weak and slow support for those opposed to colonialism would continue to mark official U.S. policy throughout broader Africa, notwithstanding moments of anticolonial rhetoric and action.[15]

American Power and Colonial Empires

Entering World War II, America's historical and ideological commitment to anticolonialism, along with its crucial resources and power, ensured that it could be a powerful voice on questions of colonialism and decolonization in the world to come. The American Revolution itself had established the first successful modern revolt against a colonial power. In the twentieth century, Wilsonian internationalism touted national self-determination, and while not directed toward non-European peoples, the language was absorbed and used worldwide.[16] Throughout World War II, the rhetoric of the Roosevelt administration placed the United States on the side of anticolonialism and freedom for all peoples. In his annual message to Congress in January 1941, Roosevelt articulated his "four freedoms," declaring, "Freedom means the supremacy of human rights everywhere. Our support goes to those who struggle to gain those rights or keep them." An elaboration of these ideals came in August 1941, when Roosevelt and Churchill met off the coast of Newfoundland to draw up a joint declaration of war aims. The Atlantic Charter outlined eight propositions that included principles of sovereign rights and self-government for all peoples, as well as a postwar peace assuring safety to all nations and freedom from fear and want for all people. The colonized peoples of the world interpreted these principles to mean that democratic freedoms would come for them, too.[17]

Other U.S. officials offered similar anticolonial rhetoric. "In this vast struggle, we Americans stand united with those who, like ourselves, are fighting for the preservation of their freedom; with those who are fighting to regain the freedom of which they have been brutally deprived; with those who are fighting for the opportunity to achieve freedom," declared Secretary of State Hull in July 1942. "We have always believed—and we believe today—that all peoples, without distinction of race, color, or religion, who are prepared and willing to accept the responsibilities of liberty are entitled to its enjoyment." And colonial subjects around the world, such as Mahatma Gandhi in India, spoke of the need to follow principles of self-determination to gain the support of colonized people for the war effort.[18]

Behind this high-minded rhetoric lay pragmatic concerns. Colonies, as sources of friction between European powers, provided potential flash points in the world system. Thus, eliminating them would presumably reduce the possibility of war. Economic concerns also underlaid anticolonial rhetoric. Since the late 1800s, the United States had pursued an Open Door policy in Asia, and colonial doors everywhere were not wide open for trade. Fears of an economic depression following the war, such as that which occurred after World War I, and beliefs that restrictive trade practices helped spiral the world into depression in the 1930s reinforced views that world trade would be better off without colonies, especially in a world the United States expected to dominate.

While the United States had few direct economic interests in Africa, it harbored a strong desire to pursue economic interests throughout the continent. Within hours of Roosevelt's death, Secretary of State Edward Stettinius, who had replaced Hull just a few months earlier, was briefing the newly sworn in president, Harry Truman, on the country's principal problems. Shortly thereafter, Stettinius gave Truman a manual on U.S. foreign affairs that identified two objectives for colonial peoples: to promote their economic, social, and educational growth, and to prepare them for independent sovereignty. For Africa, the manual offered more specific guidance: "The keystone of our policy toward Africa has long been equality of opportunity for Americans in that continent. While under the impact of war this policy has to some degree been temporarily relaxed . . . it is our intention to revert as quickly as possible, following the conclusion of hostilities, to the historic policy of the 'open door' and equality of opportunity in Africa."[19]

The desire for access to markets and raw materials placed American officials at fundamental cross-purposes with the colonial powers that sought to maintain preferential trade policies with their colonies. Europeans viewed with suspicion American motivations, readily believing that there was more to American designs than merely promoting the economic and social welfare of African peoples. American anticolonial rhetoric had raised expectations that Washington would be an anticolonial advocate, as had Roosevelt's contempt for the British and French record in colonial areas and recognition of the latent power of peoples yearning to be free.

Yet a tradition of ambivalence about revolutions marked U.S. attitudes. American policymakers were wary about social and political upheavals, especially those arising from the left. The waves of revolution from the late eighteenth through the early twentieth centuries reinforced beliefs that revolutions were best when they were conducted with a minimum of disorder, led by respectable citizens, and harnessed to moderate political goals, culminating in a balanced constitution safeguarding human and property rights. Absent these conditions, policymakers reacted to changes with attitudes ranging from disappointment to open hostility.[20]

Indeed, by the twentieth century, the United States generally acted as a more conservative power when it came to colonies and revolutions. The United States itself added overseas colonies following the Spanish-American War of 1898. Woodrow Wilson sent troops into Mexico and Russia in an attempt to shape those revolutions. Throughout the first half of the century, American troops regularly intervened in the Caribbean basin in order to impose America's prerogatives. During World War II itself, even as the Roosevelt administration spoke in anticolonial terms and held a position of strength in the Western alliance, it refused to forcefully push European allies to divest themselves of their colonies. The highest priority for U.S. policymakers during the war was defeating Nazi Germany and its Axis allies; anticolonial objectives were less immediate. Selassie's restoration to power was due more to antifascist efforts than to anticolonial imperatives.

Critics fumed that the United States was not doing enough during the war years to ensure a decolonized postwar world. W. E. B. Du Bois scathingly parsed a 1943 statement concerning the relations between America and Africa by Assistant Chief of Near Eastern Affairs Henry Villard as "an illogical mixture of the Open Door (equal right to exploit servile labor and cheap materials); God-bless-England (whose colonial record is perfect); Isolation (power without responsibility); Missions (opening wedge for trade and obedience); and Self-Rule (for the few who want it and can use it)."[21]

UN San Francisco Conference and the Emerging Cold War World

In April 1945, with Truman only weeks into office and the war still taking its toll in both Europe and the Pacific, leaders from around the world met in San Francisco to organize what would become the United Nations. Like the birthing pangs of nations around the world, the United Nations Conference on International Organization was filled with myriad debates and disputes, not least of which was what to do about trusteeships and, even further, colonies in general. Here the Truman administration for the first time directly confronted defining a position on colonies. Roosevelt had seemingly committed himself and his administration to the principle of colonial independence, believing that anything short of such a commitment would sow the seeds for another world war. Yet commitments to anticolonialism were roiled in a rapidly changing landscape in which an already fraying alliance against fascism was being replaced by growing doubts over communist Soviet intentions. The question increasingly appeared to be how to square concerns over security with desires for colonial accountability and, ultimately, self-determination.[22]

In his authoritative history of the United States and British pas de deux during the war years over the fate of the British empire, Wm. Roger Louis argues that it is "helpful to regard the American delegation as the key to the whole situation" regarding trusteeships. Within the American delegation there were competing positions, as had been the case during the war itself. The military and State Department tangled over how to handle strategic islands in the Pacific that the military considered vital for U.S. national security yet made it awkward for the United States to demand that European allies relinquish their empires. With Soviet encroachment on the Kurile Islands, military arguments for U.S. control of islands in the Pacific gained immediacy and made it all the more difficult for Washington to press European allies to divest their possessions.[23]

On the large issue of colonial independence, Louis argues that when the imperialist powers lined up against the anticolonial nations, "for no other delegation perhaps was the choice more excruciating than for the American." Understanding the stakes, outside organizations were in San Francisco to advance their views. The NAACP consultants—consisting of organization head Walter White, W. E. B. Du Bois, and Mary McLeod Bethune—focused on achieving two primary goals: a strong declaration of human rights that would convey the equality of all races and peoples; and, a forceful anticolonial section in the UN charter that would create an international body to oversee colonies and push them speedily toward self-governance and independence. White and Du Bois, who were divided personally on many issues and whose association would soon rupture completely as Du Bois resolutely moved further left than the NAACP, shared a deep concern that human rights gains could be offset by a proposed "domestic jurisdiction" clause. That clause would prohibit the UN from interfering in matters deemed completely internal to a country. White and Du Bois innately understood that colonial powers would use this "dangerous and unfortunate" clause, as Du Bois termed it, to fend off UN action, claiming colonial issues as strictly internal.[24]

Amid the tensions between supporting European allies or pushing for strong anticolonial measures, between expanding U.S. territorial claims in the Pacific or taking a stand for self-determination, U.S. officials headed toward what they saw as somewhere in between. South Africa's prime minister, Jan Smuts, had presided over the commission that hammered out the establishment of the UN General Assembly, working through four committees that devised the forms and functions of the world body. The work of the fourth committee dealt with trusteeships, using language that the principle of trusteeship applied to "all dependent peoples in all dependent territories." UN member states would be expected to adhere to a set of principles ensuring economic and social advancement and developing self-government "in forms appropriate to the varying circumstances of each territory." There were widely different ways to view the language, but Harold Stassen, the U.S. delegate who played a pivotal role, provided his view. "This document can open the door to millions of people; it can mark out a path," Stassen told his colleagues. "But only the helping hand of the . . . more advanced and privileged nations can make it live."[25]

American support for self-determination came in vaguely broad constructions while concrete action slipped into the back seat. In time, the UN would become an institution for anticolonial nationalists to challenge colonial powers, but not because Washington sought to formulate that construction. Washington essentially foreshadowed the "middle path" formulation that of course was no middle path and would mark its actions in Africa. The American anticolonial stance during the early war years had raised expectations that they might unfurl an anti-imperial banner, yet doing so risked damaging, perhaps irrevocably, relations with allies/imperial powers, including its "special relationship" with Britain. Even more, long-standing beliefs of white civilization and superiority in both the United States and Europe reinforced the shared racial politics of white control in a tumultuous world. "When it came to the test," writes Louis, "the United States sided with the colonial powers."[26]

The San Francisco conference produced no specific timetables or procedures for the independence of colonial peoples. The NAACP registered its displeasure in the conference's aftermath, and *The Crisis* called the U.S. refusal to affirm that dependent peoples have the right to independence a "bald compromise of basic American principle."[27]

• • • • • •

As tensions in the relationship between the United States and the Soviet Union took on greater prominence, differences over Germany, Eastern Europe, Iran, the control of atomic weapons, and access to markets led President Truman to believe the United States needed to follow a "get tough with Russia" line. For U.S. officials, the Soviet Union and communism swiftly replaced Nazi Germany as the greatest threat to Western democratic ideals. Domestic politics, namely fears that Republicans would outflank and pound him on the communism issue, reinforced Truman's shift away from Roosevelt's wartime policy of working with the Soviets. By the end of 1946, a hard-line U.S. policy was in place. When London informed Washington in February 1947 that it could no longer provide economic and military aid either to civil-war torn Greece or to Turkey, the Truman administration made its dramatic call for support for a global battle against communism. Truman designed his address to Congress in March 1947 to "scare hell out of the American people" in order to rally them to the conflict. Within two weeks of announcing his Truman Doctrine, the president gave impetus to the domestic counterpart of the anticommunist crusade by announcing the establishment of a loyalty program designed to root out all communist security risks from government ranks.

These actions rallied Americans to support anticommunism but did so at a steep price. Domestically, the loyalty program legitimized anticommunism as a national ideology and purpose, creating an environment in which the loosely worded directives behind the loyalty program abrogated civil liberties at home: those accused of disloyalty did not have to be told the precise charges against them nor the identities of those providing evidence, while the ill-defined concept of "disloyalty" allowed persecution simply based on thoughts or beliefs. Internationally, nuanced distinctions between threats posed by communists and crises stemming from other causes, such as nationalistic desires for self-determination, increasingly fell victim to anticommunist zeal.

Fears of communist advances led U.S. officials to actively support their Western allies—countries that also happened to be the colonial powers in Africa. By 1947, communist parties in Italy and France were threatening to take power through democratic elections. Leftist movements in Asia were gaining strength, most spectacularly in China. A world in flux seemed to offer numerous opportunities for communist intrigue and advance. Shoring up the Western allies became a top priority. Shortly after the Truman Doctrine speech, the new secretary of state, George C. Marshall, pledged the United States to making substantial contributions to the rebuilding of Europe. Within a year, the Marshall Plan started pumping billions of dollars, as well as machinery, material, and experts, into Western European governments and economies. The Marshall Plan strengthened the devastated economies of Western Europe and reduced the possibility that turmoil and privations would turn the people toward communism. It also gave the European allies more resources with which to keep their colonial empires. Europeans had argued that aid for the development of their overseas territories was indispensable to their own recoveries even as World War II hung in the balance. French authorities, hoping to use the empire for reconstruction of the metropole, thus sought to keep the empire in economic tow even while proposing some sociopolitical reforms at the 1944 Brazzaville Conference.[28]

U.S. officials largely accepted the European arguments, seeing American aid as a temporary measure, with Western European trade and investment expansion in the Third World sustaining long-term recovery. U.S. dollars would flow to Third World countries through American procurement of raw materials, Western Europe would earn those dollars through investments and exports, and eventually European economies would recover to the point that they no longer needed U.S. grants and loans. The sleight of hand did not pass unnoticed or unremarked. Testifying before the Senate Foreign Relations Committee on the proposed European Recovery Program (Marshall Plan) in January 1948, NAACP head Walter White spoke little about the specter of communism, instead focusing on the inevitable violence that would come if racism and colonialism continued. Acknowledging that European nations benefiting from the Marshall Plan received much economic strength from their colonies, White argued that "it would be utter folly for the United States to help white Europe" and still "permit it to continue to deny freedom and opportunity to colonial peoples." White, pointing to wars of liberation in Indonesia and Indochina as omens, maintained that continuing down that path "will speed revolt among hundreds of millions of brown, yellow, and black people who are determined to have freedom also." Marshall Plan dollars, he testified, should not be used to tighten Europe's grip on its restive empires.[29]

Even as White spoke, a surging nationalism was fueling change throughout Asia. America's own control of the Philippines had formally ended, with the Stars and Stripes lowered on 4 July 1946. India, Britain's jewel in the crown, slipped away the next year. The bloody war the Dutch were waging to hold Indonesia was generating international outrage, and by the following year Indonesians had won their hard-fought independence. Mounting resistance embroiled French efforts to restore control over Indochina. These wars of liberation—highlighted in White's speech—were part of a worldwide endeavor to dismantle white supremacy. Anticolonial voices were working to transcend national, racial, ideological, and historical boundaries to take on a system of oppression that had reigned for hundreds of years.

Nevertheless, the Marshall Plan's U.S. dollars did flow. Experts estimate that during the Marshall Plan years, export of dollar-earning and dollar-saving commodities from European colonies in Africa totaled some $400 million.[30] After the United States and its Western European allies established NATO in 1949, American funds made available through NATO further supported Europeans in their efforts to maintain control over their colonies. Convinced that recovering European economies relied on resources extracted from their colonies as well as on American dollars, European efforts to maintain colonial control met with little resistance from U.S. officials. Despite seeing the rising force of nationalism in Asia, U.S. officials focused on supporting European allies and, in Africa, backing friendly white rule.[31]

"Development Based on the Concepts of Democratic Fair-Dealing"

As it supported European allies, the Truman administration also sought ways to make less stark the racial policies of white rule. Facing criticism at home for continued racial discrimination and segregation, and criticism abroad for not backing anticolonialism strongly enough, the Truman administration made moves on both fronts. Domestically, a number of actions sought to shore up support among liberals and African Americans, including Executive Order 9981 and its directive to end discrimination and segregation in the armed forces. The administration also took steps to provide some assistance to those disadvantaged in Africa, Asia, and Latin America. In his inauguration speech in January 1949, Truman emphasized the global struggle against communism and his support for democracy. He also announced four major courses of action his administration would undertake in a "program for peace and freedom." The first three outlined support for the UN, continuing economic recovery efforts, and the strengthening of collective security against communist aggression. His fourth major goal was to "embark on a bold new program for making the benefits of our scientific advances and industrial progress available for the improvement and growth of underdeveloped areas." Truman sketched the daunting parameters: "More than half the people of the world are living in conditions approaching misery. Their food is inadequate. They are victims of disease. Their economic life is primitive and stagnant. Their poverty is a handicap and a threat both to them and to more prosperous areas." But he remained optimistic: "For the first time in history, humanity possesses the knowledge and skill to relieve the suffering of these people."[32]

Truman framed a vision of the United States working to share its industrial, scientific, and technical capabilities to help "peace-loving peoples . . . realize their aspirations for a better life." With an aim "to help the free peoples of the world, through their own efforts, to produce more food, more clothing, more materials for housing, and more mechanical power to lighten their burdens," Truman presented a vision of a bountiful future. Aware of the realities of a world of imperial powers and colonized peoples, he carefully noted, "The old imperialism—exploitation for foreign profit—has no place in our plans. What we envisage is a program of development based on the concepts of democratic fair-dealing." Truman sought to promote peace and prosperity while changing conditions that might lead toward communist advances, and Africa seemed a likely and fruitful ground for the work.[33]

A "fair deal" writ global, the idea was to provide a practical, positive development program without visible strings. The technical assistance program became known as Point Four due to its placement as the fourth and final foreign policy objective enumerated in the address. While earlier "development" programs in North–South relations existed, this marked a potentially significant step for the United States.[34] Yet at the announcement it was an idea, not a plan, and not an idea enthusiastically supported by either Congress or Truman's own State Department. Funding was slow to be appropriated, and when it was, it was markedly limited. There would be no Marshall Plan for Africa. The Truman administration recommended first year funding of $45 million; Congress authorized $35 million in 1950, a pittance compared to the $2.25 billion for the Marshall Plan at the same time.[35]

European allies also held reservations about Point Four. The French may have been the most suspicious that America primarily had designs on advancing its own economic interests and even displacing France as the great power in North and West Africa. This was due at least in part to postwar U.S. diplomats in West Africa stressing future investment opportunities for American businesses, particularly for engineering firms that could work with French authorities on infrastructure development projects, and banks and import/export firms that could gain market share in growing economies.[36] Historians have begun to unearth evidence pointing to the more substantial engagement of Truman and Eisenhower administration officials with French West Africa; in the early postwar years, Africa was undoubtedly in the frame for economic interests. Indeed, the Economic Cooperation Administration developed ambitious schemes to expand development in sub-Saharan Africa, with French territories slated to receive the largest share.[37]

As the Cold War grew ever more tense, some of the internal dynamics in the Western alliance did, too. In May 1950, George McGhee—the assistant secretary of state for Near Eastern, South Asian, and African Affairs—gave a speech in Oklahoma. The former Rhodes Scholar and Texas oilman outlined four U.S. objectives in Africa: ultimate self-government for colonies; economic development that mutually benefited Africans and Europeans; preservation of American commercial and economic rights; assurance that

Africans would choose to stay on the side of the West in the Cold War. His speech angered Paris, which demanded an explanation of McGhee's statement regarding self-rule. In response, the State Department went to great lengths to reassure the French, and McGhee was compelled to emphasize to French officials that the United States wanted to help France "maintain peace and security in her colonies and . . . to assist the French in an orderly development of these colonies."[38]

Opening the door to Africa by breaking down barriers to American trading interests continued in the long tradition of pursuing global economic opportunities but ran afoul of European colonial desires to ensure control of those very areas. Overarching strategic interests and deepening Cold War apprehensions, along with arguments about colonies and their significance to European economic recovery, worked to shape U.S. interest in economic concerns in Africa. Economic development in Africa, and whether a lack of development left Africans vulnerable to the appeals of America's foes, faded in the face of stiff European disagreement. Despite its strong postwar hand, the growing Cold War influenced just how willing the United States was to break down trade barriers, particularly after the 1947 Truman Doctrine established the strategic priority of resisting communism. Such concerns also influenced the degree to which the Truman administration promoted its own Point Four program for development, a path that seemed to address African wishes for economic progress and support movement toward independence yet threatened European authority.

Point Four never took off in Africa, and only a small amount of funding made it to the continent. Point Four in Africa faced buffeting winds from many directions: from European colonial powers that suspected the purity of Washington's motivations, especially given America's continuing search for raw materials and markets and its dominant capitalist position; from some Africans and African Americans, who were skeptical that no strings were attached as America advanced its interests; and from Congress, whose members balked at the expense. Disappointed supporters criticized Truman for creating a program with the "head of a lion and the body of a mouse," while anticolonial critics complained that projects focused more on U.S. interests and elites in countries than general social and economic improvement. The half measures and quick disintegration reveal potential paths that could have been taken, moments of possibilities that then hardened in particular choices. Even so, as subsequent chapters show, ideas of development and modernization continued to infuse American thinking about the relationship with Africa.[39]

The limits to Point Four also reflected the political context of the deepening Cold War. Interest in Washington about anticolonialism and African development had given way to the belief that African colonies could help the recovery of European allies who were vital to a Western alliance against the spread of communism. Economic considerations were folding into political determinations. The concrete interests of European allies and Washington's perceptions that Africans were vulnerable to communist advances drove political calculations that commonly left support for African aspirations for self-rule as merely verbal. Interest in African economic development was seen in terms of the strength of European allies and the emerging NATO alliance, not in terms of African decolonization.[40]

The Cold War emphasis increasingly framed the conversation regarding U.S. economic engagement with Africa: the concern for European economic recovery; the need for raw materials such as uranium; the use of military bases and facilities. These factors—integral parts of the approach to Africa—were reflected in the December 1950 regional policy statement on Africa south of the Sahara, which supported no "premature" granting of independence.[41]

Assistant Secretary McGhee emphasized the continuing role for colonial powers, using a June 1951 speech before Northwestern University's Institute on Contemporary Africa to extol the virtues of development programs by colonial governments. He opined that a "vast ferment of cooperative activity in the development of Africa" pervaded the continent. He cautioned that for many Africans, "only slightly touched by modern civilization," the immediate problem was not political status but health, education, and economic concerns. McGhee concluded that "the peoples of Africa must realize that the greatest danger to the full realization of their economic, social, and spiritual development lies in the menace of Communist imperialism, which threatens the security of the entire free world and assures for the Africans as colonial peoples—not self-government but a dark future of political and cultural enslavement." For McGhee and the Truman administration, the threat of a future "Communist imperialism" fully justified continuing European imperialism.[42]

Italy's African Colonies

The first postwar test for decolonization came immediately in the form of how to address the African colonies of defeated Axis power Italy. Africa's proximity to key shipping routes, its importance as a staging area for an invasion of Europe, and its vast and strategic mineral wealth had spurred

U.S. attention to the strategic value of Africa during World War II. With most of Africa under European rule, the State Department had not even created its first African desk until 1938, and then placed it in the Division of Near Eastern Affairs; by 1944 it had established a separate Division for African Affairs. At war's end, American officials trained their gaze on several immediate fronts. Military needs focused on North Africa, the Cape of Good Hope, and Roberts Field in Liberia. Strategic minerals in central and southern Africa were also of essential importance, with the advent of the nuclear age making sources of uranium a particularly high-stakes concern. European economic needs, anticommunist strategic objectives, American military requirements—these were the frames of reference that came to influence U.S. officials' view toward Africa during postwar planning discussions. Anticolonialism and African independence would be secondary, as soon became evident.[43]

Meeting in London in September 1945, the foreign ministers of the four Allied powers discussed the former Italian colonies of Eritrea, Italian Somaliland (Somalia), and Libya as part of the problem of preparing a peace treaty for Italy. The U.S. secretary of state at the time, James Byrnes, proposed placing the former Italian colonies under a UN trusteeship with an administrator subject to the Trusteeship Council. Ralph Bunche drafted the plan using Article 81 of the UN Charter, which permits the UN to be an administering authority over a trust territory. Libya and Eritrea would be granted independence at the end of ten years, while Somaliland's trusteeship would be of an indefinite duration.[44]

The other major powers responded coolly to the U.S. proposal. The proposal negated Soviet demands, raised at Yalta and Potsdam, for shared control in the former Italian colonies, a gambit to secure a place on the Mediterranean by controlling part of Libya. Paris worried about the destabilizing effect promised independence for Libya would have on France's own African colonies. Paris and London both worried about the feasibility of a collective trusteeship. The problem remained unresolved and threatened to forestall an Italian peace treaty, so the foreign ministers deferred a decision. They agreed that if the issue could not be resolved within a year of the peace treaty's enactment, it would be referred to the UN General Assembly.[45]

The Treaty of Peace with Italy went into effect on 15 September 1947, tripping the one-year clock. Given the intensifying Cold War, an amicable resolution remained unlikely. In 1947, a surging Italian Communist Party had the potential to share or even take power through the ballot box. Italian national sentiment favored the reinstatement of the country's former colonies. To make Italian voters more receptive to the Communist Party platform, Moscow shifted its position on control of the colonies, accepting Italian trusteeship. For its part, Washington sought to minimize communist involvement in the postwar administration of any territories throughout the world. The prospect of either a communist-led Italy governing the territories or an international trusteeship in which the Soviets would play a prominent role held no appeal. The Joint Chiefs of Staff strenuously argued against allowing any Soviet foothold in Libya, emphasizing that in the event war erupted, a Soviet presence in North Africa would jeopardize the airspace needed for a strategic bombing offensive against the Soviet homeland. Just as worrisome, a Soviet presence could influence ripening Libyan nationalist sentiment. Yet fundamental disagreement over Italy's role prevented a common position among the Western allies. London and Washington hesitated at returning the areas to Italian authority and thought a British trusteeship more desirable; Paris preferred Italian trusteeship as a way to ensure that France's own colonies developed no ideas about changing their status. Then when Italy's Christian Democrats soundly defeated the Italian Communists in the April 1948 elections, positions scrambled once again. The United States moved toward accepting a governing role by Italy, while the Soviets returned to supporting a collective trusteeship.[46]

None of these positions were primarily concerned with what the actual inhabitants wanted. With no agreement in place, in mid-September the issue became part of the UN deliberations at the 1948 General Assembly meetings in Paris. Anticolonial opposition formed against plans to divide the administration among Italy, France, Britain, and Ethiopia, as well as against plans to restore Italian administration to the areas. The General Assembly defeated a British and Italian plan—the Bevin-Sforza Plan—which would have given the defeated Axis and colonial power Italy a prominent role in governing African territory, but no alternate plan found majority approval either. On 18 May 1949, the General Assembly put over the problem for further consideration to September.[47]

The NAACP and other anticolonial groups hailed the defeat of the Bevin-Sforza proposal, working hard "to keep the 'wishes of the inhabitants' and Italy's shortcomings front and center during the debates." As historian Carol Anderson makes brilliantly clear, "The Association was appalled that the United States consistently put anticommunism above all else. Above principle. Above democracy. Above the Atlantic and UN Charters. Above the right to self-determination."[48]

The question at stake was whether American ideals included the right of all peoples to choose the government under which they live, indeed whether that *is* a basic human right and not simply an abstract philosophical goal. Washington was not leading with a clarion call of democratic self-determination. Anticommunism intertwined with racialized paternalism to chart a path of continuing European governance.

The NAACP, the Council on African Affairs, and other anticolonialists waged a sustained campaign to ensure that the inhabitants of Libya, Somalia, and Eritrea had their voices heard and considered, and to undermine the ambitions of both the Soviets and the West in North Africa and the Horn of Africa.[49] Notwithstanding its own internal discord at the time, NAACP leadership helped "push the reality of the Somalis', Libyans', and Eritreans' objections back onto the U.S. and UN agendas, especially when NATO considerations had muffled the cries of the indigenous peoples." The anticolonial intervention achieved, as Anderson notes, some notable results. After much wrangling, the UN voted to make Libya independent by the end of 1951; to make Somalia independent in ten years, with Italian trusteeship in the interim; and to continue the long search for a solution in Eritrea. A negotiated end to colonial rule in Libya marked a first in the rapidly dawning era that would see European rule ended, north to south, east to west.[50]

"In Those Days We Talked to Them as Friends"

As the Truman administration navigated how it would address European colonialism across the continent, thousands of miles to the south of Tripoli and Mogadishu a new government in white minority-ruled South Africa was elected on a platform of apartheid. Literally "apartness," the policy advocated social separation and, in time, the removal of all people of color from South Africa. It sought white supremacy and, ultimately, a white nation. In short, at a time when much of the world was moving away from nakedly overt policies of white supremacy, on the southernmost tip of Africa white supremacy was being shored up. Faced with Daniel Malan's election as South African prime minister in 1948, the State Department generated its first formal policy statement for an area in Africa south of the Sahara. The statement defined three general objectives: to maintain and develop friendly relations between the United States and South Africa, to encourage South African bonds of sympathy with the Western powers and its continued participation in the UN, and to encourage the economic development of South

Africa and the growth of its foreign trade. The policy statement recognized that race relations reigned as the omnipresent issue in South Africa, and it warned that unless a policy could be developed "on something other than a substratum of fear and hate," progress there "will be hampered and the development she has already achieved will be endangered."[51]

Alliance with apartheid South Africa was not an "unthinking" decision. Washington determined from the outset that its greater interest was in securing South Africa's support for the struggle against communism and in expanding markets for trade, rather than in acting on concerns about racial policy. Officials saw much in South Africa that assured them it would continue as a staunch ally. Historian Thomas Borstelmann describes the dominant impression Americans held of white South Africans immediately after World War II as "English-speaking, Christian, capitalist, anticommunist Western allies who had carved a corner of European civilization on the 'Dark Continent.'" The United States and South Africa had fought together during both world wars, and their economic connections were expanding. Most importantly, as the nuclear age and the Cold War dawned simultaneously, geological surveys revealed that the world's largest undeveloped reserves of uranium ore capable of early commercial development existed in the soil of South Africa. Any number of factors—South Africa's wealth of gold and strategic minerals, its rapidly industrializing economy, its expanding trade with the United States, its strategic location on the sea lanes around the Cape of Good Hope, its historic ties to Great Britain and the Commonwealth, its zealous anticommunism—made the country a desirable ally.[52]

Yet South Africa's discriminatory and segregative apartheid laws, its shameful domestic treatment of Indians, and its refusal to submit a trusteeship agreement for South West Africa (Namibia) swiftly gained a higher profile in the UN and around the world. Most of the world's nations opposed the white South African government's actions, and the early stages of what would grow to be a global anti-apartheid movement soon commenced. At the same time, and not unlike attention to the fate of Italy's former colonies to the north, attention south of the equator in the late 1940s focused squarely on the mandate given to South Africa after World War I. The League of Nations had assigned to it what had been German South West Africa, and South Africa harbored designs on permanently absorbing the territory. With the death of the League of Nations, the status of the mandate entered uncharted waters, and in 1946 South Africa announced its intention to annex the territory. UN member states disagreed, believing that the UN stood as the heir to the league and that South West Africa should be made part of the UN trusteeship system. Member states and international organizations worked to prevent South Africa from annexing the vast region. Newly independent India, emerging as a leading voice against white supremacy and for self-determination, became an implacable foe of Pretoria. India's links to South Africa traced back to the migration of thousands of indentured Indian workers in the nineteenth century. The racist treatment they faced prompted Mohandas Gandhi to debut his nonviolent resistance of satyagraha shortly after the turn of the twentieth century. Decades later in 1946, Gandhi continued to encourage and support South African Indians in a passive resistance campaign, now against the Asiatic Land Tenure and Indian Representation Act. India continued to broaden its efforts, ultimately leading international condemnation of the entire white supremacist structure of South Africa and its designs on South West Africa.[53]

An array of organizations in the United States joined the fight, including the International League for the Rights of Man, the American Friends Service Committee, the Council on African Affairs, the Civil Rights Congress, the American Civil Liberties Union, and the NAACP. The threat posed by Malan's retrograde government was clear. In the aftermath of the 1948 election, the NAACP's *The Crisis* warned its readers that while outgoing prime minister Jan Smuts was bad, "the Nazi-minded Dr. Malan" would try to turn back the hands of the clock of civilization on race.[54] These organizations worked to counter South Africa's ongoing press to annex South West Africa and incorporate it as a fifth province—or, in the words of Prime Minister Malan, to "knit South West Africa and the Union together in such a manner, knit them constitutionally in such a way that the countries will in the future be inseparably bound together."[55]

With the UN still defining its protocols and workings, these outside organizations were essential in raising voices opposed to South Africa's plans. The design for the UN allowed only member states to have direct access to the international body, which had caused Du Bois to point out "how consistently the Allies had disfranchised the 750 million people who lived in the colonial world. . . . According to the proposals . . . only states could join the UN, bring a complaint before the Security Council, or appeal to the International Court of Justice. Colonies had no rights." To hear directly the voices of those colonized, or even people committed to representing their interests, took massive and ongoing pressure. Colonial powers worried about the implications of providing a venue for voices that favored decolonization anywhere in the world. Nonetheless, NAACP board member and U.S. delegate to the UN's Fourth Committee Channing Tobias and others worked successfully to get direct testimony about South West Africa in New York.[56]

In South Africa itself, the Anglican reverend Michael Scott made the defense of the interests of the indigenous peoples of South West Africa a personal crusade, linking arms with the NAACP in support of the cause. At tremendous personal sacrifice, Scott concentrated his time and energy on speaking out for people who had no opportunity to argue their case at the UN.[57] Having traveled to and through South West Africa to gather evidence about conditions there, Scott's testimony helped compel the UN General Assembly to ask the International Court of Justice for an advisory opinion on South West Africa's status and South Africa's responsibilities. These efforts contributed to a 1950 ruling that the mandate was still in existence and South Africa must adhere to its rules. The ruling met with outright hostility from the Malan government while buoying those who sought to free South West Africa from Pretoria's yoke. The coalition of anticolonial groups next fought for direct testimony from indigenous Africans living in South West Africa, particularly the leaders of the Hereros and Namas. Overcoming strong pushback from Britain and other colonial powers, by late 1951 the UN issued invitations.[58]

But Malan's government threw up another obstacle: it refused to issue passports for these men and women to make the journey. The action inflamed world opinion and further isolated Pretoria. Within weeks, the UN created committees to investigate conditions in South West Africa and racial conditions in South Africa itself.[59]

Even so, the Truman administration continued to view the issues of South West Africa and South Africa's overtly racist treatment of its population as distractions from the greater issue of containing communism. Washington took no strong stance against South Africa's continued control over South West Africa. Yet what Washington treated as a minor distraction stirred up antagonism and resentment among people of color around the world. Updating its policy statement for South Africa in March 1951, the State Department spoke about South Africa's "reactionary racial policies, and the difficulties which those policies have engendered in the UN." The criticism voiced in the UN was aligning nations against white South Africa while also providing useful material for Soviet propaganda against the West. Working with South Africa linked the United States to South Africa's racial policies, damaging American efforts to win the hearts and minds of the world's colonized peoples. Cold War concerns and UN criticism prompted U.S. officials to try to encourage the South African government "to adopt a more conciliatory attitude in the UN." Yet that was as far as U.S. officials would go, reaffirming the fundamental policy objective first articulated in 1948: "It is in our interest to maintain friendly relations with South Africa because of strategic considerations and also because South Africa represents a good market for our products."[60]

Just north of South Africa, racial realities crashed down on the relationship of Seretse Khama and Ruth Williams, one of the twentieth century's dramatic romances, highlighting in deeply personal terms the consequences of Washington's priorities. Khama was the designated heir to the throne of the Bangwato, the largest Tswana chieftaincy in colonial Bechuanaland. He was the grandson of Khama the Great, who along with fellow Batswana leaders had used diplomacy to stave off Afrikaner annexation, though at the price of the establishment of a British protectorate over Bechuanaland. After the death of Seretse's father in 1925, Tshekedi Khama became regent for Seretse, who would later receive a Bachelor of Arts degree from the University of Fort Hare in South Africa, then study at Oxford for a year. Seretse then moved to London to train as a barrister, where he attended a London Missionary Society dance and met and fell in love with Ruth Williams, who was working as a typist. Despite disapproval from Seretse's regent uncle, Ruth's father, her employer, the Anglican church, and some Bangwato, Seretse and Ruth married in 1948. The price would turn out to be excruciatingly high: London not only prevented Khama from assuming his rightful chieftainship but in time would exile him from Bechuanaland. The expulsion sparked protests from the Bangwato against Britain's unwarranted incursion into its internal affairs.

South Africa's covert role added fuel to the anger. South Africa's longstanding desire to annex the British protectorates of Bechuanaland, Basutoland, and Swaziland kept Pretoria mindful of the internal politics of the protectorates. In 1949, South Africa made interracial marriage illegal, and the government shuddered at the thought of such a prominent display of interracialism so close to its borders, let alone potentially within its borders. Malan's government declared the couple prohibited immigrants, and exerted pressure on the British to remove Khama from the scene.

Across the Atlantic, outraged African Americans denounced those who placed political calculations above the right to love and marry without consequence. The issue held deep meaning, especially as roughly one-third of the United States still made interracial marriage illegal. "The blood of the African natives on Malan and his gang is dripping on the British and indirectly upon us," blazed the *Chicago Defender.* "We submit that the United States is morally obligated to crack down on the Union of South Africa and the British government for this inhuman attack upon the natives of Africa, which is now climaxed by the exile of Prince Seretse Khama and his wife." To prod action, the *Defender* noted that Britain's actions against Seretse and Ruth aided the cause of the Russians. The *Baltimore Afro-American* emphasized the color issue, declaring the South Africans to be "more anti-colored than the Rankins and Bilbos here." It, too, called on the U.S. government to end subsidies to Britain because it supported a government that discriminated against people of color. The marriage became wrapped in the symbolism of color and integration and was regular news in the Black press. The Council on African Affairs sent a letter of concern to the UN secretary general, underscoring that the British government had violated the Universal Declaration of Human Rights provision against arbitrary arrest, detention, or exile. At the NAACP's 1950 convention, the delegates condemned the British government's expulsion of Seretse Khama, passing a resolution calling the action "an arrogant attack upon two people who have participated in an interracial marriage." Du Bois boldly ventured that the case could mark "the beginning of the independence of Africa."[61]

The marriage and the Khamas' subsequent actions marked yet one more act of defiance on a continent moving to overturn white supremacy. After five years of exile, Khama renounced his throne and returned to his homeland with his family. He soon founded the Bechuanaland Democratic Party and helped chart the path toward self-determination. When Botswana gained independence in 1966, he became the nation's founding president.[62]

U.S. diplomats in South Africa and State Department officials in Washington warily watched the escalating racial tensions in southern Africa and Pretoria's moves toward a white supremacist police state. The American embassy assessed the greatest source of communist strength in the area as "the restrictive and often repressive treatment of Natives," and found that "the legitimate grievances of Natives are legion and among the few persons who espouse these grievances the majority of vocal ones are Communists." Yet this was not taken as reason to reassess whether the U.S. approach to South Africa might feed the very thing it most feared: the spread of communism.[63]

On both sides of the Atlantic, U.S. officials submerged concerns over South Africa's racial policies and how they affected the people of the country and region. With the Korean War underway and South Africa in support of the U.S.-led efforts, including military support, the Truman administration solidified its view of South Africa as an important anticommunist ally. When American ambassador John Erhardt listed objectives for U.S. policy in South Africa shortly before his death in Cape Town in February 1951, he concentrated on strengthening South Africa's support of the West, expediting the utilization of South Africa's strategic raw materials, and maintaining South African participation in the UN and the British Commonwealth. As for the racial divide, American influence should "cautiously and without giving offense" work to bring racial policies "closer to the general standards of Western democracies" and evoke a harmonious formula for the coexistence of all.[64] Erhardt's successor, Ambassador Waldemar J. Gallman, retained many of Erhardt's attitudes and beliefs, ones that mirrored the way many Americans viewed white South Africans. Reflecting on his tenure as head of the American mission to South Africa, Gallman noted that neither time nor the furtherance of apartheid had changed his admiration for the parallels he saw to the pioneer story of the United States. Gallman wrote of white Europeans moving through the African interior, taming the land, and turning it into "a bit of Western Europe." He lauded their establishment of schools and churches and a parliamentary system of government "years before the natives showed any signs of political consciousness." He waxed on the idea that, while apparently having "no political consciousness," Africans had muscles, and "the natives' help was indispensable" in mines, fields, the building of roads, and the everyday cooking and cleaning. In Gallman's formulation, European brains and African brawn had combined to create the best of Africa.[65]

His Westernized historical understanding, racism, and paternalism led Gallman to believe that Africans had no political systems in place outside European structures and contributed to why he thought white South Africa should be handled gently. "My tour as Ambassador to the Union of South Africa predated the era of scolding the white South Africans. In those days we talked to them as friends." In his telling, he tried to convince the Nationalist Party to stop pursuing an ever more "immoderate" position, but Gallman made clear that scolding—such as the UN resolutions condemning South Africa—was ill-advised and, further, unchristian-like. Using scripture ("He that is without sin—let him cast the first stone"), Gallman concluded his ruminations about the "Black-White Problem in South Africa" with a caution to those who cast judgment: "Ponder those words when one feels the urge to sermonize." Gallman eventually left South Africa to become ambassador to Iraq and then the director general of the U.S. Foreign Service.[66]

"A Serious Dilemma": Self-Determination or Colonial Rule

So it was that during the final years of the 1940s and the start of the 1950s, the Truman administration, amid a deepening Cold War, formulated its approach to potential decolonization in Africa. In mid-1948, the CIA assessed the implications of the breakup of colonial empires for U.S. security. The primary concern: "The shift of the dependent areas from the orbit of the colonial powers not only weakens the probable European allies of the US but deprives the US itself of assured access to vital bases and raw materials in these areas in event of war." Almost as worrisome, should newly independent states become oriented toward the USSR, "US military and economic security would be seriously threatened."[67]

According to the CIA, several elements had spurred the development of successful independence movements, and as a result, "further disintegration of the remaining colonial empires appear[ed] inevitable." Beginning with Japan's defeat of the colonial powers during World War II and its encouragement of nationalism in occupied areas, the postwar military and economic weakness of the colonial powers undermined their ability to resist nationalist demands. The UN itself provided a forum for agitation on the colonial issue and a mechanism for liquidating colonies. Further, within the colonial powers, "liberal-socialist elements" increasingly favored voluntary liquidation of the empires, and recently liberated and other sympathetic states such as the USSR encouraged independence movements. With the USSR "effectively exploiting the colonial issue and the economic nationalism of the underdeveloped areas," the CIA warned that communists could divide the non-Soviet world, weaken the Western powers, and gain the goodwill of colonial and former colonial areas. "The colonial independence movement, therefore, is no longer purely a domestic issue between the European colonial powers and their dependencies."[68]

The CIA assessment highlighted that the United States had a tremendous stake in the outcome of decolonization, and "its stand on the colonial issue and economic nationalism will have a major effect on the attitudes of these colonial and former colonial areas." The United States, however, was in an "unfortunate position." On the one hand, its historic sympathy with the aspirations of dependent peoples for self-government meant that those areas had come to expect U.S. backing, and "to the extent that the US acquiesces in or supports restrictive colonial policies on the part of Western European nations, it will jeopardize its positions in these areas." On the other hand, the European colonial powers "are the chief prospective US allies in its power struggle with the USSR and it is difficult for the US to oppose these powers on colonial issues." While the overall benefits of the colonial empires were open to debate, in the short term, losing the benefits of their empires "would hamper their economic recovery and possibly threaten the stability of governments friendly to the US."[69]

The tougher question was how to view the longer-term colonial situation and determining how then to proceed. The intelligence estimate made clear to all its readers—and it was circulated at the highest levels of government—that "if the colonial powers do not basically modify their present colonial policies, they will in the long run lose the very strategic and economic advantages in their dependencies and former dependencies they are seeking to retain." The estimate went even further: efforts to restrict nationalist activities or forcibly retain colonial areas "may actually weaken rather than strengthen colonial powers." The United States therefore faced "a serious dilemma": if it encouraged colonial self-determination and economic development, it might incur the immediate wrath of colonial powers and be charged itself with economic imperialism; if it supported the colonial powers, it would alienate subjugated peoples and, by laying the groundwork for inevitable future disruptions, in the long run weaken the power balance with the USSR.[70]

In early 1949, former British undersecretary of state for the colonies Ivor Thomas remarked that despite a strong anticolonial tradition in the United States, "with the growth of her own responsibilities, and an increasing awareness of the communist menace, the United States has shown a marked understanding of colonial problems; and the new spirit of American cooperation, which particularly affects Africa, is to be warmly welcomed." The European colonial powers noticed which way Washington was turning, and they appreciated the shift. Faced with opposing choices, Washington's "new spirit" of cooperation was with the comfortable familiarity of European allies and their continuing rule.[71]

By 1950, the United States had framed its policy toward decolonization and white rule in Africa, even if it had not fully explicated or announced it. When the State Department held a regional conference for Africa south of the Sahara in Mozambique, the meeting addressed problems confronting the United States in terms of its political, economic, and cultural relations in the area. The goal: to develop a preliminary statement regarding attitudes, objectives, and policies toward Africa. State Department officials characterized the conference as "an opportunity to lay the foundations for a restatement of American policy toward Africa," a curious phrasing since at that time, "no comprehensive U.S. policy had been formulated for Africa south of the Sahara," according to then assistant secretary McGhee.[72]

In preparation for the conference, the State Department consulted a panel of American experts on African affairs. Eleven nongovernmental panelists participated. The outside consultants suggested coupling the new program for technical assistance proposed under Truman's Point Four program with a bold reaffirmation of U.S. opposition to colonialism. "Such a definition would be a much more powerful weapon in our cold war with Russia than any tactical or ad hoc approach."[73]

Armed with advice to affirm opposition to colonialism and support for economic development, the conference did neither. It produced no bold new initiatives and certainly no bold reaffirmation of support for decolonization. Concerns about communism and strategic minerals consistently outweighed ideals such as self-determination and majority rule. At the Lourenço Marques meeting, foreign service officers from around the continent were called on to assess the situation. Rhodesia: "Little evidence of Communism at present." Belgian Congo: "Little evidence of Communism among natives. . . . Natives are not receptive to Communism." Gold Coast: "No Communist Party as such. Only two known Communists in territory." Liberia: "Communism is not much of a problem. There is no evidence of a tie-up with Moscow." Nevertheless, in a Washington beset by Cold War fever, many in the corridors of power—and indeed across the nation—had trouble distinguishing communist advances from the heartfelt ambitions of colonized peoples to free themselves from European rule. Deepening Cold War tensions inevitably kept concerns about communism's spread in Africa at the forefront. Faced with what they perceived as a choice between continued colonialism under European allies' control or newly independent nations potentially ripe for communist penetration, Truman administration officials preferred the first alternative, despite their own foreign service personnel's assessment that there was no serious communist threat.[74]

This, then, was not simply about communism. The Western sensibilities of U.S. officials predisposed them to believe that colonized peoples were better off under the guidance of Western powers. Few would warrant that Africans were ready for self-government. Shortly after the Lourenço Marques meetings, the Bureau of Near Eastern, South Asian, and African Affairs prepared a paper on the "Future of Africa" for the U.S. delegation to the American, British, and French foreign ministers meeting in London in May 1950. When describing the "attitudes, interest, and policy of the United States with regard to Africa," the first objective was "political and economic stability sufficient to resist domination by unfriendly movements or powers through subversion or aggression." The second objective was "advancement of the social, political, economic, and educational condition of the African peoples *at a rate commensurate with their capacity*" (italics added). The last phrase—unthinkable in a paper about the future of Europe—was added at the request of the Joint Chiefs of Staff.[75]

Participants focused on U.S. policy and Africa almost entirely from the perspective of the colonial governments; they evaluated how colonial officials, not African peoples, viewed U.S. policies and actions. "It was emphasized," came the conclusion, "that one factor which must be borne constantly in mind is that the mass of indigenous people in Africa South of the Sahara know little about our foreign policies and probably care less."[76] This belief assumed that Africans did not care how much the United States was backing their colonial rulers, and it provided little basis for officials in Washington to promote a strong anticolonial line. McGhee himself later admitted that "there was no hint of boldness with respect to the promotion of decolonization" and that at best, "there are vague references to African—as distinguished from metropolitan—opinion."[77]

By the end of 1950, the five-year "Regional Policy Statement on Africa South of the Sahara" highlighted that "the metropolitan powers need reassurances from the United States that we are not purposefully working to bring about a premature according of political independence to the peoples of Africa." The emphasis was clear: continued European rule was fine. The capabilities of Africans were suspect; "premature" independence should be avoided.[78] Western-oriented, anticommunist, and economic interests drove the objectives. The solution put forward was to "cooperate with the responsible governments in the political, economic, and social advancement of the people of Africa at the maximum practicable rate."[79]

The policy statement articulated that "sympathy on the part of the American Negroes for the aspirations of the native peoples of Africa" could affect the implementation of the objectives.[80] Yet a variety of ongoing factors—African Americans' limited voice on foreign policy, policymakers' prejudices, the Cold War's dampening influence—worked against African Americans and others seeking a stronger anticolonial position in Washington during this critical period when the United States formed its basic policy framework for addressing the rising tide of nationalism in Africa. They could not overcome the powerful intertwined forces of anticommunism and racial prejudices that helped support ongoing backing of continuing white supremacy in Africa.

Phrases such as "at a rate commensurate with their capacity," "at the maximum practicable rate," and no "premature independence" peppered State Department policy papers and speeches. While recognizing the desire for independence and its inevitable coming, American officials in the early 1950s felt little drive to end white minority rule. African independence seemed too fraught. For all intents and purposes, U.S. policy accepted the continuance of white rule in Africa. Officials determined that no colony should become independent until the West could be confident that it would be against communism and safely pro-Western. Assistant Secretary McGhee declared in his 1951 speech at Northwestern, "Immediate independence is, however, not the cure for all colonial problems. The United States government has always maintained that premature independence for primitive, uneducated peoples can do them more harm than good and subject them to exploitation by indigenous leaders, unrestrained by the civil standards that come with widespread education, that can be just as ruthless as that of aliens. Also, giving full independence to peoples unprepared to meet aggression or subversion can endanger not only the peoples themselves but the security of the free world."[81]

American officials were moving toward what in their minds was a "middle position" of supporting both their European allies and African hopes for self-determination. But there was no "middle path" here. If the dilemma was colonial rule or self-determination, by the end of 1950 Washington clarified its choice: in this bipolar world, it wanted the short-term security of continued white allies in control.

The attitude of some American officials toward decolonization and Africans was painfully illustrated once again when American consul Donald Lamm wrote to McGhee assessing the situation in Mozambique shortly after the 1950 Lourenço Marques conference. Lamm wanted to assure McGhee that "the native population does not present any problem from a political point of view." Lamm thought the reason self-evident: with no political organizing and widespread illiteracy and censorship, the people "accept the complete and autocratic rule of the white minority as the natural order of things." He opined that "native workers" were "very apathetic, performing their duties only under close supervision." Lamm casually observed that though corporal punishment had to be used extensively, he had seen more positive incentives: "special inducements, such as meat, are offered as a reward for steady work" on some large estates.[82] Lamm's message, redolent of antebellum America, reinforced any inclination to see white rule as natural,

Africans as lazy. With reports such as these, on what basis would Washington actively support decolonization?

The rising tide of anticolonial African nationalism prevented the United States from fully supporting European interests without alienating Africans. African nationalists viewed anticommunism as far less important than anticolonialism. As historian Thomas Borstelmann notes, for the majority of the world's population, "the Cold War and the supposed dangers of communism were merely distractions from the historic opportunity provided by World War II for ending the European colonialism that had long dominated the lives of most of the world's people."[83]

And by the end of 1951, the rising force of nationalism was starting to effect dramatic change on the continent. Libya gained independence by year's end, the first of the wave of North African states. South of the Sahara, Kwame Nkrumah had been released from jail in the Gold Coast (Ghana) and appointed as leader of government business, reiterating, "What we want is the right to govern ourselves, or even to misgovern ourselves."[84] The coming decade would fundamentally alter both the map and the future of Africa as Africans liberated the continent.

2 No Stopping the Torrent, 1952–1960

> One basic question transcends all others in considering what United States policy toward Africa should be, and it is this. We must make up our minds whether we stand with the metropole powers in endeavoring to maintain their centralized control over the economies and political freedoms of the developing areas in Africa, or whether we shall throw our influence on the side of those who seek political and economic autonomy. On the one hand we risk damaging our relationship with some of our NATO partners, but, on the other, we risk for all time losing the friendship of large areas of Africa which inevitably, sooner or later, will be independent. It is a serious dilemma, but we must not take refuge in equivocation.
>
> —Clarence Randall, April 1958

> No Congolese worthy of the name will ever forget that independence has been won by struggle. . . . This struggle of tears, fire, and blood makes us profoundly proud because it was a noble and just struggle, an indispensable struggle to put an end to the humiliating bondage imposed on us by force. Our lot was eighty years of colonial rule; our wounds are still too fresh and painful to be driven from our memory.
>
> —Patrice Lumumba, June 1960

On 6 March 1957, Nkrumah and his fellow nationalists readied to watch the hoisting of their newly independent nation's flag. At the center of the flag's tricolored field of red, gold, and green was a five-pointed black star that evoked the Black Star Line of Pan-Africanist Marcus Garvey. A host of dignitaries had arrived from America to mark the occasion, including future Nobel laureate Martin Luther King and future U.S. president Richard Nixon, who met each other for the first time in Accra. Dr. King arrived fresh off the Montgomery bus boycott, while Vice President Nixon arrived at the urging of President Dwight Eisenhower and Secretary of State John Foster Dulles. While King could only afford to travel a few days, Nixon visited the African continent for an extended three-week journey, with the most visible and vital stop being to officially represent the United States in Ghana.

The first country south of the Sahara to cast off colonial rule, Ghanaian independence held tremendous symbolic import for Africans and people of African descent; it also held great meaning for those locked in the Cold War struggle. Ghana seemingly had the potential to lead an entire slate of African nations into nonaligned status or, even more threatening to U.S. officials, into sympathetic alliance with the Soviet Union. Sending the vice president as a message of U.S. interest in and concern for this newly liberated nation was a meaningful gesture in the larger war.

America faced a new Africa during these pivotal years, one in which dozens of African nations moved toward political freedom. An array of liberation struggles, from the relatively peaceful moves toward constitutional change to protracted armed conflicts, appeared across the continent. The well-traveled Nixon returned to the United States championing greater attention to the emerging nations of the continent, and he found himself shortly thereafter being billed as the father of a new African policy. Belatedly, the Eisenhower administration began to expend some effort in Africa in an attempt to effectuate a Western-oriented decolonization. And yet even with a liberating Africa forcing reconsideration of policies toward the continent, on the whole the administration continued with the established approach that, for all intents and purposes, favored the colonial powers. Doing so precluded the United States from taking advantage of its legacy of never having been a colonial power in Africa.

Prime Minister Sylvanus Olympio of Togo remarked to American observer George Houser at the 1958 All-African People's Conference in Accra: "Everyone is our friend after we are independent. But our real friends are those who support us in the difficult days of our struggles." Yet Eisenhower, as uncomfortable with the rapid changes wrought by African nationalism as he was with the domestic civil rights movement, worried about the potential consequences for the struggle against communism. He and his administration generally sought stability through continuing Western influence. The United States sent no representation to the conference, offering only a belated message of greeting late in the proceedings. In recollecting the era, Eisenhower would write, "The determination of the peoples for self-rule, their own flag, and their own vote in the United Nations resembled a torrent overrunning everything in its path, including, frequently, the best interests of those concerned."[1]

Eisenhower and his leading advisers felt most comfortable with the status quo even if—or perhaps more accurately, especially if—that meant white rule in Africa. They held long-standing prejudices about those of African descent, stoking an underlying belief that Africans might not govern themselves well. These lurking preconceptions, combined with concerns about communism's potential spread, continued to convince officials that African desires for freedom could end up harming their own "best interests." After touring the continent in 1958, Clarence Randall—chair of the Council on Foreign Economic Policy—provided his unequivocal answer to the dilemma facing Washington: "We must publicly draw attention to the great danger to all of Africa that could arise from premature or disorderly independence on the part of an area that is neither politically, socially, nor economically ready for such a changed situation. We must urge caution. We must be for the evolutionary and not the revolutionary approach to autonomy."[2]

Yet by the time the Eisenhower administration neared its end, much of North, West, East, and Central Africa had gained or was on the cusp of independence. Africans were pushing aside any default to continuing white rule. Yet as more and more African nations moved rapidly toward independence, and as the end of white rule became more apparent, fears of instability and chaos encouraged thoughts in Washington that security might be found in the alternative of authoritarian governments led by those sympathetic to the West. Nixon developed early on a penchant for strongman rule among Third World allies. This inclination, which would have enormous consequences in future years, was seen as a way to keep order amid nationalist upheavals and to provide a bulwark against communist advances.

"European Governments . . . Mak[e] Substantial Contributions to the Evolution of These Peoples"

During Truman's last year in office, Africa appeared to be aflame with growing unrest. The African National Congress launched its Defiance Campaign against Unjust Laws to protest apartheid in South Africa. Tensions between supporters of the Kenya Land and Freedom Army, popularly known as the Mau Mau, and white settlers escalated into outright warfare. Anticolonial actions appeared with more frequency around the continent.

Alarmed, American officials launched a new round of internal debate over how to engage colonial areas. Africa was very much on the agenda. Discussion focused less on priorities—all agreed that keeping Africa allied with the West stood paramount—and more on how best to achieve the goal. Support for European allies was challenged by Africans' demands for change. The administration's ongoing effort to chart and follow what they termed a "middle course," a "middle position," or a "middle-of-the-road position" became more pronounced.[3] The prevailing argument remained that rapid decolonization would damage the overall anticommunist effort; that quickly ending white rule would lead to weak, unstable indigenous governments susceptible to Soviet or Chinese control. Further, with arguments that colonial markets continued to be important for postwar European economic health, "Europeanists" maintained that white rule in Africa remained necessary for economically strengthening Western European allies and enabling them to guard against communist gains. While the Europeanists understood that in the long run America's strength and security depended on friendly relations with areas in Africa that would inevitably gain independence, they nevertheless insisted that immediate, even apocalyptic, concerns meant more. In short, as Ridgway Knight, acting deputy director of the Office of Western European Affairs, put it, America's "long-term interests will have little meaning unless they are reconciled with our immediate security interests. There would be little value in throwing our support to dependent peoples with a view to developing worthwhile democratic friends in half a century, if, by so doing, we might seriously jeopardize present American security and the continued survival of democracy itself."[4]

Foreshadowing what would be a long and ongoing divide, officials involved with the UN or Third World areas countered that continued white supremacy drove Africans to communism as their only means for liberation. In addition, these officials asserted that undue support for colonial powers alienated hundreds of millions of formerly colonized peoples in countries such as India and Indonesia. These peoples could become a "third force"—what might later become a "nonaligned movement"—whose manpower and resources might be denied to the West in its struggle against communism, or, worse yet, might join with the Eastern bloc. U.S. interests lay in more strongly supporting majority rule. "'Premature independence' obviously is as bad as overdue autonomy," argued the Office of Dependent Area Affairs and the Office of UN Political and Security Affairs. "And experience has shown that Communism thrives on delayed and repressive colonial policy as much as on premature independence movements. The United States should condone or encourage neither."[5]

In truth, the apparent differences tended to be less than met the eye. While they debated the relative weight that should be accorded European interests, neither side argued for substantive and material U.S. support for anticolonial liberation movements. By and large, most believed that the United States would generally have to follow the "difficult middle course." As one participant summed up the matter, while there existed differences of approach, "there is no disagreement on the basic proposition that both our long-term and short-term interest require us to maintain the uncomfortable middle-of-the-road position."[6]

On the eve of Eisenhower's election, amid rising demands for change throughout the African continent, U.S. policy toward Africa stressed stable, white minority rule, with a soupçon of support for eventual Black majority rule. When Truman met with Eisenhower to transition administrations, in their conversations on Africa the agenda particularly noted the strategic areas of North Africa and South Africa.[7] By the time Eisenhower entered the Oval Office, the United States had left behind its more explicit anticolonial talk of the World War II years in favor of strong relations with its European allies and Cold War partners.

The early Eisenhower years saw past thinking carry forward. If consolidating a Western alliance against the Soviets meant accepting that colonial powers would stay in Africa for some indeterminate time, that was a small price to pay, especially given Washington's doubts about the ability of Africans to govern themselves. In 1953, a National Intelligence Estimate (NIE)—one of a continuing series of high-level reports created by the CIA, FBI, State Department, army, navy, air force, and Joint Chiefs of Staff—labeled the "chief problem" in tropical Africa as the "increasing African discontent and demands for self-government." Despite having to deal with the "problem" of people desiring majority rule and independence, the report reassuringly concluded, "The breakdown or overthrow of existing authority is nowhere imminent in Tropical Africa." The authors believed that the colonial powers would make the "adjustments" necessary to prevent discontent from erupting into large-scale revolt for at least a decade and probably longer. White control seemed secure. Few in Washington understood the depth of African nationalism, and even fewer were prepared to deal with it. Faced with other world problems, officials welcomed the illusion of stability in Africa and believed that colonial authority would keep that stability.[8]

While policy changed little when Truman handed power to Eisenhower, historian Thomas Noer argues that the rhetoric, style, and personalities of the incoming administration made its African policy seem even more conservative and hostile to African aspirations.[9] Speaking in October 1953, Eisenhower's new assistant secretary of state for Near Eastern, South Asian, and African Affairs, Henry Byroade, followed a favored formulation. Agreeing that "old-style colonialism" was on the way out, and that much blood and treasure might be saved if the Western world hastened rather than hampered the evolution toward self-determination, he went on to stress far more forcefully the threat of "the new Soviet colonialism." Declaring that "premature independence can be dangerous, retrogressive, and destructive," Byroade defended slow evolution toward independence over immediate change. Surveying reasons why "premature independence" served neither the interests of the West nor of colonized peoples themselves, Byroade justified the continuing colonial presence in Africa by declaring that "serious observers of the African scene agree that the European governments are making substantial contributions to the evolution of these peoples."[10]

For the Byroades of the world, the white man's burden had not ended. The following month, his boss, the new secretary of state John Foster Dulles, spoke of his view of the global battle between liberty and despotism being fought. He described "dependent areas" as a "field of dramatic contest," arguing that nationalism was being used by communism, creating a task of infinite "difficulty and delicacy" to respond to desires for independence without falling into the communist trap of immediate independence.[11] Dulles viewed nationalism with suspicion, neutralism and nonalignment with outright hostility. In 1956, as nationalism swept Africa, Dulles condemned nonalignment as "immoral and shortsighted" and warned that Soviet aggression posed a greater danger than continued white control.[12]

As for the new occupant of the Oval Office, his emphasis in remedying racial inequalities in the United States and in the world proved equally circumscribed. Just as Eisenhower followed a go-slow approach on civil rights in America, proclaiming support for a moderate stance until events in places like Little Rock forced him to act, in Africa Eisenhower was more comfortable with the security of white minority rule despite the obvious inequities that resulted. "Despite his administration's emphasis on America's proclaimed moral and spiritual superiority to communist nations like the Soviet Union," historian Thomas Borstelmann argues, "the president and his advisors failed to recognize either the central moral issue involved in racial inequality or the significance of race relations in the modern world."[13] Unable to overcome his own racial preconceptions, Eisenhower failed to adroitly accept or adjust to the powerful tide that was already sweeping through Africa.

"Did We Think at That Time . . . We Were Ready"

These attitudes and understandings, with their lack of concern about the antidemocratic and systemic racial inequities at the very heart of colonialism, were reflected across America. When *Life* magazine—that widely read purveyor of middle American standards—published a special issue on Africa in May 1953, the article introducing sub-Saharan Africa rested under the boldfaced headline "Black Africa: Primitive Society Holds Out South of the Sahara." "From the headwaters of the Blue Nile to the Cape of Good Hope, across 46 degrees of latitude and two-thirds of a continent," began the article, "many of Africa's 200 million still live in a jungle twilight of a primitive past."[14] *Life* turned to white South African author Stuart Cloete to inform its readership about South Africa. "It must be remembered," cautioned Cloete, "that we are not dealing with American Negroes who think as white men do. These Africans are the sons and grandsons of primitive warriors." *Life*'s readers should not despair, Cloete assured, for with the guiding hand of whites, already much had been accomplished. The "native population has increased by millions since the coming of the white man, who stopped tribal wars, the slave trade, and protected his servants against drought and famine." In Cloete's narrative, wars, slavery, and famine had been stayed by the hand of whites, and such work would continue unless subversive elements such as communists sought their removal.[15]

Life decried the appalling American ignorance of Africa, editorializing that "an informed American attitude towards Africa badly needs developing." Yet in addition to Cloete's piece, other parts of the issue presented the Gold Coast as a place where vendors sell "brain pills" and the Mau Mau in Kenya use "murdering and pillaging" to drive whites out. *Life*'s overall lesson for its readers was clear: white Europeans were the source of civilization in Africa.[16]

The enduring power of such depictions was reinforced in Washington by ongoing portrayals from diplomats working in Africa. While any number of Americans, from private citizens to public officials, supported ideals of freedom throughout the world, many feared that African decolonization harmed African progress and, more germanely in many minds, even aided the spread of communism. African nations moving toward independence seemed fraught with potentially disastrous pitfalls, notwithstanding hopes invested in development ideas.[17]

Reports about the Mau Mau that were generated by U.S. diplomats in Kenya fed stereotyped beliefs that already commanded thinking in Washington. The Mau Mau started receiving mention in consulate reports as early as March 1951. For at least the next year and a half, Vice Consul Robert Stookey and others did not simply excoriate the Mau Mau, which might have been expected given his position. They went further, even faulting the Kikuyu who were resisting the Mau Mau: Kikuyu efforts to defy the Mau Mau through "white" magic instead of cooperating with colonial officials "underlines the state of savagery, ignorance, and barbarism in which the vast majority of indigenous East African tribes remain."[18]

When Kenyan governor Evelyn Baring declared a state of emergency, so began a brutal four-year atrocity-filled effort to break down the insurgency.[19] As the war began, American diplomats sided with the white settlers in language that not only favored the British but also reinforced prejudices and beliefs that supported continued colonial rule as the preferred path for Africa to follow. The consulate reported that in the state of emergency's first five weeks, the government's efforts in "restoring law and order" were met by the Mau Mau "with additional shocking crimes." Further, "despite stern measures taken to deal with the current unrest, lawlessness . . . continued, with resulting bloodshed, terrorism, and property losses."[20]

Consul General Edmund Dorsz, decrying that not even the sanctity of Christmas could stop Mau Mau atrocities, informed Washington of Christmas Eve attacks (conveniently forgetting George Washington's attack on that hallowed evening as Americans fought their own war for independence against the British). The Mau Mau, Dorsz concluded, at minimum had "retarded" orderly political development. Although Dorsz acknowledged that the Kikuyu held legitimate grievances, he did not reflect on what "orderly development" under colonial auspices meant for the vast majority of dispossessed Africans.[21]

Popular culture further reinforced stereotyped thinking, perhaps most graphically in Robert Ruark's novel *Something of Value*, which became a big-screen production starring Rock Hudson, Sidney Poitier, and Dana Wynter. "Like Mr. Ruark's popular novel," the *New York Times* wrote of the film, "it tells a tormented tale of irrepressible conflict between two friends in Africa, one black and the other white. The black man, moved by racial outrage at injustices forced upon him and his witchcraft-worshiping father, falls in with the Mau Mau group and soon is pillaging and murdering in the home of his former friend. Whereupon the latter, joining forces with the defending whites, goes after the Mau Mau terrorists." Any legitimacy in the fight against racial injustice was checked, as it was characterized as being carried on by "witchcraft-worshiping . . . pillaging . . . terrorists."[22]

To be fair, a number of consular officials also spoke eloquently about the hopes and aspirations of African peoples. "The United States should stand for freedom from all forms of oppression, for self-government, and for independence based upon self-determination," argued Consul General Robert McGregor in Léopoldville. While maintaining "it is true that Africans are not ready to make a success of self-government," McGregor looked to America's own past: "But we who threw off the colonial yoke—did we think at that time whether we were ready to assume the responsibilities of self-government?" The sentiment paralleled that of Julius Nyerere's take: "They [the signers of the Constitution] were the same average age as we—and [now they] say we are too young!"[23]

Yet more often, deeply held beliefs and long-standing prejudices informed the views that consular officials sent back to Washington. With exceptions, consular reports continued to regularly depict Africans as inferior, backward, and in need of the continuing guidance of white leadership, lest they fall back into primitiveness or, even worse, fall prey to communism. Writing from Dakar, Consul General C. Vaughan Ferguson, soon to become director of the Office of Southern African Affairs and later director of the Office of West African Affairs, evoked a song popular during the 1899–1902 war in the Philippines, "Underneath the Starry Flag, Civilize Them with a Krag [rifle]." His message: not so long ago Americans accepted colonialism, and in much of Africa, the people were not ready for self-government.[24] Essentialized views of race, and attendant views of the supposed inability of Africans to govern themselves without European guidance or further education, infused the reports of U.S. officials out in the field. "The world, it is submitted," wrote the consul general in Southern Rhodesia, "is better off for the Romans having civilized the Gauls, the Franks and the blue painted Britons."[25] And so, the same week Ghana raised its flag as an independent nation, Consul General Robert Ware in Dar es Salaam again warned against "premature independence" elsewhere.[26]

"Increasing Demands for Self-Government"

But such messages could not effectively address rising anticolonial nationalism in Africa or elsewhere in the world. No matter how much Washington would have liked to focus on stopping communism, anticolonialism continued to sweep along in Africa. As scholar Cheikh Anta Babou reminds us, Africans were liberating themselves, and events unfolding in Africa rather than colonial planning in Europe "dictated the pace and trajectory of decolonization."[27]

Further, Washington worried that American race relations were undermining U.S. Cold War efforts throughout the colonial world. Perhaps the most prominent manifestation of this occurred in the *Brown v. Board of*

Education case. The amicus curiae brief filed by the Justice Department in December 1952 invoked global concerns, declaring, "The existence of discrimination against minority groups in the United States has an adverse effect upon our relations with other countries. Racial discrimination furnishes grist for the Communist propaganda mills, and it raises doubts even among friendly nations as to the intensity of our devotion to the democratic faith." In deliberations over the case, Justice Stanley Reed, persuaded to concur at the last moment, was pressed to consider the effects of segregation on America's position in international affairs.[28]

As the Supreme Court deliberated the *Brown* decision, Vice President Nixon, the high official most concerned about the continent, compelled the National Security Council's Policy Planning Staff to place Africa on its agenda. Knowing that the United States would eventually have to deal with indigenous leaders in Africa, and that American race relations created potential problems in doing so, the question for Washington became how to handle growing African aspirations for independence while maintaining the strongest possible worldwide front against communist advances. The struggles for freedom at home and abroad were combining to force the Eisenhower administration to deal with race and anticolonial nationalism to a degree that top officials neither anticipated nor entirely welcomed.[29]

By this time, American strategists had come to view virtually every corner of the Third World as potentially vital to the overall national security interests of the United States. Diplomatic and economic initiatives undertaken by the Soviets triggered an elemental shift in U.S. policies and attitudes, such that "the Soviet campaign to extend its influence throughout the periphery . . . led to the collapse of previously held distinctions between vital and marginal areas."[30] Mushrooming national liberation movements seemingly provided fertile ground for communist intrigue. And as the Soviets increasingly sought influence in Third World countries, the growing competition between the Soviets and the Chinese for worldwide leadership fanned communist interest in Africa.[31] Soviet interest, and potential advances, made every corner of the world seem vital. Indeed, by the end of the decade, U.S. national security officials warned that the movement of any additional state into the communist camp could harm U.S. security, and that such change "might be out of all proportion to the strategic or economic significance of the territory involved."[32]

In response to Nixon's request, Special Assistant for National Security Affairs Robert Cutler asked his staff to identify the principal elements of U.S. concern throughout Africa. Three primary interests were advanced: security of access to actual and potential U.S. military bases; security of access to strategic raw materials; and "support of the colonial powers' presence in the area and of their responsibility for the security, political and material progress of the African peoples, and the latter's adherence to the free world." While other parts of the administration slightly altered the ordering of these interests—the State Department ranked highest the issues of colonialism, nationalism, and the problem of "determining the proper rate of advance in the development of African territories towards democratic self-government"—by and large the lists found common ground. "Support of the colonial powers' presence"—Eisenhower administration officials knew their policies and priorities, which largely aligned with those of Europe.[33]

Yet the world, like communism, could not be easily contained. During the next two years, two events marked the emergence of a "third way" in the world, and with it a changing global landscape. First came the gathering in April 1955 of leaders from Africa and Asia in Bandung, Indonesia, representing over half the world's population at the time. The Bandung Conference coalesced forces of Third World nationalism, Global South independence, and Cold War neutrality. Leaders sought to construct an alternative postcolonial path that framed political, economic, and social concerns outside a bipolar Cold War world. In the following years, a movement gaining momentum led to the formal establishment of the Non-Aligned Movement in 1961. Membership grew as the wave of independence spread to more areas of Asia and to much of Africa.[34]

Just over a year after Bandung, Egyptian president Gamal Abdel Nasser nationalized the Suez Canal. The meetings and rhetoric of the Third World leaders who had gathered in Indonesia took on new dimensions in light of the Suez crisis, reinforcing an independent path expanding rapidly across the Global South. Diverse yet coalescing, the emerging nonaligned movement gained impetus with the perceived successes of Bandung, Suez, and, in short order, the independence of Ghana. New views and voices, ones beyond East and West and North, were muscling themselves into the conversation, creating as well as exploiting international tensions to advance their own interests.

Not surprisingly, administration officials found that cultivating friendships with African nationalists and leaders of newly emergent countries while backing continued colonial rule over other people of color was an increasingly precarious high-wire act. When British, French, and Israeli governments responded to the Suez crisis independently of Washington, it angered U.S. officials that they would do so on such a vital issue. To a degree, it fostered a disposition to chart a somewhat more independent course regarding British and French colonies in Africa, while U.S. desires for more economic opportunities in Africa further reinforced some parting from the colonial powers' lead in Africa.[35] By 1956, the National Intelligence Estimate from just three years earlier was revised, reflecting the rapid changes occurring in Africa and a greater urgency about preparing for African independence. The new estimate predicted that Africans "will make increasing demands for self-government," that the result would be "an increasingly rapid emergence of new native states," and that "regardless of how political demands are handled," interracial tensions would almost certainly increase throughout tropical Africa. The report warned that during the conflict between the metropoles and those demanding self-rule, the United States would be "bombarded" from both sides with demands for diplomatic and moral support.[36]

Domestic race relations and political concerns added to pressures to address policy toward Africa. The Black freedom struggle continued to be a public relations nightmare for U.S. foreign relations, with first Montgomery's bus boycotts and later Little Rock's desegregation confrontation ravaging America's image abroad. Nixon, the administration's world traveler, reminded Eisenhower, "Every instance of racial prejudice in this country is blown up in such a manner as to create a completely false impression of the attitudes and practices of the great majority of the American people. The result is irreparable damage to the cause of freedom which is at stake."[37]

Many in Mississippi, Alabama, Arkansas, and across the nation would have disputed Nixon's characterization of the impression as "completely false." And Nixon recommended that "in the national interest, as well as for the moral issues involved, we must support the necessary steps which will assure the orderly progress toward the elimination of discrimination in the United States."[38] Nixon might well have been making political calculations, too, for a growing number of African American voters were using political views on colonialism and decolonization as a barometer for views on racial issues in America. Someone who did not support Black majority rule in Africa faced a difficult task convincing Black voters that he supported equal rights in America.[39]

Washington's strategic assessments indicated that there would be an ever-stronger demand to shift policy toward more actively engaging African desires for independence. All these pressures, plus a growing belief that American leadership was necessary, pushed Washington to focus increased attention on Africa. The State Department soon created the position of deputy assistant secretary of state for African affairs, and in August 1958 it finally established a separate Bureau of African Affairs with its own assistant secretary of state. The Eisenhower administration knew it could not ignore Africa and African nationalism; the fact makes its resistance to change and to more or less continue past practice all the more stark.

1957: Ghana, Nixon, Kennedy

Three seminal events took place in 1957: Ghana became independent, raising interest in and hopes throughout a continent seeking self-determination; Vice President Richard Nixon traveled to the continent, helping him define it as a Cold War battleground; and Senator John F. Kennedy spoke out against the French war in Algeria, moving him along toward advocating greater appreciation of the forces of nationalism in the Third World.

In the Gold Coast, nationalists formed the United Gold Coast Convention (UGCC) in 1947, with Kwame Nkrumah as general secretary. In February 1948, demonstrations by World War II veterans in Accra prompted police to open fire and kill two of the protesters. Civil unrest spread, and over two dozen people died. Nkrumah and others were temporarily arrested, and the British were forced to reckon with growing anticolonial sentiment. The next year, Nkrumah and his supporters broke from the UGCC to form the Convention People's Party (CPP) and to push for more change. Their campaign of "positive action" pressed for self-government. The British soon declared a state of emergency and again arrested Nkrumah. Yet continuing nationalist pressure forced London to accept change, and a long series of reforms and constitutional modifications slowly inched the colony toward self-government. Still imprisoned, Nkrumah saw his CPP sweep elections in 1951, whereupon he was released to become the leader of government business, a position ranked only behind the governor in authority. Beginning in 1952, the British governor-general no longer chose the leader of government business from the Legislative Assembly; instead, the assembly itself voted for a prime minister. The Executive Council became known as the cabinet. In 1954, an amended constitution further reduced or transferred many of the British governor's discretionary powers. Going forward, the general population elected all assembly members, and the prime minister chose the cabinet. Internal self-government had been secured, yet the governor retained control over defense and external affairs. Nationalists kept up the pressure for the next stage: full sovereignty.[40]

Finally, in early 1957, the British Parliament passed the Ghana Independence Act that formally recognized independence for Ghana, with a date of 6 March 1957 for the transfer of power. Secretary of State Dulles telephoned Vice President Nixon to urge him to head the official U.S. delegation to the independence festivities. Nixon replied cautiously, affirming the strategic wisdom of the request but indicating his reluctance to go due to ongoing media speculation that Nixon himself campaigned for his extensive overseas travels and Washington gossip that the trips served no vital government purpose. Dulles made sure that Eisenhower personally asked Nixon to make the trip, noting, "These events will be watched with great interest by both colonial and anti-colonial powers. They will undoubtedly command considerable attention in the United Nations. The import of what takes place in Accra next March should be clear to the whole world: here is an instance where thanks to good will, patience, and perseverance on the part of both African and European, the political, economic, and social advancement of 4.5 million Africans has been carried out peaceably and resolutely to the point where independence has become a reality." Highlighting his belief in the European self-styled mission having advanced 4.5 million Africans, Dulles recognized that other African nations would follow the events closely. He also knew they would "follow with particular attention the degree of interest and sympathy which the United States accords these developments."[41]

The world in fact did watch this momentous day with great interest. With just Haiti, Liberia, and Ethiopia before it, Ghana's independence especially reverberated through the Black Atlantic. Indeed, African Americans who made the trip included Martin Luther King Jr., head of the Southern Christian Leadership Conference; Lester Granger, executive director of the National Urban League; A. Philip Randolph, president of the Brotherhood of Sleeping Car Porters and vice president of the American Federation of Labor and Congress of Industrial Organizations (AFL-CIO); Ralph Bunche, United Nations undersecretary for special political affairs, representing Dag Hammarskjöld and the United Nations; Congressmen Adam Clayton Powell (D-NY) and Charles Diggs (D-MI); Horace Mann Bond, president of Lincoln University; John Johnson, president and owner of the Johnson Publishing Company; Dr. C. B. Powell, editor and publisher of the *New York Amsterdam News*; John Sengstacke, editor and publisher of the *Chicago Defender*; Claude Barnett, head of the Associated Negro Press; Shirley Graham Du Bois, representing W. E. B. Du Bois, whose passport had been revoked and not yet reinstated; William Sherrill, president of the Universal Negro Improvement Association; Rev. James H. Robinson, founder of Operation Crossroads

Africa; and religious dignitaries representing the National Baptist Convention of the USA, the National Baptist Convention of America, the African Methodist Episcopal Church, the African Methodist Episcopal Zion Church, and the Christian Methodist Episcopal Church.[42] Adam Clayton Powell commented, "Nothing in my public life of 27 years has attracted the attention and attendance of colored American leadership as has Ghana."[43]

Nixon turned his attendance at Ghana's celebrations into a three-week tour through the northern half of Africa. With stops in Morocco, Ghana, Liberia, Uganda, Sudan, Libya, and Tunisia, he logged thousands of miles and scores of meetings. The trip left him championing increased attention to Africa, with his report to Eisenhower detailing a series of recommendations for U.S. policy. Nixon urged the Defense Department and the International Cooperation Administration to give higher priority to their operations in Africa, and the State Department to improve the quality and quantity of U.S. representation. Along these lines, Nixon advised reviewing aid and information programs so that they achieved the maximum possible effectiveness. Perhaps most importantly, Nixon urged planning to commence for diplomatic relations with the emerging African states. The administration was on notice: more freedom was coming.[44]

While at the time Nixon was arguably more progressive on race issues than others in the administration, White House conversations recorded during his presidency reveal the deep-seated prejudices he harbored. Nixon's motivation for paying increased attention to Africa grew not out of moral conviction but out of anticommunist fears. Throughout his Africa trip, Nixon kept a diary of notes in which he regularly jotted down his concerns about communism. He worried that "Africa [is] a vacuum" where "any Soviet moves will have great impact." Assessing communist strength and potential for growth in each country and region that he visited, Nixon wrote his impressions of emerging nations: "Their course = at present free—against Commies—but could change." Nixon stressed to Eisenhower that "the course of development, as its people continue to emerge from a colonial status and assume the responsibilities of independence and self-government could well prove to be the decisive factor in the conflict between forces of freedom and international communism." The support the United States should give to newly independent countries could "alleviate the conditions of want and instability on which communism breeds." Seeing Africa as a place changing from a region firmly aligned with the West under white rule to a continent undergoing a potentially dramatic sea change, Nixon banged the drum for a more comprehensive policy.[45]

Over the course of the ensuing weeks and months, Nixon and others who felt similarly kept pushing for the creation of a more robust policy toward the continent. Any number of issues arose, from the deceptively minor question of which areas to include, to larger questions about whether to offer aid directly to new countries or to work through colonial powers or the UN. As a National Security Council policy paper slowly took shape, foot dragging and worries over the extent of knowledge about the African situation threatened to grind progress to a halt. Still, in August 1957, discussion of the first comprehensive policy paper on Africa south of the Sahara, NSC 5719, came up for final debate.

During the meeting, Robert Cutler asked Nixon, "as the 'father' of this new African policy," for his comments. Nixon seized the opening to decry those who wanted to delay specific policy action with further study. He argued that action was needed to overcome the serious tendency to underestimate the communist threat in Africa, adding that it was not merely card-carrying communists about whom one had to worry. Dulles and Undersecretary of State Christian Herter registered their support, with Herter recommending that language be added to the paper to make clear that the potential communist threat to Africa was greater than the current threat and was a matter of growing concern.[46] With this change, the paper was adopted, and the United States had its comprehensive policy for Africa south of the Sahara.

Yet Nixon had not fathered a new, fundamentally altered policy. African nationalism and Cold War anticommunism pushed policymakers to focus greater attention on African decolonization, yet these same fears of communist advances led administration officials to continue to prioritize close alliances with European allies over ideological or moral commitments to African freedom and independence. There was no fundamental shift to backing independence for African nations. Nixon's advocacy of more attention to Africa was a matter of emphasis, not transformation. Notwithstanding arguments that siding with African nationalist movements would better serve American interests by promoting friendlier ties with Third World peoples, immediate Cold War priorities and racialized perspectives reinforced beliefs in the security of Western rule. On the all-important issue of self-rule or colonial rule, "Premature independence would be as harmful to our interests in Africa as would be a continuation of nineteenth-century colonialism, and we must tailor our policies to the capabilities and needs of each particular area as well as to our overall relations with the metropolitan power concerned." The "new" policy failed to address the full force and power of nationalism sweeping through Africa, the grip of Cold War anticommunism and racial prejudices still informing its now familiar conclusions.[47]

Notably, at the same time that the Eisenhower administration was forging this formal policy, Senator John F. Kennedy stood before the U.S. Senate to deliver a major speech on the Algerian crisis. Using the occasion as a platform to build his appeal as a friend to the world's peoples seeking freedom, he declared, "The most powerful single force in the world today is neither communism nor capitalism, neither the H-bomb nor the guided missile." Rather, "it is man's eternal desire to be free and independent. The great enemy of that tremendous force of freedom is called, for want of a more precise term, imperialism—and today that means Soviet imperialism and, whether we like it or not, and though they are not to be equated, Western imperialism." Urging Paris and Washington to recognize the powerful tide of nationalism, he encouraged both governments to adjust their policies accordingly. If the United States wanted to secure the friendship of Africans, Arabs, and Asians, Kennedy concluded, the strength of the appeal had to lie "in our traditional and deeply felt philosophy of freedom and independence for all peoples everywhere." The speech resulted in sharp criticism from France and from the Eisenhower administration, notwithstanding its own concerns with French actions. Officials in Algeria warned Americans to stay off the streets to avoid reprisals. But it secured Kennedy's reputation as a friend of the emerging Third World, something that would become more important in a few short years as he entered the White House with a more sympathetic understanding of nationalist aspirations.[48]

"To Encourage Education . . . Is to Foster Independence"

During the Eisenhower administration's second term, public diplomacy activities in Africa, Asia, Europe, and the Middle East accelerated. Goodwill tours by jazz musicians, connections to HBCUs, and other "soft power" actions began to be promoted more extensively.[49] The United States Information Agency worked to make existing programs in Africa more robust. "The U.S. Information Program . . . presents a real challenge to the staff, first to operate in the transition period of colony to independent status, and second to operate in the beginning of a vast 'awakening' of a primitive people (estimates vary from 5–10 percent literacy for the [Gold Coast] as a whole)," cited a 1956 report. Historian Jason Parker, noting that these officials knew that race relations damaged U.S. standing among people of color throughout the world, highlights how the language used—"primitive," elsewhere "natives"—reveals the fundamental lack of full comprehension by many of the very same U.S. officials.[50]

Given its ongoing views about Africans' lack of readiness for self-rule, and long-standing American faith in the efficacy of education, educational assistance in Africa was a short step for the Eisenhower administration to take. While not as conspicuous as other social and cultural efforts, the administration saw education as a way to accelerate African readiness for eventual independence while keeping African countries oriented to the West. These development efforts differed from Truman's Point Four emphasis on technical expertise and from Kennedy's later emphasis on socioeconomic modernization while reflecting in fundamental ways a continuum of a long-held presumption: that Africa and Africans needed to be "developed."

Since the enrollment of two Gold Coast students at the College of New Jersey (now Princeton University) in 1774, a handful of African students had trickled into the United States, but the number remained miniscule. Africa south of the Sahara was most underrepresented; aside from South Africa, during the 1920s and 1930s the region sent an average of just twenty-six students per year to college in the United States. Even so, the opportunity afforded these few individuals helped some toward positions of national leadership and influence, including Lincoln University graduates Kwame Nkrumah, prime minister and president of Ghana, and Nnamdi Azikiwe, president of Nigeria, as well as Meharry Medical College graduate Hastings Kamuzu Banda, president of Malawi.[51]

The number of African students in the United States began increasing in the late 1940s, aided by a growing Cold War imperative to steer newly independent countries toward democratic capitalism by training a generation of leaders with ties to the West. This goal, combined with a faith in the powerful efficacy of education, rallied diverse voices to support African educational exchanges.

But a sulfurous blend of colonial interests, racial prejudice, and anticommunism complicated these efforts. In one case, the NAACP, seeking to advance African education needs on a very human scale, championed the cause of Mugo Gatheru, a Kenyan student studying at Lincoln University. In September 1952, Gatheru was visited by an immigration official who interrogated him for more than two hours. In November, Gatheru received official orders to leave the country within thirty days or face arrest and deportation. The Immigration and Naturalization Service (INS) provided no reason; Gatheru and his supporters were convinced it was a result of pressure from British officials. The Mau Mau movement was exploding, and the British were uncomfortable with Kenyans out of their sight and control. When Gatheru fought deportation, the INS claimed that he had fraudulently obtained a visa in London by declaring that he had never been denied one previously.

Gatheru argued that he had never been denied a visa but rather had been denied a Certificate of Good Conduct, which was needed in Kenya to obtain a visa. Although he did not know for certain, Gatheru believed he had been rebuffed because he had written letters to Kenyan papers advocating rights for Africans and had worked as an assistant editor for the Kenya African Union paper. After being denied the certificate, he had traveled to India, and from there to London, where he applied for and received the now-questioned visa. Since April 1950 he had lived and studied in America.[52]

When the deportation threat came, a committee formed to help Gatheru fight it. The committee's members included Horace Mann Bond, the president of Lincoln University, and St. Clair Drake, then a sociology professor at Roosevelt University. A background report on the case concluded that Gatheru had denounced the activities of the Mau Mau and had no hint of communist affiliation. Receiving an education seemed to be his sole motivating desire. In the toxic atmosphere of the McCarthy era, it seemed safe to support Gatheru, who plainly appeared to be simply the victim of colonial pressures. NAACP youth secretary Herbert Wright traveled to Pennsylvania to meet with Gatheru, after which the NAACP supported the Gatheru defense committee's efforts. Lawyers filed for an injunction restraining the INS from deporting Gatheru, while Wright solicited all youth councils, college chapters, and affiliated organizations to send funds to aid Gatheru's defense. The NAACP appealed to the INS to extend Gatheru's visa long enough for him to complete his education. As in the struggle over desegregating public education in America, education for Africans was caught in a witch's brew of race and Cold War concerns, with an added ingredient of colonialism.[53]

With the case in the courts, in February 1953 the Justice Department rescinded its deportation order, allowing Gatheru to stay until his visa expired at the end of April. Continuing efforts by the defense committee enabled Gatheru to receive permission to stay in the United States through July 1954, allowing him to complete his studies at Lincoln. When Gatheru sought to continue his studies in graduate school at New York University, the NAACP maintained its support for his case, with Walter White writing to the INS on behalf of Gatheru and discussing the issue with Attorney General Herbert Brownell.[54]

At this point, the Eisenhower administration was clearly and actively dissuading Gatheru from continuing his education in the United States, and was doing little to set up or support mechanisms to assist African education. On the other hand, beyond the need, there was a deep-rooted albeit paternalistic basis for change. Raised in an era rife with ideas about a "civilizing mission" in Africa, Eisenhower was comfortable with the concept of uplifting Africans with education. He spoke of the need for other societies to become more like the United States, reflecting America's long-standing view of itself as a "city on a hill," and believed that "emerging peoples" had to be persuaded to follow the British and American examples. In Eisenhower's vision, organizations would heed the call to equip cultures "ancient and rich in human values" with educational resources to learn the values that underpin the United States.[55]

During his second term, these efforts grew, and in 1958 the administration started providing greater coordination of efforts through a committee on educational, technical, and cultural activities for Africa. A year later, exchange programs with eight independent countries and sixteen dependent territories were established. And yet despite insisting on no "premature independence" and promoting the value of education, U.S. support remained shockingly low. Educational grants rose from 24 in 1952 to 363 in 1959, a twelve-fold increase but far fewer than elsewhere in the world and hardly reflective of a vast continent swiftly moving toward independence. Part of this was a latent fear that the presence of African students, coming from a continent with ambitions to overthrow white supremacy, might feed into and radicalize the civil rights struggle on American campuses. When Eisenhower ruminated in a National Security Council meeting on a recent film he saw, which "had stressed the theme that the black man, under the influence of religion, was taking a more realistic view of his problems," he wondered if the United States could foster education and religion, "leaving the mother country to prepare the colony for independence." Clarence Randall, chair of the Council on Foreign Economic Policy, responded that even as more emphasis should be placed on education in Africa, "that to encourage education and religion is to foster independence," he also believed "there were risks in bringing Africans to the United States to be educated."[56]

Broader context reveals just how few African students were studying in the United States, and how little financial support they received from sources in America. In the academic year 1957–58, just fifteen hundred students from Africa studied in the United States, more than a quarter of whom came from Egypt alone. In that academic year, the U.S. government did little to advance formal education ties, supporting a mere 128 of those students. From newly independent Ghana came 135 students—three with support from the U.S. government. From Nigeria, the most populous nation in Africa, came 192 students, with three supported by the U.S. government. Educational uplift may have been central to American ideals of improving oneself and one's community, and Eisenhower officials certainly spoke to the value of education, but in Africa—which Vice President Nixon was touting as a Cold War battlefield—the administration invested relatively paltry resources.[57]

By the late Eisenhower administration, that story line slowly and belatedly began to change. The number of African students grew to two thousand during the 1959–60 school year. Even so, that was out of roughly 35,700 undergraduate and graduate students from non-Western nations studying in the United States (4,780 came from Taiwan alone). Despite the great need, just two came from the Congo, where independence dawned with fewer than thirty Congolese university graduates in that vast territory, and not a single Congolese medical doctor, lawyer, engineer, or army officer. By the end of 1960, as the Eisenhower administration was leaving office, only 3 percent of foreign students attending school in the United States came from Africa, and just 271 of those (roughly one out of six) received some support from the U.S. government.[58]

At the same time, the private sector was taking a greater interest in expanding opportunities. Beginning in 1959, new efforts to bring hundreds of African students to study at U.S. universities burst onto the scene. Kenyan labor leader and politician Tom Mboya spearheaded the efforts. The charismatic Mboya, who would come to rival Kwame Nkrumah's visibility in America, first came to the United States in 1956 under the auspices of the American Committee on Africa (ACOA). The organization was founded in the early 1950s, forming originally as Americans for South African Resistance (AFSAR) to help support the 1952 South African Defiance Campaign against Unjust Laws. Headed by ministers Donald Harrington, George Houser, and Charles Trigg, AFSAR included a range of supporters, such as Charles S. Johnson, Mordecai Johnson, Adam Clayton Powell, A. Philip Randolph, Rev. James Robinson, Bayard Rustin, George Schuyler, and William Sutherland. Soon thereafter, the group broadened its mission, becoming the American Committee on Africa to educate, lobby for, and support Africans and their liberation struggles, while maintaining a particular interest in opposing white supremacy in South Africa.[59]

ACOA brought Mboya on a speaking tour, during which he promoted a more positive image of Kenyans than the picture the British painted during the Mau Mau war. He sought to build support for Kenyan independence. He gave lectures, developed contacts with labor leaders, and, perhaps most enduringly, solicited aid for higher education for Kenyans. In 1959, the Kenyan government offered financial assistance for higher education to only 451 Africans—out of a population of 6,000,000. No African could receive a liberal arts education in Kenya; just forty-two were able to study in the United Kingdom. The racial inequities and the growing support for educational exchanges persuaded individuals and institutions alike to support Mboya's scholarship drive. Black Americans undertook particularly significant efforts to help African students at a time when they themselves faced huge odds in terms of going to college. Even those with pressing demands on their time and resources contributed. When Mboya wrote to Martin Luther King that Tuskegee had accepted Kenyan Nicholas Rabala but Rabala needed nearly $1,000 to cover costs, King promised to raise the money: half from his Dexter Avenue Baptist Church, and half from his new civil rights organization, the Southern Christian Leadership Conference.[60]

Such positive responses helped convince Mboya and William Scheinman—an ACOA board member and the president of an aircraft hydraulic equipment company—to organize the African American Students Foundation (AASF) as a way to bring African students to the United States. Board members included singer Harry Belafonte; actor Sidney Poitier; Ralph Bunche's wife, Ruth Bunche; and African nationalist leaders Mboya and Nyerere.[61] Through a fundraising effort headed by Belafonte, Poitier, and baseball legend Jackie Robinson, the AASF raised $35,000 from eight thousand contributors for the transatlantic transportation. Robinson personally contributed $4,000. How important was the fundraising? The charter aircraft alone cost approximately $330 per person in a nation where Africans earned a per capita income of $84 a year. More than five thousand exuberant Kenyans gathered at the airport to send off the students.[62]

In the final years of the Eisenhower administration, governmental support for educational assistance grew, while nongovernmental support grew even more. Educational assistance seemed to provide a daily double of positives: a way to advance American values and a way for the Eisenhower administration to indicate support for Africans without overly challenging ideas of European rule. It also provided a response to the Soviets making a stronger push for influence in Africa. In February 1960, Soviet premier Nikita Khrushchev announced his country's intention to bring thousands of African, Asian, and Latin American students to study at the new Peoples' Friendship University in Moscow. The Soviets planned to double the number of African students studying in the USSR, from an estimated 350 in 1959–60 to 775 in 1960–61, and grow from there. Egypt sent the most students, while seventy-six came from Ghana, sixty-two from Guinea, and a smattering of others from around the continent. As more and more nations became independent, the number of Africans able to go to the Soviet Union rose.[63]

Advancing educational opportunities fit well within the American frame and was part and parcel of American notions of social and economic mobility while not directly forcing extensive introspection about more systematically supporting principles of majority rule and one person, one vote in Africa. Eisenhower and like-minded individuals could see themselves as anticolonial and supportive of African aspirations while continuing to back an illusory stability based on European colonial powers.

When discussion of education in Africa made its way into National Security Council deliberations in mid-1958, President Eisenhower spoke in numerous directions. He stated that the nation must believe in the right of colonial peoples to achieve independence, but then immediately worried that if it was emphasized too strongly, that right might create a crisis in relations with the mother country. Moments later, Eisenhower again expressed the need to go with the trend toward independence, and then again the conversation steered toward education as the way to go. Impulses to engage Africa more, to support more change, were there, but they kept crashing against the rocks of colonial allies, Cold War anticommunism, and racial prejudice.[64]

At that same meeting, Eisenhower also remarked that "rather than slow down the independence movement," he would "like to be on the side of the natives for once." Secretary of State Herter and others immediately pushed back, cautioning that such a policy would raise "delicate questions" with NATO allies. Eisenhower faced his opportunity within mere weeks.[65]

Algeria, Guinea, and *Non*

With victory secured in Europe, France embarked on adopting a new constitution for the Fourth Republic, one that restructured the empire into a new political framework, the Union française (French Union). Intense debates over the meaning of citizenship and the extent of rights were elemental and hard fought. The effort to address the widely different views of status and rights ultimately led to an ambiguous final determination. While providing for some additional rights, including African representation in the National Assembly, many aspects of the new constitution left those in overseas territories in a second-tier status with limited autonomy. Nevertheless, historian Frederick Cooper argues that "Africans, who had wanted something better, were not opposed to what they got: the constitution was not an obstacle to legislation that would provide for the single college, universal suffrage, and stronger territorial assemblies." African leaders had set a process in motion; it remained unclear whether genuine change would come or whether the new constitution would be a wolf of continuing colonial oppression in sheep's clothing.[66]

Under the French Union, different areas of the empire had different designations. Algeria, constitutionally part of France since 1848, was considered part of metropolitan France. In many ways not paradigmatic of French imperialism in Africa, Algeria's independence path would not be either. French West Africa, French Equatorial Africa, and Madagascar were designated "overseas territories." The portions of UN trust territories of Cameroon and Togo administered by France were yet another element in the union, associated territories, along with Morocco and Tunisia. There was no meaningful loosening of control by Paris in any of the areas, but there was contested space for Africans to politically organize.

At the urging of Félix Houphouët-Boigny of Côte d'Ivoire, representatives from French West Africa and French Equatorial Africa came together in 1946 in Bamako to build the Rassemblement Démocratique Africain (RDA) as an umbrella political organization. The RDA's manifesto stated that it sought "progressive but rapid autonomy within the framework of the French Union," not separation and independence. Nevertheless, Paris opposed the gathering and worked to sabotage it, fearing that the new political organization was too radical. These fears were compounded by the overseas minister, Marius Moutet, who sought to align Africans with his own party, the Socialists. Instead, the RDA drifted to ties with the French Communist Party (PCF), the one political party with an avowed anticolonial position.[67]

Ties to the PCF helped cast the RDA as a radical organization, and it faced intense pressure in subsequent years to take a more moderate stance. By the early 1950s, the intensity of the pressure in the Cold War environment convinced the RDA's leader, Houphouët-Boigny, to make that step, severing ties with the PCF. Not all members of the RDA welcomed the shift, with some leaving the organization. Others, such as Sekou Touré and the Guinean branch of the RDA, remained more left-leaning, with Touré "pushed to the Left by grassroots militants, particularly trade unionists, students, women, and youth—not the other way around." The Guinean RDA faced ongoing repression from French authorities and internal divisions, but Touré would successfully navigate these shoals and continue to rally the majority of the Guinean people to the RDA.[68]

The government in Paris was finding it faced increasing challenges on multiple fronts as it fought to hold its empire. In Algeria, during the course of World War II, the sacrifices of soldiers who served, the economic deprivations suffered, and France's weakened position all contributed to a growing expectation of reforms. As the war came to an end, nationalists had scheduled celebratory marches amid rumors that the upcoming United Nations Conference on International Organization would declare Algeria independent. Bloody clashes broke out, and European settlements were attacked. In response, "authorities unleashed a ferocious repression, including aerial bombardment, naval gunfire, and summary executions." French historians total the deaths at six thousand to eight thousand; Algerians number it closer to forty-five thousand. The echoes of gunfire in Europe had barely silenced, and the struggle in Algeria was surging.[69]

Across the globe, as French fortunes in Southeast Asia dramatically worsened, the growing troop deployments to Algeria placed more pressure on Paris. Within six months of the defeat at Dien Bien Phu, the Algerian War of Independence began. The crisis intensified when the Battle of Algiers found a half million French troops battling the nationalist insurrection. Throughout the battle, amid the atrocities, and as the French fought back with brutal measures, and as thousands disappeared and significant portions of the capital's population were herded into internment centers, the Eisenhower administration withheld any public criticism, notwithstanding its skepticism about France's chances for ultimate success. By this time, reassessments of the French hold on its empire in Africa began to accelerate.[70]

Morocco and Tunisia had been restive for years; protests, boycotts, strikes, and bombings were regularly met by strong and often deadly reprisals from the French. The Eisenhower administration, with the president exasperated at French actions and concerned about steady French repression causing more radicalization and communist inroads, especially as the nationalist movements were generally pro-West and anticommunist, quietly pressed Paris to undertake reforms. With the Algerian War on its hands,

Paris sought resolution of the increasingly untenable situations in these two protectorates. Both gained independence in March 1956. With the strains on Paris hardly abated, African and Asian political leaders accelerated working through the UN to monitor Paris in an effort to prevent territories making up the French Union from being subsumed to French territorial ambitions.[71]

Faced with mounting pressures, the French National Assembly in 1956 passed a *loi-cadre* that provided the framework for devolving additional authority to elites in overseas territories. This marked an important step for increasingly autonomous Africa. Yet at the same time that the *loi-cadre* came into being, Paris remained determined to take all measures to win the war in Algeria. As conditions in Algeria worsened, Paris confronted African demands elsewhere in multipronged efforts to contain the situations. Many hard-fought political demands advanced within the *loi-cadre*: universal suffrage; territorial assemblies with actual power, including responsibility for budgets and civil service; a single electoral college. While Frederick Cooper argues that the time was marked less by "a stubborn French colonialism and strident African nationalism" than by those seeking some form of French-African community, the form and meaning of that relationship was a capacious concept to which many brought ideas, and most Africans relentlessly pushed for more rights, more autonomy, more égalité. The newly set up territorial governments pushed those claims even further, as did the 1957 independence of Ghana.[72]

The brutal quagmire of the Algerian War ultimately caused seismic changes in France, a pattern to be seen some fifteen years on in Portugal as well. As the war and its atrocities dragged on, the hundreds of thousands of European settlers, the *pieds-noirs*, and much of the Jewish population sought to retain connection to metropolitan France, while the Front de Libération Nationale (FLN) fought for independence, both militarily and diplomatically. Their transnational efforts built networks throughout the world, including south of the Sahara with African leaders that included Houphouët-Boigny, Touré, Nkrumah, Mandela, and Holden Roberto in Angola.[73] In Algeria, rebels were striking from Tunisia and Morocco, prompting the French military to widen the war by claiming a right to "hot pursuit" across borders. In the international aftermath of the bombing of a Tunisian village, Washington used some economic pressure to protect Tunisia and press Paris to seek a political settlement in Algeria. Months later, Washington would abstain on, although not support, an Afro-Asian resolution at the UN recognizing the Algerian people's right to independence.[74] Into the situation came a coalition of dissident army officers, *pieds-noirs*, and Gaullists bitter over the defeat in Indochina, angered by the conduct of the war in Algeria, and frustrated with the political instability of the Fourth Republic. Now uncertain about the leadership in Paris, the group instigated a political crisis in May 1958 that led to the collapse of the Fourth Republic and the return to power of Charles de Gaulle.

A new constitution would be written for the Fifth Republic. The status of territories was in the air and on the minds of Africans. The possibilities ranged from some to-be-defined federated status to outright independence. Léopold Sédar Senghor, the Senegalese intellectual, poet, and politician, pointed to France as always being one step behind what Africans were asking. He warned that he and other leaders could lose control of their followers if French structures were insufficiently attractive. And increasingly, short of a federation of equals—with equal resources, rights, everything—there was diminishing attraction to staying within any French structure.[75]

De Gaulle toured Africa to rally support for a draft constitution. When he reached Conakry, Touré did not publicly call for voting against it but famously declared, "We prefer poverty in freedom to wealth in slavery." Touré sought both independence and the right to join a community of equals. De Gaulle, believing France had contributed much to francophone territories and had come a long way toward African self-determination, heard Touré's words as a public rejection and humiliation, and a bitter rift ensued. De Gaulle informed Touré that Guinea could claim its independence but "it would feel the consequences."[76]

Seeking to hold on to as much of the empire, and as much of its influence, as possible, French authorities pressed throughout the territories for the colonized either to vote *oui* on the new constitution, which would allow increased colonial autonomy within a Franco-African community, or to vote *non* and take independence, triggering immediate removal of all French economic, political, and military presence and assistance. The consequences of that withdrawal would be severe; as Paris pointed out repeatedly, France had underwritten a number of administrative costs and invested close to $1 billion in the previous decade.[77] To help ensure a *oui* vote, Paris used political and economic pressure as well as dirty tricks, including manipulation of electoral lists, to influence the outcome. Under these terms and tactics, only Guinea dared to vote for independence.

Guinea's defiant no was resounding. France had made its threats clear in the days before the vote, preventing teachers vacationing abroad from returning on the eve of the new academic year, an action quickly expanded to include all civil servants vacationing abroad. It also began to move physical and monetary assets out of the country. France wanted Guineans to blink and vote *oui*; instead, on the day of the vote, 85 percent of registered Guinean voters turned out, with a staggering 94 percent of them voting *non* to the new constitution.[78]

France quickly retaliated, informing Guinea it had no standing in the French community and would no longer receive French assistance or credits. Within forty-eight hours, all French technical and administrative personnel were ordered to leave, with instructions to take with them or destroy all archives and materials. Ships en route with medicine and food were diverted. The French secret service sought to sow panic by peppering the country with counterfeit currency. On Independence Day, October 2, not a single French representative attended the ceremony.

France coldly worked to isolate the new nation diplomatically as well, pressuring allies such as the United States not to recognize the new nation. Just weeks after commenting that he wanted to be on the side of the Africans for once, Eisenhower faced de Gaulle, his former comrade in arms and current NATO ally, who asked him not to recognize Guinea. And Washington did not. Unlike the Guineans, Eisenhower blinked. And so, at first, just the few independent African states recognized Guinea, then the larger bloc of communist states did so. The situation was not simply awkward but telling of Washington's priorities. Not until Paris indicated its approval did the United States, four weeks after Guinean independence, send a letter of recognition to Touré.[79]

Even after diplomatic recognition, support for the fledgling nation was parsimonious. Paris wanted Guinea and Guineans to suffer, hoping to convince the remaining parts of its empire not to follow a similar path. Yet Touré had cards to play, and he took advantage of the East–West divide to secure a better situation for his country. Touré's overtures to Moscow convinced Western leaders that he might be moving down a dangerous communist path, albeit one Paris and its allies forced him onto in pursuit of their own purposes. A year later, Touré would visit the United States, the brutally cold shoulder to this new nation slightly thawed as Conakry navigated Cold War dynamics to improve its path forward. Eisenhower and Touré met at the White House, cordial but unproductive. As Touré toured the country, the more memorable moment—and the one that in the longer term would mean the most to relations between the countries—was his meeting in Disneyland with Senator John F. Kennedy.[80]

Racial Views and Crisis Politics

Ghana's triumphal transition to independence, soon followed by Guinea's equally successful break, encouraged other areas to press for increased autonomy and, even more, for full independence. Neither French nor British efforts to slow down the pace of decolonization seemed to have much effect as more parts of Africa accelerated toward independence. Indeed, by the end of the 1950s the British and French were working primarily to channel decolonization in an attempt to protect the metropole's economic interests and institutions of colonial domination from radical challenges.[81]

Even so, the "wind of change" that British prime minister Harold Macmillan noticed blowing created minimal turbulence in Washington. The seeming security of backing colonial powers that were Cold War allies and enabling white rule continued to outweigh alternatives. Material support for African independence remained small. After Guinea chose independence, it sought educational assistance from the United States in the form of English-language textbooks, teaching materials, and teachers. The United States provided just *one* teacher, and only after Touré personally took up the matter. The American ambassador in Conakry found himself having to answer the sharp-pointed question of why the United States was in such need of English teachers that it could spare only one. The marginalization of those lobbying for Africa in America further diminished the prospect of a fundamental shift. Despite increasing nationalism and the imminent demise of colonialism, seeds for policy change found rocky soil.[82]

Even with rapidly changing conditions, underpinning the reluctance to support change lurked the enduring prejudices of some of America's highest officials. These men remained convinced that Africans stood to benefit by remaining under colonial rule for as long as possible. In early 1960, while discussing U.S. policy toward Africa south of the Sahara, Eisenhower brought up French president de Gaulle's observation that within two years there would be thirty independent African nations. CIA director Allen Dulles opined that none of the thirty would be capable of governing themselves; the president agreed, as long as (white-ruled) South Africa was excluded. As the conversation continued, Vice President Nixon interjected that the British anticipated that many countries in Africa would develop "a South American pattern of dictatorship." Nixon counseled that the United States must not assume that the struggle in Africa would be between Western-style democracy and communism, and that while it could not be said publicly, the United States needed the strongmen of Africa on its side. Nixon pressed that it was naive to hope Africa would be democratic, and perhaps developing military strongmen would offset communist development of labor unions.[83]

The moment marked an insidious development: the use of anticommunism to support white supremacy being extended to justify the support of authoritarian strongmen. The purported father of a new African policy saw little chance for democracy to develop and flourish in Africa. Revealing chilling prejudices underlying his analysis, Nixon remarked that in his judgment, some people in Africa had been out of the trees for only about fifty years. Recently returned from a trip to the Belgian Congo, Maurice Stans—director of the Bureau of the Budget—toadied up with his view that many Africans "still belonged in the trees."[84]

The painful racial predispositions among these, the highest officials in the land, rendered unlikely any substantial shift away from highly Eurocentric policies—except perhaps toward support of strongman rule. Notably, reports from the field continued to reinforce the prejudices of these officials. In Liberia, the one long-standing independent republic of sub-Saharan Africa, U.S. ambassador Richard Jones operated from his conviction that "the average Liberian does not want to work." That attitude pervaded the embassy, where another official, Jacob Crane, advised that "Liberians do not have good work habits." He further warned that if the State Department turned over the running of the Port of Monrovia "in order to rid our government of the burden," then "the Liberians would not be able to run the project."[85]

• • • • • •

By the last year of the Eisenhower administration, political crises brought Africa center stage, putting such longstanding views into play. The bubbling cauldron of African anticolonial nationalism boiled over in two highly strategic places: South Africa and the Congo. In neither nation would Eisenhower and his subordinates unequivocally back majority rule and African independence. To the contrary, support for South Africa's white minority regime and for the most extreme measures in the Congo to ensure Western-friendly leadership carried the day.

The first crisis erupted in South Africa. As the government continued to hammer home apartheid, the Eisenhower administration handled the white minority regime with kid gloves. Even a relatively benign proposal by Mason Sears, U.S. representative to the UN Trusteeship Council, to integrate the American embassy's Fourth of July celebrations met with a cold reception. Sears, responding to the atmosphere of rising African nationalism, promoted the idea as "a very little thing to do [that] would have a very happy effect upon millions of Africans all over the continent." The State Department dismissed Sears's proposal as overly provocative.[86] For its part, Pretoria continued to advance devastatingly racist economic, social, and political policies on its own people. The totality of its efforts extended into the cultural as well, as Pretoria banned all "Negro American magazines"; censored works by Richard Wright, Zane Grey, Lillian Smith, and Damon Runyon as either immoral or dangerous to "peaceful race relations"; and suppressed a comic book version of Davy Crockett's life because it showed cooperation between whites and Native Americans.[87]

Yet American officials felt comfortable with South Africa as an anticommunist bastion and a reliable supplier of strategic minerals, even as its "disturbing course of race developments" prompted the embassy to recommend that Washington take a more active concern in South Africa's growing racial tensions. The embassy's advice stemmed not from concerns over the expansion of white supremacist activity but from fears for the strategic and economic interests of the United States and underlying doubts about Black leadership. The embassy staff concluded that although it was obviously undemocratic and oppressive, "It is in the interest of the United States that White leadership be preserved, or at least indefinitely prolonged, in South Africa."[88]

Even so, the rapid emergence of independent African states, the rising Third World, and the East–West struggle for world opinion prodded the Eisenhower administration to at least try to appear less supportive of South Africa's racial practices. In late 1958, the United States supported a UN resolution, albeit a weak one, criticizing Pretoria's racial policies. This was a first; always before, the United States had opposed or abstained on resolutions critical of South Africa.[89]

The South African government ignored world opinion and continued to implement apartheid, creating a police state to thoroughly control South African society. Imprisonment and banning orders circumscribed opposition leaders' activities and silenced their voices. Yet repression proved a double-edged sword. While critics found themselves facing increasingly stringent government sanctions, ever-harsher apartheid laws and diminishing avenues of protest generated rising frustration throughout the country's Black majority.

On 21 March 1960, tens of thousands of peaceful protesters took to the streets to rally against apartheid and especially the hated pass laws. The day turned violently bloody in Sharpeville, thirty-five miles from Johannesburg. After several hours of demonstrations, with crowd size and tensions mounting, the South African police snapped. No order to shoot was heard, no warning shot was given, before a line of police commenced firing into the crowd. As the demonstrators ran, the police shot dead 69 Africans and wounded 186 more. Most victims were shot in the back as they fled.[90]

Hearing news of the massacre, the State Department quickly released a statement: "The United States deplores violence in all its forms and hopes that the African people of South Africa will be able to obtain redress for legitimate grievances by peaceful means. While the United States, as a matter of practice, does not normally comment on the internal affairs of governments with which it enjoys normal relations, it cannot help but regret the tragic loss of life resulting from the measures taken against the demonstrators in South Africa."[91]

The ensuing political fallout reveals the crossroads at which the United States stood and the path the Eisenhower administration chose to follow. On 24 March, Henry Cabot Lodge, U.S. representative at the United Nations, telephoned Secretary of State Herter to let him know that the Afro-Asian group had met that morning and voted to extend unanimous thanks to the United States for its statement about the massacre. This small gesture, speaking out against a government shooting its own people in the back, was enough to bring much goodwill among those who wanted U.S. support. Lodge added that because he knew Herter received so many gripes and complaints, this time Herter should be pleased with the credit and good that had come from the statement.[92]

Herter was in no mood to feel pleased; he had spent that very morning trying to placate an angry President Eisenhower. Meeting in the Oval Office, Herter disowned the statement, saying he had not seen it before its release, that he regarded it as a breach of courtesy between nations, and that he was furious as well. He blamed his subordinates, explaining that a bureau chief proposed a statement and the press office released it without checking at the top policy level. Grumbling that "the fat was in the fire," Eisenhower decided that they would secretly call in the South African ambassador and tell him that although recent events distressed the United States, it regretted having made a public statement. Eisenhower added that if it were his decision, he would find the bureau chief another post.[93]

The White House's paramount concern was damaging its tight relationship with the white South African government, even in the face of the apartheid regime's horrific killings of its own citizens. Yet there were exceptionally strong worldwide denunciations, including unprecedented domestic outrage in the United States. This reaction, combined with the expectation that the Soviets would use the situation to advance their influence in Africa, made it difficult for the United States to be viewed as publicly backing the South African government. Lodge was instructed to exercise leadership at the UN Security Council to secure a resolution that might express displeasure—regretting the loss of life, deploring the use of violence, requesting the South African government to expedite an inquiry into the "riots," urging the South Africans to reconsider their policies—but to prevent any sort of continuing machinery or investigative body that might drive South Africa from the UN or diminish its strong support for the anticommunist West.[94]

Maintaining an intensely active interest in the diplomatic aftermath of the massacre, Eisenhower viewed the situations in the United States and South Africa as not all that different. Seeing parallels between ideas of U.S. domestic states' rights and international UN Charter nonintervention in domestic jurisdictions, Eisenhower believed that the South Africans had the right to make progress in the way they wanted. His thinking on Black freedom struggles abroad was similar to his views about civil rights at home, except when his hand was forced in places like Little Rock. As the UN Security Council took up the matter, Eisenhower regularly communicated with Lodge and Herter about keeping any final resolution condemning South Africa as mild as possible.

In the end, the resolution adopted by the Security Council, with American affirmation, blamed the South African government for the shootings and called on it "to initiate measures aimed at bringing about racial harmony based on equality." Lodge, assessing how the episode played out at the UN, scored it a gain for U.S. relations with African and Asian delegations. He also counted it as a victory in that the Soviets were unable to secure the role of champions of Africans or even induce Africans to insist on an "extreme resolution" calling for sanctions. Herter characterized the resolution as "surprisingly mild"; Eisenhower viewed it as "mighty tough." To underscore Eisenhower's position after the massacre, State Department officials assured the South African embassy that it had no intention of recalling the American ambassador or of boycotting South Africa in any way. The message was clear from an administration that historian Philip Muehlenbeck notes "never once cast a vote in the UN in support of African independence or self-determination."[95]

The need to address political, economic, and racial tensions in Africa confronted the Eisenhower administration once again three months later as the Belgians agreed to transfer power in the Congo. For more than a half century, Belgium had worked to prevent any body politic from forming in the Congo, making the formation of a stable regime extremely challenging in this sprawling nation. In fact, into the late 1950s, while nations elsewhere were moving toward independence, few observers predicted Belgium would be leaving the Congo anytime soon. When Clarence Randall arrived in Léopoldville in early 1958, U.S. consulate general James Green told him that "Belgium is in the Congo to stay." Green's assessment was that while the Belgians deliberately slowed political development, they were progressive on the social front. "There is no real color barrier locally," Green reported, "and the race question is advancing fairly well." Green pointed to the fact that "all white athletic teams play all black athletic teams, usually without any difficulty," as evidence.[96]

But after seventy-five years of violent, rapacious rule by King Leopold II and Brussels, allowing segregated athletic teams to compete was certainly not "advancing" enough. During the next two years, the Congolese forced the political situation to change dramatically, aided by the encouragement of fellow Africans. In late 1958, Patrice Lumumba and a group of Congolese delegates traveled to Accra to attend the All-African People's Conference hosted by Nkrumah. Delegates from independent African states, including Ethiopia, Ghana, Guinea, Liberia, Morocco, Tunisia, and Egypt (the United Arab Republic at the time), joined with anticolonial nationalists such as Lumumba and Nyerere from across the continent. Tom Mboya was elected chair of the conference and its roughly three hundred delegates. Inspired by allies from across the continent and world, Lumumba and his fellow representatives returned to Léopoldville and organized a mass meeting for 31 December 1958. With "fiery oratory" to the three thousand assembled that day, Lumumba demanded immediate independence for the Congo. The next week, on 4 January 1959, Belgian authorities brutally suppressed Congolese demonstrators who were chanting, "Independence *immédiate*!" Forty-nine were killed in the crackdown. But the anticolonial push for self-determination surged. The Belgian parliament convened in emergency session, and the following week Brussels announced plans for independence, including elections at the local level, a national election the following year, and the establishment of a Congolese parliament.[97]

As anticolonial nationalists continued to press for a rapid timetable for independence, Brussels arrested Lumumba and other leaders. At the same time, Brussels continued taking steps to set up a roundtable conference for independence talks in January 1960, to which the nonimprisoned leaders of various political parties pledged to attend as long as Lumumba was released in time to participate as well. As the roundtable commenced, Belgian officials agreed to independence date of 30 June 1960 for the Congo, less than six months hence. Parliamentary elections were swiftly arranged for May. Lumumba's Mouvement National Congolais (MNC) and its allies won 40 of the 137 seats, leaving the MNC well short of a ruling majority but far ahead of the plethora of other parties, none of which won more than 13 seats. Maneuvering to put together a coalition of twelve parties, Lumumba became prime minister shortly before independence. His rival Joseph Kasavubu assumed the more ceremonial position of president.[98]

To this stage, the Eisenhower administration mostly contented itself with observing the difficulties, expressing little sympathy or concern for the problems the Belgian policies had created for the Congolese. When CIA director Allen Dulles reported that the Belgians' "frantic efforts" to form a viable government had been handicapped by the existence of over eighty Congolese political parties, Eisenhower wisecracked that he did not know so many people in the Congo could read.[99]

The racist quips died out as the Belgian flag lowered on Independence Day and Washington's concerns about Lumumba heightened. Hearing Belgians congratulate themselves on their reign, Lumumba scathingly denounced Belgian rule: "[Ours] was a noble and just struggle, an indispensable struggle to put an end to the humiliating bondage imposed on us by force. Our lot was eighty years of colonial rule; our wounds are still too fresh and painful to be driven from our memory." Lumumba hammered home his theme by recounting, in the presence of King Baudouin, those wounds and humiliations. Ralph Bunche, representing the UN at the celebrations, described the speech as "a hard, anti-colonial, we are free now statement" that left Belgian officials shocked, some with tears in their eyes.[100] While the Belgians and their American allies had hesitated to support Kasavubu because of his history of nationalist agitation, they now worried more about what they perceived as Lumumba's increasing radicalization.

While the focus of this book is on the time before independence, this instance is illustrative of the reality that decolonization was and is a process, not simply a flipping of a switch, and that the Cold War was increasingly becoming an overt part of African decolonization. Proponents of white rule framed the events as a cautionary tale in other areas of Africa still fighting for liberation. The Congo's shaky political situation began falling apart within days of independence, when members of the Force Publique, the old colonial army, mutinied at a base ninety miles outside Léopoldville. Soldier dissatisfaction spilled over after the Belgian commander General Émile Janssens emphasized a continuation of the colonial status quo by informing them that independence would bring no change in the soldiers' rank or pay. Unrest spread to Léopoldville. Belgian refugees fleeing to the capital told wild stories of rapes and shootings, triggering panic and European flight. The sight of roaming Congolese soldiers, no longer acting under the command of Belgian officers, heightened white fears. The British and French embassies quickly ordered the evacuation of all nonessential personnel; masses of European civilians fled across the Congo River to Brazzaville. Essential services and economic activity collapsed as the Europeans decamped, the bitter fruit of the Belgian policy excluding Congolese from all but the lower echelons of work.

U.S. ambassador Clare Timberlake, fearing any Belgian intervention would inflame antagonism and play into Soviet hands, urged Congolese leaders to request UN assistance. Washington believed this maneuver could restore order under a UN umbrella without using U.S. troops. The Eisenhower administration certainly did not want the Congo, particularly its mineral rich province of Katanga, to be under communist control. Africa was an important, and sometimes the only, source of strategic minerals, those needed to supply the military, industrial, and civilian needs of the United States and the West. These holdings included 50 to 100 percent of the known reserves of chromite, cobalt, manganese, and platinum. Copper, bauxite, zinc, vanadium, beryllium, uranium, and more were needed from Africa. The Congo was one of the richest sources, and Katanga particularly so.[101]

Days after independence, Katanga seceded under provincial leader Moise Tshombe, encouraged by Belgian and South African investors. When the UN did not quickly restore Katanga to Congolese rule, a bitter rift between Lumumba and UN secretary-general Dag Hammarskjöld ensued. Lumumba soon issued urgent appeals to the Soviets for aid. Happy to project themselves into the heart of Africa, the arrival of Soviet equipment sent shock waves through Washington. Warnings that the communists viewed the Congo as a fertile field appeared to be coming true. The timing was fraught, coming in the midst of a bitter chill in American–Soviet relations due to the downing of a U-2 spy plane and the collapse of the May summit between Eisenhower and Nikita Khrushchev. While the Soviets did not have the military wherewithal to effectively support Lumumba, that finer point was not on the minds of American officials.[102]

Lumumba quickly became the focus of attention in Washington. As officials witnessed another charismatic leftist leader appealing to Moscow, they increasingly worried about a repetition of the recent experience with Fidel Castro in Cuba. Given Castro's example on their own doorstep, the idea that an African leader could turn to the Soviets with little advance warning seemed quite plausible. Lumumba's mercurial shifts contributed to the sense that he operated under Soviet guidance, with CIA director Dulles ominously referring to Lumumba as "a Castro, or worse."[103] Lumumba seemed increasingly dependent on communist advisers and aid, and U.S. efforts to use the UN to preempt communist influence appeared to be failing. By August, the Joint Chiefs of Staff concluded, and the NSC concurred, that "the United States must be prepared at any time to take appropriate military action as necessary to prevent or defeat Soviet military intervention in the Congo. Multilateral action would be preferable but unilateral action may be necessary."[104]

Faced with the decidedly unpleasant prospect of U.S. troops going into combat in Africa, officials determinedly searched to find a way to keep the UN in the Congo and to remove Lumumba from leadership. According to historian Lise Namikas, a leading expert on the crisis, CIA spending on operations in the Congo was in the same ballpark as the Bay of Pigs operation.[105] In September, the CIA advanced the process of trying to permanently eliminate Lumumba by sending poison for an assassination attempt.[106]

As the CIA moved closer to killing Lumumba, other possibilities also loomed. In early September, Congolese president Kasavubu drove to the Léopoldville radio station to announce that he was dismissing the prime minister, triggering a power struggle between the two men. That struggle continued until CIA officers succeeded in swinging army chief of staff Joseph Mobutu to Kasavubu's side. Taking power in a bloodless coup, Mobutu informed U.S. embassy officials that he would arrest Lumumba and transfer power to a coalition government headed by Kasavubu. With his life at stake, Lumumba remained in his house under UN protection, leaving Mobutu to station a cordon of soldiers around the UN contingent, restricting Lumumba's access to Léopoldville and the nation.[107]

The volatile situation generated intense debate at the fall 1960 UN General Assembly meetings. That September, over a dozen new African nations joined the world body as part of the Year of Africa. By year's end, seventeen African nations would take their seat. The rapidly changing makeup of the UN was fraught with potential problems for the West. The situation demanded consideration of the UN's changing membership and a willingness to work with new delegations, but Eisenhower had little interest in grinning and bearing the courtship. He went to New York to address the

UN General Assembly and reluctantly met with various heads of state. Once back in Washington, he was pressed to get together with more African diplomats. His new ambassador to the UN, James Wadsworth, told him that the entire U.S. delegation felt strongly that he needed to meet the representatives of the new African countries. It was a case of face and prestige for them, Wadsworth explained, and doing so would help U.S. relations with these nations. Eisenhower refused to have a meal with each delegation, complaining it would take entirely too much of his time, but agreed that if the whole group came at one time he could manage a lunch. Taking his cue, Wadsworth assured Eisenhower that lunch was not necessary, that most of these Africans did not even speak English, and that all they needed was to come to the White House and shake hands. It was "just a matter of going through the motion so that they will have met the President of the United States." A reception was arranged, and the African delegates were ushered into the Oval Office. Before anyone sat down, they were welcomed and invited to move into the garden for coffee and orange juice and conversation. The president swiftly made the rounds, chatted briefly, and excused himself. Consultation was not on the menu, merely some grip and grin to steer these independent nations toward the West.[108]

At the same time, the very need to go through these motions brought to the Oval Office the reality of a decolonizing Africa. During the relatively short span of his second term, Eisenhower had seen the rising torrent flood into his very office. For the first time, the consideration of African delegations had become important. Washington very much wanted to keep Lumumba away from power, but it had to contend with African leaders who wanted an African solution to the crisis and wanted the world to respect Lumumba as the legitimately elected leader of the nation. Nkrumah was even making overtures to withdraw Ghanaian troops from the UN Operation in the Congo and place them under Lumumba's disposal.[109]

Tensions about the UN mission swirled and came to a head over the issue of whether to seat the Lumumba or the Kasavubu delegation in the world body. In late November, the Eisenhower administration's intense lobbying succeeded in producing a majority vote by the General Assembly to seat the Kasavubu delegation.[110] This vote apparently convinced Lumumba that the UN would no longer protect him, despite assurances otherwise, so he slipped out of his house in Léopoldville and headed toward Stanleyville (Kisangani), his political base of power. After four days of frantic searching, Mobutu's soldiers captured him.[111] Six weeks later, on 17 January 1961, Kasavubu and Mobutu delivered Lumumba to Moise Tshombe in the secessionist Katanga, ostensibly to prevent any future escape. That night and the following morning, Katanga soldiers and their Belgian handlers tortured and then murdered Lumumba and his two companions.[112]

Mere hours before Eisenhower left office, a seemingly leftist threat to U.S. interests was removed from the vast and vital Congo state. While it appears that the Eisenhower administration itself did not kill Lumumba, the result unmistakably fell in with White House efforts and desires. In the ensuing months and years, Washington continued to work actively to establish a pro-Western regime in the Congo until, with U.S. backing, Mobutu ultimately seized authoritarian power.

Strongmen

As African and Asian nations gained independence, U.S. officials discussed the new regimes and how they might or might not achieve democratic ideals. They pondered the trend toward military authoritarianism in Asia "as developmental problems bec[a]me more acute and the facades of democracy left by the colonial powers prove[d] inadequate to immediate tasks."[113] The moment seemed to require a buttressing of democratic ideals and institutions. Yet the perceived imperative to ensure that these emerging countries were noncommunist meant more than anything to the people in the room. If white rule by European allies could no longer ensure that, then authoritarian friends might. The essential test was whether a military regime might responsibly confront the problems facing it—security and development—while remaining noncommunist.

U.S. officials saw many reasons to support military regimes, not least of which was the fact that officer groups were often some of the most pro-Western, disciplined, and educated people with whom to work. Decision-makers drew from lessons they perceived from America's own backyard: "Our experience with the more highly developed Latin American States indicates that authoritarianism is required to lead backward societies through their socio-economic revolutions."[114] As historian David Schmitz compellingly analyzes, "With the emergence of the Cold War, expediency again overcame American commitment to democracy as the United States came to prefer 'stable' right-wing regimes in the Third World over indigenous radicalism and what it saw as dangerously unstable democratic governments."[115]

Nixon participated extensively in these discussions, and during Nixon's presidency, Mobutu would complete his evolution into one of Africa's strongman dictators. Nixon, who contemplated the need for developing strongmen to rule in Africa in the 1950s, carried through a decade later in the execution of his Nixon Doctrine. Speaking at the start of a trip to Asia in July 1969, Nixon articulated his resolve for the United States to keep its treaty commitments and to provide a shield for allied and other vital nations who were threatened by a nuclear power. In cases involving non-nuclear aggression, there was another path: the United States would "look to the nation directly threatened to assume the primary responsibility of providing the manpower for defense."[116] While first conceived primarily as a way to retrench U.S. commitments in Asia, in short time the path evolved into a growing reliance on regional surrogate powers, such as Iran in the Middle East and the Congo in central Africa. Invariably ruled by authoritarian regimes, these Western-friendly powers provided strong anticommunist allies but at a heavy price. In the Congo, the people suffered through over a quarter century of Mobutu's authoritarian rule and devastating looting of the nation's wealth.

The willingness of Nixon not just to abide but to promote such an authoritarian regime was rooted in the views and attitudes he held well before his presidency. Nixon and Eisenhower, grounded in Western perspectives and anticommunist doctrines, came into office in 1953 believing that continued white minority rule in Africa provided a secure harbor in the stormy Cold War. As African anticolonial nationalism became a force with which the administration had to reckon, Cold War concerns pushed Eisenhower and his aides to seek continuing stability, even at the expense of democratic alternatives. As colonial governments fell, supporting the white regimes that remained or backing shifts to strongman rule seemed acceptable alternatives, given the absence of "stabilizing" European rule amid potential communist advances. Such beliefs and attitudes shaped the U.S. approach to Africa and decolonization during the critical years of African liberation. While they generally kept Africa securely in the Western constellation through the end of the Eisenhower administration, reverberating legacies would continue to unfold on both sides of the Atlantic.

3 Years of Africa, 1960–1966

> Today, Africa and America, black men and white men, new nations and old, are inextricably linked. Our challenges rise formidably before us. If we are to achieve our goals—if we are to fulfill man's eternal quest for peace and freedom—we must do it together—and together we can and will succeed.
>
> —John F. Kennedy, June 1960

> Angola will be independent. We are your friends now, but if you want us as your friends after independence, you must act now. I realize that diplomacy moves slowly, but we hope that the experience of the last few years will help the United States to avoid past mistakes. There is still time to save both Portugal and Angola and to keep friends in both places.
>
> —Roberto Holden, December 1961

The start of the 1960s witnessed a remarkable period of African nations gaining independence. In the blaze of 1960 alone, an astounding seventeen countries raised their own flag—making 1960 the seminal Year of Africa. Countries from French colonial Africa, in particular, filled the column of newly independent nations. In the following half decade, a dozen more countries achieved independence—from Algeria in the north to Lesotho in the south, from Gambia in the west to Kenya in the east—comprising an area larger than the continental United States west of the Mississippi River and almost twice the size of India.[1]

The world took in the enormous changes and the excitement of these years. Whether in the corridors of Washington, D.C., or on the streets of New York City, whether in Lagos or in Dar es Salaam, Africa was a New Frontier. The potential collective power of the newly independent countries was palpable. The possibilities seemed endless, although depending on one's perspective, endlessly uplifting or endlessly worrisome. The rising number of voices and votes in the UN and the burgeoning relationships—both real and imagined by the West—among these countries, the emerging nonaligned movement, and the Eastern bloc were part of a world undergoing changes with a decidedly unclear end point.

The rising tide of African and Asian members in the United Nations was shifting the body away from a venue heavily influenced by postwar U.S. power and concerns toward a place of highly negotiated relationships that recognized issues on the minds of colonized peoples, not least of which was more rapidly advancing decolonization worldwide. As the Year of Africa progressed, the UN General Assembly adopted the Declaration on the Granting of Independence to Colonial Countries and Peoples by a vote of 89 to 0, with nine abstentions. Prefaced by a dozen clauses supporting ideals of freedom and independence, the resolution declared that because "all peoples have an inalienable right to complete freedom, the exercise of their sovereignty and the integrity of their national territory," the General Assembly "solemnly proclaims the necessity of bringing to a speedy and unconditional end colonialism in all its forms and manifestations." Favored reasons for delay, such as oft-cited "inadequacy of political, economic, social, or educational preparedness," were categorically dismissed as never valid. They were "a pretext for delaying independence." All armed action or repressive measures against dependent peoples should cease, and immediate steps should be taken to transfer power. Subsequent resolutions were designed to put Resolution 1514 (XV) into practice to both advance the cause of decolonization and put the United States and Europe to the test.[2]

At the last minute, the Eisenhower administration changed from voting yes to abstaining. Harmony with its European allies ranked higher than publicly and symbolically supporting decolonization throughout the world. It clung to the pole of white rule in the stormy seas. But as Adlai Stevenson told Dean Rusk, the abstention "severely damaged" United States "prestige and influence among [the] Afro-Asian group."[3] The incoming Kennedy administration would have the opportunity to align itself differently.

Notwithstanding frustrations over Washington's lack of meaningful support for decolonization up to that point, Africans held a reservoir of goodwill toward the United States. Although opinion polling in Africa was rare at the time, the United States Information Agency (USIA) in 1960 contracted local interviewers to survey over two thousand educated Kenyans, Tanganyikans, and Ugandans. Without knowing that the United States sponsored the polling, 76 percent of respondents offered a "very good" opinion of America, significantly more than offered that opinion about Great Britain, the next highest country, at 54 percent. When asked why they held this view, 37 percent of respondents cited the educational help given by America, followed by "help generally" at 21 percent. When asked "which countries of the world do the most to help Africa?" 50 percent of those polled identified the United States, 46 percent indicated Britain, and just 2 percent named the Soviet Union. Mirroring previous responses among those who indicated the United States, 52 percent identified "help educationally" as the reason.[4]

Even so, views of the United States and its relationship with Africa were subject to many forces, including rising expectations for stronger and more definitive support for freedom in areas still seeking self-determination. The Kennedy administration and then the Johnson administration, seeing African countries as a rising force and witnessing fundamental changes across the continent, grappled with decisions that they knew would have "a profound effect for many years to come."[5] They also wrestled with the meaning of these changes in an America undergoing its own turbulent changes as the relationship with Africa continued its four-hundred-year influence on America.

Advent of the Kennedy Administration

When the Eisenhower administration left office, Africa and its path to self-determination and independence became—for the first time—elemental in conversations and planning by an incoming U.S. administration. The passage of time, with its intervening wars and crises and now fixed developments, conspire to narrow our historical memory. But as the Eisenhower administration prepared to give way, events in the Congo held more meaning and captured more attention than other regions undergoing anticolonial upheavals, including Southeast Asia. Africa was the place of accelerating interest and attention. Crisscrossing the nation during the final three months of his 1960 U.S. presidential campaign, Kennedy spoke of Africa an eye-opening 167 times in speeches and statements. In comparison, he mentioned Asia half as frequently, a total of 82 times.[6] Africa was on the rise, and by the end of the Year of Africa, the continent had dramatically rewritten the membership roster of the UN, growing from ten of eighty-two member states to twenty-six of ninety-nine, more than doubling its proportion to over a quarter of General Assembly votes.

America's incoming president had already established a voice on Africa, nationalism, and decolonization. After his 1957 speech on the Algerian War of Independence, Kennedy chaired the new Senate Foreign Relations Subcommittee on Africa, a position he used to political advantage in public appearances and speeches, though the subcommittee rarely met. He mentioned his chairmanship to advance his profile in foreign affairs, specifically in connection to Africa and the Third World. As he spoke of Africa, he articulated a multitude of reasons for American interest in the continent: for natural resources and strategic minerals; for military bases and allies against communism; for a sense of responsibility about the West's actions in the area; for concern for Africa and her people; for ancestral ties of race and condition. His interest in colonialism and nationalism was political more than moral; colonialism's demise was a stark reality to face, more than a moral policy to pursue. In many respects, this viewpoint mirrored his position on civil rights. Significantly, it also meant that changing political calculations could shift his views.

The incoming president spoke sympathetically about African desires for a better standard of living and the opportunity to govern their own affairs. He believed that America had to make a political decision to assist Africa, arguing that this in turn would aid the United States in a world where the balance of power was shifting "into the hands of the two-thirds of the world's people who want to share what the one-third has already taken for granted." He made proposals: establish an Educational Development Fund to emphasize the exchange of students, teachers, and trained personnel, thereby "opening our college doors to several times as many African students as now come over"; create a multinational economic development fund to provide financial help for investment and development; and provide food to alleviate conditions of want.[7]

Developing a strong Africa needed, among other things, increased U.S. economic assistance. During the immediate post–World War II decade, Africa had received less than 0.2 percent of U.S. foreign aid—less than two-tenths of 1 percent. Dollar-wise aid had grown from $10 million in 1956 to $100 million in 1959. But that still totaled less than 3 percent of the total foreign aid budget for, as Kennedy put it, the most underdeveloped continent, one that constituted 20 percent of the world's inhabited surface. "Whatever one's point of view," Kennedy liked to point out, "one fact cannot be denied—the future of Africa will seriously affect, for better or worse, the future of the United States."[8]

Kennedy came into office more engaged with Africa than any U.S. president in history. African leaders sensed his genuine interest in the continent, and his personal diplomacy reflected his courting of Africans: in his less than three years in office, he hosted twenty-eight African heads of state at the White House.[9] Historians wrestle with Kennedy's idealism and political opportunism, his promotion of new programs such as the Peace Corps and old chestnuts like strong anticommunism. These elements intertwined, of course, as did his interest in Africa. Politically opportune in its domestic appeal to Black voters yet also part of a genuine interest in nationalism and the Third World, Africa was a place to send the first Peace Corps volunteers and a place to use his personal prestige to help ensure Africa's orientation with the West in the Cold War.[10]

The earliest days of the Kennedy administration charted a changed, more engaged course, with an expanded roster of people looking toward Africa. One of the first and most public of the Kennedy appointments, G. Mennen "Soapy" Williams as the new undersecretary of state for African affairs, made this immediately apparent. Heir to a fortune made through Mennen personal-care products, Williams served as governor of Michigan and had contemplated a run for the presidency himself. Along with Chester Bowles and Adlai Stevenson, Williams brought a liberal voice to the administration's foreign policy—or, more precisely, a voice more closely attuned to African aspirations for independence.

Williams stepped into his role enthusiastically, speaking publicly on African affairs with an "Africa first" mentality that, combined with his informal style, sometimes created diplomatic upheavals. Reactions shed light on views of the time. During his first trip to the continent in his new role, Williams stopped in Nairobi, where he was asked by the press about American goals. "What we want for the African is what the Africans want for themselves," responded Williams, which in press accounts became "Africa is for the Africans." White settlers and colonial regimes up and down the continent responded angrily, denouncing Williams for calling for their removal. At his next stop, Williams was asked, "Why do you want to drive all the whites out of Africa?" And by the time he reached Northern Rhodesia (Zambia), outrage among white settlers prompted one resident to charge the podium and punch Williams in the face. At the same time, Williams struck a chord with Africans, so that when he reached Nyasaland (Malawi), Hastings Banda called him a hero for calling for an end to white rule in Africa.[11]

How different was U.S. policy going to be, then? Was this a verbal miscue taken out of context and spun out of control, or the possible opening of a stronger stance in favor of African independence throughout the continent? Dean Rusk, the new secretary of state, sent telegrams to all U.S. embassies in Africa explaining that the press reports had failed to mention that Williams meant all people in Africa regardless of race or color. President Kennedy in his next press conference used a question on the subject to reiterate that "Africa for the Africans" did not seem unreasonable to him, given that Williams meant all people, regardless of race or color. Kennedy worked to defuse the remarks ("I do not know who else Africa should be for"), and then ordered Chester Bowles to meet with Williams and tell him to clear all future public statements with the State Department.[12]

Even so, the new president, interested in Africa and its future, was playing an unprecedented role in engaging U.S. policy as well as courting African leaders, to use the phrase of historian Philip Muehlenbeck. Kennedy projected a new relationship with independent Africa, including a willingness to accept African neutralism and nonalignment. In contrast, during the Eisenhower years, Secretary of State John Foster Dulles categorically marked the world as divided into two camps, with neutralism in all but exceptional situations "an immoral and shortsighted conception."[13]

In time spent—a telling marker of the priorities of powerful people—Africa also rose much higher with Kennedy than with any previous occupant of the White House. Symbolism and style, accompanied by a change in attitude and approach by top officials, were consequential changes, especially in the context of relations with people who for generations had been treated as lesser and unequal. It mattered that Kennedy held an abiding interest in what was happening in Africa, and it mattered that he met with African leaders: sitting down with eleven African leaders in 1961, followed by ten more in 1962, and another seven before his assassination in 1963.[14] "The value of the President seeing African leaders at the White House can not be estimated too highly," encouraged Williams. "On a continent where new leaders are so directly affecting the course of history, influencing them can be of lasting and critical importance. And Presidential audiences influence them mightily." Such urgings reflected Kennedy's instincts and personal concerns, for he also engaged in less obvious actions, such as keeping abreast of developments concerning African students enrolled in America's colleges, despite all the competing demands on his time.[15]

Education and Development

Support for education of African students from a wide range of sources in America, including African American, philanthropic, religious, and increasingly government, continued to grow. Kennedy was fully on board as well. When Belafonte, Poitier, and Robinson announced the AASF's "airlift" fundraising goal for the 1960 academic year, they tripled the ambition: $121,000 to bring 243 students from Kenya primarily but also from Nyasaland (Malawi), Northern Rhodesia (Zambia), Southern Rhodesia (Zimbabwe), Tanganyika, Uganda, and Zanzibar. Unfortunately, they failed to secure financial assistance from the State Department and were unable to convince Vice President Nixon to leverage action. Mboya appealed to Kennedy to use his position as chair of the Senate Foreign Relations Subcommittee on Africa to intercede with the State Department for funds. Kennedy went a different route: he thought the Joseph P. Kennedy Jr. Foundation might be able to help. Kennedy told Sargent Shriver, at the time head of the foundation and later founding director of the Peace Corps, that in his opinion as a trustee, the foundation should fund the whole project. Within a fortnight the foundation had pledged $100,000 for the transport of three planeloads of African students. In the midst of the presidential campaign, it proved to be good for Africans and good for connecting with Black voters.[16]

Kennedy understood that expanding African educational opportunities resonated deeply among African Americans. These opportunities spoke to broad societal beliefs in equal opportunity and uplift while echoing central battlefields in the African American freedom struggle, from the courtrooms of *Brown v. Board of Education* to the streets of Little Rock, Arkansas. Black Americans seeking to help African students built broad networks in their efforts to expand African educational opportunities.[17]

The airlift prodded the U.S. government to provide more money and play a greater role in programs for African students, and its prominent backer, now in the Oval Office, did so as well. Some of this came in the form of support for airlift students, but the State Department also launched the Southern African Student Program in 1961, and awarded grants to the Institute for International Education (IIE) and the Phelps-Stokes Fund to aid students coming without sponsorship. The International Cooperation Administration and then the Agency for International Development (AID) helped fund two new programs: the African Scholarship Program of American Universities beginning in 1961, and the East Africa Junior College Program in 1962. These efforts further spurred the interest of private organizations such as the IIE and institutions of higher learning in helping more African students study in the United States.[18]

The desire to increase the number of African students studying in the United States reflected Kennedy's ongoing interest in Africa and his recognition that, in ways similar to the Peace Corps programs, personal connections were powerful components of soft diplomacy. Despite mounting issues worldwide, Kennedy remained concerned about the progress of African students. The leader of the free world asked for, and received, updates on the status of the African students studying in the country. "In view of [his] frequently expressed interest in the education of young Africans," George Ball delivered to Kennedy in October 1961 a "Report to the President on Sub-Sahara Africa Student Programs."[19] When Kennedy learned that Portuguese-speaking African students had left their studies behind the Iron Curtain to take refuge in France and Switzerland, Kennedy directed that they be given the opportunity to finish their studies in the United States if they so desired, and helped ensure that at the HBCU Lincoln University, an African Student Center was organized for the seventeen students who came.[20]

Public and private efforts to promote student exchanges faced criticism along the way. Some expressed concern that students were ill-prepared for the rigors of university coursework, others that they were attending inferior colleges and universities in the United States, and still others that they had no clear continuing means of support for the years that they would be in America. Complaints came that exchanges were depleting the best and brightest students from African universities, such as Makerere University in Uganda. Some of the objections were contradictory, and all reflected the parochial concerns—and often fears—of the governing powers involved. Colonial officials were vexed by the prospect of hundreds of Africans leaving metropole control, spending four years or more out of their view, and returning to pursue dreams of freedom and independence, just as had influential Africans such as Kwame Nkrumah and Nnamdi Azikiwe.[21]

The State Department did worry that hundreds of students would end up destitute and scattered throughout the fifty states. The stark reality was that most students did not have enough ongoing funding for expenses while they were studying. Private efforts in East Africa to raise thousands of dollars still left as many as 60 percent of the students in difficult financial circumstances for daily living expenses. In April 1961, the State Department authorized $100,000 to distribute to needy and deserving African students not already receiving U.S. government assistance. Roughly 40 percent of the estimated 1,307 eligible students applied, with not quite half of those receiving aid. The Labor Department and the AFL-CIO, among others, worked to find students summer employment, but for many, life remained a meager existence. The State Department made further efforts to alleviate the situation, contributing another $25,000 for summer emergencies and allocating an additional $100,000 to be matched by private foundation money for emergencies during the 1961–62 academic year.[22]

As was true of earlier students who studied in America, this generation of students contributed mightily to freedom struggles and nation-building in Africa. Barack Obama Sr. returned to Kenya, leaving his son to make his own mark in America. Another student joined the 1960 African airlift to study at Mount St. Scholastica College in Kansas before going on to earn her master's degree at the University of Pittsburgh. Returning to Kenya, Wangari Maathai would eventually earn her PhD, start the Green Belt movement, and become a democracy warrior before being awarded the Nobel Peace Prize in 2014 for her visionary "contribution to sustainable development, democracy, and peace." Famous or not, the transatlantic exchanges proved enduring in meaningful ways.[23]

Educational assistance also flowed into Africa with the creation of Kennedy's signature initiative: the Peace Corps. As it developed and grew, the Peace Corps chose to focus on newly independent nations. Sending Americans who were willing to mix and mingle and be a part of the host country in all settings, not just formal meetings and discussions, blazed new person-to-person relations with recently independent Africa.[24]

Kennedy administration officials believed they could navigate the changing relationship, guide hopes and expectations, and secure Africa in the liberal democratic Western alliance through development efforts that would "modernize" it. While those educational initiatives and Peace Corps workers were individual and person to person in focus, they contributed on the broader level to macro actions of development and modernization. Economic assistance for Africa had remained miserly; despite occasional talk, no "Marshall Plan for Africa" had made any headway. Truman's program for development assistance, Point Four, made just four countries in Africa eligible—Egypt, Libya, Ethiopia, and Liberia—and the Truman people considered the first three as part of the Near East/Middle East.[25] Late in the Eisenhower administration, money for development projects still trickled in to Africa, with just $20 million in 1958.[26] The growing number of African states moving from colonial subjugation to sovereign independence had great hopes and expectations that this new world would bring a new economic and social landscape along with a new political status. But that growing number also meant that there was a growing list of people and nations seeking economic assistance.

Coming into office with Kennedy were advisers who championed ideas about underdeveloped nations moving toward "modernity." Driven by social science theories, the broad umbrella of "modernization" posited explanations for how traditional societies moved toward modern societies. That the apotheosis of modern society strikingly resembled the United States provided what was, supporters hoped, a sort of self-fulfilling prophecy: traditional societies could and should be modernized, and in that process become more like the United States.[27]

Modernization theory became a guiding ideology during the Kennedy administration and, with many proponents continuing the work, in the Johnson administration. No advocate was more important than Walt Whitman Rostow, author of the influential *The Stages of Economic Growth: A Non-Communist Manifesto*, who argued that societies go through five stages of development. Rostow became a close adviser to Kennedy, serving as deputy national security adviser and then chairing the State Department's Policy Planning Council before becoming Johnson's national security adviser from 1966 until Johnson left the White House. Africa seemed ripe for modernization theory in action, especially to Kennedy's "best and brightest," who believed that their ideas would work on the ground, in varying local conditions and considerations. That abstract social science theories, often removed from a close understanding of local conditions, now faced concrete settings produced little hesitation.[28]

Modernization projects seemingly provided a path to meet rising aspirations, accelerate modernity in African states, and keep them in the Western fold. Modernization under the care of the United States would benefit Africa as well as America. "In broad perspective," wrote Secretary of State Rusk supportively, "a political and social evolution is envisaged in Africa which would in time significantly extend the area of freedom in the world, thus making our own democratic freedoms more secure. This evolution begins with self-determination—largely achieved, proceeds through the establishment of economic and social conditions which give meaning to nationhood, and ultimately arrives at societies based on genuinely free institutions."[29]

Beyond any issues in applying theory to actuality, a basic problem would be that the United States never fully committed the resources. U.S. officials believed that by fiscal year 1963 they had reached a "relatively substantial" amount of assistance to Africa. That assistance totaled $473.2 million in the form of U.S. Export-Import Bank loans, AID technical assistance, the Food for Freedom project, and an array of other programs, such as the Peace Corps. This level would not be sustained in the following years, as other demands—Great Society domestic programs, the expanding war in Vietnam—took resources. Indeed, by 1964, AID funding for African assistance had dropped to $202 million, from $312 million just two years earlier.[30] Limited resources, typically driven by Cold War calculations, were committed to Africa, and with rare exception, almost none were earmarked for countries seeking independence. In the words of the State Department, "The effectiveness of economic assistance was greatly limited in the majority of cases simply by the scarcity of resources."[31] Economic support for newly independent nations is not the focus of this narrative, but the level of support affected how these states were able to emerge from colonial rule and how they perceived the U.S. role in decolonization still happening elsewhere on the continent. Continuing past practice, finding extensive resources to advance nations toward independence was not a priority.

"The Greatest Open Field of Maneuver"

The push for modernization was situated in what was perceived as a mostly zero-sum Cold War context, in which gain for one side seemingly meant loss for the other. "The United States, as a country with no colonial heritage in Africa, has great opportunities on that continent," assessed the State Department in 1962. "But so does the Sino-Soviet Bloc. We see Africa as probably the greatest open field of maneuver in the world-wide competition between the Bloc and the non-Communist world."[32]

The Soviets were strengthening their push for influence in Africa, from establishing warm ties with newly independent Guinea, to increasing the number of African students studying in the USSR, to embracing Lumumba's appeal for assistance. Then in January 1961, Khrushchev announced the "historical mission" of world communism to "assist wars of national liberation" in an attempt to end colonialism. "A remarkable phenomenon of our time is the awakening of the peoples of Africa," declared the Soviet leader, admonishing that it would be unfortunate if communists as revolutionaries "did not take advantage of new opportunities . . . that would best achieve the ends in view." The specter of increasing communist intrigue in Africa loomed.[33]

There was less communist activity in Africa than elsewhere, still people in Washington—diplomats, military personnel, those at the CIA and White House—interpreted and argued in Cold War terms, even when communist threats in a particular situation or region did not appear imminent. The perception of Soviet interest helped propel a subtle but noticeable shift as the Cold War increasingly narrowed Kennedy's range of vision and shifted his engagement with Africa. In August 1961, the crisis over the Berlin Wall caused U.S. ambassadors in Africa to voice their concern that Cold War anticommunism threatened to undermine the United States' relationship with Africa: "To the extent that American objectives are identified with African aspirations, our task will be facilitated. In this connection, there is no doubt that the most highly-charged issues in sub-Saharan Africa today are the war in Angola and racial discrimination in the United States."[34]

Colonialism and white supremacy, not anticommunism and the Cold War, meant the most to Africans. Kennedy's proposed responses to the Berlin crisis—$3.247 billion increased funding for the U.S. armed forces, 217,000 more men under arms, $207 million more for civil defense—were no help to diplomats in Africa. Instead, the crisis drew away resources, threatening to make their job even harder. Concerns about communism could have led the Kennedy administration in either of two directions: pouring resources into Africa and pushing harder for decolonization, or tightening ranks with Cold War allies who wanted continuing white rule. The administration chose the latter path.[35]

The effects were most evident in southern Africa. Ongoing problems around the world and across Africa, particularly in newly independent Congo, consumed vast amounts of attention, but farther south a pattern of white intransigence increasingly came to the fore. British prime minister Harold Macmillan famously spoke before the South African Parliament in February 1960 about the "wind of change" sweeping the continent. This "national consciousness," which had changed Europe long before and had swept through Asia more recently, was now transforming Africa. During four weeks touring the continent, Macmillan's appreciation of the power of African nationalism had deepened. "The wind of change is blowing through this continent," Macmillan declared to his white South African audience, "whether we like it or not, this growth of national consciousness is a political fact. We must all accept it as a fact. Our national policies must take account of it."[36]

But this wind hit the doldrums ten degrees south of the equator. As the rest of the continent blew toward independence, southern Africa offered little evidence of coming change. In response to Macmillan's speech, South African prime minister Hendrik Verwoerd declared, "The world is suffering from a psychosis which makes it think only of the brown and black man and disregard the role of the White man."[37] Deadly evidence of his determination to continue on a course of white minority rule soon horrified the world. Just six weeks after Macmillan spoke, police in Sharpeville gunned down protesters, and shortly thereafter a state of emergency was used to crack down on any form of African political expression. Within a year, white voters in South Africa approved becoming an independent republic, removing Queen Elizabeth II as head of state, and severing links to Great Britain. With the passage of the Constitution Act, in May 1961 the nation became the Republic of South Africa. Beyond its borders, the South African government sought to make permanent its authority over South West Africa. And long-held visions of further expanding South Africa's domain to the British protectorates of Bechuanaland, Basutoland, and Swaziland continued to animate South African officials.

In this context, the new Kennedy administration prepared policy guidelines toward South Africa. Early on, it dipped a toe into more assertively opposing South Africa's racial oppression. Joseph Satterthwaite, previously the founding assistant secretary of state for African affairs and now the ambassador to South Africa, informed Pretoria that its racial policy "does violence to human rights provisions of UN Charter" and weakens the West's efforts to resist communist influence in newly independent African and Asian countries. This echoed anticolonial voices the world over. "As a consequence the United States for its own and for world security must continue its disapproval of a policy which arouses emotions and resentments of such large segments of population of the world."[38]

Satterthwaite offered a lifeline to Pretoria: Washington's disapproval could be turned around if South Africa would take steps toward allowing all people a greater role in the life of their country with a "view to ultimate full participation." The United States then "would gladly cooperate to the fullest extent possible with South Africa in all fields of endeavor." Absent change, however, the United States "could not be expected to cooperate in matters which it believed would lend support to South Africa's present racial policies."[39]

Pretoria pushed back. South Africa's intensely negative response condemned the U.S. position as choosing when and where it wanted to cooperate. When South Africa sought clarification on what was meant by the demand for "ultimate full participation" of Black South Africans, Satterthwaite offered assurance that this could mean a protracted period encompassing several generations.[40] Several generations until majority rule was a window that hardly fit with African hopes throughout the continent, and it was no stronger than the previous administration's stance. As months passed, the State Department settled on its guiding policy as the "basic approach" to South Africa: "to distinguish between non-cooperation in matters directly or indirectly related to South Africa's apartheid policy, and cooperation in all other fields."[41]

But "all other fields" was an elastic concept, and the extent to which the Kennedy administration stretched it revealed the tepidness of the administration's commitment to change. Washington agreed to continue cooperation in a multitude of significant areas, including common defense against threats from the Eastern bloc, missile activity, space exploration, atomic energy, and other scientific areas.[42]

Military and strategic needs competed with moral and diplomatic concerns as Washington wrestled over policy toward South Africa. Concrete actions against apartheid crashed against other Cold War interests. Gold, uranium, and strategic minerals such as chrome, manganese, and titanium all seemed vital in the ongoing Cold War, as did South Africa's developed ports. Even the use of a satellite tracking station factored in, as it enabled the U.S. Air Force to receive data providing diagnostic information in certain satellite tests. In 1961, those included the Midas ballistic missile early-warning satellite and the Advent military communications satellite. Given South Africa's worldwide unpopularity, the Pentagon agreed to abandon the station if it meant a net harm to U.S. interests, and the White House assessment aligned with that of deputy secretary of defense and former undersecretary of the air force Ros Gilpatric that the "loss of this site would be painful, but not fatal." Yet for Cold Warriors, abandoning anything that might make a difference was highly problematic, particularly when a white-ruled anticommunist ally pushed back.[43]

The idea that rhetoric alone would be enough for African nationalists, enabling U.S. actions to continue more or less status quo, now manifested with respect to South Africa. Philip Muehlenbeck notes in his examination of Kennedy's courting of African nationalist leaders, "Because the Kennedy administration never considered the ANC [African National Congress] to be an acceptable representative of African nationalism, it refused to give aid to the movement," fearing that a race war or an ANC victory would help Moscow.[44] The Kennedy administration was being pulled, like those before it, by Cold War imperatives and the seeming security of white rule. Fears of communist advances, desires for stability and continuing trade, and worries over potential racial conflict contributed to a general reluctance to pressure the white regimes in southern Africa, even among U.S. officials with a more liberal view.

Dean Rusk, secretary of state to both Kennedy and Johnson, "balanced security with ideals," according to biographer Thomas Zeiler.[45] Born and raised in rural Georgia, Rusk in many ways had an admirable record on civil rights, and he had integrated State Department functions in South Africa. But he counseled against exerting too much pressure on South Africa, or indeed on authoritarian African regimes. "National security took precedence," notes Zeiler. "Since the Second World War the United States had favored trade over morality regarding Pretoria."[46] Rusk was a neo-Wilsonian liberal, but he abandoned those principles as he engaged with Africa, which he believed "necessitated a distinctly amoral approach." The significance was profound: the secretary of state, tasked with guiding U.S. relations with the world, felt he needed an "amoral" approach to white supremacy because the stakes elsewhere seemed so high.[47]

Anticommunism and white supremacy became intertwined in the United States and in its relations with southern Africa during these postwar years. Given the omnipresent nature of apartheid in South Africa, it hardly seemed credible that the United States could distinguish between apartheid-related and non-apartheid-related matters. And it was even less credible that the broader world would see and accept this distinction, thereby "avoiding damage to our broader interests in Africa." African nationalists framed a dilemma for the United States: Would the United States act forcefully against racial oppression and for democratic principles of one-person, one-vote majority rule, even at the cost of an ally? The answer appeared to remain no.

"Impossible to Be an Ally of Portugal in Europe and an Enemy in Africa"

Relations with Cold War allies were enormously complicating the decisions of officials in Washington, particularly with white regimes in southern Africa determined to maintain control. Colonial resolve gained sustenance from António de Oliveira Salazar's government in Lisbon. Portuguese involvement in Africa dated back half a millennium, but Portugal had become a second-tier European power and had lost out on a number of its claims during the Scramble for Africa. Nevertheless, it received European recognition of its governing authority in Angola and Mozambique, as well as small fragments of West Africa and islands off the coast. Efforts to expand its authority and profitably exploit these areas faced limited success; when Portuguese chose to emigrate, the vast majority went to the United States rather than to Africa. By the 1920s, Lusophone Africa seemed likely to fade, or perhaps get snapped up by another European power.

The rise to power of former economics professor Salazar altered the equation. His view was that Portugal's overseas possessions were essential components in the country's national, economic, and spiritual well-being. He saw them not as colonies but as part of a Lusitanian community in which all were residents of Portugal, positing a worldview that meant the loss of a colony would be akin to the loss of a limb. In theory, rights would be determined by "merit" and by achieving a standard of "civilization." But the facts revealed the true nature: in 1950, only thirty thousand of four million Angolans were considered "civilized," leaving over 99 percent without political and civil rights, mired in grinding poverty.[48]

The shrinking Portuguese empire held few outposts in the world other than in Africa, and Salazar's government fervently believed in maintaining possession of its remaining overseas interests. The conviction bestowed each territory with symbolic importance, but the remaining large colonies in Africa offered the most tangible economic significance. The Salazar dictatorship left no uncertainty about its intent to keep its African possessions. "Nationalism does not exist in either Angola or Mozambique," Salazar proclaimed. "You Americans have invented it. Portugal will continue its 400 year old effort to build a multiracial society."[49]

The situation presented a dilemma for officials in Washington. They could sail with the wind of anticolonialism or tack against it toward a European and NATO ally's continuing colonial ambitions. As Salazar himself warned Kennedy's ambassador, Charles Elbrick, in March 1961, it was "manifestly impossible to be an ally of Portugal in Europe and an enemy in Africa."[50]

Events in Angola helped crystallize the situation in February 1961, just weeks after Kennedy took office. Against the backdrop of a brutally suppressed cotton workers revolt, before dawn on February 4 several hundred Angolans attacked the main prison and two police barracks in Luanda. The next day, after the state funeral for seven slain police officers, a group of Europeans turned on African bystanders, killing hundreds in retaliation. Five days later, a second prison raid prompted more reprisals that then spread outside Luanda, with security forces killing hundreds of Africans demonstrating against colonial rule; inside the impoverished slums of Luanda, vigilantes backed by security forces patrolled and shot suspects on sight.[51]

Amid worldwide condemnation of the killings, Liberia's ambassador to the United States, George A. Padmore, called for an urgent meeting of the Security Council to address the crisis. The Afro-Asian bloc at the UN was spearheading a resolution to press Portugal toward allowing self-determination in its colonies. The new administration in Washington projected its willingness to side with African nationalism and push Portugal to move its African colonies toward independence. Informing Lisbon that it could not expect American support in UN debates about Angola because it was "increasingly difficult and disadvantageous to Western interests . . .

to support or remain silent on Portuguese African policies," on 15 March 1961 U.S. ambassador to the UN Adlai Stevenson voted in the Security Council for the Afro-Asian bloc resolution calling for self-determination in Angola.[52]

The U.S. vote marked a notable change, and the shift from past policy was replayed several times in the following ten months. Stevenson again voted for resolutions condemning Portuguese colonialism in April, June, December, and in January 1962. In the bitter words of conservative columnist James Burnham, those behind the shift held "the illusion that the primitive jungles of Africa are more important than the advanced men, ideas, and machines of Europe."[53]

The U.S. votes strained relations with Portugal. So did evidence that the tens of thousands of Portuguese troops Salazar rushed to Angola were using U.S. arms to fight the rebels. This news led to added U.S. demands that the Portuguese ensure that American arms intended for NATO purposes were not used in Angola. While not the "arms embargo" that the State Department initially characterized it to be, the events bitterly soured relations between the two allies. With tensions rising, the CIA took steps toward Angolan nationalists, putting Angolan nationalist leader Holden Roberto on a $6,000 annual CIA retainer.[54]

The Kennedy administration held no illusions about the harshness of Portuguese rule. Visiting Angola and Mozambique, Assistant Secretary of State Williams reported to his boss that "the Portuguese have up until very recently conducted themselves as if this were still the 18th century."[55] Outside the Congo's deteriorating situation, Williams believed that Angola posed the most critical situation in sub-Saharan Africa. He wrote that the "abuses of the police state and feudal system" have led to revolt and required that the United States "continue to put pressure on Salazar for genuine political, educational, and economic reforms leading to self-determination." As Williams rightly understood, the Portuguese did not have "magic that will make them immune to the force of nationalism, which is sweeping the continent. The timetable may be shorter than any of us think."[56]

Yet the Portuguese government, press, and populace pushed back, denouncing U.S. actions. The press fanned anti-American anger, and demonstrators took to the streets, with between fifteen thousand and twenty thousand Portuguese gathering outside the U.S. embassy in Lisbon in the days following the March 1961 UN vote.[57] Much more worrisome to officials in Washington was the potent card held by the relatively minor NATO ally: access to the Azores. The U.S. military had come to depend on the Azores as a base during World War II, use of which neutral Portugal allowed when

America pledged to "respect Portuguese sovereignty in all Portuguese colonies." As the Cold War took hold, Portuguese control over the islands contributed to Portugal being asked to join NATO as a charter member. In 1951, Washington and Lisbon signed a defense agreement granting the United States base rights for five years in exchange for which, instead of paying rent, the United States "agreed to underwrite much of Portugal's involvement in NATO." Additionally, in a set of secret notes, the United States pledged that permission would "no doubt . . . be promptly forthcoming" if Portugal sought to use NATO equipment in its colonies. By the early 1960s, roughly 75 percent of all U.S. military air traffic to Europe and the Middle East stopped in the Azores, which served as a refueling station during the deployment of U.S. Marines to Lebanon in 1958, UN troops to the Congo in 1960, and U.S. troops to Berlin in the crisis of 1961.[58] Former secretary of state Dean Acheson, in 1961 a senior voice on foreign policy matters and a staunch friend to Lisbon, characterized the Azores as "perhaps the single most important (set of bases) we have anywhere."[59]

Tensions in Europe ratcheted higher after the contentious Kennedy-Khrushchev Vienna summit in June 1961, making ruptures with European and NATO allies even less palatable, a sensibility heightened when the Berlin Wall appeared in August. Despite being a relatively minor power with little international influence, Portugal revealed the limits of American power in a Cold War world. The initial boldness of the UN vote against Portuguese colonialism receded, such that the first year of Kennedy's forthright anticolonialism turned into an anomaly rather than a fundamental change.

Within a year of adopting a firmer position against Portuguese colonialism, Portuguese intransigence and American need for access to the Azores caused the Kennedy administration to step back. Its public criticism of Portuguese colonialism faded, and its contacts with Angolan nationalists diminished. In the UN, the United States began abstaining or voting against resolutions critical of Portugal, and sales of military equipment picked up. The U.S. approach to colonial questions at the UN "bowed to Cold War considerations," in the words of historian Mary Ann Heiss.[60] The Cuban missile crisis, and the role the Azores played in allowing the surveillance of Soviet naval activity in the Atlantic, accelerated the backpedaling. "Kennedy's hesitation and eventual retreat on Angolan policy was a bitter defeat for [Soapy] Williams," writes historian Thomas Noer. "Combined with the administration's reluctance to use force in the Congo, it showed that the

New Frontier was still closely wedded to Europe and that military and strategic interests dominated African issues."[61]

In hindsight, access to the Azores may seem less critical than it did at the time. In subsequent decades the United States shifted away from other major installations, such as Clark Air Base and Subic Bay Naval Station in the Philippines in the 1990s, without crippling effects. Even at the time, suggestions were made to seek alternative bases, and contingency planning was done. Yet the national security structure consistently and successfully made the case that the Azores bases were vital to America's defense.

The advent of the Kennedy presidency had marked a movement toward greater empathy with African views, and his early months in office reflected this seemingly fundamental shift. As it turned out, the more concrete aspects of U.S. policies and actions regarding the white-ruled states on the continent changed less than might have been expected given the tone and tenor. The Bay of Pigs fiasco in April 1961, followed by the Berlin Wall crisis of August 1961, consumed Kennedy's attention, as did the broader Cold War. While Africa was a part of the global Cold War, in the early 1960s, flaring hot spots there—the Congo, Angola—were addressed under the umbrella of Cold War concerns, and the desire for strong unity with European allies seemed ever more important in the wake of the Berlin crisis. Faced with the decision of whether the United States would support UN military intervention to end the Katanga secession from the Congo, Kennedy declined to make the commitment, believing that, with the situation in Europe, "it was the better part of valor to go slow with any bold 'New Africa' policy."[62]

For those seeking bold new policy on Africa, initial Kennedy administration moves raised hopes and expectations regarding U.S. actions toward the continent. If Kennedy was meeting with so many African leaders, would he not also listen to them? African leaders witnessed the power of the United States and expected that power to be used to aid the fight against colonialism, other concerns aside. Rising African hopes and aspirations in turn created rising expectations of concrete actions that, if not met, could sow rising frustrations. In Nkrumah's estimation, genuine support for Angolan independence by the United States would entail expelling Portugal from NATO, and "Portugal's colonial rule would collapse the day after."[63] Yet Nkrumah and others soon saw that the more traditional Europe-first orientation held constant, notwithstanding those handful of U.S. votes against Portugal in the UN.

U.S. military support to NATO allies contributed to Lisbon's ability to maintain control over its African possessions—just as its NATO support had helped colonial allies during the previous two administrations. And so Kennedy's policies on decolonization ended up being not so distant from those of previous administrations.[64] As Arthur Schlesinger, historian and adviser to the Kennedys, told Robert Kennedy, the basic policy of African states "is to try to make us choose between Portugal and South Africa, on the one hand, and the rest of Africa, on the other." Acknowledging that history and justice were on the side of the African states, Schlesinger nevertheless argued that the United States must "evade that choice." The United States needed to show support for self-determination so as not "to abandon Africa altogether" while not risking military access to the Azores and to the tracking stations in South Africa.[65]

Changes in Africa, Divisions in America

As officials in Washington wrestled with the extent and nature of support for decolonization and self-determination in Africa, powerful constituencies in America sought comfort in continuing what they believed brought stability and progress to Africa: white authority. From Americans working in Africa to politicians who never visited the continent, many wanted to hold on to the familiar, which to them meant people of European descent in charge. Soapy Williams warned President Kennedy and all who would listen that retrogressive forces "constantly pointed to the excesses and ineptitudes of the Congo, pretty much oblivious of (or refusing to recognize) such successes as Nigeria and the Ivory Coast." Given the forces arrayed against further African self-determination, ensuring the success of already independent African states held continental significance. Turmoil in the Congo raised Williams's fear that "if the Congo fails to function as a state under black control, white settler elements and racist groups will say 'I told you so' and will seek to perpetuate their dominant roles indefinitely, possibly along the South African pattern" in Rhodesia and other parts of Africa still under white rule. The path of independent Africa continued to hold great meaning for decolonization in countries still seeking majority rule.[66]

When violence broke out following Congolese independence, hundreds of American missionaries fled in any manner they could, many via a circuitous route through Katanga, then Southern Rhodesia, and on to Johannesburg. Within a month, some 118 made it to South Africa, where American consular staff met, debriefed, and aided their return to the United States. In the interviews, missionaries were "unanimous" in their view that the situation in the Congo was "inspired by communists." "Some of the missionary group attributed the attacks against the Belgians less to Belgian injustices (which some of whom had been in the Congo for 20 years or more said were very rare)," wrote Consul General Arthur Beach, "than to the fact that the Belgians had for several years past permitted indignities offered to them by lawless natives to pass unnoticed thereby lowering respect in which the mass of Congolese held them."[67]

Communist machinations and a lack of colonial discipline (in the Congo of all places!)—these explained the chaos in the Congo, not a desire for independence amid neocolonial efforts to thwart that very outcome. For these former residents of the Congo, Lumumba was a "thief . . . [who] could not possibly have written the speeches that he has made." When these missionaries returned to the United States, to their church halls and friends' living rooms, their views informed their communities' perceptions.[68]

Racism was a problem among American missionaries as they grappled with the realities of a decolonizing world and a decolonizing church, just as it was in America generally.[69] Intensely negative perspectives about the meaning of independence in Africa coursed through broader American society, combining with Cold War fears about change in Africa and America. Throughout 1961, Vice President Lyndon Johnson was peppered with concerns about communism, the UN, and Africa. "Katanga and its President are hundred per cent pro-Western," wrote A. J. Dens of Arlington, Texas, to LBJ as the crisis over the Katanga secession dragged on into late 1961. "The United Nations (including Stevenson) and Moscow want to destroy Katanga, to liquidate Tshombe. We pay for this 'operation.' How preposterous can we get? Please reconsider our Congo policy. Save Katanga from the U.N. and communism. If not, the Russians will soon dominate Congo and the rest of dark Africa."[70] More letters from his fellow Texans arrived, with *Borger News Herald* editor J. C. Phillips asking, "How will the Kennedy Administration explain victory over Katanga, forcing it into a communist controlled Congolese government?" Phillips and others saw in secessionist leader Moise Tshombe an anticommunist, capitalist, Christian leader in Africa willing to work with the West. To them, alternative views of the situation made little sense. Too many years of mistrust of the State Department, the UN, and communist subversives formed these views and moved Phillips to lament, "Our communist serving State Department does not recognize a separate entity called Katanga."[71]

As was true for those resisting change within America, the Cold War became a way people could argue against change in Africa by expressing concerns about communist exploitation and advances. One effect of the Cold War, Soapy Williams highlighted, was that "those who most violently oppose the development of African nationalism link it directly and inextricably with Communism."[72] The same was true of those who fought against civil rights in the United States.

Johnson worked to defend the Kennedy administration position, yet passions ran deep. Racist views of events in Africa were given added fuel by the United States' grappling with its own Black freedom struggle. Shelby County, Tennessee, school superintendent Bennie Nix wrote to the vice president about his anger when watching on television "your United Nations troops shoot dead some innocent Belgians—over in a land where we have no business—giving support to the wrong negroes, even if we had business there." Far from mollified upon receiving a reply from the vice president, Nix angrily scrawled across it and returned to sender the deeper meanings that he saw: "Today in America, no *thought of rights* are given Southern white people; same goes for *white Belgians*. Any fool can see that" (emphasis in original). With that, Bennie Nix returned to his duties of overseeing the education of the children of Shelby County.[73]

Americans who saw Africa through a racialized lens had experiences at home mingled with their understandings and views of events abroad. For Nix, Phillips, Dens, and others, colonial abuses first under the rule of Leopold II and then under the government in Brussels were a distant past. Perhaps they were not even aware of that past. Of more immediate concern were the threats of spreading communism and the UN expanding its authority, which made a potent cocktail when mixed with enduring racial views of the "inferiority" of Africans. Not all letters came from areas embroiled in the domestic civil rights revolution, but many did, and conveyed the racist views at home entangling with those fears abroad.

As African independence unfolded, however, there were those who wanted to help ensure its success. James Del Rio, for example, was a member of one of the increasing number of trade missions to Africa. President of a mortgage company in Detroit, Del Rio had become a pioneering African American mortgage banker and had built a successful real estate company. After the trade mission, he helped plan and lead the mass Walk to Freedom civil rights march in Detroit, was elected to the state legislature, and eventually served as a Detroit judge.

Del Rio returned from the trade mission to the Sahel in mid-1962 laden with such misgivings about how America was representing itself that he contacted Vice President Johnson's special assistant, Hobart Taylor, for action. He told Taylor that prior to the trip, there had been no orientation for members "with respect to respecting the difference in color of the African people." At a large social function given by the president of Chad, Del Rio observed delegation members who "contented themselves with escorting and attending solely the ladies of the embassy." Reflecting on why, Del Rio attributed it to trade mission members having "only experienced associations with people of color in an employee or servant capacity." The effect was that while the delegation was "striving to do a good job for our country," local citizens had the sense that "the other members of the mission considered themselves superior to everyone except the European residents." Counseling Taylor to ensure that mission members were selected carefully and given proper predeparture orientation, Del Rio offered him one last piece of advice: "It was not especially helpful to find and has not gone unnoticed by the Africans that usually the only Negro in the service of the American government abroad is the head of the public information center which is usually many blocks from the Embassy itself. It sort of conveys the impression that 'we have one.'"[74]

The problem of unconscionably low African American representation in the foreign service of the United States was long running. By 1950, only one Black American had ever served in the Foreign Service Officer Corps; twenty years later, after several efforts to increase representation, the State Department employed just thirty-seven Black Foreign Service Officers and sixty-eight Black Foreign Service Reserve Officers. As a candidate, Kennedy had addressed the lack of African American representation in the U.S. diplomatic corps, with the long-standing inequity becoming even more glaring as African nations gained independence and the United States named white ambassadors as envoys. "Do you know how many Negroes we have in our State Department Foreign Service out of 6,000? Twenty-six. Do you know how many Federal judges there are, Federal district judges? Zero out of 220. We can do better. We can do better," exhorted Kennedy before a packed crowd at the Elks Auditorium in Los Angeles.[75]

Del Rio's interest reflected the deepening connections that Black Americans felt with Africa, and the desire to influence positively the relationship with the continent. One of the more important efforts arose in the late 1950s from a group who began discussing the need for an organization that would represent and express the views of Black Americans. A. Philip Randolph, along with other labor figures such as Maida Springer and George McCray, built on their transnational labor organizing to help push along the idea. These labor connections provided critical experience working with Africans and on the continent. Indeed, by the late 1950s Springer had been to Ghana four times, Kenya and Tanganyika two times, and the Congo once, for periods ranging up to three months, before becoming the international representative for Africa in the AFL-CIO International Affairs Department.[76]

In mid-1958, Randolph corresponded with McCray, at the time the president of Chicago Local No. 1006 of the American Federation of State, County and Municipal Employees, AFL-CIO. McCray expressed interest in forming a national group that would work to have greater government and private sector support for positive programs on behalf of Africa and to develop contacts with African nationalist groups. Randolph responded that he had given the matter "quite a bit of thought." In fact, he and Maida Springer, Ted Brown—a labor economist formerly employed by the Brotherhood of Sleeping Car Porters (BSCP) and then serving as assistant director of the Civil Rights Department of the AFL-CIO—and a few others had been talking about this question "for a long, long time."[77]

By this point, Randolph had developed a steady correspondence with labor leaders in Africa, such as Tom Mboya, and used his positions as head of the BSCP and member of the AFL-CIO Executive Council to promote an exhausting range of projects: bringing Mboya to the United States on a speaking tour, establishing an AFL-CIO program to train African labor leaders in America, building a trade union educational center in Kenya, building a labor college in Kampala, aiding the defense of Kenyan labor leaders on trial for conspiracy to commit a misdemeanor and publish defamatory material, urging labor to support the American Committee on Africa's South African Defense Fund.[78]

Despite some lingering doubts about building and sustaining a new organization, by the end of 1959 Randolph had taken definite steps to launch an African American organization devoted to Africa. He invited approximately fifty people to meet, including James Farmer, then the program director of the NAACP. Farmer reported back to his NAACP colleagues about Randolph's plans. "This one is to be a 'mass Negro' organization on Africa, hoping to fill the vacuum of interest and activity in the Negro community with regard to Africa," wrote Farmer. "The projected organization apparently would work with the United Nations and seek in other ways to influence American foreign policy on Africa . . . and to build channels of communication, to use an over-worked phrase, between American Negroes and African leaders."[79]

The desire to have an organization featuring African Americans' views and voices on issues with Africa has a long history. Black Americans had long been at the vanguard of anticolonial efforts, sometimes as part of the work of broader organizations such as the NAACP and other times in more focused efforts such as the Council on African Affairs (CAA). The latter, with Paul Robeson, Alphaeus Hunton, W. E. B. Du Bois, and others, had fought for African liberation from white rule for years, even as these individuals were persecuted and the CAA itself driven out of existence as the Cold War hysteria against the Left reached new heights in early 1950s America.[80]

This new effort came soon after the demise of the CAA, while later organizations, such as TransAfrica, would build on its efforts. The scope of the project rapidly grew beyond labor activists to encompass a broader effort—and, somewhat paradoxically, in doing so moved away from a more grassroots "mass" movement. National organizations and civil rights leaders furthered efforts to create an organization controlled and operated by Black Americans, designed to raise interest in America about the situation in Africa and to influence U.S. policy toward that continent. The efforts bore fruit in 1962 with a new coalition, the American Negro Leadership Conference on Africa (ANLCA), hosting "The Role of the American Negro Community in U.S. Policy toward Africa," a conference presented at Columbia University's Arden House in November 1962.

Leaders of the prominent civil rights organizations constituted the Call Committee for the conference: James Farmer, by then with the Congress of Racial Equality (CORE); Dorothy Height, National Council of Negro Women; Martin Luther King Jr., Southern Christian Leadership Conference (SCLC); A. Philip Randolph, BSCP; Roy Wilkins, NAACP; and Whitney Young, Urban League. The principal areas of Africa to be addressed were those still under white rule, specifically Portuguese Africa, Kenya, the Central African Federation, South West Africa, and South Africa, as well as the ongoing crisis in the Congo. "The American Negro community in the U.S. has a special responsibility to urge a dynamic policy on our own country," wrote these leaders. "Although we have a serious civil rights problem which exhausts much of our energy, we cannot separate the struggle at home from that abroad."[81]

Two interrelated arguments animated this broader pan-African vision: first, that the struggles in America and in Africa were linked; and second, that Black Americans could help create a U.S. policy more favorable to

Africans, and that doing so would be beneficial for both Africa and America. When T. J. Sellers wrote executive secretary Roy Wilkins, asking, "Is it actually the view of American Negro leaders to 'link the integration struggle in the United States with the fate of the sub-Saharan African States'?" John Morsell, assistant to Wilkins, replied, "It seems incontestable that there is such a link in the minds of a great many Negroes and Africans. The conference did not undertake to create such a link but merely took note of its existence."[82]

Martin Luther King Jr. advanced the bonds of connection in his assessment of the conference: "Colonialism and segregation are nearly synonymous; they are children in the same family for their common end is economic exploitation, political domination, and the debasing of human personality. . . . In many ways the future of the emergent African nations (particularly those below the Sahara) and the American Negro are intertwined. As long as segregation and discrimination exist in our nation, the longer the chances of survival are for colonialism and vice-versa, for the very same set of complex politico-economic forces are operative in both instances."[83]

Africa then brought the civil rights leadership into the Oval Office, with President Kennedy taking note of the developments and inviting the ANLCA leadership to meet. Until that time, Kennedy had shown far more interest in meeting African heads of state than in meeting Black leaders in America. Indeed, historical memory should mark that in 1962, Africa seemed the New Frontier for Kennedy, not civil rights. In the meeting, King, Wilkins, Randolph, and the others began their comments by observing that the U.S. government had failed to play a role in the African fight for freedom commensurate with the American commitment to the precepts of the United Nations' Human Rights Charter. Advocating that the Kennedy administration could and should be doing more, the civil rights leaders counseled a positive policy and program to help secure freedom and respect in Africa. They presented Kennedy with the Arden House resolutions, which highlighted four needs of special concern: "a massive Marshall Plan of economic aid and technical assistance" to make African economies more viable; support for economic sanctions against South Africa; an embargo on the sale of munitions and weapons to Portugal, unless an adequate inspection system ensured the armaments were not used to subjugate Portugal's African territories; and more extensive use of qualified Black Americans in the foreign service and in State Department policymaking. The first three in particular locked arms with anticolonial nationalists in Africa, who pressed in the UN for such measures.[84] After collectively discussing the ANLCA resolutions, Kennedy called in Adlai Stevenson, who invited those in the room to meet with him after the New Year to discuss "in depth" issues contained in the resolutions. The Kennedy meeting lasted more than an hour, and Ted Brown described the president as providing an unhurried and attentive audience.[85]

The lengthy meeting with Kennedy marked an epochal moment in African American relations with Africa. "The historic White House meeting," wrote the *Baltimore Afro-American*, "represented the first time in American history that a group of the nation's most important colored leaders had met with a President to discuss foreign policy—on any level."[86] Formal and informal lobbying of the president and other decision-makers had been conducted by individual African Americans in the past, but this marked a first: a significant group of Black leaders meeting at length with the president, in the Oval Office, to discuss the nation's relations with Africa.

The ANLCA continued to meet and correspond with the highest officials in the land in order to influence U.S. policy, especially toward Africa. Their names, reputations, and ability to reach public opinion opened doors. People well beyond Washington understood the potential influence of the ANLCA voice on issues affecting Africa. Immediately after President Kennedy's assassination, an American public relations firm used by Salazar's government assessed the incoming president for Lisbon. The firm expected Johnson generally to hew the same line as Kennedy in foreign affairs, with any changes likely to lean in the direction of a softer policy toward Portugal. This expectation was partly because Johnson was closer to Dean Acheson than to Adlai Stevenson and Soapy Williams, and partly because the ongoing problems in the Congo would incline him to appreciate the recently improved security situations in Angola and Mozambique. But the firm cautioned that domestic considerations could scramble the assessment, informing Lisbon that in its view, "Black speakers and black journalists, concerned with domestic political issues, will suspend their campaign against Portugal, maintaining their silence regarding African affairs," but that "much can depend on the attitude of the black American 'leaders.'"[87]

When the ANLCA held its next major conference in September 1964, there was no silence on Portugal or on decolonization in Africa. Wilkins, serving as chair of the Call Committee, sent out word of the gathering in Washington, D.C., where "our major area of concern will be the American Negro's goals and responsibilities as an influencing force on this government's political and economic problems in sub-Saharan Africa."[88] A partial list of conference sponsors reveals the breadth and depth of interest, including civil rights, social, labor, business, religious, professional, and Greek-letter organizations: Alpha Kappa Alpha Sorority, Alpha Phi Alpha Fraternity, American Committee on Africa, American Society of African Culture, Bible Way Church of Our Lord Jesus Christ World Wide, BSCP, California Negro Leadership Conference, *Chicago Daily Defender*, CORE, Delta Sigma Theta Sorority, Gandhi Society for Human Rights, The Links, NAACP, National Association of Fashion and Accessory Designers, National Council of Negro Women, National Newspaper Publishers Association, National Urban League, Negro American Labor Council, Operation Crossroads Africa, Phelps-Stokes Fund, SCLC, Trade Union Leadership Council, United Automobile Workers of America–AFL-CIO, United Packinghouse Workers of America–AFL-CIO, United Steelworkers of America–AFL-CIO, Western Christian Leadership Conference.[89]

The conference built around the theme "The American Negro Citizen's Role in the Pursuit of a More Effective United States' Policy in Africa." A. Philip Randolph presided at the opening plenary, and Rev. James Robinson of Operation Crossroads Africa offered the keynote address. Secretary of State Rusk addressed the conference, and in attendance were the U.S. ambassador to the UN, Adlai Stevenson; the assistant secretary of state for African affairs, Soapy Williams; the director of the United States Information Agency, Carl Rowan; and the under secretary for political affairs, Averell Harriman. Participants in workshops during the two days included Martin Luther King Jr., Horace Mann Bond, James Farmer, Dorothy Height, Clarence Mitchell, Wyatt T. Walker, Whitney Young, John A. Davis, Martin Kilson, Adelaide C. Hill, John Marcum, Lawrence Reddick, Hugh and Mabel Smythe, Allard Lowenstein, and George Houser.[90]

The comprehensive set of resolutions adopted were broad in scope, detailed in their recommendations, and particularly pointed in urging action in areas of Africa still under white rule. The resolutions condemned South Africa for apartheid. They called on the U.S. government to take "a more dynamic approach" in support of economic sanctions against South Africa, in support of oil and arms embargoes, in prohibiting future investment in South Africa, in discouraging the continuance of American-owned plants or subsidiaries in that nation, and in abandoning the practice of excluding African Americans from its diplomatic mission in South Africa. Future battle lines were being drawn.[91]

The conference spoke forcefully against what was happening in Portuguese territories, noting that "freedom-loving Americans everywhere would be appalled and revolted by the knowledge that Africans struggling for their independence against a repressive colonial regime are being slaughtered by weapons and materials provided to the Portuguese government by the United States, ostensibly for other purposes." Participants urged specific and concrete measures, ranging from developing alternatives to military bases in the Azores in order to extricate the United States from dependence on Portugal, to supporting refugee students with a "crash program to provide them higher education." Resolutions took strong positions on issues of Southern Rhodesia (Zimbabwe); South West Africa (Namibia); and the futures of the High Commission Territories of Basutoland (Lesotho), Bechuanaland (Botswana), and Swaziland.[92]

The leaders and activists made their views clear: it was time for America to live up to its ideals, to help Black Africans as much as it had helped white Europeans. "We urge that the United States launch an imaginative and massive aid program in Africa," resolved the conference. "The time has arrived for assistance of a magnitude comparable to the aid programs offered to Europe in the near past." In fact, given Africa's relatively greater needs and size, "the Africa aid program might reasonably exceed those given to other areas." To that end, the conference proposed a ten-point program of guiding principles, offering an ambitious agenda that sought a basic reappraisal of U.S. approaches to the problems faced by African states.[93]

Through these efforts, a group of activists and leaders brought to fruition the dream of an organization of, by, and for African Americans to build on the relationship with Africa. They imagined a relationship with Africa that could transform the continent and, in doing so, change the legacy of a half millennium of slave trade, exploitation, and white supremacy. They imagined a United States changing poles to that of full and complete support for African independence. They compelled top U.S. officials to speak with them, and offered a slate of proposals on which to build a different U.S. policy and change the future.

The organizing and actions advanced these representatives and their views into the highest office in the land and helped ensure that African American voices would be reckoned with in relations with Africa. Though this push would continue to grow in the coming years, it did not always mean the voices would be listened to or even welcomed. As Black Americans worked to create a more powerful voice on policy toward Africa, they ran into President Johnson's determination to prevent Black leaders from doing just that. When the ANLCA sought a meeting to talk about African policy after its 1964 conference, as it had with Kennedy in 1962, Johnson balked. Johnson believed his leadership on domestic civil rights issues would strengthen his hand with African leaders, while his actions and interest in Africa would strengthen his hand with Black America. Yet he disliked the idea of an African American voice on African affairs. He highlighted what he saw as a paradox in the effort by Black American leaders: At the same time they sought to break down segregative walls in America, why should they have a particular voice on Africa, not Asia or Latin America? "He's working to make the American Negro fully a part of American society and overcome his segregation from the white community," wrote National Security staffer Robert Komer to McGeorge Bundy. "He doesn't think it at all a good idea to encourage a separate Negro view of foreign policy. We don't want an integrated domestic policy and a segregated foreign policy. The president recognizes the American Negro community's natural interest in African affairs but doesn't think they should make it their special province."[94] Undoubtedly the ANLCA leadership would have agreed that they did not want to be segregated on foreign policy; they wanted to be at the table equally, their voices heard in respect to Africa but elsewhere as well, such as on the expanding war in Vietnam. And they wanted their views integrated into policy action.

"A Long Way from Texas to Kayar"

Johnson looked to support from the civil rights leadership, ties with African leaders, and the relationship with Africa to be positive symbols of U.S. standing—and the president's own reputation—in the world. The strategy of using Africa to cultivate image and standing has been actively employed over the years. Kennedy used Africa to build his foreign policy credentials and court an image of sympathy with freedom struggles; George W. Bush used it to try to repair low world opinion after the Iraq War by mounting the President's Emergency Plan for AIDS Relief. Given global concerns about Johnson sending combat troops into Vietnam in March 1965 and U.S. Marines into the Dominican Republic a month later, NSC staffer Komer suggested taking "measures deliberately calculated to show that we're still for peace and progress. A new gambit to rescue the UN, new disarmament initiatives, a stronger line on racism in Africa are possibilities."[95] Press Secretary Bill Moyers suggested LBJ consider a fall 1965 trip to Africa, arguing that the key to an American president's standing in Africa was his relationship to the domestic civil rights movement, and that after his March 1965 voting rights speech and June 1965 commencement address at Howard University, LBJ stood as "a hero to the Negro at home—and it has spilled over into Africa." An African visit would enable Johnson to project his leadership in the struggle for civil rights, leadership that "is a major American asset in Africa." Moyers, tapping diasporic links, sought not just a place for LBJ to be warmly received but a place where he could strengthen his authority and stature both domestically and internationally. The president agreed that of all the possibilities abroad, an African visit might pose the fewest problems and reap the greatest returns.[96]

Johnson's "night reading" left him concerned about the engagement with Africa, and he began thinking that the United States should carry forward the development efforts that Soapy Williams advocated. Moyers met with the NSC staffer tasked with Africa, Rick Haynes, and told him that Johnson had made clear that "where State seems to be falling short in protecting and advancing the President's interests in Africa, the NSC staff should not be reluctant to take the initiative." Moyers, Haynes, and others agreed: Johnson was anxious to make his own mark on Africa.[97]

LBJ tasked Williams with taking a "new and critical look at overall African policy" in order to "develop a program with which he [LBJ] could be associated personally."[98] Williams produced a blueprint for a Strengthened African Program, but not a "new" African program. In his discussions with the chiefs of mission in Africa, Williams determined that a consensus existed that "U.S. African policy is sound but that some of the programs which implement it should be strengthened." He recommended that the fortified program should be built on four parts: (1) personal association with Africa by the president; (2) personal association by the president with the principle of self-determination; (3) the use of economic aid to serve political as well as developmental objectives; and (4) the strengthening of programs in educational and cultural exchanges, with information to promote the United States and to combat communism.[99]

After critical refinements, Rusk sent the recommendations on to the president. Unchanged was the central idea that the president himself should associate publicly with Africa and its aspirations. Personal relations held great meaning on the continent. The emphasis on public diplomacy broadened to include visits to Africa by more high officials. A few years later, for example, Vice President Hubert Humphrey and Justice Thurgood Marshall traveled to Africa together. A variety of economic and cultural programs were also strengthened, despite a Congress increasingly at odds with Johnson about money spent on the Great Society and in Vietnam, and foreign aid to Africa being an easy target for reduction. The idea that LBJ should be personally associated with the principle of self-determination, however, was watered down. Despite efforts by Williams and others to move toward self-determination, a continuing engagement with the continent without fundamental changes in policy was the path of the Johnson years.[100]

While Johnson wanted to be seen as interested in Africa on a level at least equal to that of his predecessor, in Africa he could not equal Kennedy's appeal. Memories of the slain president put the mark out of reach. When the USIA had surveyed several thousand African students studying in the United States in 1962–63, 34 percent ranked Kennedy as the most popular leader outside Africa; the second choice, India's Jawaharlal Nehru, garnered just half that support. Charles de Gaulle and Nikita Khrushchev trailed badly at 6 percent each. Even if the immediacy of living in the United States at the time influenced results, Kennedy held enormous appeal.[101] Although Kennedy's policies and actions narrowed and retreated in the shadow of ongoing Cold War imperatives, particularly in regard to white rule in southern Africa, he personally continued to generate widespread enthusiasm among Africans. From his early sympathetic speaking on African nationalism to his continuing support of African education and his many meetings with African leaders, specific differences on U.S. policy and actions were largely dissociated from Kennedy himself, especially after his death.[102]

With comparisons to Kennedy on White House minds, in the fall of 1965 officials fed material to a UPI reporter about Johnson's concern for and engagement with Africa: LBJ exchanging letters with eleven African leaders; LBJ meeting with a half dozen high-level African officials; LBJ heading a Potomac River yacht trip with African ambassadors; LBJ supporting missions by astronauts Charles "Pete" Conrad and Gordon Cooper to Africa; LBJ sending Soapy Williams on repeated trips; LBJ taking a firm stand in the unfolding Rhodesian crisis.[103]

Contrasts with Kennedy remained a concern for Johnson. That Kennedy met with more African leaders than he did was a matter of substance as well as symbol, a matter of record that he asked his own staff to rebut. Upset at a speech by Senator Eugene McCarthy chastising the Johnson administration for not doing more regarding Africa, the president requested his staff to produce a document refuting McCarthy. The draft sent to LBJ for approval offered a number of metrics to indicate the administration's efforts: during the Johnson administration, total U.S. development aid to Africa had increased more than 10 percent compared to the previous four years; aid excluding food had grown 14 percent, to $202 million from fiscal year 1966 to fiscal year 1967; food aid had increased even more, by 18 percent in fiscal year 1967; AID was financing more than eighteen hundred technicians working on health, education, and agriculture, a number 20 percent higher than in fiscal year 1966. Nevertheless, the aggregate total was not good enough for Johnson, who offered several suggestions for improvement. NSC staffer Edward Hamilton complied, but "with one exception. No matter how one cuts the numbers on visits by African heads of government, the totals for the last four years aren't as impressive as those for 1961–63." Kennedy: 28 visitors; Johnson: 20 visitors.[104]

It would be quite unfair to Johnson to reduce his interest in Africa to simply a competition with his predecessor. While he seems destined to always be linked to Vietnam, LBJ was the first U.S. president to enter the White House who had been to sub-Saharan Africa, having visited Senegal in 1961 for the first anniversary of Senegalese independence as part of his vice presidential tours.[105] While Johnson had not needed to leave his home state to see poverty and deprivation, the trip nevertheless enabled him to see that part of the world in a way no previous U.S. president had. What he saw reinforced ideas of assistance to those in need.

Upon arriving in Senegal, U.S. ambassador Henry Villard and his wife warned Johnson and his delegation to remain in the car with the windows raised and not to shake hands because of the possibility of catching disease from the "dirty people." Instead, Johnson and Lady Bird left the car—and the ambassador—to walk the streets to greet people. He shook hands until his own were sore. "You go back and tell your president," one local chief responded, "that you are the first important man from any country to visit my village."[106] Johnson and Lady Bird also visited the fishing village of Kayar, where Johnson explained that he visited Dakar "because of President Kennedy's deep interest in Africa," then added, "but I came to Kayar because I was a farm boy, too, in Texas. It's a long way from Texas to Kayar, but we both produce peanuts and both want the same thing: a higher standard of living for the people."[107]

Some back in Washington moaned that Johnson was in campaign mode during his travels, and perhaps he was, yet he enjoyed the personal interaction and understood the symbolic force of being with the people on the street. "Johnson, raised in a rural area amidst poverty, illiteracy, and hardship, could relate to the people overseas in ways that most of the Kennedy Administration simply could not," notes historian Mitch Lerner. "He more than the rest of the Kennedy team could relate to the hardships of Third World life . . . could speak about the difficulties of subsistence farming and manual labor . . . could understand the desire to hold on to traditional aspects of an indigenous culture in the face of challenges from the outside . . .

[and could] recognize the innate suspicion of the people of a lesser power, wary of foreigners promising progress and modernity while treating the locals as inferiors."[108] Johnson understood people's desire for a higher standard of living and the difficulties in getting there, and that sensibility did not stop at the border. When LBJ ordered his staff to prepare a "new and critical look" at U.S. policy, he wanted, wrote Rusk, "to shape future US policy towards Africa with same energy and imagination that generated programs of 'The Great Society' at home."[109]

The OAU Anniversary Speech: "Respect for the Diversity"

Although Johnson ultimately did not travel to Africa as president, the idea of a major policy initiative for Africa appeared to hold nearly as much intriguing promise. Staff began working on a defining speech on U.S. relations with Africa, one that Moyers thought might help "lay the foundation for a Johnson Doctrine for Africa."[110] The selected occasion was the third anniversary of the establishment of the Organization of African Unity (OAU).

The decision to mark the OAU anniversary was part of an effort to address the diplomatic fallout of America's ongoing racial discrimination. For the past decade, the United States had faced rapidly growing anticolonial strength in international bodies, including the UN and the OAU, and was struggling with shifting dynamics as memberships in these organizations expanded and diversified. Unsurprisingly, while Washington sought to forge common ground on Cold War issues, the Afro-Asian bloc sought common ground on anticolonial and antiracism efforts. The OAU made that clear from the moment of its inception. Heads of state and their representatives gathered in Addis Ababa in May 1963 for the Summit Conference of Independent African States to chart a collective vision for Africa's political future. As these leaders met to define their common goals, they turned to events in America. On the second day, Prime Minister Milton Obote of Uganda published an open letter about the appalling situation in Birmingham, Alabama: "The Negroes who, even while the [OAU] conference was in session, have been subjected to the most inhuman treatment, who have been blasted with fire hoses cranked up to such pressure that the water could strip bark off trees, at whom the police have deliberately set snarling dogs, are our own kith and kin. The only offences which these people have committed are that they are black and that they have demanded the right to be free and hold their heads up as equal citizens of the United States." The conference called on the United States to "end these intolerable mal-practices" of racial discrimination, warning that serious deterioration in relations would otherwise ensue.[111]

Notwithstanding the passage of the Civil Rights Act of 1964 and the Voting Rights Act of 1965, the African dignitaries who gathered in the White House the evening of 26 May 1966 to hear Johnson's address had racial discrimination and liberation struggles on their minds. Johnson voiced his admiration for the "truly remarkable era in which more than thirty nations have emerged from colonialism to independence." Supporting the spread of democracy and principles of majority rule, Johnson highlighted that "in Africa today [is] an increasing awareness that government must represent the true will of its citizens." The implication was made plainer as Johnson went on: "This makes all the more repugnant the narrow and outmoded policy which in some parts of Africa permits the few to rule at the expense of many." Intended to be a strong statement on the crisis in Rhodesia, which just six months earlier had unilaterally declared independence in order to perpetuate white minority rule, it also signaled a position on the Portuguese colonies and South Africa. A nation could no longer expect to achieve order and growth, Johnson argued, "unless it moves—not just steadily but rapidly—in the direction of full political rights for all its people."[112]

Interweaving the U.S. struggle for racial equality, Johnson connected the Black freedom struggle in the United States with national liberation struggles in Africa. "The United States has learned from lamentable personal experience the waste and injustice that result from the domination of one race by another. Just as we are determined to remove the remnants of inequality from our own midst, we are also with you—heart and soul—as you try to do the same." Acknowledging that "it has taken us time" to learn the lesson that a nation cannot expect to achieve order and sustain growth unless it moves toward "full political rights for all its people," Johnson declared that the American government "cannot, therefore, condone the perpetuation of racial or political injustice anywhere in the world."[113]

Black Americans from the Mississippi delta to Watts to Newark might question just how fully the lesson had been learned on the farms and in the cities of America, and similarly, Africans questioned just how much weight and action Johnson's administration would put behind his lofty words. Johnson explicitly identified the situation in Rhodesia as one in which the United States sought to restore "legitimate government," meaning British rule, so that steps could then be taken to "open the full power and responsibility of nationhood to all the people of Rhodesia—not just six percent of them."[114]

Johnson painted a portrait of an inextricably linked America and Africa. To achieve a vision of all, American and African, working together to build a growing, modern, free Africa, Johnson identified multiple areas of mutual work. He spoke of strengthening regional economic activities, for which the United States was willing to extend financial and technical assistance. He pledged to increase the number of trained Africans, with the United States going beyond its current efforts—funding two thousand African students studying in the United States and supporting some sixty secondary, vocational, and teacher training institutes, mostly through the Peace Corps—by assisting African universities to help more students attend those institutions. And he addressed the need to develop effective communication systems for Africa, in particular by helping to build ground stations to take advantage of satellite communication potential. Mentioning other potential areas for cooperation, such as improved internal transportation networks, Johnson declared that the United States wanted to respond to African needs. Ideas would be gathered, policies reviewed, and the ambassador to Ethiopia, Edward Korry, would spearhead ways to follow through with initiatives.[115]

The final passages of the speech offered the most striking admission and tone. "It is no longer a case of what we can do for or even with the people of Africa," Johnson told his assembled guests. "We have come to recognize how much we have to learn from you." Johnson professed that America has learned that "Africa has never been as dark as our ignorance of it," and that as America has learned about Africa, it has learned "about our debt to Africa and the roots of so many of our American cultural values and traditions."[116]

The president of the United States was standing before an audience of Africans, discussing America's debt to Africa, along with its "deepening appreciation and respect for the diversity of the world" and its need to allow Africans to "decide for themselves the kind of nations they wish to build." The moment revealed the powerful force of a decade of African freedom struggles. Ten years earlier, there were a bare handful of independent African nations, and the State Department would not integrate receptions at consular events in South Africa; now, Johnson was proclaiming the need to appreciate diversity and allow Africans to determine their destiny.

Africa in 1966 looked markedly different than it did in 1956, and the same could be argued for America and its own racial situation. Even so, on both sides of the Atlantic, people of African descent struggled daily toward basic goals of freedom and equality in a world that had been stacked against them for generations. Efforts to achieve that freedom and equality continued, forcing all levels of American society to confront what a changing world meant, be it on their street, in the schools their children attended, or in a world where the structure of European empires was giving way to a more chaotic jumble of independent nations and voices.

The rise of African states pushed the United States to start rethinking how it constructed its view of the world. Johnson's speech opens a window onto the changing relationship with Africa but also marks ways that the changing relationship was laying the groundwork for a new era in American life. When LBJ addressed the assembled African ambassadors and dignitaries, he had years of negative characterizations of Africa to contend with, and millions of Americans worried about the changing social and political relationships at home as well as in Africa. Standing at the podium, Johnson spoke in terms that in future years would become familiar to the American public—an appreciation and respect for diversity—but that at the time were being used to describe the U.S. relationship with Africa. In Johnson's words, "We will not live by a double standard—professing abroad what we do not practice at home, or venerating at home what we ignore abroad." As Johnson and America wrestled with the meaning of those words, Africa pushed him and others to wrestle with how to engage and incorporate increasing diversity on the world stage—and at home.

And yet Johnson's words met with an understandable skepticism. They came after years of struggle and continuing resistance to change. Those same years had also pushed expectations higher, both for America's domestic freedom struggle and for Africa's liberation struggles. African leaders did not respond as enthusiastically as Johnson had hoped—it was, after all, no longer 1956. Some saw the declarations, which would have seemed groundbreaking a decade earlier, as too little, too late. A qualified appreciation for the speech prevailed, seasoned with a wait-and-see view about whether the United States would follow the words with deeds. After the speech was distributed to the African representatives at the UN, U.S. officials learned that it was viewed as "impressive and heartening," but representatives "questioned the extent to which the president's words would be implemented."[117] Two decades of tacking toward the safe harbor of continuing white rule meant that actions, not just words, were expected, especially when it came to the large swath of Africa still under white rule and seeking self-determination. The audience that evening was listening with open minds yet waiting with some skepticism for concrete commitments to demolish the white redoubt in southern Africa.

4 The White Redoubt, 1965–1974

> The basic issue in Rhodesia is self-government for all the people, regardless of race. Our country, founded on the proposition that all men are created equal—and currently engaged in a vigorous nationwide program to make that equality real for our own Negro citizens—cannot honorably turn its back on what is happening in Rhodesia.
>
> —Arthur Goldberg, April 1966

> The action of the USA to resume chrome imports from Rhodesia under the present circumstances only goes to show that she cares more for metals than for justice and peace in southern Africa.
>
> —Ndabaningi Sithole, October 1972

In early 1965, in the wake of the brutal assault on civil rights marchers peacefully crossing the Edmund Pettus Bridge trying to reach Selma, Alabama, President Johnson spoke to Congress about taking action on the Voting Rights Act and ensuring equal rights for all Americans. Soon, Johnson received a letter from Kenyan president Jomo Kenyatta. By this time Kenya had developed a network of links with the United States that wove among labor activists, freedom movements, educational initiatives, and Lancaster House conferences. Connections continued, as LBJ sought to strengthen his hand with Africa, and Kenyatta sought to develop alternatives to links with Britain, the former colonial power. Kenyatta informed Johnson that his people had been following "with considerable interest the measures . . . being taken by the United States Government in an effort to enfranchise the Negro Communities in some parts of [the] country where they are otherwise denied the most basic rights of citizenship under democratic government." He went on to say that while international conventions may deem race relations in America a domestic affair, "in view of the wide interest and sympathy roused by incidents in the southern part of your country and the close connections between the Negro people and the people of Africa, I am writing to offer you my support in your government's efforts to remove all forms of discriminatory practices."[1]

Voices on both sides of the Atlantic were speaking and acting in concert to propel Johnson forward on civil rights in America and majority rule in Africa. Acknowledging Kenya's own efforts to "defeat racialism whenever it raises its ugly head," Kenyatta gently prodded Johnson, casting the struggles as mutual, for "our task will be made easier if your government will overcome this racial problem, especially in the Southern States."[2] Regardless of whether he needed Kenyatta's assistance at that point, Johnson recognized the powerful connections between Africa and its diaspora, and indeed, just a year later he spoke expressly about those ties in his OAU anniversary address on relations with Africa.

As Kenyatta and other African leaders observed how the United States handled its own domestic freedom struggle, they cared even more directly about how Washington addressed the ongoing freedom struggle in Africa. The seemingly straightforward idea that colonialism and white minority rule must end was a powerful force throughout Africa, a principle to embrace. Yet as the 1960s progressed, states with entrenched settler populations defied that process. Generations of immigrants from European nations had established themselves across Africa: in the highlands of Kenya, on the high savannas of Zimbabwe, on the rich soil of South Africa. And they fought to stay and hold power.

As decolonization unfolded, the problem of continued white authority proved most intractable in southern Africa. A "white redoubt" seemed entrenched across southern Africa. Kennedy administration officials had worried that "the seeds of another Algeria [had] been sown in Southern Africa. Blacks face Whites across a sea of developing hate. With this confrontation and the increasing polarization of racial relations the White supremacists are seeking to strengthen their established positions." "The White Redoubt" paper identified the territories: South Africa, the Portuguese colonies of Angola and Mozambique, and the Central African Federation, which subsequently splintered, leaving Southern Rhodesia as part of a determined group of white supremacists "taking up a defensive position along a rampart from which they feel there is no retreat."[3]

Rule in this region took different forms by the mid-1960s: Portuguese colonial rule in Angola and Mozambique; unilaterally and illegally declared independence in Southern Rhodesia; independence under a white minority government in South Africa. In each area, however, a small but long-established settler population made clear its expectation for continuing white minority rule: Angola with 250,000 Europeans in a population of roughly 5,000,000 Africans; Mozambique with 150,000 Europeans in a population of over 7,000,000 Africans; Southern Rhodesia with 240,000 whites in a population of over 4,000,000; South West Africa with 75,000 whites in a population of roughly 500,000. South Africa had a much larger population, with some 3,500,000 whites outnumbered by a population of 15,000,000 people of color that in pursuit of apartheid the government was feverishly working to racially classify and divide via the Population Registration Act.[4]

That the rest of Africa had more or less moved to majority rule did not convince most of these white populations to follow; rather, independence activities north of the Zambezi made those south of the river all the more determined to hang on. By 1967, decolonization had slowed so dramatically that in the next half dozen years only the small nations of Mauritius, Swaziland, Equatorial Guinea, and Guinea-Bissau claimed independence, none of them larger than the Netherlands.[5] The situation deeply frustrated independent Africa. Having achieved their own self-determination, these nation-states held wide-ranging hopes for rapid political, social, and economic progress. But colonial legacies and neocolonialist intrigue worked to thwart these expectations. A country's willingness to tolerate continued white dominance in southern Africa provided a ready litmus test for the depth of its support for African independence.

With the rest of the world moving away from overt forms of white supremacy, these areas under white control thus presented officials in Washington with stark and uncomfortable choices. Although Washington tried to portray its decisions as favorable to the African majorities, its strategic choices typically continued a U.S. approach enabling a status quo that favored the white minority in the parts of Africa still not free. These choices stemmed from Cold War concerns, immediate economic interests, and continuing racial prejudices—prejudices learned in America yet sometimes reinforced by the postindependence troubles in places such as the Congo. Together, these things buttressed the maintenance of white rule, as South Africa, Southern Rhodesia, and the Portuguese in Angola and Mozambique defied the decolonization trend and held on to power. It would take African liberation fighters, independent African nations, international actions, and, in time, domestic pressures in America to turn things around.

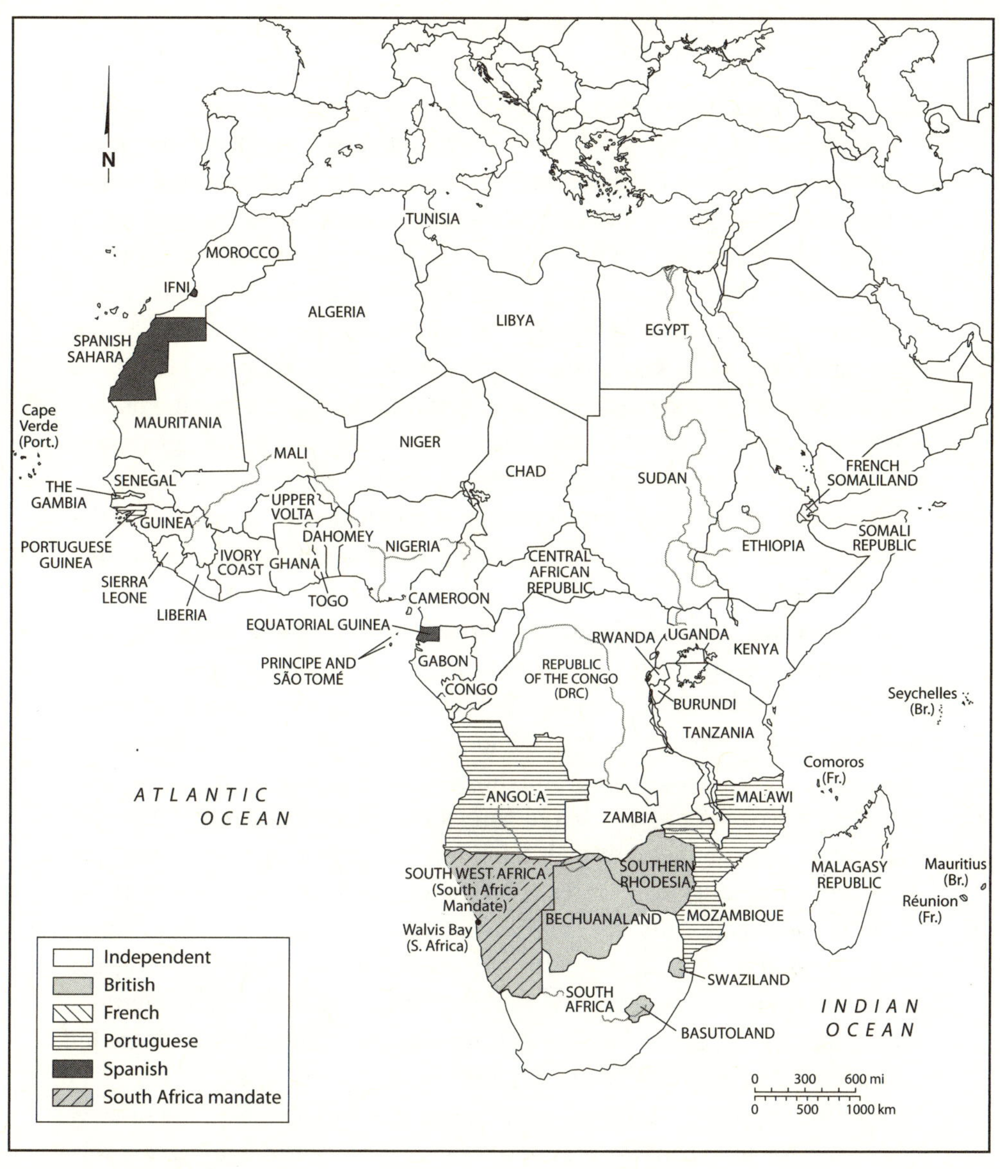

Africa, January 1966

"The Scarcity of Resources"

LBJ's 1965 speech on Africa announced the intention to review U.S. policy and programs and as nations became independent and the Cold War raged, economic assistance to new African nations took on great meaning. Assistance could strengthen the Cold War fight—the rationale being that "a soundly conceived and well-administered basic economic development drive was the most effective long-range defense against Communist penetration, in addition to serving other fundamental U.S. objectives."[6] The framing of aid in Cold War terms reflected politics in the United States and influenced who received assistance and in what form. The results did not always line up with actual needs in Africa, nor address in meaningful ways the ongoing structural inequities of the modern world economic system.

The internal State Department history of relations with Africa during the Johnson years noted that the United States had "fewer formal treaty or special commitments in Africa than in any other area of the world," yet its "interests in the continent [we]re . . . substantial." It was essential that "African states remain independent and free from excessive influence of blocs or power systems hostile toward us." Defining this relationship in the negative—risks to avoid—reflected a long entrenched pattern of seeing Africa less as a place where things might go right, a new frontier of possibilities, and more as a place to avoid things that might go wrong. "Equally important" was the need to maintain "internal political stability and the achievement of satisfactory rates of economic development," because these were "shields against disorder and chaos that could invite outside interference." Further, the mineral wealth of the African continent was "of great value and in some cases essential to the American economy and to our defense industry." America had compelling reasons to give assistance, maintain access, and promote trade and investment opportunities.[7]

Yet after the review initiated by Johnson, the Task Force on the Review of African Development Policies and Programs cautioned against any sort of "Marshall Plan for Africa" or Alliance for Progress. Named for its chair, ambassador to Ethiopia Edward Korry, the Task Force's Korry Report advised, "With $220 million annually, plus agricultural surpluses, we cannot pretend to conduct economic development programs in 33 countries."[8]

Johnson had declared his desire to shape U.S. policy toward Africa "with the same energy and imagination that generated programs of 'The Great Society' at home." But there would be no Great Society for the many needs and vast continent. The United States, the report posited, should instead narrow its focus to a few, select African countries that seemed readier for major development efforts. The Korry Report favored concentrating on development infrastructure, including communications, transport, and power, along with a "more vigorous attack" on the problems of agriculture and "a particular effort" in education. The Korry Report perceived limits on what the United States could do, stemming from the daunting challenges posed by the vast scope of Africa itself and from competing demands on U.S. resources, most prominently the cost of the expanding war in Vietnam and the Great Society programs at home. In Congress, a growing preference to limit spending abroad dovetailed with questions about the role former colonial powers should play in aid and development. Fewer than twenty years had passed since the Marshall Plan, but already concerns about the limits of U.S. economic strength were on hand, and Africa was perceived as a lower priority.[9] As the State Department lamented, "The effectiveness of economic assistance was greatly limited in the majority of cases simply by the scarcity of resources."[10]

The Korry Report thus recommended targeted efforts, preferably done with some coordination among international organizations such as the World Bank. Legislation from Congress limited the number of countries outside Latin America that could receive new development loans or technical assistance grants from AID. In response, AID placed a moratorium on new bilateral projects in all but ten African countries, with State Department officials bemoaning "the loss of flexibility in the use of AID assistance as a foreign policy tool in promoting bilateral US objectives in individual African countries," making it difficult for U.S. officials "to answer the fears of some African leaders that the new emphasis in aid to regional projects was not a device for partial US disengagement from Africa."[11]

Modernization plans and development assistance on a limited scale would leave much unaddressed, and even while the United States might expect aid to influence the degree to which an individual African country would openly criticize the United States, no amount of aid could alter African views on remaining white rule in Africa. And the United States, as the most powerful country in the Western bloc, was in a unique position to push political change and democratic principles in colonial Africa. Liberation struggles in southern Africa faced daunting challenges, but they enjoyed broad support among African states, and those states wanted the United States and other great powers to "take action that would terminate white rule in Southern Africa." Otherwise, the states might look elsewhere for support, and the Soviets, Chinese, and increasingly the Cubans were ready to promote, at relatively little cost, support for and appreciation from liberation movements. Washington had to decide how to address the ongoing drive for decolonization and self-determination south of the Zambezi in the face of determined massive resistance from Cold War allies.[12]

From Angola to Zimbabwe: The Fight for Majority Rule

By the mid-1960s, "the question of white minority domination of black majorities in southern Africa [had] emerged as the most difficult problem facing US policy in Africa."[13] In South Africa, the government's bloody and brutal repression of the Black majority in the wake of the Sharpeville massacre and its subsequent crackdown on both the African National Congress and the Pan Africanist Congress was followed by ongoing repression, perhaps most famously illustrated in the Rivonia Trial, which sent Nelson Mandela, Govan Mbeki, Walter Sisulu, and others to be imprisoned on Robben Island.

The ongoing intransigence of Portugal about its overseas territories meant continuing battles with liberation movements as Lisbon poured in troops to maintain control. Most U.S. officials believed the Portuguese would keep control for years, the U.S. intelligence community assessing liberation struggles as standing "little chance of significant progress through 1970, and probably for some considerable time thereafter."[14] And in spite of Washington's concerns about Portuguese rule, there was little drive for change. As Secretary of State Rusk explained to Salazar's successor Marcello Caetano, "The U.S. was not leading a crusade on the African question and had no interest in the disappearance of the Portuguese presence from Africa."[15]

It was in Rhodesia, where settlers strongly resisted the sweeping movement toward majority rule underway north of the Zambezi, that the next major conflict over white supremacy and decolonization came. White rule in the region had solidified ever since the late nineteenth century, when Cecil Rhodes used his British South African Company (BSAC) to extend European rule northward. After the infamous Rudd Concession was signed by the powerful local ruler Lobengula, Rhodes sent a relatively small "Pioneer Column" past him into Mashonaland to establish Fort Salisbury in 1890. Within a dozen years, twin defeats—of Lobengula by white settlers and, further south, of the Boers by the British—left the British with power over the region. White settlers in Rhodesia soon welcomed the opportunity to shift away from BSAC rule: in 1922, they voted to reject joining South Africa and instead become a British colony. An agreement the following year allowed

Southern Rhodesia to become self-governing, with control over internal affairs. In short order, white settlers used their new authority to allocate 50 percent of the land, including 80 percent of the most arable land, to the 5 percent white population.

In the aftermath of World War II, Britain moved to create a federation of states in the region. For ten years, Southern Rhodesia joined with Northern Rhodesia and Nyasaland in an uncomfortable Central African Federation. Ultimately, federations of states found little success, but in the 1950s and 1960s these combinations were seen as offering an answer to any number of issues. In this instance, London officials hoped a strong federation would check Afrikaner influence and result in a prosperous multiracial state that would economically advance Northern Rhodesia and Nyasaland while bringing more African participation into government structures. In reality, white Southern Rhodesians reaped wealth from the Zambian copper belt, while giving Africans little in the way of political power. As independence swept other parts of Africa, internal resentment of the federation grew, and after racial tensions erupted in Nyasaland in early 1959, questioning in London grew as well. Britain authorized new constitutions for each of the three territories, and by the end of its ten-year run in December 1963, African nationalists rejoiced at the federation's dissolution. Within a year, Northern Rhodesia and Nyasaland gained long-sought independence as the new nations of Zambia and Malawi.[16]

African nationalists in Southern Rhodesia faced a different landscape. When political movements among the African population had hoped to work with the government in the mid-1950s, the relatively liberal political stance of Garfield Todd, a man characterized as one of the last British liberals in Africa, proved unacceptable to white voters. As independence spread across Africa, white Rhodesians flocked to leaders who preached continued white rule.[17] Southern Rhodesia, with its white settler population of roughly 220,000, chose a path of resistance to democratic majority rule by the approximately 4,000,000 Africans. In November 1960, the highly restrictive franchise meant that the total electorate numbered only 75,061 voters, of whom a mere 3,129 were Black. Constitutional changes in 1961 expanded the number of legislative seats from thirty to sixty-five, with fifteen intended for Africans. Yet when Prime Minister Edgar Whitehead dared to declare before the UN that, under this system, the Black majority might achieve a legislative majority in fifteen years, his white constituents reacted with even more vehemence. The opposition Rhodesian Front trounced Whitehead and his party in the December 1962 elections, sending a clear message: no Black majority rule.[18]

While maintaining their racist structures and rejecting democratic one person, one vote, Rhodesian Front supporters nevertheless believed that independence should arrive in Southern Rhodesia, just as it was scheduled to come in Zambia and Malawi. They wanted it on their terms, though, and seeing former British possessions gain majority rule across Africa, these voters were losing faith that their interests would be protected by London. Their fears and dissatisfactions helped Ian Smith engineer his rise to power in April 1964. Upon assuming power, Smith imprisoned African nationalist leaders such as Joshua Nkomo without trial, in the arid hinterlands of the nation. Smith, the first prime minister born in the country, ruled on a platform of continued political domination by whites. In the May 1965 general election, Smith and his party received more than two-thirds of the white electorate votes and captured all fifty parliamentary seats on the exclusively white "A" roll. Given the restrictions on Black voters, that was the only vote that mattered. A few months later, when the archbishop of Canterbury spoke in support of Southern Rhodesia's majority, white Rhodesians burned bibles in response.[19]

As British prime minister Harold Wilson sought a solution, his government pressed for little substantive change but expected at least token acknowledgment that at some point in the future—fifty years, one hundred years—there would be majority rule. Smith steadfastly refused to accept such a possibility even in "a thousand years." As *Time* magazine noted, "Few communities in the world can match the sun-drenched affluence that Rhodesia's hardy settlers have achieved for themselves." The stalemate remained, prompting questions as to whether London would use military force to end any unsanctioned move to independence.[20]

Anticipating that the Smith government might break from the Crown, the CIA produced a Special National Intelligence Estimate on the "Repercussions of a Unilateral Declaration of Independence by Southern Rhodesia." "[Rhodesian Front supporters] are confident," assessed the CIA, "that the West will soon acknowledge the justice of their argument that black African governments are inherently unstable and rapidly coming under Communist influence."[21] In the event of the Unilateral Declaration of Independence (UDI), the CIA estimated that "for the next several years at least, political and economic sanctions would not dislodge white rule in Southern Rhodesia and that effective military intervention from any quarter is highly unlikely." The CIA warned that Rhodesia's ability to sustain itself would frustrate Africans, bring greater pressure on "moderate" African governments to take stronger action, and thereby increase pressure and raise difficulties for the West.[22]

The Johnson administration monitored the situation, concerned about the unfolding events. When Smith flew to London in October 1965 for talks, National Security Adviser McGeorge Bundy told Under Secretary of State George Ball, "For Smith to go to London with the idea the Americans don't give a damn about UDI is a mistake." Worried that "we have not stated it as strongly as we may want to," President Johnson warned Smith, and the U.S. ambassador in London then reinforced U.S. opposition to any UDI. None of it changed the matter. With Smith on the verge of unilaterally taking the country to "independence," the British government did not take strong action. It neither detained him nor put the screws to him, as it had done to Seretse Khama just a few years earlier; to the contrary, the British left it clear that force would not be used against the white residents or government.[23]

Days later, on the morning of 11 November 1965, Smith and his cabinet voted to declare independence and signed the UDI. They did so not quite two hundred years after the last time British colonies declared independence in defiance of the British Crown. London welcomed the news with no more pleasure than it had in 1776. No longer the dominant world power as its colonies pushed toward self-determination, Britain was doing what it could to steer toward independence on terms it found acceptable; a white minority-ruled Rhodesia was not that. But short of military action, Wilson would have to force Salisbury to comply through international condemnation and economic sanctions.[24]

Upon sending word to Wilson about his government's break, Smith telegrammed President Johnson, leader of the last nation to unilaterally declare independence from Britain. The news received a cold reception, notwithstanding the fact that the UDI was modeled after the United States' own Declaration of Independence. From his ranch in Texas, LBJ and his team contemplated what further measures to take to help Britain rein in the Rhodesian rebels. Having already stated its opposition to any form of a UDI and voiced support for a resolution acceptable to the nation's entire population, the question now was how much further the Johnson administration was prepared to go. It seemed inevitable that, in time, the Black majority in Southern Rhodesia, with an almost 20–1 numerical advantage, would gain majority rule. Siding with it aligned the United States with the broad sentiment across Africa, in the UN, and throughout the world. It supported a key ally, Britain, and spoke to an important domestic constituency that supported a strong stance against any UDI: African Americans.[25]

Secretary of State Dean Rusk quickly and publicly deplored the Smith government's action, emphasizing that the United States did not recognize the rebel regime. In short order, Washington recalled the consul general, reduced the staff, closed the U.S. Information Service office, and discouraged Americans from traveling to Rhodesia. More substantive measures followed, with the United States announcing it would not import any Rhodesian sugar in 1966 and, when learning that a shipment of sugar was already on the high seas and scheduled to dock soon in New York, refusing to allow the shipment to be unloaded.[26]

In the ensuing weeks, the State Department requested American importers of chromite and tobacco products to comply with restrictions on those items, and it supported the British oil embargo against Rhodesia. The United States aided the airlift of petroleum to newly independent Zambia, in time spending $4.5 million to get petroleum to that landlocked nation. The oil airlift illustrated the multifaceted nature of the engagement in southern Africa. U.S. actions were designed to apply pressure on Salisbury while keeping Zambia, the African state most vulnerable to Rhodesian reprisals, from bearing the brunt of the consequences. While this brought welcome relief to Zambians and appreciation from fellow Africans, the significant copper production Zambia provided—important in America for uses ranging from the manufacture of consumer goods to the provision of shell casings for soldiers fighting in Vietnam—helped make the decision to airlift oil a higher priority. Oil was sent not so much for the average Zambian but to keep the machines in the mines running. Even so, the economic incentives were intertwined with the public value of the airlift; indeed, the amount of oil brought in barrels by the chartered Boeing 707s was ultimately less than the amount used to fuel the planes on their airlift flights. The Johnson administration's willingness to undertake stronger international involvement on Rhodesia was made easier, as historian Thomas Noer points out, because the United States had fewer direct interests there than in other parts of white-ruled Africa—no missile tracking stations, no vulnerable NATO alliances, no major economic investments.[27]

U.S. policymakers faced a conundrum. In years past, U.S. policy was generally amenable to the European colonial powers and their ruling and running of colonies, even as American business and religious constituencies pursued their particular interests. But now U.S. officials found British actions frustrating and potentially debilitating. Wilson's government seemed unable to corral Smith's rebel regime. Washington urged London to take a firmer approach, but arrogating a primary role for Washington would mean greater U.S. involvement at a time when Johnson's people already saw Vietnam taking its toll in attention and resources. As the situation unfolded,

LBJ worried "about the mounting gravity of the Rhodesian crisis and . . . the apparent lack of any British plan which gives much confidence that the rebel regime will soon be brought to heel." Johnson asked for a comprehensive analysis of the prospective outcome of the crisis, the risks of escalation, and alternative courses of action.[28] Working groups formed to stay on top of the crisis, with ongoing situation reports from NSC staffers for McGeorge Bundy, in-house efforts to coordinate actions, and regular updating of the president.[29]

The White House understood one high-profile domestic litmus test at stake. "The American Negro community," observed George Ball, "regards this as a test case of the bona fides of the Administration."[30] Special Assistant Jack Valenti pointed out, "The United States is inescapably involved in Africa by reason of its large, increasingly politically-conscious Negro minority. A 'Zionist' type of emotional concern, affecting local voting, could emerge."[31] A. Philip Randolph and Donald Harrington, co-chairs of the American Committee on Africa, telegrammed the president immediately after news broke of the UDI, hoping to spur vigorous opposition to the establishment of a "new white supremacy state in Southern Africa."[32] Martin Luther King quickly contacted Johnson, warning him that UDI was "one of the most serious threats to freedom and justice to emerge on the African continent since the establishment of apartheid in South Africa." King urged severing diplomatic and economic ties with Rhodesia. NAACP head Roy Wilkins suggested that Black Americans "fully support whatever measures may be necessary to crush this racist revolt."[33]

By any means necessary, by whatever measures necessary: the language Malcolm X used about white supremacy in America was now being used by the civil rights leadership about white supremacy in Africa. It marked a mainstreaming of once "radical" positions, which were becoming part of the broader discourse. The Johnson administration's position provided an international barometer for its broader position on anticolonialism and ending white supremacy in the United States and Africa. When the administration's actions did not go far enough or fast enough, groups such as the ANLCA and the NAACP pressed it onward, as did King and others.[34]

These efforts mattered, and not simply because Johnson did not want to be susceptible to criticism by Black constituents and by Africans. The stance on Rhodesia spoke to the place of freedom, equality, and human rights in American foreign affairs. Pressuring the White House to take a strong stand against the discriminatory and repressive Smith regime, "activists firmly signaled that rights of black Africans were a human rights concern. Their activism shaped U.S. policy and set the stage for movements against apartheid and racial discrimination elsewhere" in the years ahead.[35] Historian Sarah Snyder, analyzing the activists and language of human rights in the 1960s, argues that LBJ and others in his administration were broadening the use of human rights as a framing consideration, along with the Cold War, relations with Africa, and domestic political considerations. "The problem in Southern Rhodesia is a matter of basic human rights," Johnson assured Jomo Kenyatta. "We continue to share your concern about the unjust effect of the situation on the people of Southern Rhodesia and the abrasive effect on relations among the races throughout the world."[36]

Johnson's words were reassuring, but Kenyatta and others wanted action—if not military intervention, then mandatory sanctions. With talks between London and Salisbury yielding no progress, the UN Security Council passed Resolution 232 on 16 December 1966 with U.S. support. Previous resolutions had called on member states not to recognize or render assistance to the illegal regime and to sever diplomatic relations with the Smith regime. Resolution 232 called on member states to prevent the importation of listed products, including asbestos, iron ore, pig iron, copper, chrome, tobacco, sugar, meat, and meat products. Trade in arms, ammunition, military equipment, and materials for the manufacture and maintenance of these, along with motor vehicles and aircraft generally, were to be stopped. So were oil and oil products. In the following days, LBJ signed an executive order to implement sanctions. These were the strongest sanctions ever passed by the UN, despite being short of comprehensive. U.S. ambassador to the UN Arthur Goldberg explained these votes to his colleagues in an NSC meeting: "We were obliged to vote in the U.N. as we did because to do otherwise would have caused us domestic racial difficulties and hurt our business interests in every African country."[37] NSC staffer Robert Komer summed up the situation this way: "Rhodesia itself isn't very important to us. But the point is that it's critical to all the other Africans. They see it as a straight anti-colonial issue, and all their anti-white instincts are aroused. So our stance on this issue will greatly affect our influence throughout Africa—it will be a test of whether we mean what we say about self-determination and racialism."[38]

Officials in Washington remained unconvinced that sanctions would be effective in overturning the Smith regime. White Rhodesians were committed to UDI, the country had great self-sufficiency, and South Africa and Portugal supported the Smith regime. The CIA's assessment before UDI was that "for the next several years at least, political and economic sanctions would not dislodge white rule in Southern Rhodesia." A year into UDI, the analysis had hardly wavered: "Mandatory economic sanctions imposed by the UN against Rhodesia are not likely to have the desired result."[39]

The sanctions did pinch Rhodesia and were meaningful in the eyes of millions around Africa, indeed the world. Yet they would not be the primary undoing of the Smith regime as much as were the freedom fighters of the Zimbabwe African National Union and the Zimbabwe African People's Union. And one can question just how determined the West was to isolate and overturn white-ruled, anticommunist Rhodesia. Presaging fierce debates over economic sanctions and South Africa, LBJ's special adviser, John Roche, argued that the "net judgment" of the intelligence community was that "economic sanctions will not work" and that they may be "counterproductive" by hitting the Black population first and hurting Zambia. Roche reasoned that "only great power, armed intervention on a major scale" could bring down white governments, so Roche offered his Machiavellian advice: "This is an escalator we do not want to get onto. What we have to do—I think—is find a way of expressing approval of the sanctions (it is too late now to take patently evasive action) *with the full intention of ignoring their active implementation*"[40] (emphasis added).

The words of Roche call into question the vigor with which sanctions, even those adopted, were pursued: Rhodesian exports grew by over 45 percent in the four years following UDI, and Rhodesian GDP grew at an average of 3.5 percent per year in the ten years after UDI. Roche gave voice to what a number of businesses and states did. Alois Mlambo details the international evasions of sanctions, even after UN Resolution 253 imposed comprehensive international sanctions in 1968.[41]

White Rhodesians hardly appeared to be suffering. Actions taken seemed to be well short of the full measure of what the United States and Britain could do. And therein was the rub: no tangible results seemed forthcoming from the actions of either Washington or London. At the end of the day, the Smith regime was in power and the sum total from the most powerful nation on earth appeared to be little more than removing some diplomats, helping Zambia get some oil, and importing/exporting less with Rhodesia. Longtime scholar on Africa William Minter makes a telling comparison to the American pursuit of sanctions against Cuba, which were comprehensive and debilitating. The potential consequences of this limited approach by the Western powers were severe: "To expect Africans . . . to continue to remain docile under minority rule is not being realistic," Zambian president Kenneth Kaunda pointed out to an American journalist. "The people of the

West have refused to help the freedom fighters. . . . This leaves these young men and women with no choice at all but to go to the only area where they will be supplied, namely the East."[42] From that perspective, it is difficult to see why one would not expect liberation movements to find support from the Eastern bloc, the very thing Washington did not want.

On the other hand, historian Andrew DeRoche points out that the Johnson administration actions marked "one of the first times that the U.S. government responded to black Africans with concrete steps against white Africans."[43] The American South, solidly Democratic for one hundred years, was already shifting toward the Republican Party, and LBJ was accelerating the political shift with his support for the Civil Rights Act of 1964 and the Voting Rights Act of 1965. His administration now seemed to be supporting Black Africans over white interests. It sought an end to the white minority regime, and it supported sanctions in that effort. Washington's actions seemed inadequate to those who wanted faster, more fundamental change, yet they outraged a more conservative America.

"Anticolonialism Is . . . an Attitude of Mind and Not a Very Sensible One"

The situation in Rhodesia brought to center stage an ongoing critique of decolonization in Africa that had been made since the 1940s but was advanced most stridently when whites found that their rule or interests were being visibly threatened and fought to maintain control. The critique spanned the entirety of decolonization: in the early stages during the Mau Mau struggle in Kenya, during the highwater Year of Africa whence came the onset of violence in newly independent Congo, and now when white settlers in Southern Rhodesia faced rule by the majority.

The most extreme proponents intertwined racism, paternalism, and acceptance of oppression in their view of white rule in Africa as bringing numerous blessings to the entire world system. In 1950s and 1960s America, this meant above all staunch anticommunism, backed by Christian faith and Western ideals. In late 1962, Senator Allen Ellender (D-LA) visited Southern Rhodesia and South Africa, where, contrasting these white-ruled areas with newly independent African nations, he stated, "I have yet to meet any Africans who have the capability to run their own affairs." In his view, Africans were "incapable of leadership except through the assistance of Europeans." Appalled, the State Department hastily arranged to send Senator Vance Hartke (D-IN) to retrace Ellender's steps in an effort to mitigate the damage done.[44] Segregationist senator James Eastland (D-MS) saw it in starkly racist terms in his own 1969 trip to Rhodesia and South Africa, criticizing his hosts in Salisbury for allowing Black and white to mix at a hotel, thereby having "inserted the thin end of the wedge by allowing stinking n——s into such a fine hotel."[45] These men, seeking to hold the support of their white constituents back home, defended white supremacy in Africa and pushed to have U.S. policy do the same.

Their aggressively racist perspectives may not have been articulated as openly or as extremely by others, but many still shared a general sense that the story of colonialism and white settlers in Africa mirrored their image of the Manifest Destiny story in North America: hardy Europeans coming to tame a primitive land, cowboys fighting Indians, pioneer wagon trains settling a landscape and making it productive. In their view, these mythologized images were simply swapped out by intrepid explorers fending off wild animals, the European civilizing hand subjugating primitive natives, settlers moving in to make something of dense jungles and limitless savannas. These conflated images prompted Senator Barry Goldwater (R-AZ), his presidential campaign behind him and on a trip to southern Africa, to write to his children, encouraging them "to include South Africa on their travel list. They are delightful people, just like Western Americans and Johannesburg is a great thriving city looking far bigger than San Francisco."[46]

On the first anniversary of UDI, Ian Smith happily rang the Rhodesian "Liberty Bell," a gift from conservative allies in the United States. A festive mood among white Rhodesians marked the occasion, with some celebrating at a club serving a defiant menu offering "turtle soup a la [Harold] Wilson" and "fried filet of Martin Luther King."[47] King never set foot within two thousand miles of Rhodesia, let alone met these men and women in Salisbury. Yet the global nature of the Black freedom struggle meant that the event organizers connected struggles on both sides of the Atlantic—only in this manifestation, the struggle was to resist ending white supremacy. Rhodesia was a symbol for those who argued against civil rights in the United States. Conservative newspaperman James J. Kilpatrick, a vocal advocate for the South's "Massive Resistance" to desegregation, noted that the United States had yet to reach one person, one vote, so why should it be forced on Rhodesia?[48]

Bedrock democratic values of all men are created equal, of one person, one vote, and of rule by the majority while protecting the rights of minorities, proved not so straightforward for many in the United States. Eisenhower had written of decolonization as a torrent overrunning everything.

But these unreconstructed supporters of white rule in Africa, joining with Rhodesia, South Africa, and Portugal, were a mighty dam trying to stop the flow—the flow of majority rule, of liberty and justice for all.

Americans from both major political parties saw Rhodesia as a bulwark against instability and the spread of communism. Most prominently, former secretary of state Dean Acheson made it a veritable crusade to support the white Rhodesian quest for independence, arguing that Rhodesia had enjoyed de facto independence since 1923 and that any interference by the UN in its affairs was violating the domestic affairs of a sovereign state. "Whatever may be said about colonialism," wrote Acheson, "one thing must be said about our attitude toward it, an attitude which we have had for nearly a hundred and fifty years, and that is that anti-colonialism is not a policy. It is merely an attitude of mind and not a very sensible one at that."[49] Others rallied to the Rhodesian cause as well. Accentuating the anticolonial nature of UDI and its similarity to the American effort two hundred years prior, the *National Review* labeled Ian Smith "the George Washington of Africa."[50] Senator Goldwater declared, "We need more men like Ian Smith."[51] Goldwater estimated that Rhodesia was not being hurt by sanctions, "but our country is being hurt by our attitude toward South Africa and Rhodesia." The U.S.-based Friends of Rhodesian Independence, with connections to other right-wing domestic groups such as the John Birch Society, reportedly had 122 branches and 25,000 members by 1967.[52]

As sanctions took hold, powerful business interests in America increasingly chafed despite the relatively limited trade that America conducted with Rhodesia. Tobacco could be found elsewhere, but need for high-level chromium forced importers to turn to the Soviet Union for alternative supplies. Chromium was of high value due to its strength and resistance to corrosion, and vital to the production of numerous products, including stainless steel. Rhodesia produced some of the highest-grade chromite ore on the planet, and loss of access meant a reliance on the Soviet Union, of all countries, as a supplier, with its inferior product and escalating prices. The prohibition on purchasing high-quality chrome ore from a white-ruled, anticommunist friend seemed an illogical proscription made worse by then having to purchase inferior product from an archenemy. The whole thing made little economic or geopolitical sense for this coalition of racial and business conservatives. Businesspeople upset at sanctions spoke out for what they wanted: trade with a stable, white-ruled, allied nation. Former Chrysler chief L. L. "Tex" Colbert tried to take Rhodesia's case directly to LBJ, but when Johnson refused to meet with him, Colbert went to National Security Adviser Walt Rostow. Colbert, apparently losing track of South Africa, the Portuguese colonies, and Great Britain—let alone the vast world—explained to Rostow that whites had "no place to go" if Blacks in Rhodesia took power. And lest anyone believe the situation paralleled the civil rights struggle in the United States, Colbert assured Rostow that Africans did not want integration and were grateful for white guidance and protection. Colbert felt no compunction in judging the desires of millions of Africans and dismissing the notion that they might want independence, majority rule, and equal rights despite—or, perhaps more accurately, because of—his limited knowledge of Africa.[53]

This paternalistic bigotry often allied with racist views about Africans and sometimes mixed with a deep-seated fear that the UN was an avenue for a worldwide government that would suppress Americans and their rights, a view shared without any sense of irony that Africans might view their subjugation by distant European capitals in much the same way. These combustible ingredients led to clashes on the campus of UCLA when pro-Rhodesian demonstrators attempted to burn a UN flag, sparking further confrontation between Black students and members of the John Birch Society and the American Nazi Party.[54]

As advocates of America's liberal democratic tradition across the country demanded more action against the Rhodesian regime, opponents of actions against Rhodesia and the other white-ruled states in Africa pulsed with concerns. These apprehensions were about potential spreading of communism; about potential instability; about potential undermining of economic interests; and about abandoning the white settlers who these officials, businesspeople, and private citizens saw as equivalent to American pioneers. Knitting together these transatlantic concerns, white supremacist allies gave comfort to one another in a world of crumbling color lines. And into the unresolved situation stepped a familiar player, now pursuing his own domestic "Southern strategy."

Nixon and the "Tar Baby"

In the early stages of his long career, Congressman Richard Nixon had been granted an honorary membership to a local NAACP chapter. As vice president, he had been one of the Eisenhower administration's more prominent voices on civil rights. He endorsed the *Brown v. Board of Education* decision, supported the 1957 Civil Rights Act, and chaired the President's Committee on Government Contracts, which both investigated charges of racial discrimination in federally related employment and sponsored education campaigns to promote equal opportunity.[55]

His trip to Ghana's independence celebrations in March 1957 and his grueling three-week tour through the northern half of Africa convinced him that the continent was a Cold War battlefield that needed more of America's attention. Emphasizing the communist threat throughout his report back to the president, Nixon endorsed U.S. action to support newly independent countries in order to "alleviate the conditions of want and instability on which communism breeds." Rep. Frances Bolton (R-OH), the first woman elected to Congress from Ohio, was chair of the House Committee on Foreign Relations' Subcommittee on Africa at the time. She had led a major three-month-long study mission to Africa in 1955, which left her determined to create a separate Bureau of African Affairs in the State Department. Nixon now lent his weight to creating that bureau, which Congress finally did in July 1958.[56] Even as Nixon made his 1960 presidential run, he declared an obsession with Africa in National Security Council meetings, pushing for more attention while Eisenhower was in office, notwithstanding two recently completed NSC papers on the continent.[57]

Manifestations of more progressive views on race and interest in Africa, both laced as they were with disturbing prejudices, faded as Nixon embarked on his Southern strategy. Whereas in his 1960 campaign Nixon had spoken of Africa on a fairly regular basis, by 1968 that was not part of his strategy. One limited exception was the war in Nigeria and the humanitarian plight of those in Biafra. During the campaign, he advocated for more relief aid for Biafra, and just days after his inauguration, one of the first National Security Study Memorandums ordered by his national security adviser, Henry Kissinger, was on Biafra. But then Nixon did little else on the subject.[58] Nixon and his administration would generally abandon even the modest development efforts undertaken by previous administrations.[59]

Whether Nixon's racial views were always there but held in check, or whether in time they descended deeper into contempt and racism, by the time he occupied the Oval Office he had little inhibition in voicing his racial views, at least behind closed doors. The man who in the late 1950s promoted the need to engage Africa now told Kissinger, glum after Secretary of State William Rogers returned from a successful trip to Africa, that it did not matter. "Henry, let's leave the n——s to Bill and we'll take care of the rest of the world."[60]

Kissinger might have been content with focusing elsewhere. He certainly had limited knowledge or curiosity about the region, as evidenced in his meeting with Marcello Caetano, Portugal's prime minister, a few years later. Sitting down in Lisbon, Caetano pressed for more support and resources from Washington, claiming the fall of Angola would lead to the downfall of Rhodesia and South Africa. Insurgent operations needed to be stopped. Kissinger wondered from where the guerrillas came. Caetano explained that they infiltrated from Zambia, and this affected Mozambique as well. "But does Zambia have a common border with Angola?" asked Kissinger of the nearly seven-hundred-mile border, almost three times the length of his native Germany's border with France. And does Portugal have a "serious military problem in Mozambique?"[61]

Despite such prejudices and priorities, Africa would remain very much part of the conversation. And with southern Africa embroiled in the fight for freedom, the white regimes south of the Zambezi found a stronger and more active friend in the White House than they had in recent years. As Nixon pursued a global strategy that sought regional partnerships and allies that would effectuate continued anticommunism and American influence without need for U.S. intervention, he found allies on the "periphery" that did not need to be democratic. Africa proved no exception.[62]

Recommending to Nixon that the U.S. review its policy toward southern Africa, Kissinger presented his case in a way that would interest his boss in shaping policy there. Citing "black terrorist raids into Rhodesia" and "white reprisals," Kissinger framed the situation in southern Africa: Black men and women willing to use violence to achieve majority rule were terrorists, not freedom fighters; whites who fought against that outcome were merely and legitimately responding. Kissinger warned of the "presence of the Soviets and Chinese as patrons of the terrorist groups" operating against Rhodesia, Angola, and Mozambique. He pointed to the United States' other meaningful interests in the region as well, including a NASA tracking station, overflight and refueling rights, U.S. investment, and major trade potential.[63]

Kissinger was convinced the white regimes would "easily" contain any military threat for the next three to five years but acknowledged that long term, "the black–white confrontation in Southern Africa will be with us with growing insistence politically throughout the '70s." In his assessment, the United States needed to be involved with white authorities while trying to avoid being associated with the repressive racial policies of those regimes. He recommended that all options be put on the table for internal debate.

Kissinger carefully referenced Dean Acheson, who fiercely supported the Smith government in Salisbury, as having a point that the State Department had been too stubbornly tied to one track. "There is clearly a legitimate case," Kissinger concluded, "for a quite different policy than the current posture toward the white regimes."[64]

The next week, the now notorious National Security Study Memorandum 39 initiated a comprehensive review of U.S. policy toward southern Africa. Because of the sensitivity of where NSSM 39 could lead, the review was conducted in secret.[65] The stakes were clear: "Racial repression by white minority regimes in southern Africa has international political ramifications extending beyond the region itself. Politically conscious blacks elsewhere in Africa and the world deeply resent the continuation of discrimination, identify with repressed majorities in southern Africa and tend in varying degrees to see relationships of outside powers with the white regimes as at least tacit acceptance of racism."[66] And if the political stakes were not high enough, additional factors were considerable: economically, investment in southern Africa yielded "a highly profitable return," while trade ran a favorable balance; strategically, southern Africa was important for U.S. defense, it had essential overflight and landing facilities, and it housed a crucial NASA space tracking facility. Racial problems in the region would "probably . . . grow more acute over time, perhaps leading to violent internal upheavals and greater involvement of the communist powers," and U.S. policy should take these into account even though developments "may be years or even decades ahead."[67]

Current policy, trying "to balance our economic, scientific, and strategic interests in the white states with the political interest of dissociating the U.S. from the white minority regimes and their repressive racial policies," evoked the "middle path" dating back to the Truman years. It had left the Afro-Asian members of the UN demanding further measures: excluding South Africa from the UN, sanctions against South Africa and Portugal, even the use of force to implement UN actions. Yet Washington's position had steadily made clear "that we have gone as far as we can in the direction of greater UN pressures on the white regimes."[68]

The world was changing, though, and making any "middle" even more retrograde than ever. The Kennedy and Johnson administrations had edged away from supporting colonialism and white rule; now Nixon would go the other way and embrace the white redoubt. He planned to move U.S. policy more firmly to the pole of white minority rule.

The review initiated by NSSM 39 offered six options for approaching the region and continuing decolonization, ordered to represent a spectrum of policy approaches:

1. Movement toward normal relations with the white regimes
2. Broader association with both black and white states in an effort to encourage moderation in the white states and cooperation in the black states to reduce tensions and encourage improved relations among states in the area
3. Increased identification with and support for the black states of the region while pursuing the minimum necessary U.S. economic, strategic, and scientific interests in the white states
4. Closer association with black states and limited association with white states "in an effort to retain some economic, scientific, and strategic interests in the white states while maintaining a posture on the racial issue which the blacks will accept"
5. Dissociation from the white regimes and closer relations with black states "in an effort to enhance our standing on the racial issue in Africa and internationally"
6. Increased U.S. coercion, short of armed force, "to induce constructive change in white-regime race policies"[69]

In a rather generous self-assessment, especially regarding South Africa and Portugal, officials believed that Option 4 represented the current approach. The approach could be continued, they suggested, on the premise that the situation in southern Africa would likely not change appreciably in the foreseeable future. Doing so would retain some economic, scientific, and strategic interests in the white states, while limiting the nature and scope of those relations might help protect America's standing on the racial issue. Giving economic aid to the Black-ruled states of the region and standing firmly against the Smith regime could also be used as an offset, allowing the United States to reduce criticism of Portuguese policy in Africa and maintain relations with South Africa in a rough status quo.[70]

Nixon chose a different direction: Option 2—charting a path to broader association with white states—and began moving to strengthen relations with white supremacist regimes. His premise: "The whites are here to stay and the only way that constructive change can come is through them." The decision meant that the United States "would maintain public opposition to racial repression but relax political isolation and economic restrictions on the white states." His administration would come to the aid of the beleaguered white redoubt. It would try to soften any blowback by providing increased and more flexible economic aid to majority-ruled states.[71]

The White House believed it could persuade independent states in Africa that they should accept remaining minority white-ruled states, that "their only hope for a peaceful and prosperous future lies in closer relations with white-dominated states." The lure of continuing white rule was such that Nixon himself argued in National Security Council discussions that "we have to be realistic on this question and straddle it." For Nixon, "realistic" meant determining "where our national interest lies and not worry[ing] too much about other peoples' domestic policies" while somehow, in some inconceivable way, avoiding "the colonialist label."[72]

Nixon's approach reflected a calculating realpolitik, his disparaging racial views, and thorough disregard for democratic principles. Examples used in debates over the path ahead made clear what the chosen option meant: "Maintain public stance against apartheid but relax political isolation and economic restrictions against the white states." Help enable white supremacist states to hold on to power by enforcing the arms embargo against South Africa "but with liberal treatment of equipment which could serve either military or civilian purposes." The same for the Portuguese: publicly continue the arms embargo "but give more liberal treatment to exports of dual purpose equipment." For all the white redoubt, the United States would maintain its cloaking rhetoric but enhance the work-arounds, including for Namibia. "Without changing the U.S. legal position that South African occupancy of South West Africa is illegal, we would play down the issue and encourage accommodation between South Africa and the UN."[73]

For the illegal regime in Rhodesia, now on the table was to "gradually relax sanctions (e.g. hardship exceptions for chrome)." That change would put the United States dramatically out of step with most of the world and particularly the Afro-Asian bloc. Nonetheless, the Nixon administration contemplated going even further: it might "consider eventual recognition" of Rhodesia. Recognizing that wholesale condemnation would rain down if this came to pass, the administration considered using economic incentives for Black states, including development funds and bilateral technical assistance. A few pieces of silver to try to buy cooperation and continued white rule by anticommunist allies. "By diplomatic means," hazarded Option 2, the United States would "seek to persuade black states (importantly Zambia and Tanzania) to adopt policy of peaceful coexistence with white regimes."[74]

For a White House known for its realpolitik approach to international relations, in this region of the world Nixon and Kissinger displayed remarkably unrealistic expectations. Africa was moving away from white minority rule, and "peaceful coexistence" with white supremacy was a Cold War option that did not reflect the decolonization impetus. African states and peoples sought a fully free continent, which meant strengthening sanctions, not weakening them; increasing pressure, not decreasing it; speaking and acting in alliance, not speaking with them but then acting against them.

When the National Security Council met to debate the issues of southern Africa and the policy to follow, Nixon opined that "the whites can't go home. . . . They are there to stay." Under Secretary of State Elliot Richardson—later secretary of defense and then attorney general (a post he chose to resign rather than fire the special prosecutor in Watergate's Saturday Night Massacre)—then articulated the underlying presumptions of those in the room: "I agree there is no real solution. A white minority ruled by a black majority will not work and a black majority ruled by a white minority does not work."[75]

Richardson crystallized the view of these powerful men: no substantial white population should be ruled by a Black majority. These men had no doubt that whites were there to stay, but they could not envisage them being governed by Blacks. Vice President Spiro Agnew asked why the Rhodesian government was any more illegal than "we were when we declared independence." Richardson posed one solution: "There must be a partition." He veered closely toward the homeland policy of apartheid South Africa.[76]

Option 2 was debated, and plans were adopted, in secret. State Department critics derided it as the "Tar Baby" option, one that would adhere America to the side of the white minority regimes.[77] Viewed in the longer frame, the attitudes and actions embodied in the Tar Baby option had long shaped Washington's approach to decolonization in Africa. Now, however, these views were increasingly retrograde and isolated as Africa and the broader world moved in the opposite direction. The Nixon White House, in short, pulled toward white minority regimes as Africa and the world moved away from them. Although the United States had never thrown its full weight behind decolonization, the Nixon administration's policy shift meant that the United States, now more than ever, was aiding and abetting the continued control of the remaining white regimes of Africa.[78]

The Byrd Amendment

The recalibrations that brought the Nixon administration closer to the white regimes soon found the debate over chrome imports from Rhodesia highlighting the shift. Conservative backers of Rhodesia sought to repeal sanctions, and with a new administration in Washington, Sen. Harry F. Byrd Jr. (I-VA) introduced legislation to allow the importation of "strategic and critical minerals" from Rhodesia. The son of arch segregationist and former senator Harry F. Byrd, this scion of Virginia's long political dynasty saw much to like in the white, capitalist, anticommunist Smith regime and much to dislike in the supporters of majority rule, most of whom were Black and some of whom were Marxist. Allies of Byrd included fellow segregationist Southern senators, such as John Stennis (D-MS) and Strom Thurmond (R-SC). These men saw their era passing by yet believed that their fight to hold on to it in America should be extended to parallel places in Africa. Allies in the House of Representatives, such as Rep. James Collins (R-TX), even used the lack of African American representatives in the U.S. Congress to commend white Rhodesians for the Salisbury Parliament's higher proportion of Black representation. Collins did not comment on what that comparison said about U.S. voting rights and democratic traditions.[79]

These men joined forces with others, particularly in the business community, to find a way to work around or even end sanctions. Not surprisingly, the Byrd Amendment backers based their arguments on Cold War logic: sanctions against Rhodesia made the United States more dependent on the Soviet Union for chrome and other strategic minerals. Businesses like Union Carbide and Corning Glass Works lobbied hard to loosen sanctions or receive exceptions to them. Dean Acheson, "to his last breath . . . an unrepentant, unreconstructed colonialist where black Africa was concerned," made his final appearance on the public stage to argue for the Byrd Amendment at the Senate Subcommittee on African Affairs, three months before a stroke felled him.[80]

As the issue came to a boil in late September 1971, the U.S. Senate readied itself to vote. Senator Gale McGee (D-WY) articulated the stakes: if adopted into law, the Byrd Amendments would represent "formal defiance" of the UN embargo on importing Rhodesian chrome, and that would impair U.S. relations with "virtually all African countries."[81] Mauritanian president Moktar Ould Daddah, chair of the Organization of African Unity (OAU), girded to confront Nixon about the OAU's opposition to the Byrd Amendment and the damage it would do to U.S. relations with African states. Prepping his boss for the meeting, Kissinger shared his assessment that the Byrd Amendment could not be defeated. Nixon reassured Kissinger not to worry about it. "I agree with [the] Byrd Amendment. No public statement should be made by the W[hite] H[ouse]. Let State continue to take the position it needs to for African purposes."[82] Nixon's meeting with Daddah came and went, and Nixon told Kissinger to ignore what he had said to "that OAU fellow." "Well, I was being nice to them," Nixon recounted to Kissinger, "and, actually, I am for the Byrd Amendment." Nixon directed Kissinger not to let the State Department "pucker out of this and sink the goddamn—we want to continue to buy that chrome."[83]

As the two talked further, Nixon started rambling about "those poor, child-like Africans," and Kissinger fawned with compliments on Nixon's superb job in handling the conversation with an "almost incoherent" Daddah "and these other savages." Enjoying the flattery and shared bigotry, Nixon explained to his national security adviser that "a lot of patting them on the ass goes a long way."[84] A week later, still chewing on the Daddah meeting, Nixon, with no hint of irony, told British foreign secretary Sir Alec Douglas-Home that Africans should worry about the troubles in their own countries rather than those elsewhere in the world.[85]

With the Byrd Amendment clearing the Senate and moving toward a vote in the House, Rhodesia and Africa remained on Nixon's mind. He shared with Kissinger "my attitude towards the whole African problem." Complaining that the Africanists in the State Department were a thorn in his side, his irritation boiled over: "I know that State in the past has had this African policy and for two reasons. Forget all the goddamn principles. One is because they are concerned about the position of the United States among the new African countries. . . . The other point that they're concerned about is the domestic American political situation. They're afraid of it." Nixon was not going to let "goddamn principles" or worries about what Black Africans and Black Americans thought stand in the way. Instead, "The domestic American political situation should be completely taken out of their [State Department] feeling on this. I make that decision." And it was nakedly political: "You don't gain any votes from the blacks who give a shit what happens to Zambia."[86]

Having choreographed the Southern strategy on his way to the White House, Nixon largely dismissed African American votes domestically. In pursuing a "white redoubt" strategy for southern Africa, he was following suit with his international policies. The low regard for Africans in his geopolitical thinking left their interests well below European interests, for, in his words, "I do not believe that it is worth our while to do something for the Africans that's against the British or somebody else."[87]

Nixon reflected long-standing racial attitudes that coursed through much of America: Blacks should know their place. He resented Africans for even voicing an opinion that went beyond their own countries. "For the Africans to come in and see the President of the United States, as they did the other day, and to waste their time and my time for 40 minutes talking about the problems that didn't affect their own countries is an indication of the problem."[88] In Nixon's view, Americans had legitimate interests everywhere; Africans had no legitimate interests beyond their borders—not even for forty minutes. Nixon had long ago seen Africa as a front in the Cold War; now Africans who came in to talk about democracy, majority rule, and independence were wasting his time. Chrome, needed for a variety of purposes and sourced from Rhodesia rather than the Soviet Union, was more important than any "goddamn principles."

Having passed through the Senate, the Byrd Amendment cleared the House of Representatives, too. Historian Sarah Snyder points out that the Byrd Amendment was the only instance when "Congress pressed for and passed legislation that undermined rather than enhanced U.S. policy regarding human rights."[89] Nixon quickly signed it into law. Section 503, the Byrd Amendment, of the Military Procurement Act of 1971 officially eliminated bans on the importation of "strategic and critical" minerals from a country as long as imports from the Soviet Union were allowed. This effectively authorized the importation of strategic minerals from Rhodesia, including chrome ore, notwithstanding UN sanctions. The State Department opposed the Byrd Amendment, but the Commerce Department, the Treasury Department, Kissinger, and, most importantly, Nixon himself supported it.[90] President Johnson's executive orders to enforce the sanctions were reversed. The chrome came. Over the next two years, American businesses imported tens of millions of dollars of Rhodesian chrome and other minerals, violating mandatory UN sanctions on Rhodesia with every shipment.[91] The minority white regime was thus supported, the white redoubt strengthened.

"Cares More for Metals Than for Justice"

Washington undermined sanctions and thereby the economic strategy to seek a peaceful solution, strengthening the Smith regime and ensuring that those seeking change would feel even greater need to turn to armed struggle. Africans voiced their anger. From his prison cell in Rhodesia, Ndabaningi Sithole—a founder of the Zimbabwe African National Union—declared, "The action of the USA to resume chrome imports from Rhodesia under the present circumstances only goes to show that she cares more for metals than for justice and peace in southern Africa." The *Zambia Daily Mail*, during a visit by U.S. ambassador to the United Nations George H. W. Bush a few weeks later, wondered "whether Ambassador Bush and his colleagues in the Nixon Administration would be so vehement in their arguments [for peaceful approaches to UDI while breaking sanctions] if the situation were reversed and it was an African regime that had rebelled against the British Crown."[92]

The U.S. decision to join Portugal and South Africa in defying sanctions on Rhodesia outraged many on both sides of the Atlantic. As chrome deliveries sailed toward American ports, hundreds of protesters joined Black dockworkers in Louisiana to block deliveries from Rhodesia. African American students at Southern University, Lincoln University, Swarthmore, and elsewhere rallied to the cause. Longshoremen in Baltimore and San Francisco protested the importing of Rhodesian chrome.[93] The *New York Times* blamed "a well-financed Rhodesian lobby which has shrewdly exploited the racism of Southern Senators and Congressmen, the anti-Communist sentiment on Capitol Hill, the current hostility to the U.N. arising from the expulsion of Taiwan, and the wrath of importers forced to pay inflated prices for Soviet chrome." The paper lambasted Nixon for his inaction on the issue and wondered whether this was one more example of the high price of his Southern strategy.[94]

Black and white Americans rallied to keep pressure on the Smith regime and to oppose white supremacy in the region more generally. In the late 1960s and early 1970s, a wide range of groups and efforts populated the landscape. Actions focused on boycotts and disinvestment, the very things that the Nixon administration was moving away from. Companies targeted included Polaroid, Gulf Oil, Shell Oil, Ford, and General Motors.

Outraged that the company for which they worked sold products used to support the apartheid system in South Africa, Black labor activists launched the Polaroid Revolutionary Workers Movement (PRWM) in 1970. A world leader in photographic technology and a large multinational corporation, Polaroid's products were used for the photos in the passbooks that Africans were forced to carry, serving as an everyday tool of apartheid. Passbook laws had helped launch the protests that led to the Sharpeville tragedy, and a decade later American companies and products continued to help create the very face of apartheid. Polaroid workers led by design photographer Ken Williams and his wife, a research chemist, Caroline Hunter, along with sales representative Clyde Walton, tried to influence Polaroid policies through internal discussions. When that failed to change anything, in October 1970 the PRWM presented demands that Polaroid disengage from South Africa, that it announce the policy publicly, and that any profits from South Africa be donated to African liberation movements. Polaroid maintained it had no plant or direct investment in South Africa but instead worked through a distributor, and denied ties to the South African government. While only numbering a few Polaroid employees, the PRWM drew support from the local community and national organizations such as ACOA. Pressure grew on Polaroid. Finally acknowledging that its products were actually being used to take passbook photos, the Polaroid Corporation sent a study group to investigate conditions in South Africa. Upon the group's return, the company created a plan known as the "Polaroid Experiment": stop sales to the government, including police and military; improve wages; increase worker training. Foreshadowing debates over the Sullivan Principles and "constructive engagement," Polaroid argued that the best way to improve circumstances for Black South African workers was to remain in South Africa, and found support for its position among many in both South Africa and the United States. The PRWM judged the "experiment" insufficient and promoted an international boycott of Polaroid products. In February 1971 Hunter and Williams, joined by ACOA, testified before the UN committee investigating apartheid, after which Polaroid fired Hunter (Williams had previously resigned). It would be several more years before Polaroid, in the wake of the Soweto uprisings and faced with incontrovertible evidence from anti-apartheid activists that its film was still being used for passbooks, announced that it was pulling its business from South Africa.[95]

Helping to shine a spotlight on the costs of white supremacy in southern Africa, and in support of the PRWM and other anti-apartheid activists, Congressman Charles Diggs (D-MI) used his position on the House Subcommittee on Africa to launch hearings on U.S. business involvement in southern Africa in 1971. Nicknamed "Mr. Africa" by colleagues, Diggs had become the first Black chair of the House Subcommittee on Africa in 1969. He used the position as a platform to keep attention trained on anti-apartheid efforts and to help pioneer roles for nongovernmental organizations (NGOs) on Africa policy. The NGOs were crucially important given the intransigence of the Nixon administration, and Diggs used his position to help give voice to those organizations and activists. Outraged by the Nixon administration's willingness to break UN sanctions on Rhodesia and help fund Portugal through a generous extension of the Azores military base lease in 1971, Diggs became the first U.S. delegate to the UN to resign during a General Assembly session. His resignation speech to the UN resulted in a standing ovation. That year, Diggs, Shirley Chisholm, William Clay, John Conyers, Ronald Dellums, Charles Rangel, Louis Stokes, and other African American representatives formed the Congressional Black Caucus (CBC), whose members fought to keep pressure on the white regimes and the Nixon administration.[96]

Anticolonial supporters also sought action against Gulf Oil because of its major operations in Portuguese-controlled Angola. In 1971, activists affiliated with organizations including ACOA and the United Church of Christ formed the Gulf Boycott Coalition. Shortly afterward, students at Harvard University, including future head of TransAfrica Randall Robinson, formed the Pan-African Liberation Committee (PALC), which had an initial focus on spearheading a boycott of Gulf Oil. The PALC prepared a fifteen-page pamphlet indicting Harvard University for its role in repression in southern Africa: "African men, women, and children are being napalmed, machine gunned and bombed daily in Angola and Mozambique," began the authors. "The Portuguese government does not bear the sole responsibility for the suffering and death which plague the people of Angola and Mozambique," the PALC argued. "Although these policies are instituted by the Portuguese government, were it not for the economic and military support of the Western powers, that government would be totally incapable of implementing such policies and resisting the liberation armies within the colonies. In short, only through the support of institutions like Harvard University can Portugal maintain its colonial empire." At the time, Harvard had more than $300 million worth of Gulf Oil stock.[97]

When Harvard president Derek Bok announced that the university would not divest, student protesters took over Massachusetts Hall, home to the president's office and the oldest surviving building on campus. On day five of the takeover, Harvard's administration agreed to send a representative to Africa to investigate and make recommendations. The conclusion: there was no need to divest. When the decision was announced, fifteen hundred students protested by blocking President Bok from his office.[98]

The African Liberation Day demonstration in Washington in May 1972 drew between thirty thousand and fifty thousand people. Planning for the event involved well-known figures from a coalescing Left, including Amiri

Baraka and Angela Davis. Endorsement and participation came from elected officials Charles Diggs, John Conyers, Louis Stokes, and Julian Bond. Comedian Dick Gregory, poet Don Lee, and others gave speeches at the base of the Washington Monument. "Support for African liberation movements," writes historian Brenda Gayle Plummer, "became the new face of Pan-Africanism for diaspora groups unable to penetrate government-level decision making." Slowly building and advancing, these activists reflected the growing sense of frustration with the ongoing situation in southern Africa and Washington's support for white regimes.[99]

Grassroots efforts such as these varied expressions have been critical to Black freedom struggles on both sides of the Atlantic. From the Defiance Campaign and anti–pass law demonstrations to the Montgomery Bus Boycott and sit-in campaigns, the ongoing need and subsequent action manifested time and again. Grassroots efforts certainly had less immediate mechanisms for change than did the inner sanctum of the White House, but they could build a powerful force for societal change. The liberation struggles against white supremacy in the Portuguese colonies, Rhodesia, and South Africa built a transnational solidarity encircling the globe. More radical activists sought a socialist vision that, at times, also held vibrant Pan-Africanist overtones. Black Power leaders, particularly drawn to the liberation movements in the Portuguese-held territories, sought international support. Vehicles were created to promote solidarity, such as the film *A Luta Continua* by African American Robert Van Lierop. Part of a genre of films critiquing Cold War capitalism and promoting leftist alternatives, the 1972 film depicted Mozambique's struggle and the Mozambique Liberation Front's hoped-for revolution of equality and social cohesion. The African Liberation Support Committee (ALSC), which formed in 1972 to promote transnational solidarity work, used the film for education and recruitment purposes. Within the year, the ALSC had thirty-five U.S. chapters and networks in the Caribbean as well as Africa. Although riven by ideological debates, the ALSC carried on the legacy of organizational work by those interested in Africa and transnational anti-imperialism extending back to the Universal Negro Improvement Association and the CAA.[100]

Boycotts of Rhodesia and South Africa, along with companies doing business in these places and in the Portuguese colonies, increasingly blossomed and started extending into noneconomic areas as well. This development came first in the sporting world and, in short order, the world of music and the arts. Prominent athletes used their unique position to shine a light on apartheid's injustices. Arthur Ashe used his fame from the tennis court to challenge South Africa's color line, meeting with Secretary of State William Rogers in anticipation of applying for a visa to compete in South Africa. When Ashe's visa application was denied in January 1970 after cabinet-level discussions by the apartheid regime, it led to worldwide protests and pressure, including congressional hearings at which Ashe testified. Global outrage and pressure ultimately culminated in South Africa's expulsion from the Davis Cup and, two months later, from the International Olympic Committee.[101]

The Nixon administration's support for the white redoubt was helping provoke the activism that would harden the pressure on the white regimes, and these grassroots efforts both presaged and contributed to future efforts aimed more directly at the apartheid regime. It would take time for boycott campaigns and the disinvestment movement to move the needle, but activists like TransAfrica's Randall Robinson were honing their ideas and tactics as they worked to change the landscape in southern Africa. And while the White House offered support for white minority rule, these transnational activists joined with the expanding liberation struggles in Rhodesia, Mozambique, Angola, South Africa, and Namibia to keep the pressure on for majority rule and human rights throughout southern Africa.

5 Rapid, Just, and African Solutions, 1974–1980

> What gives Zambia and Africa great pause for concern is, Mr. President, America's policy towards Africa—or is it the lack of it. . . . American policy . . . has given psychological comfort to the forces of evil. . . . Southern Africa is poised for a dangerous armed conflict. There is not much time. . . . The patience of the oppressed has its limits.
>
> —Kenneth Kaunda, April 1975

> Most colored peoples of the world are not afraid of communism. Maybe that's wrong but communism has never been a threat to me. I have no love for communism. I could never be a communist. . . . But—it's never been a threat. Racism has always been a threat—and that has been the enemy all of my life.
>
> —Andrew Young, January 1977

Africa's decolonization at the start of 1974 reveals starkly contrasting portraits: nearly all of North, West, East, and Central Africa were a decade or more into independence, even as postcolonial difficulties troubled the regions; in contrast, nearly 75 percent of southern Africa remained under minority white rule. Liberation struggles were just that: struggles. Freedom fighters across southern Africa—FRELIMO in Mozambique; the MPLA, the FNLA, and UNITA in Angola; ZAPU and ZANU in Rhodesia; the ANC and PAC in South Africa; SWAPO in South West Africa—had met with mixed success. There was little indication that anything was about to change.

Yet these liberation struggles, along with that of the PAIGC in Guinea and Cape Verde, were building pressure. And that pressure helped prompt the April 1974 military coup in Portugal that irreversibly changed the dynamics of the region.

While the lily pads of white rule in Africa diminished, Washington's involvement inversely expanded. By the mid-1970s, southern Africa was very much on the front burner as Washington found itself contesting a burning hot Cold War there. For the white regimes, U.S. involvement was a regular matter of concern and had sometimes been a reservoir of hope, but now liberation struggles, independent African states, and the growing involvement of the Cubans and Soviets made their existence increasingly tenuous. The extent to which Washington pushed for majority rule would be critical. The scorecard would be uneven, but more than at any previous time, the Carter years saw the United States definitively and meaningfully help secure majority rule to Zimbabwe. By 1980, Angola, Mozambique, and Zimbabwe—covering an area larger than all the former European colonial powers in Africa combined—were independent nations. It was still a struggle: guerrilla movements continued to wage ruinous wars against the Black majority governments in the former Portuguese territories. But by 1980, the seismic shift in southern Africa's political landscape left only South Africa and the former mandate Namibia (South West Africa) still under white minority rule.[1]

Carnation Revolution and Lusophone Africa

When at the start of the 1960s the Kennedy administration initially pushed Portugal's Salazar regime to take steps toward allowing more African political participation, the administration had one eye on self-determination, while the other focused on the NATO alliance and the strategic value of access to the Azores. Faced with Lisbon's intransigence, over time the administration quietly eased back from applying pressure. And subsequent administrations continued this course.

The battle against Portuguese rule instead took place on the ground in its colonies. In Angola, three primary groups fought against Portuguese rule. The Popular Movement for the Liberation of Angola (MPLA), led by Agostinho Neto, emerged in the 1950s and took up arms in early 1961. The son of a Methodist minister, Neto had received a scholarship to study medicine in Portugal, where he was imprisoned for protesting the Salazar dictatorship. Able to finally complete his degree, Neto, a rather quiet poet and intellectual, returned to Angola with his family to start his medical practice. He also maintained his political activities. When Portuguese authorities arrested him, patients and supporters marched in protest, prompting the massacre of some twenty to thirty protesters by Portuguese soldiers. Exiled first to the Cape Verde islands and then to Portugal, Neto escaped and made his way to the Congo to direct the MPLA's armed struggle.

Also resisting Portugal's rule was the National Front for the Liberation of Angola (FNLA), led by Holden Roberto. Roberto's family had moved to the Congo while he was a young boy, where he was educated and found work for the Belgian Ministry of Finance. Roberto became increasingly active politically, helping found the Union of Peoples of Angola (UPA) in 1954. As its president he attended the 1958 All-African People's Conference in Accra, where he met Tom Mboya, Patrice Lumumba, Kenneth Kaunda, and other African nationalists. Acquiring a Guinean passport, Roberto traveled to the UN to promote the cause. By 1961 Roberto had met with President Kennedy, had named Jonas Savimbi as secretary-general of the UPA, and had launched armed uprisings. The next year the UPA united with another small nationalist group to create the FNLA. During these politically active years, Roberto also secretly established a relationship with the CIA that secured for him an annual stipend and divorced his wife to marry the sister-in-law of Joseph Mobutu in an effort to strengthen ties with one of the region's power brokers.

The third major group fighting the Portuguese came when Savimbi split from Roberto and the FNLA to create the National Union for the Total Independence of Angola (UNITA). Savimbi had worked his way through mission schools to eventually receive a scholarship to study in Portugal. He met Neto and, facing similar pressures from Portuguese authorities, decided to move to continue his studies in Switzerland. Charismatic and opportunistic, Savimbi slowly grew frustrated with Roberto's leadership and lack of military progress, and he broke with the FNLA. After receiving military training and support from the Chinese, he formed UNITA in 1966.

All three leaders were authoritarian; none of the groups had clear, strong ideological underpinnings beyond the desire for self-rule. The MPLA was most inclined to think in terms of class rather than race or ethnicity, and its ideology blended some elements of Marxist-Leninist thought. "However murky the MPLA's ideological commitment may have been," writes historian Piero Gleijeses, "it set it apart: the leaders of the FNLA and UNITA espoused no political doctrine."[2]

As the 1960s progressed, these groups fighting against Portuguese rule sought help where it could be found. In 1963 and 1964, Roberto—already on the CIA payroll—turned to China and elsewhere for assistance. The conservative *Washington Star*, one of the capital's two leading newspapers, advised that the U.S. government needed to "stand up for the Portuguese (white and black) who are our allies in NATO." The newspaper believed that Roberto's record of activities "suggests that he is a quite sinister admirer of Red totalitarianism" who accepts their aid in order to "carry out his 'revolution' against the Portuguese in Africa." The *Washington Star* pilloried Roberto's efforts as not a real revolution but rather the work of agents of totalitarianism whose cause "has expressed itself in unspeakable atrocities not only against whites, but much more severely against Negro Angolans, who regard themselves as full citizens of Portugal and who have no desire to be 'liberated.'" The newspaper's position—Europeans were natural allies; Africans wanted to be like Europeans; there was little purpose or true support for seeing the Portuguese go—was countered by the reality on the ground.[3]

The NSC staffer who photocopied the editorial and forwarded it to McGeorge Bundy added an accompanying note: "McG. B.—This would seem to be Secretary Rusk's point of view."[4] Wherever Portuguese authority remained, liberation movements grew. In Mozambique, nearly as large as Angola, Eduardo Mondlane led the Mozambique Liberation Front (FRELIMO), formed from a coalition of smaller nationalist groups that came together in mid-1962. Mondlane had been in the United States for most of the previous decade, having earned his BA from Oberlin and PhD from Northwestern. He married and was hired by the UN Trusteeship Department, but resigned because being a UN employee restricted political activity. He instead accepted a position as an assistant professor at Syracuse University. In early 1963, after completing his obligations to Syracuse, Mondlane and his family moved to Dar es Salaam to lead the liberation struggle. Mondlane had met with Attorney General Robert Kennedy the previous year, and while Kennedy was impressed with him and floated the idea of support, there would be no military aid or long-term commitment.[5] Nevertheless, under Mondlane's leadership, FRELIMO launched a guerrilla war in 1964 and was soon making notable inroads in rural areas. "The government [in Lisbon] knows how ill it can afford to lose the colonies," Mondlane explained as to why he turned to armed struggle. "For similar reasons it cannot afford to liberalize its control of them." Portugal's colonies, Mondlane argued, contributed to its economy only because of exploited labor and taking of resources and profits for the metropole, while giving discontented Portuguese a place to go with a position of special privilege. And because the dictatorship in Lisbon had eliminated democracy within Portugal, Mondlane continued, "it can scarcely allow a greater measure of freedom to the supposedly more backward people of its colonies." As a consequence, armed struggle for the now avowedly Marxist FRELIMO was the only solution.[6] Its successes on the ground in Mozambique soon led to Mondlane's assassination: in early 1969, he opened a parcel bomb sent by Portuguese agents. By the end of the year, Samora Machel emerged as the new leader of FRELIMO to continue the guerrilla war.

The most advanced liberation struggle was in relatively small Portuguese Guinea (Guinea-Bissau) and Cape Verde, collectively less than half the size of Portugal. Led by Amílcar Cabral, the African Party for the Independence of Guinea and Cape Verde (PAIGC) had formed in 1956. Cabral had returned from Portugal after completing his degree and traveled extensively through Portuguese Guinea as an agronomist for the colonial regime, using the time to deepen his understanding of and connections to the rural communities. The PAIGC tried labor strikes and political action without success, and after colonial authorities fired on and killed dozens of striking dockworkers in August 1959, the PAIGC turned to rural areas and armed struggle in the early 1960s. By 1969, PAIGC controlled at least half the country, despite Lisbon sending in forty times more troops—from one thousand in 1961 to forty thousand in 1969. Cabral's influence, as leader and revolutionary, spread.[7]

Salazar's government was determined to crush these liberation movements and, after Salazar suffered a debilitating stroke, his successor, Marcello Caetano, fought on. Becoming Portugal's first new leader in thirty-six years in the fall of 1968, Caetano vowed to continue to resist change in Africa. But the struggle increasingly drained resources and required evermore conscription of young Portuguese men. The strains on Portugal went mostly unremarked by the Western powers, including the United States. The highest U.S. officials were more engaged elsewhere, and the signs were largely missed by the intelligence and foreign affairs communities.

By the beginning of 1970, Nixon had decided that he and Kissinger should concentrate on "the big battles" and delegate matters that would not have "any major effect" on the success of his administration. East–West relations, policy toward the Soviet Union and China, NATO and the major countries of Western Europe: these should be the areas receiving the highest level of attention. Other problems, such as the Middle East and Vietnam, might make the cut, depending on the particulars. Beyond that, Nixon preferred that foreign policy issues stay off his desk unless they absolutely required presidential decisions. Latin America, all of the Western Hemisphere besides Cuba (as part of the East–West conflict), most of Asia, and of course Africa were to be delegated. This meant that in Nixon's words, the "weak sisters" of the Africa bureau at the State Department would be on point for Africa.[8]

But the world rarely packages itself so neatly. Africa soon commanded Kissinger's attention and became a major front in the Cold War. April 1974 brought one of those moments when events in one part of the world clearly and unequivocally alter the landscape in another: the government in Lisbon was overthrown. The authoritarian regimes of Salazar and then Caetano had clung to the belief that Portugal could retain its overseas territories, even as mounting costs drove more military officers and soldiers to the opposite conclusion. On 25 April a group of officers who had joined the Armed Forces Movement launched their coup. Within hours, they removed Caetano, and thousands of Portuguese were celebrating in the streets of Lisbon, sporting red carnations.[9]

"The virtually bloodless coup that toppled the government of President Thomaz and Prime Minister Caetano on April 25, 1974," explained Kissinger, "was triggered by Lisbon's African policies and the divisions within the military to which they gave rise."[10] Decolonization in Africa continued to shake the foundations of governments in Europe and would do so further as the new leaders in Lisbon struggled over exactly how to handle its colonies. The new head of government was Portugal's most decorated military officer, former general Antonio de Spinola. Spinola had helped spark the coup with his public declaration that a military approach would not defeat African insurgencies and a political solution needed to be achieved. The new regime found itself divided: to seek cease-fires and the space to—after generations of rule—build functioning democratic institutions, followed by votes on self-determination, or to immediately and outrightly commit to self-determination. The issue divided the government, and so it was that African liberation fighters helped make the decision: none of the movements laid down arms.[11]

Three months after Caetano's overthrow, on 27 July 1974, President Spinola announced that independence would come to all of Portugal's African colonies. Publicly declaring the government's recognition of the right to self-determination for the overseas territories, including the right to independence, Spinola announced Portugal's readiness to transfer power to the peoples of Angola, Mozambique, Guinea, and Cape Verde. Spinola welcomed initiatives to start planning and carrying out the decolonization process forthwith, with the headline priority being to agree on the terms and dates for independence. With that, he asked that over a dozen years of fighting cease.[12]

Almost a year earlier, on 24 September 1973, the PAIGC had already declared independence for Guinea-Bissau and Cape Verde, although by this time Cabral had been assassinated in a plot orchestrated by Lisbon. While not recognized by Portugal at that point, the UN General Assembly expressed its support for independence in a resolution passed on a 93–7 vote, with the United States joining Portugal in opposition. With Spinola's announcement, Portugal also formally recognized independence. On 10 September 1974, Guinea-Bissau became the first of Portugal's African colonies to gain full sovereignty. The PAIGC had been less active in Cape Verde, but negotiations led to independence for the island archipelago the following July.[13]

Mozambique as well had a unified nationalist movement. Spinola's address led to an informal cease-fire in the country and negotiations with FRELIMO in Lusaka. Six weeks later, a signed agreement created the blueprint to implement a formal cease-fire, form a transitional government appointed by FRELIMO and Lisbon, and achieve full and formal independence on 25 June 1975.

In Angola, however, the decolonization of Lusophone territories ran directly into multiple competing nationalist movements, with tensions exacerbated by Cold War divisions. With the MPLA, FNLA, and UNITA all claiming to be the rightful leaders of a free Angola, transitional efforts focused on establishing cease-fires and creating a working coalition government. UNITA stopped fighting in June 1974, but the FNLA and the MPLA did not agree to official cease-fires until mid-October. It would take until the beginning of 1975 for the three groups, now all official political parties, to agree to a united front, an essential Lisbon prerequisite for final independence negotiations. On 15 January 1975, Portugal and the three liberation groups signed the Alvor Agreement, providing for equal representation in a transitional government that would organize elections and draft fundamental laws in preparation for Angolan independence on 11 November 1975.

"We Can't Let the Communists Win There"

The three Angolan groups failed to remain united, an unsurprising development. They had competing interests, years of differences, and, most importantly, different Cold War backers. By this point, the MPLA itself was riven by internal factions that sought leadership of the group as well as control of enough of Angola to emerge ahead of the FNLA and UNITA. As 1974 progressed into 1975, Soviet envoys, seeking to deepen their ties with Angolan nationalists, worked to promote a unified MPLA and to convince MPLA leadership to create a liberation front with the FNLA. Yet the very fact of Soviet involvement paved the way for the FNLA and UNITA, in this starkly divided Cold War environment, to solicit support from Soviet rivals, namely the United States and China. In January 1975, only days after the signing of the Alvor Agreement, the CIA increased aid to Holden Roberto and the FNLA to $300,000 annually, and funneled more economic and material aid through the Mobutu regime. The escalation was not done in response to Soviet assistance, but to Soviet presence. Notably, Washington would give diplomatic recognition to Mozambique and the avowedly Marxist FRELIMO government on the day of its independence; Angola, with Soviet and Cuban presence, was prompting a different response.[14]

Regional African leaders worked to find a path forward. In April 1975, Zambian president Kenneth Kaunda arrived in a Washington still reeling from the Watergate scandal and resignation of Nixon. Kaunda met with Nixon's successor, Gerald Ford, as well as Kissinger, who remained on the scene as secretary of state. They discussed Kaunda's decision to shift support to Savimbi, a leader who Kaunda had "ignored" but now saw as a compromise figure who "could save the situation." Kaunda represented that he and his fellow regional leaders—Julius Nyerere of Tanzania and Mobutu Sese-Seko (née Joseph Mobutu) of Zaire (the once and future Congo)—agreed that Neto and Roberto should lead their respective parties while Savimbi should serve as the compromise leader of all three. Adding that Mozambique's imminent new leader Samora Machel was also impressed with Savimbi, Kaunda made the case that while it was for the people of Angola to decide, this might be the solution that all parties should back.[15]

Kaunda's representations seem not to have decisively shifted U.S. support away from Roberto and the FNLA, as Angola faced growing involvement from outside forces. Six weeks later the secret "40 Committee" of the NSC, which for years reviewed covert operations before approval by the president, debated whether to expand covert assistance to Savimbi as well as Roberto. CIA director William Colby and State Department officials endorsed Roberto as "the best" for the United States, given his anticommunist credentials and long relationship with U.S. ally Mobutu. Kissinger fumed that he did not want another situation like Chile—"to give money to everybody and then lose to the Communists." Conveying his typical frustration with the State Department, Kissinger derided the "weeping response" and lack of policy recommendations, rendering his opinion that the State Department wanted to do nothing. When Under Secretary of State for Political Affairs Joseph Sisco ventured that doing nothing might actually be best, Kissinger made clear the stakes as he saw them: "We can't let the Communists win there."[16] Seeking policy direction, in late May Kissinger had Ford order up a National Security Study, NSSM 224. Delivered within weeks, it presented three options: stay neutral, and out; actively promote a peaceful settlement; or provide support to aid the FNLA and UNITA in order to prevent the MPLA from taking power.[17]

Having watched his erstwhile ally in Saigon utterly defeated as all of Vietnam unified under communist rule, Kissinger was determined not to allow Angola to "go Communist" on the heels of the bitter U.S. defeat in South Vietnam. Confessing that he had not focused on the situation in Angola early enough, Kissinger sought to address the situation: "What real choice do we have? If Angola is taken by the Communists, what conclusions can the African leaders draw about the United States." Advised that it was not clear that Neto and the MPLA actually were in a position to come out on top, Kissinger remained adamant: Luanda was at risk of being MPLA controlled. He demanded action. "Forget for a moment how important Angola itself may be," Kissinger sketched. "I am concerned on the impact on Nyerere, and Kaunda, and Mobutu when they see we've done nothing."[18] Of particular concern was Mobutu. The Congo's vast size and mineral wealth, along with Washington's long working relationship with Mobuto (notwithstanding his larcenous authoritarianism), was seen as too valuable a chip to lose in the Cold War. Warned that U.S. involvement would make America "fairly pregnant" by deepening its role, Kissinger demanded that it be done in a way that "makes us the least pregnant, but most decisive."[19]

There were those who may have sought to push Africa to the margins, but in 1975 Angola was the "center," the primary crucible of an East–West, Global North–Global South, Cold War–fed engagement. Indeed, the specter of even more revolutionary change fueled a rapidly mushrooming belief that the United States needed to project a more visible presence. By late June, Angola was the priority at the National Security Council. In free-ranging discussions, various options were tossed about. Secretary of Defense James Schlesinger raised the possibility of encouraging Angola's disintegration, so that the Cabinda enclave could be "in the clutches of Mobutu," thereby securing resources. CIA director William Colby pointed out that the South Africans "would like us to join with them in an effort." When it came down to it, summed up President Ford, doing nothing was unacceptable and relying on diplomatic efforts would be naive.[20]

The CIA presented options for assisting Roberto and Savimbi, ranging from limited financial support for political activity combined with covert action to stop the flow of weapons to the MPLA, to large-scale support to the FNLA and UNITA, which would include supplying one-third of all the weapons and supplies they needed. The latter would be on such a scale that no longer could it be covert. Pushing against Kissinger, the CIA, and others backing covert action, Under Secretary of State Sisco offered an alternative view: that U.S. interests in Angola were not enough to warrant covert action. Kissinger put the question to Sisco, framed as a definitive consequence: Was he willing to let Angola go communist? Sisco was unequivocal: yes.[21]

The Ford administration was defining southern Africa as another Cold War test of will. Kissinger began offering a 1970s' African version of the domino theory. If Angola went communist, then so would go Zaire, then Zambia, Tanzania, Rhodesia, and eventually South Africa. Thinking that once informed U.S. actions in Southeast Asia in the 1950s and 1960s was now at work in southern Africa in the 1970s. Kissinger dismissively brushed aside skepticism about increasing U.S. involvement. He was pressed on the matter: Should the United States support Roberto, who has a ragtag army and refuses to venture into Angola himself? Kissinger: Yes, the army is ragtag precisely because the United States had not been supportive. And so it went. "If all the surrounding countries see Angola go Communist, they will assume that the U.S. has no will," Kissinger argued. "Coming on top of Vietnam and Indochina their perception of what the U.S. can and will do will be negative."[22]

Ford and Kissinger were convinced that U.S. credibility was again at stake and that the U.S. response would determine the fate of the entire region. The administration's driving motivation was never a positive framing of support for one of the Angolan leaders but rather the perceived need to stop Neto, the MPLA, and any potential communist threat. Who to back was little more than finding the strongest alternative. On the ground in Luanda, U.S. consul general Thomas Killoran offered little enthusiasm for any possibility: "I trust no one in this drama—not the Portuguese, who have no will, not the MPLA, which has no scruples, not the FNLA which has no sense and not UNITA which has no power, at least for the moment. All of the factors driving the leaders of the three liberation movements are negative—hate, greed, ambition—and the final solution in Angola has to be by force of arms." Killoran advised that "the denouement will come after independence and it will be bloody."[23]

As the White House grew more convinced that the MPLA was on the rise with Soviet backing, it grew more determined to influence the conditions on the ground to create a favorable situation before independence day, 11 November 1975. President Ford made his decision: he would act and approve covert operations in Angola. Those who counseled otherwise would not deter him; he was convinced that "if we do nothing, we will lose Southern Africa."[24] In the following months, the United States would step up its dealings with Mobutu and supply both Roberto and Savimbi with money and weapons, largely funneled through the CIA. Some $50 million would be allocated for the CIA to train, equip, and transport forces fighting against the MPLA. While it could find little to financially assist dozens of African nations establishing their independence, Washington was spending tens of millions of dollars to influence internal power struggles.[25]

While Kissinger and others argued strenuously for intervention, in this raw post-Vietnam environment all understood there would be no sending American military. Throughout the country, from Congress to the public more broadly, there was little appetite for overseas military action. Yet as the impending transfer of power in Angola loomed, the MPLA and its Soviet allies were not collapsing; more funds, more weapons, more training, did not seem enough for anti-MPLA forces.[26]

A long-standing ally in the region had the power to act, however, and by August, small teams of South African forces had arrived on the ground in Angola, and by September they were undertaking missions with and training FNLA and UNITA fighters. Barely a month before Angola's independence, then, Prime Minister John Vorster authorized launching Operation Savannah, the invasion of Angola with thousands of troops and hundreds of vehicles. On 14 October 1975, South African regular troops crossed into Angola.[27]

The government in Pretoria saw an opportunity to shape Angola's postcolonial government to its advantage. Deeply fearful of communist activity outside its borders as well as within, South Africa had powerful motivation to prevent the MPLA from taking power or, failing that, to simply create a buffer zone above the border with Namibia.[28] A second rationale entered as well: the belief that the Americans would be beholden to Pretoria for its efforts. While views differ over whether Washington pushed Pretoria to enter the fray or whether Pretoria initiated action on its own accord, Pretoria made its choice, just as it is now generally accepted that Cuba entered Angola on its own volition rather than at Soviet behest. Indeed, Mobutu in Zaire, Kaunda in Zambia, Nyerere in Tanzania, Machel in Mozambique, and each of the other regional actors were navigating their own paths in ways that did not merely conform to superpower desires. Even so, for a White House that wanted to act but faced post-Vietnam constraints, South Africa's gambit offered possible high reward in advancing the campaign against the MPLA. But it also threatened severe blowback for the United States to be associated with a pariah white minority regime invading an African state liberating itself from colonial rule.[29]

South African troops in Angola dramatically reshuffled the deck. MPLA troops found themselves increasingly pressed by the FNLA in the north and

UNITA in the south. Both were supplied by external powers, including China, the United States, and Zaire. They were supported by hired mercenaries, and now troops from South Africa. By late October, the MPLA controlled less than 25 percent of the country. Yet the MPLA had its own allies. Along with the Soviets, Cuban involvement had been meaningful in the run up to independence, with Cubans supporting and training MPLA forces. After the invasion by South Africa, Cuban leader Fidel Castro swiftly concluded that the moment had come for Cuban troops to enter the fighting. Castro rushed hundreds and ultimately thousands of Cubans to fight on the side of the MPLA. In concert with Cuban forces and Soviet materiel, MPLA forces defeated the FNLA forces in the north, notwithstanding their support from the CIA, Zaire, China, and hired mercenaries, while in the south the MPLA defeated UNITA forces, despite their South African allies.[30]

Angola's path to independence had quickly become a bubbling cauldron of Cold War, regional, and internal conflicts. As Washington debated what to do, for the second time in Africa's decolonization era the U.S. Congress meaningfully asserted itself to shape policy (the Byrd Amendment being the first time). In the post-Vietnam era in Washington, Congress was challenging White House latitude in foreign affairs, and no more so than as the Ford administration drew deeper into Angola. With the MPLA in charge in Luanda on independence day, and with little desire for deeper U.S. involvement without its approval, the U.S. Senate in mid-December voted to adopt the Tunney Amendment to the Defense Appropriations Bill, cutting funds for covert operations in Angola. Two months later, the Senate extended this action by approving the Clark Amendment, which prohibited U.S. security assistance to insurgent groups in Angola without congressional authorization. Congress was in no mood for sliding into another Vietnam. The Senate vote left Ford angry, taking to television to deplore the action; and it left Kissinger fuming, soliciting Middle East allies to send money to support the FNLA and UNITA.[31]

Frustration in the Ford administration deepened as, with vital support from Cuba and the Soviets, Neto and the MPLA firmed their grip. On 12 January 1976, the OAU met to decide the fate of Angola. In the narrowest of votes, recognition of the MPLA won out over recognition of a unity government. By the end of March, forty-one of forty-six OAU member states had recognized the MPLA government, and the last South African troops had withdrawn from Angola. The Neto government was securely in place, backed by Moscow, Havana, and ten thousand Cuban troops with MiG aircraft and three hundred tanks.[32]

Kissinger in Southern Africa

Angola's decolonization had become a Cold War battleground. Those in Washington who had made it an anticommunist imperative and a question of U.S. prestige believed that the stakes were high—southern Africa mattered, the Soviets and Cubans were advancing, and America was on the run, looking weak. The Ford administration could not look away, and the Angola debacle fueled high-level efforts to address regional issues: the escalating struggle between the Smith regime and liberation movements in Rhodesia, the ongoing fight over the status of Namibia, and the now deeply frayed relationship with South Africa's white minority government, which remained committed to an increasingly isolated white supremacist system.

With African nations recognizing Neto's MPLA government in Luanda, Kissinger told Ford that if the Cubans became involved in Rhodesia, "Namibia is next and after that South Africa itself. We must make the Soviets pay a heavy price. If the Cubans move, I recommend that we act vigorously. We can't permit another move without suffering a great loss."[33] Kissinger saw dominoes falling, and to prevent that, he was willing to "crack the Cubans. . . . I think we have to humiliate them. If they move into Namibia or Rhodesia, I would be in favor of clobbering them." President Ford asked what the United States would do if the Cubans ignored its demands that they get out of Africa. "I think we could blockade [Cuba]," replied Kissinger, who began planning for that contingency.[34]

While much of the Ford administration's attention to southern Africa had been on Portuguese territories and particularly Angola in recent months, the entire region was a new crisis point in the Cold War, with the White House seeing the need to more fully address issues of white rule and decolonization. Historian Eddie Michel takes note of the different makeup of the newest occupant of the Oval Office: "President Ford entered the White House with a sincere commitment to moral principles, including racial justice, both domestically and globally. Both publicly and privately the president stated unequivocally his commitment to majority rule in Rhodesia. This alone signified a major change from the calculating realpolitik of his predecessor."[35]

Ford and his team also faced continuing pressure from African leaders as they contemplated initiatives to counter the real threat of the region sliding toward Cuba and the Soviets. At a black-tie dinner at the White House in his honor, Zambian president Kaunda used his remarks to forcefully express his dismay that Washington seemed content with the status quo of racial oppression, saying that the United States had "not fulfilled our expectations." Kaunda pulled no punches: the failure to intervene by the United States provided "psychological comfort to the forces of evil." "If we want peace we must end the era of inertia in Rhodesia and Namibia and vigorously work for ending apartheid." The root causes of conflict—colonialism and institutionalized racism—must be put to an end.[36]

In April 1976, Kissinger embarked on a six-nation journey in Africa that took him from Kenya to Tanzania, Zambia to Zaire, Liberia to Senegal, and then back again to Kenya. Known for his frequent trips to the Middle East, Kissinger had a steep learning curve on Africa. At the same time, he walked into meetings with words that leaders of the Frontline States—Botswana, Tanzania, and Zambia originally, joined by Mozambique upon its independence and then later by Angola, who worked together in the fight against colonialism and apartheid—wanted to hear: "You have seen reports of my motives for coming here—to set up an American-sponsored liberation movement, or to support the white Rhodesian regime. With respect to the latter, I am prepared to put the power of the United States behind the liberation of Rhodesia, in unmistakable terms, so Smith and Vorster cannot possibly misunderstand."[37]

Arriving in Lusaka, Kissinger intended to execute a public pivot for the Ford administration and reverse the Tar Baby course that the United States had followed since early in the Nixon administration. The white regimes were no longer "here to stay"; majority rule was now the accepted goal. Catching Kaunda before his address, Kissinger informed him, "While it is true that within the United States there will be resistance to my speech today, we have made our decision. We are totally behind majority rule, and we will work with the four [Frontline State] presidents."[38]

Kissinger delivered his remarks at a luncheon hosted by Kaunda. "Morally and politically, the drama of national independence in Africa over the last generation has transformed international affairs," began Kissinger. He called the colonial era "a thing of the past" and described the great tasks of nation-building, keeping the peace and integrity of the continent, developing economically, and achieving racial justice as the major challenges in building a humane and progressive world. Detouring to boldly claim that "the United States was one of the prime movers of the process of decolonization," Kissinger asked those in the room not to look backwards, not to get into "a debate about whether in the past America has neglected Africa or been insufficiently committed to African goals." That debate he could not win.[39]

Kissinger suggested looking forward and seeking practical solutions. "Of all the challenges before us, of all the purposes we have in common,"

Kissinger reflected that day, "racial justice is one of the most basic." Echoing John F. Kennedy's words following the strife in Birmingham in 1963, Kissinger called it "not simply a matter of foreign policy but an imperative of our own moral heritage." Kissinger did not mention his role in NSSM 39 and the adoption of the Tar Baby option. Instead, he reaffirmed "the unequivocal commitment of the United States to human rights, as expressed in the principles of the U.N. Charter and the Universal Declaration of Human Rights." And in a measure of how the world had changed in less than a generation, Kissinger declared U.S. support for "Africa's genuine nonalignment and unity."[40]

Words were hollow without deeds, and perhaps especially words of high morality from this speaker, yet at this moment Kissinger seemed prepared to push for majority rule in Rhodesia. On the question of whether to tackle Rhodesia or Namibia first, there were those who prioritized Namibia, including the presidents of the Frontline States. But Kissinger believed it best to handle them sequentially, with Rhodesia first.[41] Frontline States' leaders, who would be critical in convincing nationalist leaders to negotiate with Ian Smith, were willing to accept this arrangement if it meant the United States would finally use its strength to fully support majority rule. A decade had passed since LBJ told the assembled OAU delegates at the White House that the American government "cannot, therefore, condone the perpetuation of racial or political injustice anywhere in the world."

Boxed in by not wanting to side with an illegal racist regime while desperately wanting to fend off communist influence, the solution was to get the Smith regime out. The liberation forces in Rhodesia were gaining strength and seeking support from allies. With Marxist governments in Mozambique and Angola, resolving the Rhodesia situation on terms favorable to Western interests seemed imperative. Kissinger described a specific ten-point policy in support of "a rapid, just, and African solution" in Rhodesia, and four steps toward self-determination in Namibia. Measures included asking Congress to repeal the Byrd Amendment and providing aid to nations hurt economically by sanctions on Rhodesia. Restoring the United States' participation in sanctioning Rhodesia provided pragmatic value in aligning with the world and strengthening relations with African states, as well as moral justice in doing so.[42]

Nyerere and Kaunda responded positively to Kissinger's overtures, which included promises of assistance for the states bordering Rhodesia that had closed their borders to it. Not seeing the inconsistency in his own words, Kissinger told Kaunda, "If foreign intervention is kept out of southern Africa, the United States can give you its maximum support."[43] For Kissinger, foreign intervention meant the Eastern bloc; the Western bloc was supposed to be there. The African leaders were understandably wary of all outside involvement in the region, yet they were quick to understand that Smith would not leave without Western involvement or, absent that, a long and costly liberation war. In the weeks that followed, Nyerere and Kaunda became convinced that Kissinger and the United States might help push Smith from power.

But Kissinger significantly hedged the U.S. position regarding white minority rule with South Africa, where Kissinger sought to keep alliance with the government. He framed the situation as "no one" challenging the right of white South Africans "to live in their country"; they were not colonialists but rather "an African people." He promised that U.S. policy would encourage the South African government to remedy the institutionalized separation of races within a "reasonable time," hardly a bold new position for majority rule or strong stance against racism but one that reflected the arc of past practice and policy toward South Africa. At the same time, Kissinger's approach reflected a plan to use the Vorster government in Pretoria as an ally in turning Rhodesia toward majority rule, while apartheid would remain something to address in the future. Pretoria could show its "dedication to Africa" by using its influence in Salisbury "to promote a rapid negotiated settlement for majority rule in Rhodesia."[44]

On the face of it, Pretoria's willingness to pressure the Smith government in Rhodesia might appear confounding, given the similarly isolated and pariah state of the two white minority governments. Nonetheless, differences existed between the countries and between Smith's British and Vorster's Afrikaner backgrounds. Internal and international factors pressed Vorster. With the collapse of the Portuguese empire, regional dynamics had taken a dramatic turn and Pretoria embarked on its own policy of détente, perhaps insulating it from external criticism by promoting peaceful coexistence and respect for the internal system of each state in the region. Détente with neighboring majority-ruled states at the cost of encouraging majority rule in Rhodesia could possibly prevent further Soviet and Cuban inroads, and open opportunities elsewhere, maybe even secure terms that would allow South Africa to control Namibia. If push came to shove, Rhodesia was less important to South Africa than Namibia, and Smith more expendable than the extensive network of Afrikaners and economic control in the "fifth province." Action on Rhodesia might also decrease the likelihood that ongoing war would further radicalize any future majority government there, while an engineered change might lead to a pliable majority-ruled neighbor.[45]

Still, Kissinger knew it was a big step for South Africa to pressure its ally in Rhodesia, one of the few it had in the world, to accede to majority rule. As he sought inroads with the Frontline States, Kissinger sent signals to Pretoria that the United States would allow South Africa a free hand on domestic actions if it cooperated with U.S. interests in Rhodesia, even commiserating with South African ambassador Pik Botha that if he was in Botha's position, he too would not allow one person one vote.[46] During the summer of 1976, Vorster met with Kissinger in West Germany and agreed to use South African leverage in order to pressure Smith to accept a transition to majority rule. The two men hammered out details of how they would move toward securing majority rule in Rhodesia and in Namibia on terms that might not be embraced by the Smith regime or by SWAPO but were acceptable to both the Ford administration and the apartheid regime.[47]

The strategy fell under the banner of the ends justify the means: weighing the value and utility of pushing for majority rule in one place (Rhodesia) while enabling white supremacy in another (South Africa). And events in South Africa made clear just how deadly a bedfellow one had in Pretoria. Kissinger's meeting with Vorster came a week after the Soweto uprising, which had been sparked by the Ministry of Education decree that half of school subjects be taught in Afrikaans. On 16 June 1976, thousands of primary and secondary students left Soweto schools in protest, intending to rally at the local stadium. As the children marched through the streets, police arrived. In the ensuing confrontations, police shot and killed numerous protesters, including thirteen-year-old Hector Pieterson. Photographs of his lifeless body shocked the world, as did the ruthless and bloody repression that followed. By the next day, the official death toll had reached fifty-eight, while unofficial counts went to over one hundred killed.

While the white regime cracked down, Kissinger exhibited little interest in discussing the brutal repression; he sensed an opening to steer Vorster toward helping push change in Rhodesia. To get South Africa on board to pressure Smith, the White House was willing to accept the status quo in South Africa.[48]

Kissinger also needed British involvement and cooperation to make meaningful progress, outlining a transition plan that London reacted to cautiously. This would become the rough basis for the Anglo-American Initiative that had Kissinger returning to the region for a second time in September 1976. Meeting in Pretoria, Kissinger and Vorster pressed Smith to accept the principle of majority rule. Smith was facing the changed circumstances of now having an avowed enemy on his over eight-hundred-mile-long eastern flank in Mozambique, an ongoing and escalating bush war, a deteriorating military situation, and a weakening economy. GDP had declined for the first time in 1975, then again in 1976. Over fifteen hundred whites a month were emigrating. And now his closest ally and friendliest superpower were pressing him to accept majority rule. Cornered, he sought the best deal. On 24 September, he announced on television his government's acceptance of majority rule within two years. Kissinger later recalled talks with Smith as "the most painful negotiations I have spent in my eight years in Washington." In sympathy with the minority white settlers, Kissinger believed that Smith saw acceptance of this proposal as the end, as accepting "the destruction of everything that they and their fathers had built."[49]

The struggle against white minority rule in southern Africa reverberated domestically in the United States. In the presidential campaign, the incumbent Ford was walking a tightrope. He was struggling against a challenge from Ronald Reagan on his right, the very flank of his party that would be most outraged by actions against the Smith regime. Where Ford and his administration saw a need to prevent communist advances by changing out white minority rule in Rhodesia, hard-line conservatives saw the abandonment of an anticommunist regime as aiding that very outcome. As Reagan campaigned in the Republican primaries, he criticized Kissinger for pursuing a policy that might lead to a "massacre" in Rhodesia. On the other side, if Ford won the primaries, he faced a close general election in which the African American vote might prove crucial. And Black voters, strongly in support of majority rule in Zimbabwe, were using that as a measure of a candidate's support for Africa and for Black Americans.[50]

As Ford sought to navigate the shoals of domestic politics and international geopolitics, on the ground in southern Africa came the most elemental of questions for any transition of power: On what terms would majority rule come? Kissinger believed he had Smith, Vorster, and the African presidents of the Frontline States lined up in rough accord, although Kissinger had represented the details differently to these leaders as well as to the British. But details mattered. When the African presidents met in Lusaka, there was "great confusion as to what had been agreed" during Kissinger's shuttle diplomacy. For those seeking authentic majority rule, the racial composition of transitional ruling bodies and white control of security ministries for defense and for law and order were not small issues. The very details that Smith pressed for were nonstarters for the liberation fighters and the African presidents. Two days after Smith's public announcement, the Frontline State presidents just as publicly rejected Kissinger's proposals.[51]

Just when the initiative was supposed to find culminating success, everything unraveled. A conference under British auspices was convened in Geneva, but proceeded disastrously. London saw little hope for success, and by all measures managed that along even as, not inconsequentially for the longer-term, Mugabe appeared to strengthen his position at the expense of Nkomo. As it all collapsed at the end of the year and in the last days of Ford's time in office, the leaders of the Frontline States voiced their anger and frustration. "I changed my approach in early September because I had been brought to believe (as I have continued to believe until now) that American power would be brought to bear, and maintained as long as necessary, in support of a transfer of power from the minority in Rhodesia," Nyerere fumed at Kissinger. "With this background you will appreciate why I feel slightly irritated to find now that Smith's power, together with American, British, and South African combined 'powerlessness,' is being advanced as the reason why the front-line states must ask the nationalists to abandon their legitimate demands." In the end, Kissinger's missteps, Britain's fumbles, Smith's dogged clinging to power, and liberation movement leaders' belief that they could strengthen their negotiating position by further gains on the battlefield, even as they sat at the table, sounded the death knell. Smith was still in power, the liberation fighters were still at war, and Kissinger's great post-Vietnam effort was down for the count.[52]

Still, the change in Washington from when the Nixon administration ascended to power in 1969 to when the Ford administration left the scene in 1977 was stark. In 1969, Nixon and Kissinger talked of southern Africa as a place where whites were "there to stay" and of Africans as "child-like" and "savages" to be dealt with. By 1977, the white regimes had collapsed in Angola and Mozambique, and the Ford administration was actively seeking to remove the white regime in Rhodesia, with an eye toward doing the same in Namibia. And, unmistakably, it was those unwilling to remain quietly under white rule on "the periphery" who forced these changes in the ongoing transformation of a continent.[53]

"Burning Problems"

As the Ford administration initiatives stalled out, the domestic upheavals in America saw Ford voted out of office and the White House welcoming its third occupant in less than thirty months. As the Jimmy Carter presidency embarked, the calculating realpolitik of the Nixon years seemed ready to give way to an agenda defined more by ideals and rights. Relations with African nations, and particularly dealings with the diminishing white redoubt, seemed likely places for a bracing wind of change in the U.S. approach to white minority rule. "At the beginning of my Administration," Carter would write to South African prime minister P. W. Botha, "I decided that the United States would make a major diplomatic effort to resolve peacefully two burning problems—the Middle East conflict and the mounting violence in southern Africa."[54] As time has passed, Carter is understandably remembered for his Middle East breakthroughs and the Camp David accords. Yet his efforts in southern Africa played their own meaningful role in moving U.S. policy toward greater alignment with liberation struggles when his administration could have easily hewed a line that favored continuing white control in Rhodesia.

As Carter entered the White House, he initiated a full-scale review of policy toward Rhodesia, South Africa, and Namibia. The highest officials, including Vice President Walter Mondale, Secretary of State Cyrus Vance, National Security Adviser Zbigniew Brzezinski, and Ambassador to the UN Andrew Young all engaged actively with seeking to end white supremacy in southern Africa. For the first U.S. president from the Deep South since before the Civil War, doing so held special meaning. Asked by historian Nancy Mitchell why he was able to view insurgents in Rhodesia as freedom fighters rather than terrorists, Carter replied, "I felt a sense of responsibility and some degree of guilt that we had spent an entire century after the Civil War still persecuting blacks and to me the situation in Africa was inseparable from the fact of deprivation or persecution or oppression of Black people in the South."[55]

This was a significant shift, one brought by conviction rather than crisis, and Jimmy Carter soon received his South African George Wallace moment. From the outset, Carter's change in tone and policy was felt in South Africa, and Vorster quickly decried the change with a private letter plaintively opening, "Why must we confront one another, why must we quarrel with each other?" He sought a high-level meeting, which came in May when Vice President Mondale met with top South Africans in Vienna. The meetings went poorly and ended with a bitter divide between Mondale's position of "one man, one vote" and South African foreign minister Pik Botha's rejoinder: "We shall not accept [one man one vote]. Not now, not ever, never ever."[56]

A few weeks into the Carter presidency, the National Security Council held a meeting devoted to southern Africa. At the end, Carter "concluded that the central focus of U.S. policy toward South Africa would be to promote a gradual transformation of South African society." This was a front-burner concern for this administration. National Security Adviser Brzezinski shortly thereafter provided Carter with a set of "Ten Central Objectives" for the next four years that embedded dual hopes: "To set in motion a progressive and peaceful transformation of South Africa towards a biracial democracy and to forge . . . a coalition of moderate black African leaders in order to stem continental radicalization and to eliminate the Soviet-Cuban presence from the continent." Brzezinski elaborated on three specific areas: "(1) Promote transition to majority rule in Zambabwe [*sic*]; (2) Promote independence for Namibia under Majority Rule; (3) Set in motion substantial domestic change in South Africa." Each objective had specific markers and timetables, including keeping up a broad range of pressure "so that by 1980 there is a marked progress in dismantling apartheid, creating equal economic opportunity, development of a fair electoral system, and abandonment or radical restructuring of the homelands concept." If by 1978–79 there was "no clear indication of progress in the areas listed above," Brzezinski argued that it would then be time to "deploy [a] full range of economic sanctions against RSA [Republic of South Africa]." Comprehensive economic sanctions touted by one of the most powerful members of any administration was relatively uncharted territory.[57]

Brzezinski's approach was a potentially defining step against white supremacy in Africa: deploying a full range of economic sanctions within two years, if need be. But as had been the case throughout Africa's decolonization, when Washington considered Africa, following clear democratic principles frequently became muddied and hedged. Brzezinski noted that complicating regional factors meant that "if possible, . . . [economic sanctions] should be delayed until the Zimbabwe and Namibia situation are settled."[58]

Then, in September 1977, events in South Africa once again brought worldwide attention—and the Carter administration to its first crossroads. Just over a year prior, the killings in Soweto had led to further repression, with more dead, more wounded, and twenty-four hundred Africans arrested and detained between June 1976 and September 1977.[59] Now just eight months into his presidency, Carter learned that Stephen Biko had been taken into South African custody. With the widespread imprisonment or exile of anti-apartheid South African leaders after Sharpeville, Biko, representing a younger generation of leaders, had emerged as the most visible activist in

South Africa. His Black Consciousness Movement energized younger South Africans and helped inform the student protests in Soweto and elsewhere. Banning orders against Biko had not dampened the spread of his influence or indeed the seething discontent in South Africa.

Taken into custody, Biko was held in detention, naked and in leg irons, purportedly so he would not hang himself with his own clothes. His jailers beat him with ferocity, after which they transported him seven hundred miles from Port Elizabeth to Pretoria—still naked, horrifically injured, and in the back of a truck. The next day, 12 September 1977, he died in police detention. Two weeks later, the U.S. ambassador joined fifteen thousand mourners at his funeral.

As happened after the Sharpeville massacre, the South African government chose not to reconsider its policies but instead to clamp down harder. On Black Wednesday in mid-October, more organizations were banned, two newspapers were shut down, and scores of activists were arrested or banned. Yet anger and unrest mounted. Over the next four months, some 575 people were killed, including at least 134 under the age of eighteen. Opposition to apartheid could not be stamped out.[60]

The circumstances surrounding Biko's murder and the subsequent brutal and extensive clampdown added to the already long list of South African violations of human rights, and pushed the Carter administration to at long last put U.S. support behind a mandatory UN arms embargo against South Africa. The United States also banned gray area sales and withdrew a U.S. naval attaché. In some ways, support for the UN action held more symbolism than substance, as the United States, like most countries, had already ended arms shipments to South Africa. Yet the moment held larger significance: it was the first time the UN had approved a mandatory arms embargo against South Africa and only the second time ever, after the previously taken action against Rhodesia.

However, when African nations sought stronger measures—at the UN, additional steps to impose economic sanctions; at the OAU, a call for armed struggle in South Africa—Washington worked against both. The Carter administration was not the Nixon administration, yet Cold War concerns, other regional objectives, and economic interests still worked against adopting more human-rights and majority-rule-oriented approaches. Long-standing European allies shared some of the same concerns, and they also opposed mandatory economic sanctions. As had been the case for forty years, the preferences of these European allies typically carried more weight than did those of African allies.[61]

For any number of people, particularly in liberal and civil rights communities, Biko's murder and the repression that followed provided still more evidence—as if more were needed—that the United States needed to take stronger measures. A year earlier, members of the Congressional Black Caucus (CBC), including Andrew Young, had convened the Black Leadership Conference on Southern Africa, bringing together 120 leaders from government and labor, business, civil rights, religious, and community organizations including the NAACP, the National Council of Negro Women, People United to Save Humanity, and the African Heritage Studies Association. The conference's "African-American Manifesto on Southern Africa" provided another strong expression of the connections across the Atlantic. "We, the descendants of Africa, meeting in Washington, D.C., on this 200th anniversary of the first modern war for independence, proclaim our unswerving commitment to immediate self-determination and majority rule in Southern Africa. We do this because we are African-Americans, and because we know that the destiny of blacks in America and blacks in Africa is inextricably intertwined, since racism and other forms of oppression respect no territories or boundaries."[62]

Decrying the root causes for strife in Namibia, South Africa, and Zimbabwe (the term used throughout the manifesto), participants called out the economic exploitation, the "despotism and racism that serve to polarize the white government and the African majority," and the "violence by the Europeans to sustain institutions of racism and exploitation." They issued an eleven-point program for change, with measures that ranged from action at the UN to military assistance for liberation movements should current negotiations be unacceptable to African leaders and peoples. The manifesto condemned the government in Pretoria for "crimes against humanity," citing its "wanton killing of hundreds of African youthful demonstrators and its wholesale detention without legal redress of Africans and their allies." It demanded that South Africa release political prisoners and begin negotiations with Black leaders.[63]

As Washington and America grappled over the decades with how to handle the fight for majority rule in Africa, voices in America time and again offered approaches that would align America more firmly behind African aspirations. Conference participants declared their total support for "the liberation of Southern Africa from white minority rule by means of armed struggle, where necessary, and affirm the right of the African liberation movements to seek necessary assistance from whatever sources available to achieve self-determination and majority rule." Members of Congress, other elected officials, and representatives of wide-ranging groups committed themselves to support armed struggle against white minority governments and, notwithstanding the Cold War, accept support for that struggle from any source. For them, the fight against white supremacy meant more than Cold War considerations.[64]

These voices argued that there was another path that better aligned with America's ideals. Their defiance of past Cold War framing of priorities embodied a progressive spirit that worked hand in glove with America's national interests, argued those attending the conference. "The policies we have recommended are not only morally just, they are in America's best interests. Africa's economic and strategic importance to the United States in an increasingly interdependent world must be fully recognized." U.S. support for the white minority regimes in Africa necessarily worked against that interest.[65]

Conference organizers hoped a mobilized Black America could help press for more change. The gains of the civil rights struggle in America, and most particularly the Voting Rights Act of 1965, had helped bring more African American politicians to the local and national stages. The CBC continued its advocacy for greater economic and diplomatic sanctions, and it expected more out of the Carter administration. With Biko murdered by South African authorities, Pretoria brutally repressing resistance to apartheid, and the Afro-Asian group pressing for greater action at the UN, the new administration was at a critical juncture. The CBC questioned whether it would rise to the moment.

The CBC demanded a meeting, and Carter's people anticipated that the most elemental question would be asked: Why has the administration made such a limited response? With little basis on which to claim that it had made strides, the administration attempted to change the framing, calling theirs a "measured response" and arguing that a fuller response would leave less range of action if future events in South Africa, Rhodesia, or Namibia warranted it. The logic that doing less now meant more *might* be done later offered cold comfort to those who sought action in the fight against global white supremacy and for democratic majority rule.[66]

The CBC pressed Carter to consider a number of possible measures, including economic sanctions, downgrading the U.S. mission to South Africa, and ending nuclear cooperation. While the Carter administration supported UN Security Council Resolution 418 imposing a mandatory arms embargo on South Africa, it worked against resolutions that imposed comprehensive mandatory sanctions in economic, commercial, and nuclear fields. "We cannot support the resolution calling for an end to economic cooperation," Brzezinski told the CBC, "because it requests the Security Council to consider mandatory economic sanctions against South Africa. We are opposed to the use of mandatory trade sanctions as a political instrument except in the most exceptional circumstances." The earlier Brzezinski, who had put forward metrics and timelines for progress that, if not met, would trigger the deployment of mandatory sanctions, was nowhere to be found.[67]

Human Rights and Economic Sanctions

On the campaign trail, Carter had repeatedly highlighted the need for resolution in southern Africa, "with an understanding that there would be no yielding on our part on the issue of human rights and majority rule."[68] His campaign position paper on policy in Africa was similarly explicit: "The United States should move immediately toward using leverage on South Africa to encourage the independence of Namibia and the beginning of majority rule in Rhodesia."[69]

Less clear was the use of economic sanctions. During the campaign he spoke both ways on the issue. One time he took the position that "the economic dependence of South Africa on the United States is such that an aggressive diplomacy need not include economic sanctions," yet another time he told the Black press that he could not foresee sending military assistance to those fighting for majority rule because there were many other options at hand: public forums such as the UN, influence through business interests, the arousal of public opinion, and "the universal insistence on human rights and economic sanctions, if necessary, to expedite the purposes that we have espoused."[70]

Standing before the nation on his inauguration day, Carter proclaimed to all, "Because we are free, we can never be indifferent to the fate of freedom elsewhere. Our moral sense dictates a clear-cut preference for those societies which share with us an abiding respect for individual human rights." A few months later, Carter used his commencement address at the University of Notre Dame to offer a fuller vision of the role of human rights in his foreign policy. "Being confident of our future, we are now free of that inordinate fear of communism which once led us to embrace any dictator who joined us in that fear," Carter told his audience. "For too many years, we've been willing to adopt the flawed and erroneous principles and tactics of our adversaries, sometimes abandoning our own values for theirs. We've fought fire with fire, never thinking that fire is better quenched with water." Carter proposed bringing America "back to our own principles and values," and to that end he sketched the outlines of the fundamental premises on which he and his administration operated. "First, we have reaffirmed America's commitment to human rights as a fundamental tenet of our foreign policy. In ancestry, religion, color, place of origin, and cultural background, we Americans are as diverse a nation as the world has ever seen. No common mystique of blood or soil unites us. What draws us together, perhaps more than anything else, is a belief in human freedom." Notably, Carter added a less remarked upon disclaimer that day: "This does not mean that we can conduct our foreign policy by rigid moral maxims. We live in a world that is imperfect and which will always be imperfect."[71]

During his first months in office, Carter spoke more than any predecessor about human rights and their place in the U.S. engagement with the world. Yet this greater emphasis on human rights in U.S. policy came with the expansive qualifier that it need not be done rigidly. Given this elastic mix, how would Carter extend these tenets to southern Africa? Near the end of his address to the assembled graduates that day, he charted a course for the region, remarking that "the time has come for the principle of majority rule to be the basis for political order, recognizing that in a democratic system the rights of the minority must also be protected."[72]

The new administration put its weight behind quickly eliminating the Byrd Amendment. As the only country to actually pass a law to break sanctions, rescinding it held symbolic meaning that surpassed any economic dimension. Ambassador to the UN Andrew Young testified that "there is a sense in which the repeal of the Byrd Amendment is a kind of referendum on American racism." Carter himself phoned and pressed members of Congress. Just two months after taking office, Carter signed legislation repealing the Byrd Amendment, once again banning the importation of chrome from Rhodesia and bringing the United States back into compliance with UN sanctions.[73]

South Africa, however, posed difficult challenges. Despite the racial segregation and systemic economic inequality of apartheid, despite the arrests and bannings and repressive use of state power, despite the murder of political prisoners in jail and the shooting of children in the street, supporting human rights via economic sanctions was not so clear-cut for the White House. Early on, the Carter administration supported a UN resolution mandating an arms embargo of South Africa, and the question continually confronted Carter: Should further action be taken? For a president committed to support of human rights, should economic sanctions be applied to this Cold War ally?

Economic sanctions, used for years against Cuba, had supporters and detractors. But when it came to South Africa, just as had been true in previous administrations, sanctions found little support in the Carter White House. Carter and his advisers found any number of reasons not to press South Africa harder. Both Carter and Andrew Young, his most active adviser on southern Africa, had lived through the civil rights struggle in the American South. They came through the experience believing that cooperation could yield more results than confrontation, especially if business interests could be brought to bear to press for change. At an NSC meeting six weeks into his presidency, Carter told Young that he had been impressed by "the apparent concern that you have that we should not be too abusive to South Africa and that maybe there should be some means of accommodation." Carter directed Young "to evolve a position on South Africa which is correct but as easy on them as possible."[74]

The ongoing need for strategic minerals and other resources from South Africa also meant that, more than with Rhodesia, leverage was a two-way street. South Africa held much of the noncommunist world's reserves of chrome, manganese, and vanadium. In the view of C. Fred Bergsten, assistant secretary of the treasury, "The U.S. is more vulnerable to South African economic sanctions than South Africa is to U.S. action."[75] Further, not only was South Africa a long-standing source of nuclear material and cooperation, it also had reached—and possibly passed—the threshold of being a nuclear power. Signs that Pretoria, which had not signed the Non-Proliferation Treaty, had potentially tested a nuclear weapon in the Kalahari Desert could have led to worldwide economic sanctions. But the CIA and others warned that sanctions might further antagonize Pretoria, now possibly a nuclear state. Once again, hovering in the background was the concern that had influenced all previous administrations: that being too "aggressive" toward Pretoria would drive white South Africa to entrench in a "laager mentality." It now contributed to the Carter administration stepping lightly while seeking a carrot-and-stick approach that might be effective.[76]

Further mitigating against turning up the pressure on South Africa was the enduring hope that Vorster would help to convince Ian Smith to accept majority rule in Rhodesia. Even before entering office, Carter believed that Rhodesia was the area in the region most ripe for resolution, especially with the aid of the South Africans. Mixing the need for change in southern Africa with his rhetoric on human rights, Carter declared, "We should use South Africa's good offices in trying to resolve the Rhodesian question, which might be of a more crucial nature in achieving a majority rule, and overall, never forget that in Africa, in particular, we've got the overriding question of human rights which still has a long way to go."[77] When Mondale reported to Carter in May 1977 that Vorster might give some help with Namibia and "has agreed that in Zimbabwe the government would be based on majority rule," it was just as evident that "on change in South Africa itself, Vorster retained his own long-standing commitment to apartheid, insisted that blacks were a different kind of human beings, and was recalcitrant about changing the attitude or structure of the government." Faced with an ally with these retrogressive views, Carter hoped "that our quiet but persistent pressure along with [that of] other nations might force evolutionary changes in South Africa. They are not going to give up the white-controlled government, however."[78] And so the United States voted in the UN for the mandatory arms embargo but vetoed resolutions that would have imposed comprehensive mandatory sanctions on South Africa in economic and nuclear areas.

It was in this context that the Sullivan Principles appeared. A Baptist minister in Philadelphia, Leon Sullivan had promoted the use of "selective patronage" to support businesses that hired Black workers and to boycott those that failed to provide equal employment opportunity. In the 1970s, he expanded his empowerment and social justice efforts to Africa as well. The first African American member on the board of directors for a major U.S. corporation, in 1971 Sullivan joined the board of automotive giant General Motors. Sullivan used his role to persuade GM and other corporations toward greater activism and to adhere to a code of conduct for businesses operating in South Africa. Publicly announced on 1 April 1977, the Principles of Equal Rights commonly became known as the Sullivan Principles:

1. Nonsegregation of the races in all eating, comfort, and work facilities.
2. Equal and fair employment practices for all employees.
3. Equal pay for all employees doing equal or comparable work for the same period of time.
4. Initiation of and development of training programs that will prepare, in substantial numbers, blacks and other nonwhites for supervisory, administrative, clerical, and technical jobs.
5. Increasing the number of blacks and other nonwhites in management and supervisory positions.
6. Improving the quality of employees' lives outside the work environment in such areas as housing, transportation, schooling, recreation, and health facilities.

Twelve major corporations were charter signatories: 3M, American Cyanamid, Burroughs, Caltex, Citibank, Ford, General Motors, IBM, International Harvester, Mobil, Otis Elevator, and Union Carbide.[79]

For those hoping to promote change without resort to sanctions, these guiding principles provided an alternative, expected "moral economic engagement." From the outset, the Sullivan Principles had detractors who believed they were damaging and counterproductive because they provided only an illusion of change. As the scholar Francis Njubi Nesbitt points out, "South Africa had welcomed Sullivan's principles, which . . . posed little threat to the system of apartheid but could be used as leverage in international relations."[80] Journalist and anti-apartheid activist Donald Woods, best known for his work with Stephen Biko, testified before the U.S. Congress at the start of 1978 that "the argument that investments benefit blacks by giving them employment is rejected by all, I repeat all, of the most widely respected and representative black leaders since 1962."[81]

Carter and his people championed human rights, and soon after entering office the administration joined in support of the UN Security Council's mandatory arms embargo on South Africa. They had gone further in pressuring the South African regime than past administrations. Yet calculations of U.S. interests, and the perceived willingness of South Africa to help bring about majority rule elsewhere in the region, contributed to the administration's unwillingness to use economic sanctions against the world's most white supremacist regime. They saw in the Sullivan Principles an alternative path to support that they hoped might still prompt change.[82] The early rhetoric and intent of the Carter team had been to pursue color-blind democracy across southern Africa, and supporters of majority rule throughout the region had rallied to the hope that Carter would pursue change in deed. By late 1977, such hopes gave way to tempered expectations vis-à-vis South Africa as U.S. officials generally became less vocal about apartheid. Yet the Carter administration did support majority rule elsewhere in the region with meaningful concrete measures. In doing so, it promoted majority rule to a historically unprecedented degree in Washington.

"Who Has Been Strengthening Rhodesia for Twelve Years?"

By mid-1977, the two main Zimbabwean liberation groups—ZAPU led by Joshua Nkomo and ZANU headed by Robert Mugabe—had been pressured into forming an uneasy alliance known as the Patriotic Front (PF). Although tenuously allied by the common aim of ending white minority rule, the groups nonetheless nurtured deep and bitter differences. Their international supporters differed as well, with ZAPU backed by the Soviet Union and ZANU by China and Romania. Nkomo led the older of the two groups, having become involved in nationalist politics during the 1950s when his trade union work with the Railway African Workers Union led him into political activities and election as head of the local African National Congress. As he revitalized the organization and it grew in strength, the Rhodesian authorities banned it. Nkomo then became president of the successor organization the National Democratic Party, which authorities soon banned. Nkomo and other nationalists then formed ZAPU in late 1961, which within a few months authorities also banned. At this point, ZAPU established a headquarters in exile in Dar es Salaam. Differences of opinion developed by 1963, leading Ndabaningi Sithole, Herbert Chitepo, Edgar Tekere, and others to break away and form ZANU, with Robert Mugabe appointed secretary-general on the ZANU Central Committee. At the time, Mugabe was little known, but a skilled organizer who would prove to be a ruthless political infighter. Both liberation groups began training fighters for guerrilla warfare, and shortly after UDI, ZANU sent the first wave of insurgents into Rhodesia in April 1966.

By that time, the Smith regime had imprisoned many ZAPU and ZANU leaders, including Nkomo and Mugabe, both of whom spent a decade behind bars. During these years, Nkomo retained his leadership of ZAPU and his stature as founding elder of Zimbabwean nationalism; ZANU faced periodic internal divisions and leadership challenges, with Mugabe eventually emerging as the political leader of ZANU in the mid-1970s. Mugabe's ascension was not universally supported, and internal struggles continued. Even so, ZANU grew into the larger and more important of the groups, drawing support from the largest ethnic group in the country, the Shona, and finding a welcoming base of operations in Mozambique after its independence.[83]

By 1974, guerrilla warfare had increased significantly, with ZAPU units (the Zimbabwe People's Revolutionary Army) operating primarily in the northwest and ZANU units (the Zimbabwe African National Liberation Army) in the northeast. Salisbury was forced to double the intake of white draftees and, with the worldwide rise in oil prices, to ration fuel. By 1977, the combined ZANU and ZAPU forces fielded several thousand guerrilla fighters, and many more were in training. While not yet a severe military threat to the Smith government, pressure was mounting in the field as well as in international circles. By 1977–78, Salisbury's military budget was increased by 44 percent, compulsory military service was extended to two years, and the death toll had climbed into the thousands for Blacks and the hundreds for whites.[84]

The Carter administration pursued action from the outset. Internationally, it maintained regular contact with the Frontline States and other leading African states, such as Nigeria, trying to address their concerns regarding southern Africa. Carter had lots of ground to make up. When Samora Machel, who had refused even to meet with Kissinger, first met Carter, he let Carter know in no uncertain terms his view after years of struggle: "We see discrimination, hangings, and massacres every day in Zimbabwe, Namibia, and South Africa. . . . We must ask, where lies the responsibility for these conditions? Who has been strengthening Rhodesia for twelve years?" He then provided the answer: "The United States is deeply involved in economic investment in Southern Africa, which . . . leads to killing and humiliation. . . . With the consent of the United States, South Africa has acquired a nuclear capacity. . . . That is a crime, and why we think of North America when we think of imperialism, because North America has always been involved in unjust causes."[85]

Intent on changing perceptions and improving relations with countries throughout Africa, Carter became the first sitting U.S. president to make an official state trip to sub-Saharan Africa. (FDR traveled to Casablanca during World War II for wartime talks with Churchill, making brief stops in Gambia and Liberia.) Carter chose large and vital Nigeria for the trip. The president's remarks highlighted "the new spirit of United States involvement in Africa and, by extension, in the Third World."[86] A cornerstone of that involvement was the effort to bring majority rule to more, if not all, of southern Africa. Carter believed that change in Rhodesia would resolve one of decolonization's most intransigent problems and improve relations across the continent. Working with a broad range of stakeholders—the Frontline States, South Africa, the Smith government, the Patriotic Front, and the British—Carter consistently put the weight of his administration behind progress toward rule by the Black majority in Zimbabwe.[87]

On the other hand, having pushed through Congress the repeal of the Byrd Amendment, the administration faced howls of protest from Smith regime supporters, who saw the regime as a bulwark of white anticommunist rule.[88] Ronald Reagan had taken up the cause of supporting Smith and blaming the liberation struggle. "I'm sure an effort—a herculean effort—will be made to place the blame for the breakdown in negotiations on the Ian Smith regime; to charge that Rhodesia is balking at giving up white rule," Reagan declaimed after the collapse of the Geneva conference in early 1977. "That is not the case. The real struggle is between a Soviet backed black minority that wants to rule over a black majority." Reagan disparaged "self-anointed" nationalist leaders, claiming that they were not chosen by the "tribes of Rhodesia": "They are Robert Mugabe and a man named Nkomo. They have made it clear . . . their guerrilla troops supported by the Marxist dictator of Mozambique will fight on until there is a socialist government in Rhodesia."[89]

American supporters of Smith continued to minimize the illegal, racist basis of his regime, and the basic contradiction of its existence with democratic values and human rights. Instead, they highlighted his white Christian capitalist profile in a region where Cuban troops were ensconced and Soviets were making inroads. They did not accept the now decades-long argument that repressive white minority rule aided the very things that they decried: the spread of more radical action and openings for more communist inroads. But the Carter White House did see it that way, and it was reorienting policy toward the view that the white regimes were not bulwarks of stability and anticommunism but instead ripened conditions for instability and communism.

Faced with internal and external pressures but encouraged by words of support from Reagan and others, Smith embarked on a new gambit. In late 1977, he launched talks to find an "internal settlement" with Bishop Abel Muzorewa and Ndabaningi Sithole. Muzorewa had initially entered nationalist politics to oppose Smith's earlier efforts to arrange for a sham majority rule; Sithole was the past founder of ZANU, who had split with Mugabe two years earlier. Both men had studied in the United States before returning to their homeland. Smith's hope was that this "internal settlement" might co-opt support for the Patriotic Front, satisfy internal demands for majority rule, keep much power in the hands of the 4 percent white minority, and garner international recognition.[90]

Smith reached agreement on an "internal settlement" with Muzorewa, Sithole, and Chief Jeremiah Chirau in 1978. The agreement called for elections in early 1979, creating the distinct prospect of Black voters choosing a Black prime minister to head a country to be called Zimbabwe-Rhodesia. At the same time, it left power in the hands of whites until the elections; reserved twenty-eight of one hundred seats in Parliament for whites; provided measures to ensure white control over the police, judiciary, and defense for years to come; and denied the vote to any supporters of ZANU and ZAPU unless they renounced the armed struggle.[91]

The prospect of Black voters electing a Black prime minister brought more pressure on the Carter administration from conservatives in Congress. Senator Robert Dole (R-KS) called on Carter to give this path a chance, and Jesse Helms (R-NC) and S. I. Hayakawa (R-CA) led efforts to force Carter to lift U.S. sanctions on Rhodesia. They were joined by other senators, including Harry Byrd (I-VA), the original sponsor of the Byrd Amendment. In the words of NSC staffer and future U.S. secretary of state, Madeleine Albright, "Suspension of sanctions would be a godsend to the Internal Settlement regime, which is floundering badly and is rapidly coming to the conclusion that it will fail. . . . The Patriotic Front, on the other hand, would see suspension of sanctions as clear evidence that the United States was not to be trusted." Albright believed that ending sanctions would help Smith survive while inviting Patriotic Front forces to turn to the Cubans or Soviets for more support. Her boss Brzezinski, however, found good in the settlement, believing it would allow "moderate Africans [to] take over from Smith" and thereby provide an avenue to ward off communist designs on Rhodesia.[92]

In the wake of Salisbury's efforts to create the "internal settlement," American critics remained adamant that the United States take no measure that would afford Smith any legitimacy. Some of the activists who rallied Americans to the larger, global anti-apartheid movement in the 1980s were part of this earlier effort to bring majority rule to Zimbabwe. People and organizations that would soon become more familiar honed their skills in the fight to keep in place sanctions on Rhodesia. The Black Leadership Conference on Southern Africa, for example, having committed itself to "mobilizing black Americans and others of good will to formulate and support a progressive U.S. policy toward Africa," worked to build a new African American foreign policy advocacy organization, an heir to the Council on African Affairs of the 1940s and 1950s and the American Negro Leadership Conference on Africa of the 1960s.[93]

The initiative eventually took the form of TransAfrica under the leadership of Randall Robinson, who had led the student push for Harvard University to divest its holdings in Gulf Oil while in law school there and had subsequently served on the staffs of Congressmen William Clay and Charles Diggs. Mayor Richard Hatcher of Gary, Indiana, served as TransAfrica's first chairman of the board. Robinson helped create and then lead the effort to situate TransAfrica as a formidable organization to educate, lobby, mobilize, and act on behalf of a more progressive U.S. policy toward Africa and the African diaspora. In one of their first actions, TransAfrica leaders

Hatcher and Robinson wrote to President Carter opposing a visa for Ian Smith when his American supporters invited him to visit the United States: "By extending American hospitality to the current Rhodesian leadership, the Administration would devastate a fledgling constructive relationship between the United States and all of independent Africa by appearing to give at the very least a tacit endorsement to Mr. Smith's own legitimacy as well as to his plans for an internal settlement." TransAfrica wanted Carter to understand the domestic consequences: "A polarized nation can easily be anticipated. With near unanimity, black Americans would view such an action as a United States certification of Mr. Smith and his preference for de facto if not de jure white minority rule."[94]

Similar missives came from a range of Black Americans, including the National Conference of Black Lawyers, Atlanta mayor Maynard Jackson, and Carlton Goodlett of the National Black United Fund. On the streets of America, African Liberation Day rallies drawing thousands of participants reinforced such messages. As the CBC monitored the Rhodesian situation, it worried that Carter might backslide on maintaining pressure on Smith. The White House found itself on the defensive with the CBC, having to produce a fact sheet of all the good it was doing, both in America and in Africa.[95]

Indeed, the Carter administration faced a broad multiracial, progressive mix of elected officials and concerned citizens opposed the "internal settlement." One of the leading voices on the issue was Stephen Solarz (D-NY), chair of the House Subcommittee on Africa, who, along with a range of liberal organizations, continued to press for authentic majority rule. They wanted maximum pressure against Smith and his regime. When the State Department issued Smith a visa, allowing him to visit Washington—and Disneyland—the battle lines were drawn for the larger issue: What would Carter do after the "internal settlement" elections?

As elections loomed in April 1979, Black voters faced decidedly contrasting choices: state-controlled forces and the Muzorewa and Sithole groups insisted they participate; ZANU and ZAPU exhorted them to boycott the entire election. Something over 60 percent of eligible Black voters cast a ballot. Muzorewa's party won fifty-one of the one hundred seats, while Smith's party claimed all twenty-eight seats reserved for whites. The results—a majority of people voting, electing a Black prime minister who would lead a Parliament with a majority of Black members—heightened debates in Washington over whether to recognize the new government and the state of Zimbabwe-Rhodesia.

Patriotic Front leaders vowed to continue fighting, arguing that there could be no such thing as a free and fair election when 95 percent of the country was under martial law. The Frontline States decried the election as a sham. The OAU released a clear shot across the bow: "No true African can accept a government based on such a constitution. . . . The war will not stop until the black majority achieves real power in Zimbabwe." A letter organized by TransAfrica and signed by 185 Black leaders, ranging from singer and activist Harry Belafonte to members of Congress, argued, "No election setting aside 28 percent of the parliamentary seats for 4 percent of the population (whites) solely on the basis of race can be characterized as free elections."[96]

Carter then provided his strongest, and certainly his most critical, support for genuine majority rule. Carter's stance was all the more significant as the British government's position was less than entirely clear, with Margaret Thatcher, having just swept into power, still shaping her position. Carter faced enormous pressure from conservatives to lift sanctions. A Black prime minister was being sworn into office with a Black majority in Parliament, and Carter was legally required to end sanctions if he found the elections to be free and fair, and Zimbabwe-Rhodesia officials prepared to negotiate seriously about all relevant issues at an "all-party conference."

Carter's resolve was buttressed by the strong—although not necessarily more numerous—pro-sanction voices on Capitol Hill and across the country. An important ally continued to be Solarz, who fought a prolonged battle to prevent Congress from mandating the lifting of U.S. sanctions on Rhodesia. Outside the beltway, the White House identified a coalition of groups that supported holding the line on sanctions. These included labor and foreign policy organizations, as well as businesses that had investments in other parts of Africa and relied on good working relations. AFL-CIO president George Meany pointed out to Carter that the AFL-CIO had urged policies with "a single standard: what actions by the United States will effectively promote the prospects of democratic majority rule?" At its 1971 convention, the AFL-CIO had supported the embargo on Rhodesia; at its 1977 convention, the organization had called "upon the U.S. Government to place maximum political pressure on the governments of South Africa and Rhodesia to end the odious system of apartheid and immediately begin the process of transition to majority rule." Meany and the AFL-CIO believed the elections under the "internal settlement" were the beginning of progress toward democratic majority rule, but not enough progress to warrant lifting sanctions.[97]

Crucial to the pro-sanction coalition were Black leaders, organizations, and churches. African American support for continuing sanctions crossed party lines. Samuel C. Jackson, chair of the Council of 100, a national group of Black Republican businessmen, called the Senate vote urging Carter to lift sanctions a "grave mistake." "Aware that you normally consider the opinion of prominent Jewish organizations before adopting positions that affect Israel," the Council of 100 called on policymakers "to seek the opinion of the Black organizations and Black Republicans before adopting positions that affect the United States' relations with African countries." Jesse Jackson appealed to Carter's human rights principles: "You cannot afford to side with apartheid in southern Africa and maintain your human rights policy abroad and your moral authority in world opinion." Jackson pointed out the domestic cost Carter would suffer in terms of his support from African Americans, as well as the cost to relations with Black Africa. "Thus, we urge you, as quickly as possible, to stand up for justice in southern Africa."[98]

Frontline State leaders Kaunda and Nyerere were also critical in pressing leaders in Washington to be stronger advocates for majority rule. The cause was a matter of deep meaning for these leaders, whose nations, particularly Kaunda's, were making tremendous sacrifices. African leaders across the continent worked to keep the pressure on Carter and the British. Gathering in Liberia for its annual summit, the OAU declared that recognizing the Zimbabwe-Rhodesia and Muzorewa government would be "an act of war against the Frontline States" because it would open the door to Salisbury legally purchasing weapons. The OAU passed a resolution recognizing the Patriotic Front as the "sole, legitimate and authentic representative" of the people of Zimbabwe.[99]

Carter announced his decision: the elections fell short of the free and fair mark. "The actual voting in the April elections appears to have been administered in a reasonably fair way under the circumstances," Carter informed the nation. "But the elections were held under a constitution that was drafted by and then submitted only to the white minority, only 60 percent of whom themselves supported the new constitution. The Black citizens, who constitute 96 percent of the population of Zimbabwe-Rhodesia, never had a chance to consider nor to vote for or against the constitution under which the elections were held." Carter pointed to additional flaws: "The constitution preserves extraordinary power for the 4-percent white minority. It gives this small minority vastly disproportionate numbers of votes in the country's parliament. It gives this 4 percent continued control over the army, the police, the system of justice, and the civil service, and it also lets the 4-percent minority exercise a veto over any significant constitutional reform." U.S. sanctions would not be lifted.[100]

Acknowledging that he did not have majority support in the U.S. Senate and likely did not in the House either, Carter argued that beyond bedrock principles, lifting sanctions would violate international law, abrogate past agreements stretching back to the Johnson presidency, and damage relations with countries in southern Africa and beyond. In short, Carter maintained, it would not contribute to the interests of the United States or the people of Rhodesia-Zimbabwe. As such, "I intend to do everything I can within my power to prevail on this decision." Carter had made his case: "It is a matter of principle to me personally and to our country."[101]

For more than a generation of decision-making, when offered the perceived security of continuing white control, leaders in Washington had felt a gravitational pull to that pole. Here, clearly and unequivocally, Carter had gone the other way. In taking this action, historian Nancy Mitchell points out that Carter made a decision unique in America's Cold War: he treated left-wing liberation movements as freedom fighters, not as terrorists.[102] Carter's decision was not one lightly taken; the situation in southern Africa was no obscure foreign policy trifle. The broader American public had come to see African issues as more important. A Roper poll after the election of the Muzorewa government asked, "When it comes to looking out for American interests around the world, would you say that what happens in Rhodesia is very important to the United States, fairly important, not so important, or not important at all?" A majority 55 percent of respondents answered that the situation was very or fairly important; just 10 percent said it was not important at all.[103]

Carter's stance garnered wide appreciation among African leaders. "It is indeed a proud day to be US Ambassador in Mozambique," cabled Willard De Pree to Secretary of State Vance. De Pree later recalled seeing President Machel at a large diplomatic reception shortly after Carter's decision: "Machel walked diagonally across the open space, lined with foreign dignitaries and diplomats—and this was a time when Mozambique's relations with the United States were not considered good—and took me by the hand and walked me across the square and asked me to send a cable to President Carter congratulating him for his courageous decision not to lift the embargo."[104]

With resolve in the White House for full and complete self-determination, with international sanctions still in place, and with the Patriotic Front guerrillas still fighting in the field, the Muzorewa government struggled to gain international recognition. Senator Jesse Helms and like-minded supporters in the United States worked to force sanctions to be lifted, while Carter and allies fought to keep them in place. Although certainly not the only factor, U.S. commitment to majority rule and the end of white supremacy made a meaningful difference. The leaders of the Frontline States and a preponderance of Commonwealth leaders also worked to convince Thatcher not to toss in with the Muzorewa government and instead to pursue new elections under new conditions. And with Thatcher's support, British officials brought all the principal players to the same table in order to discuss a transition to an internationally recognized independence under majority rule.

The meeting came together in September 1979 at Lancaster House in London, and it lasted into December. The United States had no formal role, but it worked toward free elections and majority rule, and played a crucial role in helping the different sides come to agreement. When it looked as if the Patriotic Front might balk at certain conditions within the final framework, Carter acted on British requests to lift U.S. sanctions, asking for assurances that the road to free elections was in place and that lifting sanctions at this stage would help convince the Patriotic Front to sign. Five days later, the leaders did so. Ironically, the most recalcitrant person at the signing was Robert Mugabe, the man who would later be elected as the prime minister of an independent Zimbabwe. "The successful settlement of the Rhodesian problem was important not only because it satisfied the legitimate aspirations of the Zimbabwean people," Brzezinski wrote, wedding democratic ideals with Cold War concerns, "but because it foreclosed a major avenue for Soviet and Cuban meddling in southern Africa."[105]

With the accords signed, independence and majority rule came swiftly. For a brief period, Britain once again ruled the nation as a colony before the transfer of power to a newly elected government could take place. A week after the Lancaster House accords concluded, a cease-fire went into effect; within two months, elections were held; and on 4 March 1980, Mugabe and ZANU-PF won an outright majority in Parliament with over 60 percent of the vote. At the stroke of midnight on the morning of 18 April 1980, Britain's Prince Charles handed power over to Prime Minister Robert Mugabe. The red, white, and blue Union Jack was hauled down in Salisbury (which became Harare in 1982) to be replaced by the iconic Zimbabwe bird on a flag of red, black, yellow, green, and white. South Africa and Namibia, still controlled by Pretoria, were now the last citadels of white rule in Africa.[106]

6 Majority Rule, 1980–1994

> I'm sure [Desmond Tutu] is sincere in his belief that we should turn our back on S.A. & take actions such as sanctions to bring about a change in race relations. He is naïve. We've made considerable progress with quiet diplomacy . . . but there is still a long way to go. The Bishop seems unaware, even though he himself is Black, that part of the problem is tribal not racial. If apartheid ended now there still would be civil strife between the Black tribes.
>
> —Ronald Reagan, December 1984

> You hear people say sanctions don't work. That may be so. But if they don't work, why oppose them so vehemently? If they don't work, why did Margaret Thatcher apply them to Argentina during the Falkland war? Why did the United States apply them to Poland and to Nicaragua? . . . If sanctions are so ineffective, why does the United States still maintain a blockade of Cuba? Yet we have all this wonderful sophistry when it comes to South Africa. . . . Are you on the side of oppression or liberation?
>
> —Desmond Tutu, June 1986

In March 1965, shortly before the first major teach-in about the expanding war in Vietnam began, the American Committee on Africa hosted the first U.S. national meeting organized to discuss specifically American involvement in apartheid. By then, South Africa's National Party had worked relentlessly for over fifteen years to extend the systemic white supremacy of apartheid. All persons were forced to register into racial categories; racial segregation in public areas was required nationwide in schools, hospitals, trains, beaches, and on down the list; marriage between races was prohibited, as were sexual relations; Africans were forcibly relocated, often to impoverished "homelands." To enforce it all was a police state predicated on brutality, including the regular imprisonment, banning, and assassination of political foes. But resistance to apartheid and its architects was growing in size and scope throughout South Africa and the world.

Marking the fifth anniversary of the Sharpeville massacre, the thirty-seven national organizations that joined with ACOA for the National Conference on the South African Crisis and American Action rang the bell for immediate comprehensive economic sanctions. Knowing there would need to be an implementation period, ACOA also demanded specific stopgap measures, including discontinuing International Monetary Fund (IMF) and World Bank loans to South Africa. A delegation from the conference sought meetings at the White House; Lyndon Johnson's NSC staffers in turn worked to keep the anti-apartheid activists away. The NSC wanted no part in meeting with ACOA leaders such as George Houser ("a high pressure type") and Peter Weiss ("emotional, [a] zealot"). Like the antiwar protesters, these anti-apartheid activists would not find a wide-open door at 1600 Pennsylvania Avenue, though a delegation met with Secretary of State Rusk and National Security Adviser McGeorge Bundy.[1]

Twenty years later, an extraordinary transnational, multiracial, and multigenerational effort came together to help enact the Comprehensive Anti-Apartheid Act of 1986. With support from grassroots activists, including some of the original ACOA conference participants, the U.S. Congress overrode a veto by President Ronald Reagan—the only time during Reagan's presidency that Congress overrode his veto on a foreign policy matter. More than at any other point during the era of decolonization, this grassroots activism helped shape U.S. policy toward Africa in a direction determinedly in favor of Black liberation.

With the benefit of hindsight, the end of white minority rule in Namibia and South Africa may have seemed inevitable. Yet as the 1980s dawned, South Africa was in full control of Namibia as the liberation struggle continued; Nelson Mandela was locked away on Robben Island as the African National Congress languished in exile; and the repressive police state was clamped down as hard as ever. South Africa's ruling white minority saw itself as of Africa, while seeing themselves as superior to others in Africa. They were not going to decamp. Reagan was heading to the White House, and it seemed unclear, even unlikely, that the United States would assume much of a role in promoting change. International pressure had had little traction to date. Despite the daunting challenges, after over three hundred years of expansion and entrenchment the white redoubt in southern Africa would finally be forced to take its last ruling breath.

"Help Our Brothers in Namibia"

The victorious allies of World War I had stripped all African territories from German control and placed them under League of Nations mandates administered by Belgium, Britain, France, and South Africa.[2] A generation later, with the demise of the league and more years of destructive war, the mandates became part of the new United Nations trusteeship system except South Africa rejected the UN General Assembly recommendation and proposed instead to formally annex the vast expanse of South West Africa. The UN referred the case to the International Court of Justice (ICJ), which ruled that the UN held the supervisory functions of the League of Nations and that South Africa still had international obligations to it. In 1966, the UN General Assembly, determining that South Africa had not fulfilled its obligations, terminated the mandate and created the UN Council for South West Africa, soon to be renamed the Council for Namibia, to administer the territory until it achieved independence. In theory, the UN was directly responsible for overseeing the territory, a unique position for the UN. In reality, Pretoria refused to cede control, and it continued to administer the area, an expanse larger than Texas or Mozambique.[3]

Resistance in Namibia grew. Large-scale strikes and other oppositional actions undermined the credibility of local authorities who cooperated with South Africa and helped build support for the South West Africa People's Organization (SWAPO) and its longtime leader, Sam Nujoma. Nujoma had helped found the Ovamboland People's Organization (OPO) in the late 1950s, after his labor activism while working for the railroads led to his dismissal. In December 1959 the forced relocation of Africans from Windhoek's Old Location by South African officials, as they furthered apartheid where they could, had led to mass demonstrations. Presaging events three months later at Sharpeville, authorities fired on protestors, killing eleven and wounding over fifty more. Nujoma and other nationalists fled into exile, but not before broadening and changing the OPO name to SWAPO to appeal more broadly throughout the territory. In exile, Nujoma worked to rally international support, but failure to make progress in freeing the country from South African rule led to the decision by Nujoma and SWAPO to establish a military wing and, in 1966, to launch the armed struggle.[4]

Even so, Pretoria felt little threat from the liberation struggle, and with the UN unable to carry out its task, the Security Council took up the issue. In 1969, it affirmed the General Assembly's revocation of the mandate, described the presence of South Africa as illegal, and called on it to withdraw.

Refusing to do so and refusing to accept the June 1971 ICJ ruling that the mandate was legally terminated and South Africa should immediately withdraw, Pretoria worked to enact its own plans for the territory. Western powers did little more than ineffectually voice objections. Namibia was too far away, an arid land with too small a population, to hold significant meaning.[5]

Flouting the UN actions, Pretoria assembled a gathering in Windhoek's historic Turnhalle to create a constitution for a self-governing Namibia that would be friendly to white-ruled South Africa. Instead of promoting "separate development" and a homeland policy as in South Africa, Pretoria pivoted to Namibian self-rule on terms it would help construct. Representatives of various groups, vetted by Pretoria, joined with delegates from the National Party in September 1975. African delegates were dominated "by old-line tribal chiefs who usually have gone along with South African tutelage," according to CIA analysis.[6] SWAPO boycotted, and the Turnhalle Constitutional Conference with its "internal settlement" failed to change world opinion. The UN General Assembly condemned the convention and recognized SWAPO as "the sole and authentic representative of the Namibian people." Security Council Resolution 385 repeated the call for South Africa's withdrawal and UN-supervised elections. The United States voted for the resolution, yet Washington seemed generally willing to give Pretoria wide latitude to create a friendly government in Windhoek. Doing so helped secure Pretoria's support for resolving the situation in Rhodesia and aligned with the Ford administration's own desires for a "moderate" government in Namibia.[7]

Adding to the outrage of most UN member states was South Africa's incursion into Angola, which came at almost the very moment South Africa was packaging the Turnhalle conference as a solution to majority rule in Namibia. Threads connecting the ongoing conflict in Angola and the independence of Namibia would soon become more tightly woven. With Neto and the MPLA consolidating power in Luanda, SWAPO had a friendly regime just across the nearly nine-hundred-mile border. As Neto remarked shortly after taking control, "[We] will help our brothers in Namibia with all the means at our disposal. . . . The struggle is not over with the liberation of Angola."[8]

The Carter administration, coming into office with a priority of making progress on southern Africa, soon acted on Andrew Young's suggestion to form the Western members of the UN Security Council into a "Contact Group" to press South Africa to accept free elections and independence for

Namibia. The United States, Britain, France, West Germany, and Canada intended to use the UN resolution as the north star for Namibian independence; the problem was getting SWAPO and South Africa to agree to terms and details. Complicating the matter, the Turnhalle conference now announced its own scheme for independence for Namibia by year's end. Plans for the puppet regime threatened a sham "internal settlement" that met stiff resistance from Nujoma and SWAPO and their supporters. Spurred on by the deteriorating situation, the Contact Group presented its proposal: free elections open to all, supervised and controlled by the UN. The group reinforced to South African prime minister Vorster that the Turnhalle internal settlement "was unacceptable to the international community" and warned, "If South Africa did not agree to early negotiations for Namibian independence, the Western five would have to reconsider their previous positions in the Security Council." The threat held ominous overtones: accept, or the Western nations might no longer oppose mandatory UN economic sanctions against South Africa. The threat proved a powerful stick; on 25 April 1978, South Africa agreed to the plan.[9]

For those fighting for Namibia's liberation, there was plenty to dislike in the Contact Group's proposal, not least of which was allowing South Africa to control the economically vital Walvis Bay enclave and to maintain a strong presence in any transition period. The Western powers saw both as necessary concessions to finesse land mines that would immediately blow up the proposal. Continuing South African depredations in the region, however, further embittered opponents of the plan, particularly the May 1978 raid 150 miles into Angola that slaughtered hundreds of Namibian civilians at a refugee camp at Cassinga. Although Pretoria claimed the camp was a SWAPO military base, authoritative scholar Piero Gleijeses assesses that "all the evidence indicates that Cassinga was indeed a refugee camp, administered by SWAPO with the assistance of the United Nations and protected by a small SWAPO military force." Even in the face of the atrocity, the Contact Group and the Frontline State presidents desperately wanted resolution. Neto particularly hoped to reduce the military threat to Angola, while Nyerere sought to prevent escalating regional fighting in both Rhodesia and Namibia. The Frontline State presidents pressured Nujoma to swallow the bitter pill and sign on. Six weeks after Pretoria's announcement, SWAPO publicly declared that it also agreed to the plan.[10]

For a moment in mid-1978, the plan moved forward. The UN, with resolutions endorsing the Contact Group's work, started preparations for its role in supervising and monitoring a transition in Namibia. Progress seemed tangible. Yet while Nujoma and SWAPO were reluctant participants, the bigger sticking point—soon and not surprisingly—proved to be the South Africans. Unwilling to cede control, they wanted to at least be sure that their client party, the Democratic Turnhalle Alliance (DTA), would gain sufficient power in any election to give Pretoria unofficial sway over the region. Perhaps because they feared the DTA would not emerge as the dominant party, or perhaps because they never expected SWAPO to sign on, the South Africans ended their cooperation, citing disagreements over the details of the UN role.[11]

In late September 1978, Prime Minister Vorster went on television with two major announcements. First, South Africa was rejecting the Contact Group's plan for Namibia. Pretoria instead intended to proceed with the Turnhalle formulation, with elections by the end of November. Second, he would be resigning for "health reasons." He would move instead to the more ceremonial post of president.

Soon after Vorster's announcement, the actual reason for his resignation emerged: the long-running misappropriation of vast sums of government funds to support a secret propaganda war. International in scope, the scandal was soon dubbed "Muldergate," after the minister of information, Connie Mulder. For several years, top officials had been illegally siphoning government funds to support covert efforts to influence opinion about the apartheid government. They used the money to bribe journalists, buy and control media outlets (including trying to purchase the *Washington Star*), secretly fund a domestic newspaper—the *Citizen*—to counter the influential *Rand Daily Mail*, and create slush funds to shape newspaper opinions and influence government allies in the United States and Europe. The extensive illegal activities brought down several top South African officials along with the prime minister; they also revealed the lengths to which the Vorster government went to secure favorable opinion domestically, in the West generally, and in the halls of power in Washington.

The following week, the National Party elevated Defense Minister P. W. Botha to prime minister, and with him an even more hard-line approach. "South Africa intends in the future," the CIA analyzed, "to rely more on self-sufficiency than on international cooperation to solve its problems." The day after Botha ascended to prime minister, the Security Council adopted Resolution 435, endorsing UN plans for transition in Namibia and authorizing Secretary-General Kurt Waldheim to make necessary arrangements. Botha immediately and emphatically rejected it.[12]

The situation was collapsing; progress on first Rhodesia and now Namibia had stalled, and apartheid South Africa was turning more inflexible than ever. The Contact Group had threatened, at least implicitly, economic sanctions if discussions failed. Carter's National Security Council met to discuss the situation, and Vance warned that sanctions were necessary to create any meaningful change in South African positions. But Brzezinski, abandoning his past view that economic sanctions might be needed by 1978 or 1979, saw it differently. More importantly, so did Carter. The president summarized the steps he wanted taken, which amounted to keeping the South Africans engaged and not pushing them too hard.[13]

Global pressures and priorities left Carter willing to forgo actions over Namibia for progress elsewhere, namely on his higher priority Rhodesia. The presence of Cuban troops and Soviet activity in the region rendered Washington reluctant to push harder. Conflict between Ethiopia and Somalia in the Horn of Africa took on Cold War urgency and demanded attention.[14] Further, Carter worried that conservatives in Congress might unify against and block sanctions. The chair of the Senate Foreign Relations Committee, Frank Church (D-ID), predicted that Congress would "vote to roll back sanctions against South Africa within 6–9 months of the United States voting for them in the Security Council." Other members of the Contact Group were also not entirely keen on sanctions, and as the five members weighed in, the list of possible further sanctions became relatively narrow: restrictions on landing rights for South African civil aircraft and on South African access to export financing. It would add a bit more pressure but was well short of comprehensive sanctions.[15]

Carter and his people sought to salvage negotiations. When the "Western Five" foreign ministers went to seek solutions in Pretoria in October 1978, Carter entrusted Vance with a handwritten letter to Prime Minister Botha. Carter offered to receive Botha at the White House for discussions provided Pretoria pull back from its decision to follow the Turnhalle path and instead resume the path laid out in UN Security Council Resolution 435. But a White House visit was a tiny carrot without the big stick of more comprehensive economic sanctions. Botha and his government were unmoved. SWAPO, rejecting Pretoria's approach, called on the Security Council to pass mandatory sanctions, and the African states agreed. The United States and Western allies were holding an empty bag.[16]

Hopes for any breakthrough faded. Carter continued to press Botha to accept the UN's Namibia plan, urging him to consider how two years of "painstaking" negotiations had produced a plan that SWAPO accepted, that the Frontline States pledged to support, and that forced a guerrilla organization to test its strength at the ballot box. Carter dangled the possibility that "the positive experience of cooperation in solving the Namibian problem can create a new atmosphere in your country's relations with your neighbors and with the outside world, including the United States."[17] Yet Botha had little inducement to change the equation. The UN's effort to end South Africa's illegal rule over Namibia had stopped in its tracks. And then Zimbabwean independence itself produced a new threat for Pretoria: Mugabe's victory at the polls suggested, in very tangible terms, that SWAPO might win elections in Namibia.[18] While Zimbabwe could celebrate the coming of majority rule, SWAPO and Namibia struggled on, and the Cold War raged in southern Africa. Then onto the scene stepped an actor who had long viewed with sympathy the anticommunist regime ruling South Africa.

"The U.S. Should Recognize Transkei and Stop Acting Foolish"

On an October evening in 1971, the United Nations General Assembly voted to admit the delegation from the People's Republic of China and to remove the delegation from Taiwan. Supporters of the motion celebrated the outcome. Delegates from Tanzania even danced in the aisles. In California, however, Governor Ronald Reagan danced no jig. He telephoned the White House to vent his displeasure, but President Nixon had already gone to bed. After a night to sleep on it, Reagan still boiled about what he had seen and called Nixon again the next morning. "Last night, I tell you, to watch that thing on television as I did. . . . To see those, those monkeys from those African countries—damn them, they're still uncomfortable wearing shoes!" Nixon chuckled in sympathy. These fellow Californians shared a bond beyond a home state.[19]

Reagan evinced a sunny optimism and he valued personal relationships. In one of the more unexpected twists of his presidency, he struck a friendship with Mozambican president Samora Machel, an erstwhile Marxist liberation fighter with a degree from Moscow State University. Yet Reagan had also opposed the Civil Rights Act of 1964 and the Voting Rights Act of 1965. In his bid to secure the Republican Party presidential nomination in 1976, he supported a constitutional amendment to end busing, denounced affirmative action, and started his condemnation of "welfare queens." He also chose to launch his 1980 presidential bid speaking on "states' rights" in Neshoba County, Mississippi, not far from the site where three civil rights workers were killed while trying to register voters in one of the most notorious hate crimes of the 1960s.[20] Active in speaking on a range of national and international topics as he sought the presidency, Reagan shared his views on issues in Africa. During his radio addresses in the late 1970s, he spoke specifically and repeatedly on apartheid in South Africa, the struggles in Rhodesia and Namibia, and the conflicts in Angola and Mozambique. In these wide-ranging broadcasts, he expressed discomfort with the racial segregation of apartheid, but more pronounced was his strong anticommunism and sympathy for the situation of whites in Rhodesia and South Africa. His future policies and actions, such as constructive engagement and the vetoing of comprehensive economic sanctions, would build on these early views.

After Cuban troops and Soviet resources in Angola turned the tide in favor of the MPLA, Reagan spoke of the growing role of these communist states in southern Africa. "It is unrealistic for us to fail to recognize [that] the Soviet U[nion] has opened a new stage in it's [*sic*] campaign to achieve strategic dominance over Africa with all its mineral riches. Mozambique, a home base for the terrorists who slaughter innocent villagers in Rhodesia[,] has declared itself dedicated to the goal of becoming a Marxist, Leninist state. Angola's conquerors the M.P.L.A. is following suit bolstered by Castros [*sic*] thousands of mercenaries."[21] In Reagan's worldview, the Smith regime in Rhodesia was not motivated by holding on to white rule and privilege; it was holding out against terrorists and communists. "Ronald Reagan, a true proponent of democracy and individual liberty, was," gently recalled his former secretary of state George P. Shultz, "at the same time, disposed to give the benefit of the doubt to an anti-Communist leader, even if authoritarian and dictatorial."[22] And even if racist. In contrast to Carter, Reagan saw the forces of Joshua Nkomo and Robert Mugabe as "terrorists," a view in future years he extended to Nujoma and SWAPO in Namibia. On the other hand, Reagan, with his Cold War framing, saw the Contra forces in Nicaragua as "freedom fighters."[23]

Reagan opposed economic sanctions against South Africa, instead favoring investment by American companies to provide jobs and potentially elevate employment practices and pay. He asked whether "our own experience made us intolerant and quick to criticize—indeed to punish this other nation without trying to understand complexities we were never faced with?" The complexities, he believed, were such that if "the black majority came into power tomorrow, there could very easily be outright tribal war as each tribe refused to be ruled or dominated by one of the others." In short, whites needed to be in control to prevent a bloodbath.[24]

Reagan's view of potential tribal warfare mirrored that of National Party officials in Pretoria, as did his support for South Africa's effort to set up "independent homelands," such as Transkei and Bophuthatswana. South Africa's homeland policy and "separate development" made sense to Reagan, even as the world rejected it. When Pretoria created these nominally independent "Bantustans" in the mid-1970s as part of its effort to create a whites-only South Africa, no nation in the world recognized them as legal entities. Nevertheless, Reagan pilloried the United Nations for not recognizing Transkei despite having "happily accepted a number of puppets whose strings are tied to Moscow." He charged that the UN was not recognizing "independent" Transkei because "the new little Republic is pro-western & anti-communist, two characteristics the United Nations does not possess." Reagan concluded that "these may be reasons why Transkei can't get into the U.N. but they sound like good reasons why the U.S. should recognize Transkei and stop acting foolish."[25] When South African foreign minister Pik Botha went to Washington to meet with the new Reagan administration, he reported back home: "I believe that in the entire period since the Second World War, there has never been a United States government as well disposed towards us as the present government."[26]

Constructive Engagement

As the Reagan administration entered office, two defining features of the twentieth century—the ongoing Cold War and the ongoing struggle against white supremacy—remained deeply intertwined in southern Africa and would remain prominent throughout the administration. The Cold War was very hot in Africa, and the advancing global anti-apartheid movement caused some of the sharpest criticism and worst domestic defeats Reagan suffered. Nonetheless, major works on Reagan's presidency marginalize issues relating to Africa, reconsideration of which is overdue.[27]

With Reagan in office and sympathetic to the position of the white minority in South Africa, the administration prioritized Cold War concerns, economic investments, continuing trade, and advances elsewhere in the region, much as administrations had over the previous three decades. Yet now, despite the administration's best efforts, the democratic and human rights battle against the world's most notoriously racist practices increasingly came to define the U.S. relationship with South Africa. And anti-apartheid forces, from liberation fighters in South Africa to activists in the United States and the world, forced change in Washington.

Anti-apartheid activists in the United States worked to oppose actions aiding the apartheid regime, to educate public officials and private citizens, and to build a coalition that would help end white supremacy in South Africa. For many years, these anti-apartheid activists toiled in relative obscurity and with scant support. During the 1940s, 1950s, and 1960s, U.S.- based groups—such as the Council on African Affairs and the American Committee on Africa—labored to advocate stronger action against the apartheid regime. Dedicated anti-apartheid activists campaigned against loans to South Africa and opposed American corporations doing business there. A small but growing number of politicians, often African American, worked in Washington to make forceful opposition to white supremacy part of U.S. policy. While pressure elsewhere—most notably on the Carter administration to reject the "internal settlement" in Rhodesia—was a notable success, less progress had been made against apartheid South Africa. The shrinking white redoubt in southern Africa offered some hope for activists, yet Pretoria was matching its increasing isolation with ruthless crackdowns on domestic dissent. And anti-apartheid activists seeking stronger measures from Washington faced an administration that viewed the global struggle against communism as its priority, a cause for which the administration seemed willing to give any anticommunist government—or insurgent force fighting a Marxist regime—the benefit of the doubt.

Shortly after taking office, constructive engagement became the Reagan administration's guiding policy for southern Africa. The approach was framed as one that would bring change through friendly persuasion and helpful support of a strategic ally, rather than through harsh condemnation and punitive sanctions. Chester Crocker, the new assistant secretary of state for African affairs, had first written of this in his 1980 *Foreign Affairs* article "South Africa: Strategy for Change." The policy rested on a generous and unfounded premise that the Botha government in Pretoria could and would act as an agent of racial reform and progress. Quite consequentially, the approach sought as well to resolve regional issues by linking the independence of Namibia with the withdrawal of Cuban troops from Angola. Resolution of regional impasses, Crocker posited, were necessary to achieve change in South Africa.[28]

It is worth pausing to note that at the time, people in the United States generally viewed apartheid as wrongheaded but held widely differing views on what to do about it. The Reagan administration's approach had support well beyond his conservative base. "Mr. Reagan is under no obligation to have black Africans write his South Africa policy for him," editorialized the

Washington Post a few weeks after his inauguration. "He does not have to contribute, from his side, as Jimmy Carter seemed to from his, to the debilitating notion that the United States must choose between black and white in Africa. A respect for efforts at peaceful change within South Africa could have a positive fallout here as well as there."[29] When the Reagan administration announced the policy of constructive engagement in May 1981, the *Post* opined, "The new policy sounds good."[30]

Against these headwinds, anti-apartheid activists sought to change U.S. policy and to transform South Africa. The grassroots transnational movement connected people from around the globe, ratcheting ever higher the pressure to end segregation and white supremacy in South Africa. Across America, individuals came to the issue with various motivations: appalled by the violence of apartheid, troubled at the blatant legalized segregation that the United States itself had rejected at home, committed to a belief that the fundamental values of America meant supporting democracy and majority rule. The reasons were multifaceted and individual. Unconvinced that the Reagan administration was on the correct path, a broad coalition of American people and their representatives in Congress built a growing and sustained movement toward stronger backing of stricter economic sanctions. The combined efforts of many organizations and activists—including the Congressional Black Caucus, ACOA, TransAfrica, and the Free South Africa Movement—elevated the fight against apartheid to one of the prominent issues in American life during the Reagan years.

Washington's stance became increasingly out of touch as opposition to the racist regime grew globally. When South African forces moved deep into Angolan territory in mid-1981, killing hundreds of people, the Reagan administration vetoed a UN Security Council resolution condemning South Africa for the invasion. A year later, the administration supported approval of the largest loan to South Africa in its history, over $1 billion from the IMF. In some respects, these actions were in line with past efforts in Washington to protect the relationship with the white regime in South Africa, but at a time when an active and growing global anti-apartheid coalition was rising, U.S. policy grew more isolated. Washington seemed more nakedly aligned with white minority rule than with the Black majority. Ongoing uprisings in South African townships continued to keep the racist brutality of apartheid in plain view as the world watched violent images of armed police attacking unarmed protesters.[31]

A rising tide of anger across the United States reflected a deepening conviction: years of the Sullivan Principles and constructive engagement were not working. By 1983, six years after the principles were announced, Leon Sullivan could point to a few important successes, yet there was diminishing support for the approach in the business community itself. By 1982, metrics of progress showed that less than one-third of participating companies qualified as "making good progress." The number shrank the next year, and more companies declined to even submit reports.[32]

On the ground in South Africa, the government waged its merciless campaign to keep apartheid firmly entrenched. In the two years of 1983 and 1984, police arrested more than five hundred thousand Africans for pass law violations and continued forced removal of African families from "black spots" in white-designated areas. South African hospitals allowed blood drawn from those classified as white to be given to anyone, but refused to give blood drawn from Blacks to whites.[33] Extending beyond its borders, the regional power destabilized neighboring states to undermine their ability to support resistance in South Africa. In Mozambique, South Africa applied economic pressure and provided clandestine support for the depredations of the Mozambican National Resistance, which Ian Smith's Rhodesian government had created to destabilize Mozambique after independence.[34] And on it went.

For those opposed to apartheid's racism and the white minority's anti-democratic rule, the reelection of Reagan to a second term seemed to guarantee that the situation would continue. They feared that the majority in South Africa would continue to be brutally oppressed—stripped of their democratic and human rights—while the world's most powerful nation and putative leader of the free world would do little substantively to change the situation.

Just two weeks after Reagan's reelection, four African Americans walked into the South African embassy in Washington, D.C., for an appointment with Ambassador Bernardus Fourie: Professor Mary Frances Berry of the U.S. Civil Rights Commission; Professor Eleanor Holmes Norton, former chair of the Equal Employment Opportunity Commission (EEOC); Representative Walter Fauntroy, Washington, D.C.'s delegate in Congress; and Randall Robinson, president of TransAfrica. They had arrived to discuss United States–South African relations; they stayed to launch a sit-in protest. While the other three remained in the embassy, Norton went outside to brief the press and picketers about the protest action. The police were called, and after Fauntroy waived his congressional immunity, they arrested the activists. The Free South Africa Movement (FSAM) had begun. The movement spread rapidly, and within a week, protests at corporations and consulates reached twenty cities. In Washington, members of Congress, celebrities, and ordinary folk came to protest at the South African embassy. Many were arrested throughout the following days and weeks. Coretta Scott King was arrested for the first time in her life. So were her children. More than forty-five hundred people would be arrested in the next year. The fight in America against apartheid had entered a new, very public phase.[35]

"South Africa Is the Most Burning Issue of the Day"

During that fall of 1984, Reagan regularly evoked the image of a dewy, uncomplicated golden era in the "American Century," captured in the reelection ad "It's Morning in America Again." With an almost entirely monochromatic image of a white America, the thirty-second television spot mirrored the administration's policy toward the white government in South Africa. Constructive engagement harked back to 1950s officials discussing their middle path: continued support for white minority rule while speaking about change. As more and more diverse voices joined the world stage, ever sharper, stronger condemnation of apartheid joined with rising calls for action. But Reagan held firm to his conviction that constructive engagement would enable the United States to gently steer South Africa away from apartheid.

As scenes of horrific violence in South Africa played out on television screens around the world in late 1984 and early 1985, Reagan shared his priorities in a letter to Joan Joyce Sellers of Camarillo, California. Saying again that he found apartheid repugnant and that his administration was working quietly to persuade the South African government to improve the situation, he emphasized that he believed U.S. national security and economic interests were at issue. "You are right about the importance to us and the free world of South Africa as a trade partner. Indeed our own national security is at stake. I'm sure we can be of greater help to the disadvantaged blacks in South Africa by continuing our present policy than by taking to the streets in demonstrations." Reagan added, "We've had some real success." The formulation, that "U.S. national security" was at stake and administration policy had "some real success," indicated just how little further pressure there would be from the White House to end white supremacy in Africa's last holdout.[36]

Reagan's interactions with South African leaders at the time offer a telling window. With South African townships seething and with expressions of dissent being brutally suppressed, Bishop Desmond Tutu had become one of the leading anti-apartheid voices in South Africa. Unlike most South Africans, he was able to travel the world, a compelling speaker telling a very different story than that of the apartheid regime and its propaganda arms. In the fall of 1984, while spending three months in New York City as theologian-in-residence at the General Theological Seminary of the Episcopal Church, he learned that he would be South Africa's second recipient of the Nobel Peace Prize. Tutu's voice and stature, along with the pressure of the toxic situation in South Africa, pushed Reagan to meet with him. With FSAM protesters picketing outside the South African embassy, Reagan and Tutu sat down in the Oval Office. "Bishop Tutu of S. Africa came in," Reagan wrote in his diary of that cold December day in 1984:

> I'm sure he is sincere in his belief that we should turn our back on S.A. & take actions such as sanctions to bring about a change in race relations. He is naïve. We've made considerable progress with quiet diplomacy. There are S. Africans who want an end to Apartheid & I think they understand what we are doing. American owned firms in S.A. treat their employees as they would in Am[erica]. This has meant a tremendous improvement for thousands & thousands of S.A. Blacks. There have been other improvements but there is still a long way to go. The Bishop seems unaware, even though he himself is Black, that part of the problem is tribal not racial. If apartheid ended now there still would be civil strife between the Black tribes.[37]

To Reagan, Bishop Tutu, who had lived and struggled his entire life under pervasively oppressive white minority rule, was the naive opponent of apartheid. Considering Tutu "unaware," Reagan clung to enduring tropes about tribalism in Africa. In that spirit, he sympathized with what he perceived as a continuing and difficult role for the white minority regime. With little actual evidence but strong personal conviction, Reagan believed that white South Africans would see their way clear to ending apartheid; in the meantime, this goal and the lives of those oppressed would be advanced if American companies and the American government stayed constructively engaged.[38]

Reagan had never set foot on the African continent and had shown limited curiosity about it. His conviction that he understood the situation better than South Africa's own Nobel laureate might have been seen as breathtaking except that it reflected the attitudes of generations of Westerners, attitudes that many still held: that whites best understand how to improve life for Africans. This attitude was part and parcel of the comfort that Reagan had with a white, Christian, capitalist minority holding on to power in South Africa, even as he encouraged incremental change.

In a radio interview in August 1985, Reagan lauded progress in South Africa. "They have eliminated the segregation that we once had in our own country," Reagan said, evoking a sense that those in glass houses should not cast stones. He then created a fiction that in South Africa, "the type of thing where hotels and restaurants and places of entertainment and so forth were segregated—that has all been eliminated." Reagan later partially walked back his remarks, stating that he did not mean to give the impression that racial segregation had been totally eliminated but that there had been "great improvement." Yet Tutu was the one who was "naive" and "unaware."[39]

In contrast to Tutu, when Reagan met Chief Mangosuthu Buthelezi, head of the Zulu-based Inkatha Freedom Party, a staunch anticommunist, and a prominent critic of the ANC, Reagan believed he had found "a very impressive man—well educated & while dedicated to ending apartheid in S. Africa still is well balanced & knows it will take time. I'd quoted him in my own speeches before I ever met him." Reagan remained impressed as the two stayed in touch, some months later remarking, "At lunch I read a letter & speech sent to me by Buthelezi the Zulu Chief in S. Africa. Both were the most statesmanlike works I've seen in a long time. I've never heard nor read the case against sanctions expounded better. Geo. S[hultz] came by and I gave them to him to read. I wish everyone could see them." The words of someone who was anticommunist, pro-capitalist, antisanctions, and willing to work toward incremental change on white minority rule fit like a comfortable shirt.[40]

The Reagan administration's opposition to economic sanctions against South Africa was juxtaposed against its simultaneous support for economic sanctions against Cuba and Nicaragua. The administration argued that the average person in South Africa would suffer from sanctions and that constructive good would come through engaging the regime. At the same time, for Nicaragua and Cuba, the administration maintained that constructive change would only come through sanctioning these regimes, even if that meant that the average person would suffer. In the words of Bishop Tutu, "If [sanctions] don't work, why did Margaret Thatcher apply them to Argentina during the Falkland war? Why did the United States apply them to Poland and to Nicaragua? Why was President Reagan so annoyed that his European allies did not want to impose sanctions against Libya?" Emphasizing that he was unaware of any change that came to South Africa without pressure, Tutu argued sanctions were "the last nonviolent option left." He chastised the Reagan administration's 1980s version of the middle path, stating that there was no room for neutrality. He demarcated a clear binary choice: "Are you on the side of oppression or liberation? Are you on the side of death or of life? Are you on the side of goodness or of evil?"[41]

South Africa continued sliding further into confrontation and violence. Unrest spread through 1984 into 1985. Widening student boycotts of classes to protest expulsions of activist students and teachers coincided with massive rent boycotts and street demonstrations by impoverished township residents fighting back against increased rents. White-owned stores were boycotted. When elections for Indian and "Coloured" representatives in a new parliament took place, over two-thirds of eligible voters boycotted.[42] The government, as ever, cracked down, but the diffuseness of the protests and boycotts made it impossible to stamp them out. The apartheid regime had done its best to ban and destroy organizations like the ANC, but new ones such as the United Democratic Front (UDF) inevitably emerged. Even more, people were organizing themselves; there was no single leader to eliminate, no clear organization to disband. Seeking to divide and rule, the white regime fostered divisions and differences among Africans, trying to turn the oppressed against one another rather than the oppressor.[43]

Unable to establish control of the situation, in July 1985 Botha took the dramatic step of declaring a state of emergency in large portions of the country, bestowing vast powers on the police and military. The decree also immunized from civil or criminal proceedings any person acting in service to the state. Within four days, over six hundred people were detained. Twenty-five years after the Sharpeville massacre, the South African government was once again using extraordinary powers in service of white supremacy. In Washington, the National Security Council convened at the White House to discuss the situation. Briefing materials indicated that in the previous ten months, 460 Black South Africans had been killed, 350 at the hands of the police. The materials showed that South Africa had launched raids into neighboring countries in pursuit of its aggressive campaign to maintain white control, including the notorious assault on an alleged ANC safe house in Gaborone, Botswana, that killed a dozen people, most not involved with the ANC. At the White House, NSC members were concerned and wanted to promote peaceful change, yet the clearest resolve to come out of the meeting was to improve the public messaging of Reagan administration policy.[44]

But no amount of better messaging could tamp down growing public outrage. The brutal crackdowns, the raids into neighboring countries, and the declaration of a partial state of emergency all gave the lie to claims of meaningful progress. Lack of positive change in South Africa reinforced the view that U.S. policy was not only failing to improve conditions but also allowing white South Africa to hold on to power. P. W. Botha's belligerent and tone deaf "Rubicon" speech in August 1985 further angered those who opposed apartheid and decried Washington's lack of action.

As the debate over apartheid became a more potent political issue in the United States, focus centered on two longtime goals of anti-apartheid activists: (1) to press U.S. institutions to divest all holdings in companies with business in South Africa, and to convince American businesses to disinvest and withdraw from South Africa; and (2) to move the U.S. Congress to pass comprehensive economic sanctions against the apartheid state.

Divestment campaigns scored the earlier victories, growing in number and significance as a variety of universities, religious organizations, and foundations began to take steps. Stretching back to the 1970s, some low-stakes actions had been taken. Harvard and Yale, for example, sold off Morgan Guaranty stock after the bank announced it would be making direct loans to the South African government. The 1980s saw small steps turn into a mass movement. The state of Connecticut became a front-runner in using investments as a tool for change, passing legislation in 1982 to tie investment decisions to a high Sullivan Principles grade. While short of the sweeping divestment bill activists sought, it caught the attention of state and municipal officials around the country. These entities began adopting strategies that progressively moved from sale of specific stocks to sale of non-Sullivan-compliant stocks to broad divestment. Aided by evidence that divestment did not necessarily hurt, and in fact might help, an investment portfolio, more states and municipalities found themselves willing to consider the decision. The first full divestment of a state pension plan came in Massachusetts in early 1983, when the state legislature overrode the veto by Governor Edward King.[45]

Anti-apartheid activists persevered, grinding out small advances and counting individual victories. They worked hard to win over public opinion on the need for stronger action against apartheid. Jennifer Davis, working for ACOA, made the case in an op-ed in the *Washington Post* titled "Face It: The Sullivan Principles Haven't Worked": "What the state [South Africa] fears is not a code of conduct that makes it easier for foreign corporations to stay," she concluded, "but pressure on them to pull out."[46] By spring 1985, dozens of universities, religious denominations, and foundations were divesting. State legislatures were working on passing divestment legislation, pension funds began withdrawing investments from companies doing business in South Africa, and local municipalities did both. By fall 1986, 19 states, 68 cities, and 119 colleges and universities had some type of restrictions in place. The University of California had voted in July to sell $3.1 billion in stocks and bonds in twenty-nine companies with South African operations. A month later, California's Senate approved divestment of South African–related stock from all three of the state's major public pension plans, affecting more than $11 billion in securities. The pressure on corporations such as General Motors and IBM to quit South Africa grew more intense.[47]

As the battle progressed on multiple fronts, pressure also was increasing on Congress to act on an even bigger prize: comprehensive economic sanctions. The previous year, in June 1985, the House of Representatives had passed bipartisan legislation to increase sanctions on South Africa. The Senate passed a weaker version the next month. Anti-apartheid protests continued apace, with the ongoing violence in South Africa adding to the outrage. In a bid to take the wind out of the demonstrators' sails and forestall congressional action, the White House put together token measures for Reagan to sign as an executive order: banning sales of U.S. computers to South African government agencies, ending nuclear cooperation, banning imports of Krugerrands. Anti-apartheid activists dismissed Executive Order 12532 as embarrassingly limited, especially as the United States continued to veto comprehensive sanctions in the UN Security Council. The fight continued.[48]

Economic sanctions against South Africa soon reached a defining moment. Efforts by British prime minister Margaret Thatcher and her Commonwealth counterparts to seek solutions in South Africa had seemed to make some progress when, yet again, South African forces attacked alleged ANC bases in neighboring countries. Worldwide outrage and condemnation was immediate. The Reagan administration even expressed its displeasure. Calls for sanctions grew louder. At the same time, tensions within South Africa worsened, and with the tenth anniversary of the Soweto uprising approaching, Botha expanded the already sweeping state of emergency nationwide. Days later, the U.S. House of Representatives took bold action. During debate over a more moderate sanctions bill, sponsored by William Gray (D-PA), to prohibit new investments in South Africa, the House voted to substitute a far more sweeping bill by Ronald Dellums (D-CA). The Dellums bill called for a full trade embargo and the immediate, complete disinvestment of U.S. firms from South Africa. A thrilled Dellums was sure passage would be "a tremendous boost to the anti-apartheid movement in this country." He then added, "I'm still shocked that it happened."[49] As historian Benjamin Talton notes, at this moment, African Americans as a bloc "directly shaped U.S. foreign policy and the social and political narratives that influenced public opinion." The effort was making substantial difference across America and in the Capitol, where the matter moved swiftly to the Republican-controlled Senate.[50]

By this point the Reagan administration could not rely on the Senate, even though it was controlled by the president's own party. Reagan found himself increasingly isolated in his stance, yet as in the past, an archly conservative wing pressed to support white allies in Africa. "While President Botha is moving at a fast and furious pace to end the apartheid system," wrote the conservative weekly *Human Events*, "Mandela remains as adamant a revolutionary as ever. He's still a Marxist, still a man of violence, still a supporter of the communist-run ANC." The *National Review* underscored the same point shortly thereafter: "All the reforms the Botha government has introduced . . . [would] vanish entirely on the coming to power of Nelson Mandela." A group of conservative organizations once again coalesced under the banner of anticommunism to support continuing white rule, issuing an open letter to Reagan titled "Mr. President: Why Is Chester Crocker Trying to Sell 20 Million Black Africans into Communist Slavery?"[51]

These views had a strong ally in the Oval Office, yet his advisers offered Reagan competing perspectives about the path to follow. Secretary of State Shultz and Assistant Secretary Crocker argued that the United States should clearly express its hostility to apartheid and its abhorrence of Pretoria's behavior. They counseled a more moderate stance on sanctions, contending that hard resistance to sanctions unnecessarily exposed Reagan to being labeled a supporter of the white minority government in South Africa. From the other side, hard-line Reaganites, including CIA director William Casey, National Security Adviser John Poindexter, and White House communications director Patrick Buchanan, pushed Reagan to oppose sanctions to the fullest extent possible.[52]

Buchanan pressed the president to take to the airwaves, fearing that "where emotion and media momentum are against us, only presidential intervention can save the President's policy." Reagan would have to put his personal prestige on the line. Was it worth it? "South Africa is the most burning issue of the day," Buchanan argued to Reagan's chief of staff, Donald Regan. "Our people are bailing out left and right. If the President will not defend his policy, his subordinates cannot." Buchanan pressed for a speech that would make a powerful case against sanctions while aligning the president with those who sought to end apartheid "with all deliberate speed." Inside the White House, officials were using the same 1955 language that fed massive resistance to ending segregation in America to address white supremacy in Africa.[53]

With public pressure mounting, Reagan spoke to the nation on 22 July 1986. The battle among his advisers raged, up to the very delivery of the address. Where exactly would the president land on apartheid, sanctions, and the regime in Pretoria? Beginning on the safest of notes, he offered his noncontroversial view: "America's view of apartheid has been and remains clear. Apartheid is morally wrong and politically unacceptable. The United States cannot maintain cordial relations with a government whose power rests upon the denial of rights to a majority of its people based on race." Put that way, the case seemed straightforward: the United States stood for majority rule and against racism. It was political and moral. And yet, as Reagan continued, clarity disappeared. South Africa faced "calculated terror by elements of the African National Congress," intent on a campaign "to terrorize blacks into ending all racial cooperation and to polarize South Africa as prelude to a final, climactic struggle for power." Characterizing the situation in these stark terms, Reagan defended the South African government as having "a right and responsibility to maintain order in the face of terrorists." Once again—and in sharp contrast to Carter's framing of the situation in Zimbabwe a scant half dozen years earlier—those fighting white supremacy in South Africa were terrorists.[54]

In the face of overwhelming evidence to the contrary, Reagan insisted that "in recent years there's been a dramatic change" for the better in South Africa. He opposed sanctions. He suggested steps to take, such as the elimination of apartheid laws and the release of political prisoners, while offering no substantive proposals—carrots or sticks—to push the Botha government in that direction. Quite the opposite, Reagan urged the U.S. Congress and Western European nations "to resist this emotional clamor for punitive sanctions."[55]

In the end, Reagan's speech turned the situation upside down: he recognized that basic human and democratic rights were at stake but emphasized the need to respect the security of white people "in this country they love and have sacrificed so much to build." His words, more in stride with hardline white South Africa than with the rest of the world, thrilled his conservative advisers, demoralized the moderate voices, and utterly failed to stem the rising tide of support in the United States for comprehensive economic sanctions. Bishop Tutu found the speech "nauseating" and made his anger clear: Reagan "sits there, like the great, big white chief of old to tell us black people that we don't know what is good for us."[56]

Casting aside the customary and long-standing deference shown to presidents on foreign affairs, the Senate moved forward on the sanctions bill. Members of the Congressional Black Caucus understood that the Republican-controlled Senate was not inclined to go quite as far as the House bill, so they agreed to a somewhat less sweeping Senate version that prohibited new investment, banned imports of steel and other products, denied landing rights to South African Airways, and imposed restrictions on government and commercial ties.[57] Despite efforts by conservatives and old-time segregationists such as Jesse Helms and Strom Thurmond to block and filibuster, the Senate easily passed the legislation, imposing far-reaching economic sanctions on South Africa by a vote of 84 to 14. A full 75 percent of Republican Senators voted in favor. Rapid passage by the House of Representatives sent the legislation to Reagan's desk. He promptly vetoed it.

Reagan's veto was in vain: the House overrode it 313 to 83, the Senate 78 to 21. Deciding whether to override the veto of their own party's leader, more than half of the Republican Senators stayed the course. On October 2, 1986, the Comprehensive Anti-Apartheid Act (CAAA) became law. The CAAA required U.S. sanctions banning new investments and loans by U.S. businesses in South Africa, banning the importation of many South African goods, and ending direct flights between South Africa and the United States. The sanctions were to remain in place unless and until the South African government took a series of transformative steps: ending the state of emergency; releasing political prisoners, including Nelson Mandela; lifting bans on political parties; establishing a timetable for ending apartheid laws; and beginning negotiations toward majority rule. While not entirely "comprehensive," the impact was real and went beyond the sanctions alone. Within three weeks, both General Motors and IBM announced they were leaving South Africa.

It was the first time since Richard Nixon vetoed the War Powers Resolution in 1973 that a president faced such a resounding defeat on a foreign policy issue. In the words of Senator Richard Lugar (R-IN), "I would not have persisted in opposing the President if after all these conversations, debates, and statements I had developed reasonable confidence in his comprehension of what the South African situation was all about." Reagan seemed more out of touch with national and world opinion on this issue than perhaps any other, including the Iran-Contra affair.[58]

For forty years Washington had wanted to contain the march for self-determination, and struggled to support democratic principles in a decolonizing Africa, for the most part worried about what might happen if and when white authority ended. This time, a worldwide multiracial movement rallied to the issue, with those who lobbied and gathered for Africa—Black and white, young and old, grassroots and politically powerful—joining together to compel stronger U.S. action. This undaunted coalition of activists harnessed the effectiveness of people power in creating change in the world's most powerful nation. The stance against apartheid had become a measure of commitment to democratic human rights in Africa and, in many ways, in America too.

Resolving Namibia

Sanctions and boycotts were a means to the end goal: self-determination and majority rule in South Africa and Namibia. In the following months, trade sanctions, financial sanctions, measures to isolate, and corporate disinvestment from the United States, Europe, and much of the rest of the world took an increasing toll on South Africa's economy. Cultural and sporting boycotts inflicted further pain. So did ongoing military engagements, especially in Angola. And connected to all this was the struggle over Namibia.

Pretoria resisted fundamental change. Throughout southern Africa, the white minority regime sought to maintain political power and economic security by undermining, destabilizing, bullying, and bribing its neighbors in an effort to keep a cordon sanitaire around its borders. As nations gained independence, Pretoria made their efforts to secure better lives for their citizens and fellow Africans continually more challenging. Wanting no cross-border incursions from liberation fighters, Pretoria matched its domestic ruthlessness with a regional counterpart to weaken its neighbors. From its perspective, these borders included Namibia, and Pretoria engaged in a sustained effort to keep SWAPO at bay, including making SWAPO's refuge across the border in Angola as inhospitable as it could.

While continued white rule in South Africa garnered more world attention, the ongoing struggle for independence in Namibia presented an equally immediate issue for the Reagan administration. Its policy of constructive engagement, and its linkage of the situations in Angola and Namibia, meant the Reagan administration tied self-determination in Namibia to its own bête noire: the continuing presence of Cuban troops in Angola. Washington pushed forward the operating premise that South Africa would implement UN Security Council Resolution 435—which endorsed UN plans for transition to self-rule in Namibia—if and when Cuban troops departed Angola. Such a linkage "blurred the distinction between a legal act (Cuba's troops were in Angola at the express invitation of the government) and an illegal one (South Africa was occupying Namibia despite the express disapproval of the United Nations)."[59]

Reagan officials worked to convince Pretoria that the linkage served its interests by removing Cuban troops from Angola, sidelining a powerful communist military presence and minimizing support for SWAPO. Pretoria accepted the linkage with the stipulation that there would be no establishment of a Marxist regime in Windhoek, designed to elide any role for SWAPO or to push it from a Marxist orientation. The Reagan administration forged ahead with the linkage, the "sleight of hand," as Gleijeses points out, "shift[ing] the blame for the failure of South Africa to end its illegal occupation of Namibia onto the Cubans, who were legally helping the Angolans defend their country from the South Africans."[60]

Further complicating the picture was Washington's desire to provide military support to Jonas Savimbi and UNITA as part of its ongoing efforts to oust the MPLA from power in Angola. Providing support to Savimbi, however, required repeal of the Clark Amendment, which had banned covert or overt U.S. aid for antigovernment rebels in Angola. With strong Reagan administration lobbying, congressional repeal came in 1985; funds and weapons soon began flowing to Savimbi and UNITA. Washington was more intent on expelling Cuban troops and regime change in Angola than on removing South African forces and regime change in the illegally occupied nation of Namibia.[61]

In efforts echoing those a decade earlier, Pretoria still sought an internal resolution to its liking in Namibia, maneuvering behind the shield that linkage and constructive engagement provided. As he faced growing unrest at home, Botha flew to Windhoek in June 1985 to preside over the opening of the Transitional Government of National Unity, which did not include SWAPO or support from the international community. The Reagan administration did not support the move, yet took no steps beyond reiterating a commitment to linkage. Four years into the Reagan administration, Pretoria was still doing as it pleased in Namibia. Even close U.S. allies denounced the linkage policy as unacceptable in the context of the repressive white regime. The Canadian ambassador to the UN told the Security Council, "Linkage . . . has no warrant in international law, . . . is incompatible with Resolution 435 and . . . has been rejected by this Council. Perhaps worst of all, . . . [it] is totally unnecessary, is a deliberate obstacle and is the cause of grievous delay."[62]

The festering situation dragged on, with no side able to gain a decisive advantage. Then, seeking decisive victory, in August 1987 Angolan forces with Soviet support launched an offensive against UNITA to establish control over southern Angola. UNITA and its South African allies withstood the assault, then in counterattacks drove northward, threatening to crush Luanda's forces. The prospect of a catastrophic defeat—one that might even expose Angolan president José Eduardo dos Santos and his government to potential collapse—stared Luanda and its allies in the face. In Havana, Castro made his decision: send Cuban troops into the fray. From fighter pilots to tank commanders, he committed his best troops and equipment, "stripping Cuba's defences at home down to the bone." The Cuban forces repulsed the counteroffensive.[63]

Over the course of these months, the battle around Cuito Cuanavale became the largest conventional battle in Africa since World War II. South Africa's role was in such plain sight that it publicly stated its presence, helping provoke the UN Security Council to demand that Pretoria "withdraw all forces occupying Angolan territory." The United States voted in support, but privately Crocker reassured Pretoria that the reason the UN did not call for comprehensive sanctions or any assistance for Angola "was no accident, but a consequence of our own efforts to keep the resolution within bounds."[64]

The protection that the Reagan administration provided was one thing; Cuban resolve was another. Castro committed not only to blocking the UNITA and South African advance but also to launching an offensive toward the Namibian border. As events unfolded, Cuban forces flanked by SWAPO and Angolan units advanced toward the Namibian border in such strength that in time they posed a significant threat to Pretoria's grip on Namibia. Within the increasingly restive country, worker strikes and school boycotts spread. The drawn-out border war was imposing heavy costs on Pretoria, and the situation was becoming ever more tenuous.[65]

The costly fight to hold on to Namibia and the diminishing likelihood of a resolution on favorable terms was compounded by the reality that Pretoria would find no U.S. administration as friendly as Reagan's, which would be termed out of office in less than a year. Pretoria agreed to negotiations. On the other side of the table, Cuba seemed willing to continue its support of Luanda and the struggle in Namibia, but in order to keep absorbing significant costs, it needed material support from the Soviets. Moscow, struggling to maintain pace in the Cold War, was reassessing its commitments to Third World revolutions in light of the substantial financial and military outlays they required. The Angolan offensive itself had entailed nearly a billion dollars of equipment, along with extensive use of Soviet advisers. Mikhail Gorbachev sought to retrench, preferring to resolve far-flung conflicts in order to reduce external commitments and allow him to concentrate on domestic urgencies as the Soviet Union teetered on collapse.[66]

The Reagan administration previously had refused to accept Cuban participation in Namibian settlement talks. Faced now with Cuba's strength on the ground, with significant troop numbers advancing toward the Namibian border, and the White House roiled by the Iran-Contra debacle, strictures against Cuba's participation dissipated. Crocker embarked on a series of quadripartite negotiations involving Angola, South Africa, Cuba, and the United States, the high-stakes negotiations beginning with meetings in London in May 1988, followed by another round in Cairo in June.[67]

UN Security Council Resolution 435 still formed the foundational basis for the talks. A decade previously, details about implementing the resolution had been Pretoria's pretext for walking away. The prospect of SWAPO in power and Sam Nujoma as leader of an independent Namibia was too unpalatable. Realities on the ground had now changed precipitously, with Cuban-led advances in southwestern Angola bringing them, along with their SWAPO and FAPLA (People's Armed Forces for the Liberation of Angola) allies, to Namibia's doorstep. Other factors were shifting as well, with the Soviets turning away from southern Africa, and Angola modifying its Marxist-Leninist language and applying for membership in the World Bank. Paired with a Cuban departure from the region, UN supervised elections and Namibian independence seemed less disagreeable, even necessary.[68]

Just a month before the Reagan administration left office, the Angola-Namibia agreements were signed in New York on December 22, 1988. The accords stipulated the implementation of UN Resolution 435 leading to Namibian independence. South Africa agreed to withdraw its army from Namibia within three months and end its support for UNITA. The Cubans agreed to withdraw their troops from Angola, while Luanda committed to not allowing the armed wing of the ANC any bases in Angola. The degree to which the accord finally came about due to the policy of constructive engagement, the actions of Cuba and its troops, the uprisings in South Africa, the decline of Soviet strength and communist presence, changed strategic thinking in Pretoria, or the grinding economic damage inflicted by sanctions and disinvestment remains contested; what is clear is that at the end of the Reagan administration, the terms on which Namibia gained independence, and the ensuing political results of that independence, were little different from what was on the table when the administration took office. But much brutal violence and human cost had occurred in between, a reality driven in no small measure by the Reagan administration's determination to view the situation through a Cold War lens, linking resolution in Namibia to its view of the situation in Angola. In doing so, the administration struggled to move away from the pull of anticommunist, white minority rule toward the values enshrined in political freedom, self-determination, and majority rule.[69]

The culmination of a century-long struggle in Namibia helped usher in a series of momentous events across the globe in 1989, some more obvious at the time than others. In South Africa, F. W. de Klerk was elected as leader of the National Party in February and then in September as president of South Africa, replacing the hard-line P. W. Botha. In Europe, Gorbachev's glasnost and perestroika were contributing to rapid changes, not least of which was the unexpected and dramatic toppling of the Berlin Wall in November. And as much of the world focused on this signal event in Europe and the Cold War, on the very same day voters in Namibia—most for the first time in their lives—were going to the polls to vote. They handed SWAPO an overwhelming victory, with 57.3 percent of the popular vote, more than doubling the 28.6 percent for the Pretoria-friendly Democratic Turnhalle Alliance.[70]

1990s: Dawn of a New Era

At long last, on 21 March 1990 Namibia became the last nation in Africa to cast off the external rule of an imperial age. Its achievement ended an era that in parts of Africa extended back five hundred years but for much of the continent was concentrated in the long century from the Scramble for Africa to the independence of Namibia. As UN Secretary-General Javier Pérez de Cuéllar gave the oath of office to Sam Nujoma as president, an eclectic mix of political leaders were there to mark the moment, including U.S. secretary of state James Baker, Soviet foreign minister Eduard Shevardnadze, Cuban president Fidel Castro, and South African president F. W. de Klerk.[71]

Newly released political prisoner Nelson Mandela was there, too. White minority rule carried on in one last bastion, but the bricks on that edifice were falling. The ongoing resistance in South Africa was keeping an unceasing pressure on the government and on society. Namibian independence

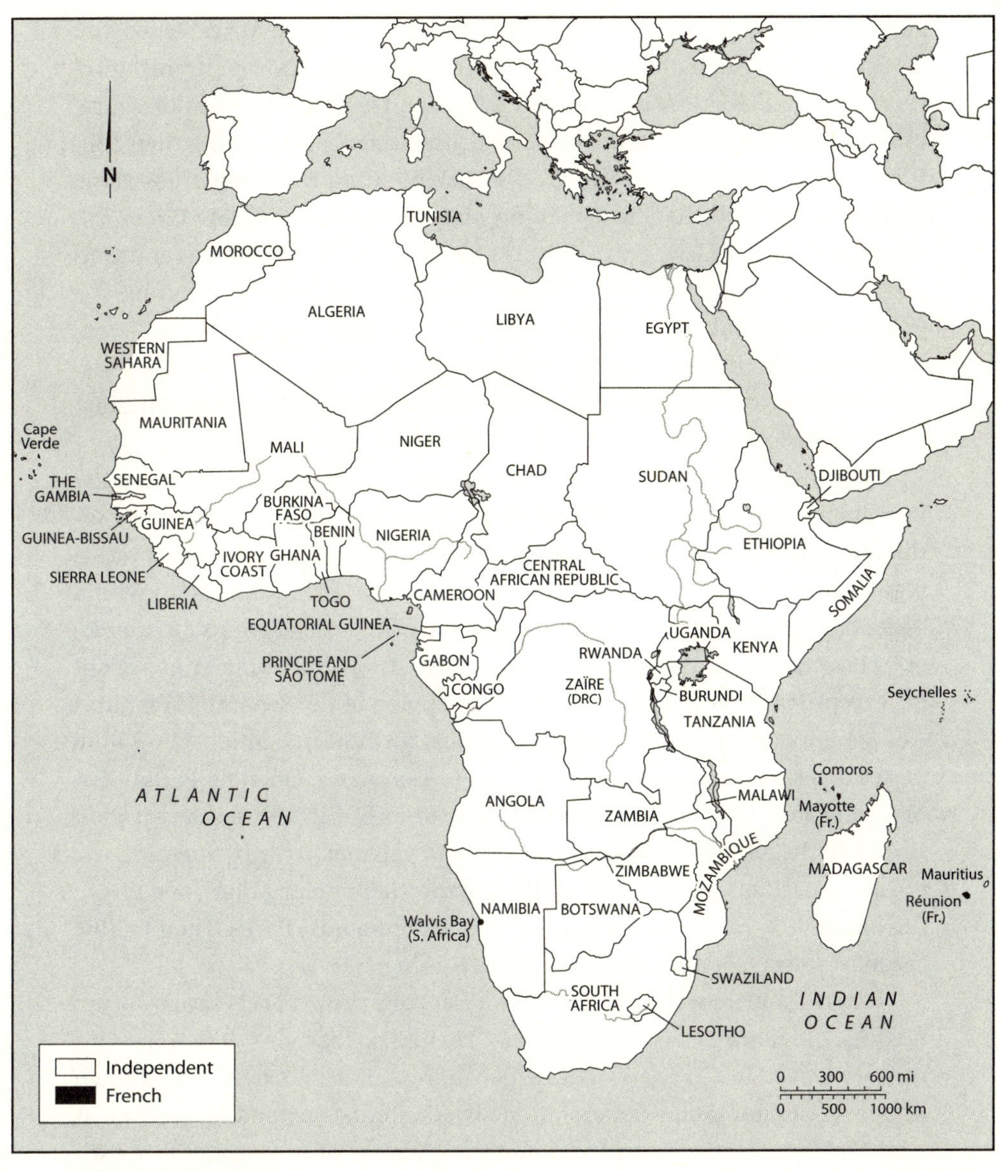

Africa, January 1991

also helped pave the way for dismantling apartheid in South Africa, especially as changes on the global stage rendered communism a rapidly receding threat to white South Africans.[72] Even further, tremendous world pressure, international sanctions, and business disinvestment were taking their toll. From January 1986 to April 1988, over one hundred U.S. companies alone pulled out of South Africa, including major firms such as Dow Chemical, Eastman Kodak, Exxon, Ford, General Electric, Goodyear, Merck, and Unisys.[73] By the end of the 1980s, these pressures had collectively caused a growing number of white South Africans to recognize that apartheid, "separate development," homelands, even white supremacy itself, were not sustainable. Economic, political, and social pressures, more than moral suasion, brought this reckoning.

There also needed to be change in the National Party leadership from the intractable "Great Crocodile" P. W. Botha. After suffering a mild stroke, Botha was slowly pushed from power. F. W. de Klerk, a seemingly conservative replacement, became president in 1989, and soon startled the nation with a series of reforms. Within weeks, he reined in police use of whips on protesters, permitted large outdoor protests, and released all Rivonia Trial prisoners except Mandela. He announced the scrapping of the Separate Amenities Act, which had segregated parks, benches, restaurants, and other public places. De Klerk then met with Mandela in December. Opening Parliament on 2 February 1990, de Klerk sketched a series of further measures, then turned to the most momentous: he was ending all media restrictions, removing all restrictions on the UDF and thirty-two other organizations, and lifting the ban on the ANC and the South African Communist Party. Then finally, the most seismic of all: he would release Prisoner 46664.

Nelson Mandela walked out of Victor Verster prison on 11 February 1990, holding the hand of his wife, Winnie. He had spent more than a quarter century locked behind bars, in time becoming the world's most well-known political prisoner. Four months after his release, he stepped off a plane at New York's Kennedy Airport and into the embrace of America. Police estimate that 750,000 people saw Mandela either during the ticker-tape parade through Manhattan or at the city hall rally that day. That night, the Empire State Building was lit in the ANC colors of black, green, and gold. A smattering of voices expressed displeasure at Mandela's refusal to disavow some of the figures who supported the ANC during the long struggle, including Yasser Arafat, Fidel Castro, and Muammar Gaddafi. But they were drowned out by those celebrating Mandela as he strode across the nation, lionized as a hero. Massive rallies and expensive fundraisers were held wherever he went, raising over $7 million for the continuing struggle against white supremacy in South Africa. Mandela visited President George H. W. Bush at the White House. He addressed a joint session of Congress, becoming the first Black man who was not a head of state to do so. Mandela was not merely a foreign dignitary—he had transcended that during his years behind bars—Mandela had become the noble embodiment of what human beings can overcome and become. He personified the historic Black struggle for liberation from white rule in Africa. No part of the nation rejoiced more than African Americans. To see Mandela walking in freedom, to be with him, was the living fulfillment of many dreams.

In his address to Congress, after thanking the assembled for the invitation, Mandela emphasized immediately what was at stake: "Our people demand democracy. Our country, which continues to bleed and suffer pain, needs democracy." Mandela evoked the ideals that the assemblage knew well yet too often had seen the nation struggle to achieve. And now this former political prisoner was reminding them of the role still to be played. To that end, Mandela called for sanctions to remain in place "because the purpose for which they were imposed has not yet been achieved." Ending, he invoked the continuing struggle that both nations had grappled with for hundreds of years. "Let us keep our arms locked together so that we form a solid phalanx against racism, to ensure that that day comes now. By our common actions, let us ensure that justice triumphs without delay." Democracy, justice, an end to racism. The struggle continued, in both nations.[74]

An epochal moment, but in itself Mandela's release did not end apartheid, let alone establish a multiracial system of one-person, one-vote majority rule. Mandela's emergence from prison is sometimes conflated in historical memory with the end of apartheid and the coming of majority rule, but more years of struggle and pain lay ahead. While some laws began to be repealed earlier, it would not be until February 1991 that de Klerk announced that all remaining apartheid laws would be struck down. Parliament repealed the Population Registration Act, the Group Areas Act, the Native Lands Act, the Native Trust and Land Act, and the Asiatic Land Tenure Act in the following months. The ANC came to an agreement with the de Klerk government to suspend the armed struggle. Finally, in late December 1991, nearly two years after Mandela's release, the ANC, the National Party, and sixteen other political organizations began the fraught, complicated work of drafting a new constitution.

In Washington, as these developments unspooled, President Bush indicated his intention to end all economic sanctions. He determined that the conditions laid down by the CAAA five years earlier had been met: ending the state of emergency; unbanning the ANC, PAC, and other liberation organizations; beginning negotiations with representatives of the Black majority; repealing apartheid laws; and releasing political prisoners. The ANC, however, remained firmly opposed to ending sanctions at this stage. There was still no fixed commitment to elections or to majority rule. The Congressional Black Caucus and others urged Bush to wait, arguing that the CAAA stipulations had not been fully met and, even if they had, that multiracial elections were the true measure. Nevertheless, the European Union had lifted sanctions, and on 10 July 1991, President Bush lifted U.S. economic sanctions on South Africa. With the federal government's ending of sanctions, state and local actors took a variety of paths: some lifted sanctions while others left theirs in place until the summer of 1993, when the ANC itself called for sanctions to end. At this stage, South Africa was heading toward multiracial elections, and the nation needed an economic boost.[75]

In April 1994, South Africans went to the polls, millions for the first time in their lives. Over the course of four days South African voters, often waiting hours just to cast a ballot, resoundingly elected Nelson Mandela as president, the nation's first leader chosen with universal suffrage. The last bastion of white minority rule was torn down, in the end, by citizens of all races, creeds, and colors armed with pieces of paper to put in a ballot box. It marked the historic end of an era, even as political, economic, social, and cultural legacies would continue to reverberate.

Four weeks later, on 10 May 1994, Mandela was sworn in. "Today, all of us do, by our presence here, and by our celebrations in other parts of our country and the world, confer glory and hope to newborn liberty," Mandela told the assembled guests and the world. "Our daily deeds as ordinary South Africans must produce an actual South African reality that will reinforce humanity's belief in justice, strengthen its confidence in the nobility of the human soul, and sustain all our hopes for a glorious life for all." Striking chords of reconciliation, he declared, "The time for the healing of the wounds has come. The moment to bridge the chasms that divide us has come. The time to build is upon us." With a final moment of grace, he then ended with a benediction: "Let freedom reign. The sun shall never set on so glorious a human achievement. Let freedom reign. God bless Africa!"[76]

Epilogue

Africa has this single aim: our goal is a united Africa in which the standards of life and liberty are constantly expanding; in which the ancient legacy of illiteracy and disease is swept aside; in which the dignity of man is rescued from beneath the heels of colonialism which have trampled it. This goal, pursued by millions of our people with revolutionary zeal, by means of books, representations, demonstrations, and in some places armed force provoked by the adamancy of white rule, carries the only real promise of peace in Africa.

—Albert Lutuli, 1961

Each time a man stands up for an ideal, or acts to improve the lot of others, or strikes out against injustice, he sends forth a tiny ripple of hope, and crossing each other from a million different centers of energy and daring those ripples build a current which can sweep down the mightiest walls of oppression and resistance.

—Robert F. Kennedy, June 1966

"Let freedom reign." Mandela evoked words spoken some thirty years earlier across the Atlantic by Martin Luther King Jr., another leader who at great cost had dedicated his life to defeating injustice. Throughout Africa, the effort to reclaim the land, end colonialism, and overturn white supremacy transformed the continent. African pursuit of "the dignity of man . . . rescued from beneath the heels of colonialism"—as Lutuli so elegantly put it as he accepted the Nobel Peace Prize—transformed modern world history during this remarkable half century. Yet as Africans embarked on independence, the hard, multifaceted work that Mandela pointed to still lay ahead. After generations of colonial rule, there was much that needed to be built. These new nations had achingly under-resourced national networks of political administration and economic integration in states grappling with boundaries by and large artificially constructed in European parlors. Business and trade often remained under control of Western companies. And legacies of reliance on systems of cash crops and mineral extraction left many new nations subject to the vagaries of global markets. People up and down Africa sought adequate living conditions, improved health care, increased access to education, and progress on a multitude of other social needs. A hard road lay ahead, and it was beset by people and governments still determined to exploit Africa's economic and cultural wealth for their own.

In many ways the postcolonial work of decolonization has extended beyond political transfers of power into realms of economic, social, and cultural change. After centuries of white supremacy and the imposition of Eurocentric views, the reckoning continues to unfold. Overturning long-standing hierarchies and intellectual, social, and cultural ways is an ongoing process, one often resisted. And just as international coalitions resisted ending white rule in Africa, transnational networks still seek to keep hierarchical racial structures that perpetuate inequities and their consequences.

As the great continent of Africa fought to decolonize and end white minority rule, the United States struggled over how to support that effort. For a nation born in its own anticolonial struggle, conceived in liberty, and dedicated to the proposition that all men are created equal, supporting African self-determination and majority rule could have been a straightforward proposition. But for generation upon generation, as America has engaged with Africa it has struggled to define the relationship in terms that matched its national ideals. The consequences of U.S. policy—which prioritized Cold War concerns, European alliances, and economic interests—made it a harder road to freedom and more difficult to overcome the resistance to treating Africans and those of the global diaspora as equal partners.

The hard work continues, in both Africa and America, in ways big and small. A dozen years after Mandela's election as president of South Africa, U.S. secretary of state Condoleezza Rice strode up Capitol Hill to testify before Congress. "This is a country with which we now have excellent relations, South Africa," Rice pointed out in April 2008, "but it's frankly a rather embarrassing matter that I still have to waive in my own counterpart, the foreign minister of South Africa, not to mention the great leader Nelson Mandela." Some twenty years after the Reagan administration placed Mandela and other ANC members on a terrorist watch list, they remained there. History has its own measures, and men and women whom U.S. policy had deemed terrorists were now celebrated freedom fighters. A few weeks shy of Mandela's ninetieth birthday, President George W. Bush finally signed legislation that removed him from the terrorist watch list; Rice would no longer have to issue waivers to allow Mandela and other ANC members to enter the United States.[1]

Not long before he left the White House, Onyango Obama's grandson returned to Nairobi. There, President Obama was met by his half-sister Auma and Kenyan president Uhuru Kenyatta, son of independence leader Jomo Kenyatta. After his three-day visit, Obama traveled on to Addis Ababa, the place where Haile Selassie in 1941 returned to reclaim his throne and start the half century that would cast out European rule across Africa. In his remarks to "the people of Africa" at the headquarters of the African Union, Obama gave voice to the underappreciated truth that for hundreds of years, "Africa and its people helped to shape America and allowed it to become the great nation that it is." He spoke of America's great debt to Africa and highlighted the influence of Africa on the course of the nation, and wove in a personal note that "Africa and its people have helped shape who I am and how I see the world." Obama declared to those assembled that he had "worked to transform America's relationship with Africa—so that we're truly listening to our African friends and working together, as equal partners. And I'm proud of the progress that we've made."[2]

Progress will require an engagement that sees the continent and its peoples as equals, a relationship that recognizes, in Lutuli's words, "equality between nations and peoples."[3] It stands as a global parallel to an individual nation's duty to protect and preserve humanity by answering to all its people. Robert Kennedy's words, spoken at the University of Cape Town on a cold winter's day, still point a way forward: When one "stands up for an ideal, or acts to improve the lot of others, or strikes out against injustice, he sends forth a tiny ripple of hope, and crossing each other from a million different centers of energy and daring those ripples build a current which can sweep down the mightiest walls of oppression and resistance."[4]

Notes

Abbreviations in the Notes

CBC	Congressional Black Caucus
CDF	Central Decimal File
DDEL	Dwight D. Eisenhower Presidential Library
FRUS	*Foreign Relations of the United States*
HSTL	Harry S. Truman Presidential Library
JCL	Jimmy Carter Presidential Library
LBJL	Lyndon B. Johnson Presidential Library
LOC	Library of Congress
NAACP	National Association for the Advancement of Colored People
NARA	National Archives and Records Administration
NIE	National Intelligence Estimate
NSA	National Security Affairs
NSC	National Security Council
NSF	National Security File
OSANSA	Office of Special Assistant for National Security Affairs
PSF	President's Secretary's Files
RAC	Remote Archives Capture
RG	Record Group
RNL	Richard Nixon Presidential Library
RRL	Ronald Reagan Presidential Library
WHORM	White House Office of Records Management

Introduction

1. Shachtman, *Airlift to America*, 4–12.

2. Obama, *Dreams from My Father*, 105.

3. Obama, "Remarks by President Obama to the Kenyan People."

4. Young, *Postcolonialism*, 4.

5. Abundant concerns about the term "Third World" and the negative connotations it can imply make the term problematic. The point of origin of the term—that in a binary Cold War world there was a third way, a Third World—helped the term gain currency at the time, and the common use of it during the period being discussed is the basis for using it as a historical term, part of the context of the era. The newer term "Global South," with an emphasis on geopolitical relationships more than development or cultural difference, also carries its own set of issues,

including precise definition and imprecise geography. Each effort to generalize will be met by the vast diversity of the world itself.

6. *Prospects of Mankind*; Nyerere in Muehlenbeck, *Betting on the Africans*, 99.

7. Donald Lamm to Deputy Director McGhee, 21 Apr. 1950, box 2, Papers of George C. McGhee, HSTL.

8. George C. McGhee, "Africa's Role in the Free World Today," in *Department of State Bulletin* 25 (16 July 1951): 98.

9. Henry Byroade, "Address before the World Affairs Council of Northern California," 31 Oct. 1953, in *Foreign Relations of the United States Diplomatic Papers, 1952–1954*, 11:54–65 (hereafter cited as *FRUS*).

10. Memorandum of discussion at the 432nd Meeting of the National Security Council, 14 Jan. 1960, in *FRUS, 1958–1960*, 14:74–77.

11. Noer, *Cold War and Black Liberation*.

12. See, for instance, Connelly, *Diplomatic Revolution*, 8.

13. Memorandum from Schlesinger, "Our Policy in Africa," 1 July 1963, in *FRUS, 1961–1963*, 21:497, https://history.state.gov/historicaldocuments/frus1961-63v21/d315.

14. McMahon, introduction, 2.

15. Broadening of our understanding has come from studies that have examined conflicts ranging from Angola to Vietnam, analyzed the power of ideas from modernization theories to human rights, and explored issues of race and gender in areas throughout the world. See the foundational Westad, *Global Cold War*.

16. Numerous examples of the eliding of Africa in magisterial works, ones that speak eloquently and meaningfully of America's foreign policy and "the World," populate the landscape. Recent examples include Hitchcock's *The Age of Eisenhower*, whose few sentences on Ghana's independence and on the Congo crisis cover Africa in roughly 1 percent of the text; Colman's *The Foreign Policy of Lyndon B. Johnson*, which has barely a glancing reference to Africa; Logevall and Preston's *Nixon in the World*, which has no discussion of Africa; and Suri's *Henry Kissinger and the American Century*, which offers a "narrative of global change" (p. 4) yet, with the exception of two paragraphs on Angola, chooses worldwide places and events outside Africa to make his case.

17. See, for instance, Lyons, "Keeping Africa off the Agenda."

18. Irwin, "Wind of Change?," quote on 909.

19. Stith, epilogue, 214.

20. George Meany to Jimmy Carter, 7 June 1979, folder "Zimbabwe (Rhodesia), 6/79," box 89, collection 6, NSA, Zbigniew Brzezinski Collection, JCL.

21. Nyerere, "African and Democracy," 158.

22. Memorandum of conversation between Acheson and Green, 25 Mar. 1952, box 70, Dean G. Acheson Papers, HSTL.

23. Acheson, *Present at the Creation*, 379.

24. Fine historians have maintained that into the 1960s, "no U.S. administration had ever formulated an African policy." Zeiler, *Dean Rusk*, 86.

25. U.S. Congress, Senate, Committee on Commerce, *Freedom of Communications*, pt. 1, 1291–93, 1299; U.S. Congress, Senate, Committee on Commerce, *Free-*

dom of Communications, pt. 2, 1263, 1266–67. For more on the role of Africa in the 1960 presidential campaign, see Meriwether, "'Worth a Lot of Negro Votes.'"

26. Just a few of the recent excellent works include Mitchell, *Jimmy Carter in Africa*; DeRoche, *Kenneth Kaunda, the United States, and Southern Africa*; Gleijeses, *Visions of Freedom*; Michel, *White House, White Africa*; Irwin, *Gordian Knot*; Plummer, *In Search of Power*; Muehlenbeck, *Betting on the Africans*.

27. Thomas, "Innocent Abroad?," 49.

28. See, for instance, Plummer, *In Search of Power* and *Rising Wind*; Gaines, *American Africans in Ghana*; Von Eschen, *Satchmo Blows Up the World* and *Race against Empire*; Meriwether, *Proudly We Can Be Africans*; Swindall, *Path to the Greater, Freer, Truer World*; Grant, *Winning Our Freedoms Together*; Nesbitt, *Race for Sanctions*; Borstelmann, *Cold War and the Color Line*; Dudziak, *Cold War Civil Rights*; Noer, *Cold War and Black Liberation*.

29. Luthuli, "Nobel Lecture."

30. McMahon, *Colonialism and Cold War*.

31. Duara, introduction, 2.

32. Mir, "Roundtable."

33. Bradley, "Decolonization, the Global South, and the Cold War," 465.

34. Getachew, "Kwame Nkrumah and the Quest for Independence," quotes on 35, 39. For important work on Africans conceptualizing, investigating, and debating political frameworks beyond nation-states and European-carved boundaries, see, for instance, Wilder, *Freedom Time*; Cooper, *Citizenship between Empire and Nation*; Byrne, *Mecca of Revolution*.

35. Memorandum of conversation, 27 Apr. 1976, in *FRUS, 1969–1976*, 28:494–97, quote on 495.

36. Westad, *Global Cold War*, 21.

37. Campbell, *Middle Passages*, 17–18.

38. An Act to Prohibit the Importation of Slaves into Any Port or Place within the Jurisdiction of the United States, Pub. L. 9-22, 2 Stat. 426, 2 Mar. 1807.

39. The lodge was previously known as African Lodge No. 1. The petition can be found at www.pbs.org/wgbh/aia/part2/2h59.html.

40. Campbell, *Middle Passages*, 43–56. At the same time, Southern supporters of slavery largely controlled U.S. foreign policy with a vision of the nation as a champion of slavery and white supremacy. See Matthew Karp, *This Vast Southern Empire*.

41. Moses, *Wings of Ethiopia*, 141.

42. Barnes, *Journey of Hope*.

43. Clendenen and Duignan, *Americans in Black Africa*, 1–44; Clendenen, Collins, and Duignan, *Americans in Africa*, 11–26.

44. Jeal, *Stanley*, 42–69.

45. Williams, *Black Americans and the Evangelization of Africa*.

46. Redkey, "Meaning of Africa to Afro-Americans," quote on 16. See also Campbell, *Songs of Zion*, 83.

47. Gaines, "Black Americans' Racial Uplift Ideology," 433–55.

48. Fredrickson, *Black Liberation*, 149–51, quotes on 150. On Du Bois and his efforts at the Versailles Peace Conference, see Marable, "Pan-Africanism of W. E. B. Du Bois," 199–202; Plummer, *Rising Wind*, 15–19; Lewis, *W. E. B. Du Bois*, 561–80.

49. Sundiata, *Brothers and Strangers*, 99–100; Saigbe Boley, *Liberia*, 32–44.

50. Saigbe Boley, *Liberia*, 45–60; Schuyler, *Slaves Today*; Plummer, *Rising Wind*, 225.

Chapter 1

1. Thomas, "Innocent Abroad?," quote on 54.

2. Adi and Sherwood, *1945 Manchester Pan-African Congress Revisited*, 80. See also Munro, *Anticolonial Front*, chap. 2; Høgsbjerg, "Remembering the Fifth Pan-African Congress."

3. Itote, "'Mau Mau' General," quote on 81.

4. Ellison, *Invisible Man*, 271–72.

5. Chief of Division of Near Eastern Affairs (Murray) to Under Secretary of State (Phillips), 17 Dec. 1934, in *FRUS, 1934*, 2:768–69; Secretary of State (Hull) to Chargé in Ethiopia (George), 18 Dec. 1934, in *FRUS, 1934*, 2:769–70. For Secretary of State Cordell Hull's account of and reasoning behind avoiding involvement in mediating the clash, see Hull, *Memoirs of Cordell Hull*, 1:418–43.

6. For more on the Neutrality Acts and Roosevelt's response to the Italo-Ethiopian crisis, see Dallek, *Franklin D. Roosevelt and American Foreign Policy*, 101–21.

7. Walter White to Cordell Hull, 21 Mar. 1935 and 11 Apr. 1935, NAACP Papers, pt. 11, Special Subject Files, 1912–39, series A, reel 30, frames 579 and 583.

8. Resolution on Italy and Ethiopia, 1935 Annual Conference, NAACP Papers, pt. 1, Meetings of the Board of Directors, Records of Annual Conferences, Major Speeches, and Special Reports, 1909–50, reel 9, frame 852; monthly report by Walter White, executive secretary, July 1935, NAACP Papers, pt. 1, reel 5, frame 1888; NAACP press release, 3 July 1935, NAACP Papers, pt. 11, series A, reel 30, frame 683.

9. Secretary of State to Chargé in Ethiopia (George), 5 July 1935, in *FRUS, 1935*, 1:725.

10. William Bullitt, ambassador to the USSR, to Cordell Hull, 6 July 1935, 765.84/451, Central Decimal Files, 1930–39, U.S. Department of State Records, RG 59, NARA; Secretary of State to Chargé in Ethiopia (Engert), 12 Sept. 1935, in *FRUS, 1935*, 1:751–52; Secretary of State to Ambassador in United Kingdom (Bingham), 27 Sept. 1935, in *FRUS, 1935*, 1:767–68.

11. Secretary of State to Ambassador in the United Kingdom (Bingham), 14 Oct. 1935, in *FRUS, 1935*, 1:775–76.

12. Anderson, *Bourgeois Radicals*, quotes on 136–37.

13. Plummer, *Rising Wind*, 54–56.

14. Selassie's address on 5 May 1941 is printed in volume 2 of his autobiography, *My Life and Ethiopia's Progress*, 161–66, quotes on 164. See also Schmidt, *Foreign Intervention in Africa*, 21–22.

15. Plummer, *Rising Wind*, quote on 77.

16. For more on the perceptions and actions of people in the colonial and non-European parts of the world to the "Wilsonian moment," see the masterful Manela, *Wilsonian Moment*.

17. Rosenman, *Public Papers and Addresses of Franklin D. Roosevelt*, 9:672; Louis, *Imperialism at Bay*, 121–25.

18. Nielsen, *Great Powers and Africa*, quote on 247; Munene, *Truman Administration and the Decolonisation of Sub-Saharan Africa*, 37–38. For further discussion on U.S. anticolonial expressions during World War II, see Louis and Robinson, "United States and the Liquidation of the British Empire," 32–37; Borstelmann, *Apartheid's Reluctant Uncle*, 12–16; Noer, *Cold War and Black Liberation*, 15–17.

19. Munene, *Truman Administration and the Decolonisation of Sub-Saharan Africa*, quote on 49.

20. Hunt, *Ideology and U.S. Foreign Policy*, 92–124, 159–70.

21. Du Bois, "Chronicle of Race Relations," 77.

22. Louis, *Imperialism at Bay*, 513.

23. Louis, quote on 514. See also Nielsen, *Great Powers and Africa*, 249–50; Louis and Robinson, "United States and the Liquidation of the British Empire," 33, 40–41.

24. Louis, *Imperialism at Bay*, 532; NAACP press release, 2 May 1945, NAACP Papers, pt. 14, reel 18, frame 25; NAACP press release, 10 May 1945, NAACP Papers, pt. 14, reel 18, frame 550; Walter White to the board of directors, 9 May 1945, NAACP Papers, pt. 14, reel 18, frame 58; Roy Wilkins to NAACP branch offices, 3 May 1945, NAACP Papers, pt. 14, reel 19, frames 175–76.

25. Irwin, "Imagining Nation, State, and Order," quotes on 14–15.

26. Louis, *Imperialism at Bay*, 532

27. Walter White to Edward Stettinius, 18 May 1945, NAACP Papers, pt. 14, reel 19, frame 261; NAACP press release, 17 May 1945, NAACP Papers, pt. 14, reel 18, frame 211; Walter White to the Committee on Administration, 28 May 1945, NAACP Papers, pt. 14, reel 18, frame 340; NAACP press release, 21 June 1945, NAACP Papers, pt. 14, reel 18, frame 320; "San Francisco," editorial, *The Crisis*, June 1945, 161. For more on African American attitudes toward and actions at the San Francisco conference, see Plummer, *Rising Wind*, 125–65; Harris, "Racial Equality and the United Nations Charter," 126–48; Horne, *Black and Red*, 33–39.

28. Bamba, "Transnationalising Decolonization," 335. The limits of any loosening would be dramatically underscored in France's unequivocal rejection of postwar independence for Madagascar and subsequent brutal repression of the revolt that ensued starting in March 1947. See Little, "Cold War and Colonialism in Africa."

29. Anderson, "Histories of African Americans' Anticolonialism," 178–79, quotes on 178.

30. Kent, "United States Reactions to Empire, Colonialism, and Cold War," 198.

31. Wood, "From the Marshall Plan to the Third World," 201–14; Kent, "British Policy and the Origins of the Cold War," 148–49; Borstelmann, *Apartheid's Reluctant Uncle*, 58–59; Nielsen, *Great Powers and Africa*, 251–54.

32. Truman, "Truman's Inaugural Address to the Nation."

33. Truman.

34. For the tracing of intellectual underpinnings of development assistance back to the Scottish Enlightenment, see McVety, "Wealth and Nations" in *The Development Century*, part of a robust and growing literature historicizing development ideas and practices. For a small sampling of important works, see Cullather, *The Hungry World*; Immerwahr, *Thinking Small*; Macekura and Manela, *The Development Century*.

35. Paterson, "Foreign Aid Under Wrap," 122.

36. Thomas, "Innocent Abroad?," 53.

37. Thomas, 55; Kent, "United States Reactions to Empire, Colonialism, and Cold War," 198. For more on U.S. officials' awareness of French concerns, see the policy paper prepared by the Bureau of Near Eastern, South Asian, and African Affairs, "Future of Africa," 18 Apr. 1950, in *FRUS, 1950*, vol. 5.

38. Munene, *Truman Administration and the Decolonisation of Sub-Saharan Africa*, 153–54, quote on 154.

39. Paterson, "Foreign Aid Under Wrap," quote on 125; Kent, "United States Reactions to Empire, Colonialism, and Cold War," 198; Munene, *Truman Administration and the Decolonisation of Sub-Saharan Africa*, 107–12, 124–27. For French concerns about potential loss of funds, see Bamba, "Transnationalising Decolonization," 337.

40. Kent, "United States Reactions to Empire, Colonialism, and Cold War," 200. For American commercial interests downgraded after 1947 for European allies' interests, see Munene, *Truman Administration and the Decolonisation of Sub-Saharan Africa*, 78–91.

41. Thomas, "Innocent Abroad?," 55–56; Kent, "United States Reactions to Empire, Colonialism, and Cold War," 203.

42. George McGhee, "Africa's Role in the Free World Today," in *Department of State Bulletin* 25 (16 July 1951): 101.

43. Borstelmann, *Apartheid's Reluctant Uncle*, 16–18; Plummer, *Rising Wind*, 109.

44. Ralph Bunche to Walter White, 17 June 1949, NAACP Papers, pt. 14, reel 10, frame 589.

45. Leffler, *Preponderance of Power*, 75–77; Rivlin, *United Nations and the Italian Colonies*, 9–14.

46. On U.S. officials' concern with communist takeovers through the ballot box in both Italy and France and their extensive efforts to prevent such an occurrence, see Leffler, *Preponderance of Power*, 121–22, 189–98, 206–7, 213–14.

47. Rivlin, *United Nations and the Italian Colonies*, 27–41.

48. NAACP press release, 19 May 1949, NAACP Papers, pt. 14, reel 6, frame 906; Anderson, *Bourgeois Radicals*, 202.

49. Anderson, "Rethinking Radicalism," 385–423. In this article and her *Bourgeois Radicals*, Anderson elegantly undermines the historical interpretation that as World War II ended and as anticommunism became the sine qua non in the United

States, only the Left and individuals such as W. E. B. Du Bois and Paul Robeson battled for colonial peoples, while liberal organizations such as the NAACP withdrew from the international struggle.

50. Anderson, *Bourgeois Radicals*, 133–203, quote on 202.

51. Policy statement of the Department of State, 1 Nov. 1948, in *FRUS, 1948*, 5:524–32.

52. Borstelmann, *Apartheid's Reluctant Uncle*, 48–50, quote on 48.

53. For U.S. relations with South Africa and the issue of South West Africa, see Borstelmann, *Apartheid's Reluctant Uncle*, 77–78, 106–7, 121–22, 161–62; Noer, *Cold War and Black Liberation*, 25–26, 31–32. For relations between India and South Africa in the years immediately following World War II, see Irwin, "Imagining Nation, State, and Order"; Lauren, *Power and Prejudice*, 167–71; Kapur, *Raising Up a Prophet*, 129–32.

54. "From Bad to Worse," editorial, *The Crisis*, July 1948, 201. For more on the African American struggle against apartheid and annexation of South West Africa in these years, see especially Grant, *Winning Our Freedoms Together*; C. Anderson, "International Conscience, the Cold War, and Apartheid," 297–325; Von Eschen, *Race against Empire*, 83–93.

55. Anderson, "International Conscience, the Cold War, and Apartheid," quote on 313.

56. Anderson, quote on 306.

57. Scott continued to face challenges in obtaining a visa and overcoming limitations on his movements in the following years, and the NAACP regularly lobbied the State Department on his behalf. See NAACP Papers, pt. 14, reel 4, frames 3, 157, 161, 188, 260, 282, 293, 308, 424, 426. For more on his life and work, see Scott, *A Time to Speak*.

58. Anderson, "International Conscience, the Cold War, and Apartheid," 313–23.

59. Anderson, 324–25.

60. Department of State policy statement, 28 Mar. 1951, in *FRUS, 1951*, 5:1433–42, quotes on 1433–34, 1441.

61. "The Blockheads in Britain," editorial, *Chicago Defender*, 18 Mar. 1950, 6; "Great Britain Has a Nerve," editorial, *Baltimore Afro-American*, 1 Apr. 1950, 4; 1950 Annual Convention Resolution, NAACP Papers, pt. 1, reel 12, frame 948; "The Background and Significance of the Seretse Khama Case," *New Africa*, Apr. 1950, Du Bois Papers, reel 84, frame 243. For other protests, see "Is Seretse a Menace to His People?" editorial, *Pittsburgh Courier*, 1 Apr. 1950, 14; "British Get Hotfoot," editorial, *Chicago Defender*, 29 Apr. 1950, 6; "Seretse Khama," editorial, *The Crisis*, Apr. 1950, 239; "Britain's Hot Potato," editorial, *Pittsburgh Courier*, 18 Mar. 1950, 16; "Tragic Happenings," editorial, *New York Amsterdam News*, 29 Apr. 1950, 8; "The Odor Is Terrible," editorial, *Baltimore Afro-American*, 2 Sept. 1950, 4; International President, Brotherhood of Sleeping Car Porters (Randolph), to President Eisenhower, 17 June 1953, in *FRUS, 1952–1954*, 11:45; Kirby, "'Our Bantustans are Better than Yours,'" 863.

62. For a fuller recounting of the story, see Williams, *Colour Bar*.

63. Sweeney (for Ambassador in South Africa Erhardt) to Secretary of State, "Communist Influence in South African Trade Unions," 3 Oct. 1950, in *FRUS, 1950*, 5:1834–35; Noer, *Cold War and Black Liberation*, 27–28.

64. Ambassador in Union of South Africa (Erhardt) to Dominion Affairs Officer, Office of British Commonwealth and Northern European Affairs (Shullaw), 30 Jan. 1951, in *FRUS, 1951*, 5:1428–29.

65. Amb. W. J. Gallman, "Some Thoughts on Foreign Affairs," unpublished manuscript, 1972, General Historical Documents Collection, HSTL.

66. Gallman, "Some Thoughts on Foreign Affairs."

67. "The Breakup of Colonial Empires and Its Implications for US Security," ORE 25–48, 3 Sept. 1948, box 214, Central Intelligence Reports File, Intelligence File 1946–1953, PSF, HSTL.

68. "Breakup of Colonial Empires and Its Implications for US Security."

69. "Breakup of Colonial Empires and Its Implications for US Security."

70. "Breakup of Colonial Empires and Its Implications for US Security."

71. Munene, *Truman Administration and the Decolonisation of Sub-Saharan Africa*, quote on 80.

72. "Political and Economic Problems of Africa," n.d., in *FRUS, 1950*, 5:1504; memorandum by Assistant Secretary of State for Near Eastern, South Asian and African Affairs (McGhee) to the Secretary of State (Acheson) and to Under Secretary of State (Webb), 12 Apr. 1950, in *FRUS, 1950*, 5:1515; McGhee, *Envoy to the Middle World*, 114.

73. "Political and Economic Problems of Africa," n.d., in *FRUS, 1950*, 5:1503–9; memorandum by Assistant Secretary of State for Near Eastern, South Asian, and African Affairs (McGhee) to Secretary of State and to the Deputy Under Secretary of State (Rusk), 17 Feb. 1950, in *FRUS, 1950*, 5:1510. See also McGhee, *Envoy to the Middle World*, 115–17.

74. Report on Lourenço Marques Conference, folder "East-West African Conference, Lourenço Marques, Feb 27–March 2, 1950," box 1, George C. McGhee Papers, HSTL.

75. Policy paper prepared by the Bureau of Near Eastern, South Asian, and African Affairs, "Future of Africa," 18 Apr. 1950, in *FRUS, 1950*, 5:1528n5.

76. McGhee to Acheson and Webb, 12 Apr. 1950, in *FRUS, 1950*, 5:1514–23, quote on 1519.

77. McGhee, *Envoy to the Middle World*, 123–25.

78. "Regional Policy Statement on Africa South of the Sahara," 29 Dec. 1950, in *FRUS, 1950*, 5:1588.

79. "Regional Policy Statement on Africa South of the Sahara," 29 Dec. 1950, 5:1590.

80. "Regional Policy Statement on Africa South of the Sahara," 29 Dec. 1950, 5:1590.

81. McGhee, "Africa's Role in the Free World Today," 98.

82. Donald Lamm to Deputy Director McGhee, 21 Apr. 1950, box 2, George C. McGhee Papers, HSTL.

83. Borstelmann, *Apartheid's Reluctant Uncle*, 195.

84. Kalu, "Postcolonial African State and Its Citizens," 21.

Chapter 2

1. George M. Houser, "A Report on the All African People's Conference Held in Accra, Ghana, Dec. 8–13, 1958," in African Activist Archive, https://africanactivist.msu.edu/document_metadata.php?objectid=32-130-D84; Eisenhower, *Waging Peace*, 572.

2. Muehlenbeck, *Betting on the Africans*, quote on 7.

3. Draft memorandum prepared in Office of Dependent Area Affairs with the Office of UN Political and Security Affairs, 8 May 1952, in *FRUS, 1952–1954*, 3:1111–15, "middle course" quote on 1114; Hickerson (Assistant Secretary of State for UN Affairs) to Matthews (Deputy Under Secretary of State), 13 May 1952, in *FRUS, 1952–1954*, 3:1116–17, for "middle position"; Perkins (Assistant Secretary of State for European Affairs) to Matthews, 4 June 1952, in *FRUS, 1952–1954*, 3:1118, for "middle-of-the-road position." Historians Thomas Noer and Thomas Borstelmann have examined the evolution of U.S. efforts to follow a middle path, taking as a prime exemplar the need to carve out policy toward South Africa. See Noer, "Truman, Eisenhower, and South Africa," 75–104; Noer, *Cold War and Black Liberation*, 1–60; Borstelmann, *Apartheid's Reluctant Uncle*, esp. 139–44 and 177–79.

4. Memorandum by Acting Deputy Director of the Office of Western European Affairs (Knight), 21 Apr. 1952, in *FRUS, 1952–1954*, 3:1103–4.

5. Draft memorandum by Dependent Area Affairs and UN Political and Security Affairs, 8 May 1952, in *FRUS, 1952–1954*, 3:1114.

6. Draft memorandum by Dependent Area Affairs and UN Political and Security Affairs, 8 May 1952, in *FRUS, 1952–1954*, 3:1114; memorandum by Assistant Secretary of State for European Affairs (Perkins) to Deputy Under Secretary of State (Matthews), 4 June 1952, in *FRUS, 1952–1954*, 3:1118.

7. "Draft Agenda for Truman and Eisenhower," n.d., Memorandum of Conversations file, box 71, Dean G. Acheson Papers, Secretary of State File, 1949–1953, HSTL.

8. "Conditions and Trends in Tropical Africa," 22 Dec. 1953, in *FRUS, 1952–1954*, 11:71–89, quote on 72–73.

9. Noer, *Cold War and Black Liberation*, 34.

10. Henry Byroade, "Address before the World Affairs Council of Northern California," 31 Oct. 1953, in *FRUS, 1952–1954*, 11:54–65.

11. Kent, "United States Reactions to Empire, Colonialism, and Cold War," 209–10.

12. Noer, *Cold War and Black Liberation*, quote on 44.

13. Borstelmann, *Cold War and the Color Line*, 86.

14. "Black Africa," 91.

15. Cloete, "'I Speak for the African,'" 111.

16. "Americans and Africa," 178.

17. Grubbs, *Secular Missionaries*.

18. "Semi-Monthly Politico-Economic Summary—British East Africa," 745P.00/5-2652, CDF, 1950–54, RG 59, NARA.

19. For important histories of British efforts to denigrate and destroy the Kenya Land and Freedom movement, see Anderson, *Histories of the Hanged*; Elkins, *Imperial Reckoning*.

20. “Fortnightly Survey, British East Africa, November 13–26, 1952,” British Africa-East, 745P.00/11-2652, CDF, 1950–54, RG 59 NARA; “Fortnightly Survey, British East Africa, November 27–December 10, 1952,” British Africa-East, 745P.00 /12-1052, CDF, 1950–54, RG 59 NARA.

21. “The Mau Mau Movement,” Edmund Dorsz, 2 Jan. 1953, British Africa-East, 745R.00/1-253, CDF, 1950–54, RG 59 NARA; “Weekly Review, Kenya, December 25–31, 1952,” British Africa–Kenya Colony, 745R.00/12-3152, CDF, 1950–54, RG 59 NARA.

22. “Racial Conflict; Mau Mau Story Told in ‘Something of Value,’” *New York Times*, 11 May 1957. For more on film and colonialism, see Cowans, *Empire Films and the Crisis of Colonialism*, 158–70, for “Something of Value.”

23. Memorandum by Consul General (McGregor), 28 Dec. 1955, in *FRUS, 1955–1957*, 18:28; Nyerere quote in Muehlenbeck, *Betting on the Africans*, 99.

24. Consul General Dakar to State Department, 6 Sept. 1955, quoted in Kent, “United States Reactions to Empire, Colonialism, and Cold War,” 213.

25. Consul General Salisbury to State Department, 8 May 1953, quoted in Kent, “United States Reactions to Empire, Colonialism, and Cold War,” 204.

26. Kent, “United States Reactions to Empire, Colonialism, and Cold War,” 214.

27. Babou, “Decolonization or National Liberation,” 49.

28. Dudziak, “Desegregation as a Cold War Imperative,” quote on 110–11.

29. Memorandum by Harry H. Schwartz of the Policy Planning Staff to the director, Policy Planning Staff (Bowie), 2 Mar. 1954, in *FRUS, 1952–1954*, 11:97.

30. McMahon, “How the Periphery Became the Center,” 27.

31. Westad, *Global Cold War*, 67–68; Mazov, *Distant Front in the Cold War*.

32. McMahon, “How the Periphery Became the Center,” quote on 31; Mazov, *Distant Front in the Cold War*, chap. 1.

33. T. B. Koons to Robert Cutler, 15 Mar. 1954, Africa South of the Sahara (3), Special Staff Files, NSC Staff Papers, DDEL; memorandum by Schwartz to Bowie, 2 Mar. 1954, in *FRUS, 1952–1954*, 11:97; editorial note, in *FRUS, 1952–1954*, 11:101; Robert Cutler to Mr. Koons, 3 Mar. 1954, Africa South of the Sahara (3), Special Staff Files, NSC Staff Papers, DDEL; memorandum from Bromley Smith, “State Papers on Africa,” 13 Mar. 1956, Africa South of the Sahara (3), Special Staff Files, NSC Staff Papers, DDEL; paper prepared in the Department of State, “List of African Problems,” n.d., in *FRUS, 1952–1954*, 11:102–3; editorial note, in *FRUS, 1952–1954*, 11:107–8.

34. There is a steadily growing literature on the Bandung Conference; see, for instance, Lee, *Making a World After Empire*; Parker, “Cold War II,” 867–92; Fraser, “An American Dilemma.”

35. Westad, *Global Cold War*, 123–26; Noer, *Cold War and Black Liberation*, 48. The Suez crisis did not, however, mean that “‘the middle of the road’ had clearly come to an end.” Connelly, *Diplomatic Revolution*, 120.

36. “Conditions and Trends in Tropical Africa,” 14 Aug. 1956, in *FRUS, 1955–1957*, 18:45–47.

37. Richard Nixon, “The Emergence of Africa: Report to President Eisenhower,” in *Department of State Bulletin* 36 (22 Apr. 1957): 636–37.

38. Nixon, “Emergence of Africa,” 636.

39. Historian Brenda Gayle Plummer argues that Kennedy compensated for his "demonstrably poor civil rights voting record" by using Africa as a bridge to the Black electorate. Plummer, *Rising Wind*, 296. During the campaign, Kennedy regularly referred to Africa in his speeches, charging repeatedly that the United States had lost ground to the Soviets in Africa because it failed to address the needs and aspirations of Africans. Meriwether, "'Worth a Lot of Negro Votes,'" 737–63.

40. For more on the events in the Gold Coast, see Ahlman, *Living with Nkrumahism*, esp. chap. 2; Babou, "Decolonization or National Liberation," 47–48; Munro, *Anticolonial Front*, chap. 7; Nwaubani, *United States and Decolonization in West Africa*, 2–15.

41. Memorandum from Dulles to Nixon, 24 Jan. 1957, Nixon Pre-Presidential Papers, series 351, box 1, Africa Trip—1957 Administration, National Archives—Laguna Niguel, RNL; memorandum from Eisenhower to Nixon, 29 Jan. 1957, Nixon Pre-Presidential Papers, series 351, box 1, Africa Trip—1957 Administration, National Archives—Laguna Niguel, RNL; memorandum of conversation of Dulles call to Nixon, 8 Jan. 1957, Telephone Calls, box 6, Memoranda Tel Conv—Gen Jan 1957 to Feb 28 1957, John Foster Dulles Papers, DDEL; memorandum of conversation of Nixon call to Dulles, 28 Jan. 1957, Telephone Calls, box 6, Memoranda Tel Conv—Gen Jan 1957 to Feb 28 1957, John Foster Dulles Papers, DDEL; memorandum of conversation of Nixon call to Dulles, 29 Jan. 1957, Telephone Calls, box 6, Memoranda Tel Conv—Gen Jan 1957 to Feb 28 1957, John Foster Dulles Papers, DDEL; memorandum of conversation of Dulles conversation with Nixon, 2 Feb. 1957, box 6, VP Nixon, Subject Series, John Foster Dulles Papers, DDEL.

42. "Ghana Sets High Goals as Independence Nears," *Chicago Defender*, 28 Feb. 1957, 3; "Lincoln, Morgan Fete Ghana," *Baltimore Afro-American*, 9 Mar. 1957, 11. Church leaders represented all the large African-American denominations, with memberships totaling over eight million. "The Negro Church in America Has Been a Powerful Voice for Good," *Pittsburgh Courier*, 9 Mar. 1957, Ghana Supplement, 26.

43. "Powell's Trip to Ghana Stirs Political Pot," *Baltimore Afro-American*, 16 Mar. 1957, 11.

44. "Report to the President on the Vice President's Visit to Africa," 5 Apr. 1957, in *FRUS, 1955–1957*, 18:65–66.

45. 1957 Africa trip notes, Nixon Pre-Presidential Papers, series 351, box 1, Africa Trip—1957; Nixon, "Emergence of Africa," 635, 638.

46. Memorandum of discussion at the 335th meeting of the NSC, 22 Aug. 1957, box 9, NSC Series, Ann Whitman File, DDEL; briefing notes by C.A. Haskins for Robert Cutler for 335th NSC meeting, Africa South of the Sahara (3), box 1, OSANSA, Special Staff File, DDEL.

47. "Statement of U.S. Policy toward Africa South of the Sahara Prior to Calendar Year 1960," NSC 5719/1, 23 Aug. 1957, in *FRUS, 1955–1957*, 18:76–87, quote on 79–80. The continuing rapid pace of events in Africa compelled the NSC to issue a new report within a year, yet aside from an increased emphasis on providing economic and technical assistance to emerging nations, the framework continued. See "Statement of U.S. Policy toward Africa South of the Sahara Prior to Calendar Year 1960," NSC 5818, 26 Aug. 1958, in *FRUS, 1958–1960*, 14:24–37.

48. "The Challenge of Imperialism: Algeria," speech by John F. Kennedy, U.S. Senate, July 2, 1957, in Kennedy, *"Let the Word Go Forth,"* 331, 337; Mahoney, *JFK*, 20–26; Muehlenbeck, *Betting on the Africans*, 36; Stephanson, "Senator John F. Kennedy," 1–24.

49. For an excellent analysis of public diplomacy and the Third World, see Parker, *Hearts, Minds, Voices*, and Von Eschen, *Satchmo Blows Up the World*. For a fascinating exploration of everyday consumer goods as part of American influence in French West Africa during this period, see Bamba, "'Mightier Than Marx.'"

50. "Inspection Report: USIS-Ghana," USIA 1956, quoted in Parker, *Hearts, Minds, Voices*, 105.

51. "Recent Actions on African Students," memo for McGeorge Bundy from Philip Coombs, 4 Aug. 1961, box 2, National Security File, Presidential Papers, JFKL.

52. Martin Kilson, "Mugo-Son-of-Gatheru," *The Crisis*, Apr. 1953, 140; background report, "The Case of Mugo Gatheru," 2 Dec. 1952, NAACP Papers, pt. 14, reel 2, frame 861; Gatheru, *Child of Two Worlds*, 172–80.

53. Gatheru, *Child of Two Worlds*, 180–81; "Kenya's Whites Seeking Return of Lincoln University Student," *Pittsburgh Courier*, 15 Nov. 1952, 1; "Sue to Prevent Ouster of Mugo," *Chicago Defender*, 6 Dec. 1952, 1; background report, "The Case of Mugo Gatheru," 2 Dec. 1952, NAACP Papers, pt. 14, reel 2, frame 861; minutes, board of directors, 8 Dec. 1952, NAACP Papers, pt. 14, reel 2, frame 857; Herbert L. Wright to Gloster Current, 29 Dec. 1952, NAACP Papers, pt. 14, reel 2, frame 862; Wright to NAACP Youth Councils, College Chapters, and Affiliated Organizations, n.d., NAACP Papers, pt. 14, reel 2, frames 863–68; Wright to Walter White, 13 Jan. 1953, NAACP Papers, pt. 14, reel 2, frames 872–73; Horace Mann Bond to Wright, 23 Jan. 1953, NAACP Papers, pt. 14, reel 2, frame 880; Wright to Bond, 27 Jan. 1953, NAACP Papers, pt. 14, reel 2, frame 879; Wright to U.S. Immigration and Naturalization, 17 Feb. 1953, NAACP Papers, pt. 14, reel 2, frame 895.

54. Gatheru, *Child of Two Worlds*, 181–84; "Rap Gatheru Ouster Order," *Baltimore Afro-American*, 28 Feb. 1953, 9; St. Clair Drake to Walter White, 2 July 1954, NAACP Papers, pt. 14, reel 2, frames 928–32; White to Drake, 23 July 1954, NAACP Papers, pt. 14, reel 2, frame 927; White to Bureau of Immigration and Naturalization, 23 July 1954, NAACP Papers, pt. 14, reel 2, frames 934–35.

55. Gerits, "Hungry Minds," quotes on 599, 603.

56. Memorandum of discussion at the 375th meeting of the NSC, 7 Aug. 1958, in *FRUS, 1958–1960*, 14:20–21, https://history.state.gov/historicaldocuments/frus1958-60v14/d6.

57. "African Students in the United States," *Africa Report* 6 (March 1961).

58. "African Students in the United States"; "Educational Exchange," box 993, Kennedy Pre-Presidential Papers, JFKL; Philip Coombs to McGeorge Bundy, "Recent Actions on African Students," 4 Aug. 1961, box 2, National Security File, Kennedy Presidential Papers, JFKL.

59. Minter, Hovey, and Cobb, *No Easy Victories*, 62–67. See also Houser, *No One Can Stop the Rain*.

60. Tom Mboya to Martin Luther King, 16 June 1959, box 26A, Martin Luther King Jr. Papers; King to Mboya, 8 July 1959, box 26A, Martin Luther King Jr. Papers; King to William Scheinman, 18 Aug. 1959, box 32, box 26A, Martin Luther King Jr. Papers; Branch, "Political Traffic," 816.

61. Smith, "East African Airlifts," 22–25; Goldsworthy, *Tom Mboya*, 118–20; A. Philip Randolph to Tom Mboya, Oct. 14, 1959, box 18, Brotherhood of Sleeping Car Porters Papers, LOC.

62. Harry Belafonte, Sidney Poitier, Jackie Robinson appeal letter, Aug. 24, 1959, container 3, Jackie Robinson Papers, LOC; Smith, "East African Airlifts," 25–43.

63. Rosen, "Soviet Training Programs for Africa," 1–2. For more on African students going to Central and Eastern Europe, see Branch, "Political Traffic"; Guillory, "Culture Clash in the Socialist Paradise"; Mazov, *Distant Front in the Cold War*, chap. 4.

64. Memorandum of discussion at the 375th meeting of the NSC, 7 Aug. 1958, in *FRUS, 1958–1960*, 14:19–22, https://history.state.gov/historicaldocuments/frus1958-60v14/d6. After he retired to his farm in Gettysburg, Eisenhower shared with longtime friend and aide Andrew Goodpaster his desire to spend time in Africa as part of his "bucket list" of final major travels: visit de Gaulle in France, followed by "visiting a country or two in Black Africa, together with Ethiopia or Kenya on the Eastern side," before heading to Pakistan and India, seeing the situation in South Vietnam, visiting Australia and New Zealand, then coming home via Tahiti and Hawaii. Folder "Eisenhower, Dwight D., General," box 2, NSF—Name File, LBJL.

65. Memorandum of discussion at the 375th meeting of the NSC, 7 Aug. 1958, in *FRUS, 1958–1960*, 14:20, https://history.state.gov/historicaldocuments/frus1958-60v14/d6.

66. Cooper, *Citizenship between Empire and Nation*, chaps. 1–2, quote on 123.

67. Cooper, 167–69, quote on 168.

68. Schmidt, *Cold War and Decolonization in Guinea*, 3; Nwaubani, *United States and Decolonization in West Africa*, 206–11.

69. Connelly, *Diplomatic Revolution*, quote on 23–24.

70. Schmidt, *Foreign Intervention in Africa*, 48–54; Connelly, *Diplomatic Revolution*, chap. 5.

71. Schmidt, *Foreign Intervention in Africa*, 46–48; Thomas, "Innocent Abroad?," 61–63; Bamba, "Transnationalising Decolonization," 327–49; 335.

72. Cooper, *Citizenship between Empire and Nation*, chap. 5, quote on 277.

73. For an important work, see Byrne, *Mecca of Revolution*.

74. Connelly, *Diplomatic Revolution*, chap. 6; Schmidt, *Foreign Intervention in Africa*, 51–52.

75. Cooper, *Citizenship between Empire and Nation*, 284–302.

76. Cooper, quotes on 315, 316.

77. The Fonds d'investissement pour le développement économique et social (Investment Fund for Economic and Social Development, or FIDES) had been established in 1946 for metropolitan funds to be used for late-colonial developmentalism as part of a French effort to help preempt the collapse of the empire. See Chafer, *End of Empire in French West Africa*, 88.

78. Nwaubani, *United States and Decolonization in West Africa*, 21; Cooper, *Citizenship between Empire and Nation*, 304–6; Chafer, *End of Empire in French West Africa*, esp. chap. 7; Schmidt, *Cold War and Decolonization in Guinea*, esp. chap. 6.

79. Schmidt, *Cold War and Decolonization in Guinea*, 166–78; Nwaubani, *United States and Decolonization in West Africa*, 211–15.

80. Muehlenbeck, *Betting on the Africans*, 24–28. For more on Soviet activity, see Mazov, *Distant Front in the Cold War*; Iandolo, "Rise and Fall of the 'Soviet Model of Development,'" 683–704.

81. Nwaubani, *United States and Decolonization in West Africa*, 18; Schmidt, *Foreign Intervention in Africa*, 175–76.

82. Macmillan, "The Wind of Change"; Nwaubani, *United States and Decolonization in West Africa*, 215–16.

83. Memorandum of discussion at the 432d meeting of the NSC, 14 Jan. 1960, in *FRUS, 1958–1960*, 14:74–77

84. Memorandum of discussion at the 432d meeting of the NSC, 14 Jan. 1960, in *FRUS, 1958–1960*, 14:74–77.

85. Notes taken by Clarence Randall during oral discussion, Mar. 1958, Africa Trip (March 1958) Final Report (3), box 3, Trips Subseries, Randall Series, Office of the Chairman Records, U.S. Council on Foreign Economic Policy, DDEL.

86. Memorandum from the representative at the Trusteeship Council (Sears) to the Secretary of State, 15 Feb. 1956, in *FRUS, 1955–1957*, 18:37–38; editorial note, 15 Feb. 1956, in *FRUS, 1955–57*, 18:39–40; U.S. Department of State Records, RG 59, Lot File No. 62D417, "Subject Files Relating to the Union of South Africa, 1946–1959."

87. Noer, *Cold War and Black Liberation*, 46.

88. "Embassy Staff Study on the South African Race Problem I," 11 Apr. 1957, in *FRUS, 1955–1957*, 14:807–15; "Embassy Staff Study on the South African Race Problem II; Diplomatic Policy Recommendation," 11 Apr. 1957, in *FRUS, 1955–1957*, 14:816–22, quote on 821.

89. Noer, *Cold War and Black Liberation*, 52–53.

90. Gerhart, "Eve of Sharpeville and Afterwards," 332–34; Lodge, *Black Politics in South Africa since 1945*, 205–10.

91. Statement by Lincoln White, director of the Office of News, 22 Mar. 1960, in *Department of State Bulletin* 42 (11 Apr. 1960): 551.

92. Dictated note left by Lodge for Herter, 24 Mar. 1960, CAH Telephone Calls 1/1/60–3/25/60 (1), box 12, Christian A. Herter Papers, DDEL.

93. Memorandum from Herter to Andrew Goodpaster, 24 Mar. 1960, Africa (General) (3), box 1, International Series, Office of the Staff Secretary Records, DDEL; editorial note, in *FRUS, 1958–1960*, 14:741–42.

94. Memorandum from Herter to Andrew Goodpaster, 24 Mar. 1960, Africa (General) (3), box 1, International Series, Office of the Staff Secretary Records, DDEL.

95. Editorial note, in *FRUS, 1958–1960*, 14:749; memorandum of conversation among A. B. Burger, counselor of the South African Embassy, and C. Vaughan Ferguson, director of AFS, William Wight, deputy director of AFS, and Robert Schneider of AFS, 21 Apr. 1960, 745A.00/4-2160, CDF, 1960–63, RG 59, NARA; "State Department Items Reported to the President," 4 Apr. 1960, Briefings, April 1960,

box 48, DDE Diary Series, Ann Whitman File, DDEL; Gerhart, "Eve of Sharpeville and Afterwards," 336; Muehlenbeck, *Betting on the Africans*, 8.

96. Notes taken by Clarence Randall during oral discussion, Mar. 1958, Africa Trip (March 1958) Final Report (3), box 3, Trips Subseries, Randall Series, Office of the Chairman Records, U.S. Council on Foreign Economic Policy, DDEL.

97. O'Malley, *Diplomacy of Decolonisation*, 13–14.

98. O'Malley, 13–15; Weissman, *American Foreign Policy in the Congo*, 17–19.

99. Editorial note containing memorandum of discussion at 443d meeting of the NSC, 5 May 1960, in *FRUS, 1958–1960*, 14:274.

100. For Lumumba's speech, see Merriam, *Congo: Background of Conflict*, 352–54; "Diary Notes," Congo, June–July 1960, box 178, Ralph J. Bunche Papers, Young Research Library, University of California Los Angeles.

101. Worger, Clark, and Alpers, *Africa and the West*, 134–35.

102. Iandolo, "Imbalance of Power," 32–55; Mazov, *Distant Front in the Cold War*, chaps. 2–3.

103. Telegram from the embassy in Belgium to the Department of State, 1 May 1960, in *FRUS, 1958–1960*, 14:272–74; memorandum of discussion at 452nd meeting of the NSC, 21 July 1960, in *FRUS, 1958–1960*, 14:338–42, quote on 338.

104. Memorandum of discussion at the 454th meeting of the NSC," 1 Aug. 1960, in *FRUS, 1958–1960*, 14:372–76, quote on 375.

105. Namikas, review of *FRUS, 1964–1968*, vol. 23.

106. De Witte, *Assassination of Lumumba*, 47–48.

107. Kalb, *Congo Cables*, 89–97; Weissman, *American Foreign Policy in the Congo*, 95–99.

108. Minutes of cabinet meeting, 7 Oct. 1960, box 16, Cabinet Series, Ann Whitman File, DDEL; memorandum of conversation of Herter call to Eisenhower, 13 Oct. 1960, Presidential Phone Calls 7/60-1/20/61, box 10, Herter Papers, DDEL.

109. O'Malley, *Diplomacy of Decolonisation*, 48.

110. For more on this period, see O'Malley, *Diplomacy of Decolonisation*, 38–58; Kalb, *Congo Cables*, 152–55; Weissman, *American Foreign Policy in the Congo*, 106–7.

111. De Witte, *Assassination of Lumumba*, chaps. 3–4.

112. Memorandum prepared in the Central Intelligence Agency, "Death of Patrice Lumumba," [Mar. 1961?], in *FRUS, 1961–1963*, 20:93–94; editorial note, n.d., in *FRUS, 1961–1963*, 20:16–18; Weissman, "What Really Happened in Congo," 14–24; Namikas, *Battleground Africa*; De Witte, *Assassination of Lumumba*, esp. 93–124; Kalb, *Congo Cables*, 184–86; Weissman, *American Foreign Policy in the Congo*, 137–38. Ongoing work on the killing of Lumumba also includes Gerard and Kuklick, *Death in the Congo*.

113. Policy Planning Staff memorandum discussed at the 410th meeting of the NSC, 18 June 1959, box 11, NSC Series, Ann Whitman File, DDEL.

114. Policy Planning Staff Memorandum, 18 June 1959, Ann Whitman File, DDEL.

115. Schmitz, *United States and Right-Wing Dictatorships*, 2.

116. Kissinger, *Diplomacy*, 708.

Chapter 3

1. Countries in Africa gaining independence from 1961 to 1966 included Sierra Leone and Tanzania (1961); Algeria, Burundi, Rwanda, and Uganda (1962); Kenya (1963); Malawi and Zambia (1964); Gambia (1965); and Botswana and Lesotho (1966). Totaling 2.22 million square miles, the area was larger than the continental United States west of the Mississippi River (2.10 million square miles) or India (1.27 million square miles).

2. Declaration on the Granting of Independence to Colonial Countries and Peoples, adopted by General Assembly resolution 1514 (XV), 14 Dec. 1960, http://undocs.org/pdf?symbol=en/A/Res/1514(XV).

3. Heiss, "Whistling in the Dark," quote on 138.

4. "Political Attitudes of Educated Africans in Kenya, Tanganyika, and Uganda," 1962, S-44, box 23, Office of Research, Special Reports, 1953–1963, RG 306, USIA, NARA.

5. "Guidelines for Policy and Operations: Africa," Department of State, Mar. 1962, box 2, National Security File, JFKL.

6. U.S. Congress, Senate, Committee on Commerce, *Freedom of Communications*, pt. 1, 1291–93, 1299. Arthur Schlesinger uses the figure of 479 references to Africa by Kennedy during his 1960 campaign speeches, a figure that may come from the entire campaign but more likely from duplicate citations. Schlesinger, *Thousand Days*, 554.

7. "Africa—the Coming Challenge," Kennedy remarks at Democratic luncheon, Watertown, Wisc., 13 Nov. 1959, box 1030, Pre-Presidential Papers, JFKL; remarks of John F. Kennedy at Saint Anselm's College, Manchester, NH, 5 Mar. 1960, box 1030, Pre-Presidential Papers, JFKL.

8. "The United States and Africa: A New Policy for a New Era," remarks at the Second Annual Conference of AMSAC, 28 June 1959, box 1030, Campaign: Press and Publicity: Speeches, Statements, and Sections, 1958–1960, Pre-Presidential Papers, JFKL.

9. Muehlenbeck, *Betting on the Africans*, xv.

10. Meriwether, "'Worth a Lot of Negro Votes'"; Muehlenbeck, *Betting on the Africans.*

11. Telegram from Rusk to Williams, 25 Feb. 1961, box 2, NSF, JFKL; telegram from Williams to Rusk, 26 Feb. 1961, box 2, NSF, JFKL; Noer, *Soapy*, 238–41, quotes on 239.

12. Noer, *Soapy*, 239–41, quotes on 240.

13. Muehlenbeck, *Betting on the Africans*, 46–47. For detailed and thorough accounts of Kennedy's interest in Africa, see Muehlenbeck, *Betting on the Africans*; Mahoney, *JFK*.

14. Noer, *Soapy*, 232.

15. Mennen Williams to John Kennedy, "Report of Second Trip to Africa," 9 Sept. 1961, box 2, NSF, JFKL.

16. "The Facts on Grant to African Airlift Students-Summary," background report prepared by Sen. Kennedy's office, [Aug. 1960?], box 1044, Kennedy Pre-Presidential Papers, JFKL. For more, see Meriwether, "'Worth a Lot of Negro Votes.'"

17. For an excellent discussion of HBCUs in decolonization, see Parker, "'Made-in-America Revolutions'?"

18. Rich, "United States Government Sponsored Higher Educational Programs for Africans," 103–8.

19. Memo for Kennedy from George Ball, Acting Secretary of State, 13 Oct. 1961, box 2, NSF, JFKL; "Report to the President on Sub-Sahara Africa Student Programs," [Oct. 1961?], box 2, NSF, JFKL.

20. Memorandum from George Anderson to McGeorge Bundy, 16 July 1962, box 2, NSF, JFKL.

21. In September 1959, the colonial attaché at the British embassy in Washington reported that all but one of the Kenyan students in the 1959 airlift had school certificates but were in the lower bracket and would be taking courses "leading to educationally inferior degrees that will place them at a disadvantage vis-à-vis Makerere graduates." Six months later, the minister of education for Kenya complained to U.S. officials that if a 1960 airlift occurred, most of the top-grade students would go to the United States and none would be left for Makerere or the Royal Technical College. D. Williams, report on students from Kenya, 1 Sept. 1959, 511.45R3/9-159, CDF, 1955–59, RG 59, NARA; Charles Withers in Nairobi to Secretary of State, Feb. 3, 1960, 511.45R3/2-360, CDF, 1960–63, RG 59, NARA.

22. Philip Coombs to McGeorge Bundy, "Problems of African Students in the United States," [May 1961?], box 2, NSF, JFKL; "Report to the President on Sub-Sahara African Student Programs," [Oct. 1961?], box 2, NSF, JFKL; Samuel Belk to Bundy, Oct. 25, 1961, box 2, NSF, JFKL; Philip Coombs to McGeorge Bundy, "Recent Actions on African Students," 4 Aug. 1961, box 2, NSF, JFKL.

23. For more on African students and their actions, see Shachtman, *Airlift to America*.

24. There is a large literature on the Peace Corps, including Fischer, *Making Them Like Us*; Hoffman, *All You Need Is Love*; Schwarz, *What You Can Do for Your Country*.

25. McVety, *Enlightened Aid*, 106.

26. Lerner, "Climbing Off the Back Burner," 580.

27. Immerwahr, "Modernization and Development in U.S. Foreign Relations"; Latham, *Modernization as Ideology*.

28. Rostow, *Stages of Economic Growth*.

29. Memorandum from Rusk to Johnson, 14 Oct. 1965, in *FRUS, 1964–1968*, 24:311, http://history.state.gov/historicaldocuments/frus1964-68v24/d201.

30. DeRoche, *Black, White and Chrome*, 97.

31. "The Place of Africa in US Foreign Policy," State Department Administrative History, 1968, vol. 1, chap. 5: Africa, pp. 7, 12, quote on 12, box 2, Administrative Histories, LBJL.

32. "Guidelines for Policy and Operations: Africa," Department of State, Mar. 1962, box 2, NSF, JFKL.

33. Muehlenbeck, *Betting on the Africans*, quote on xi–xii. On the Soviet "rediscovery" of the Third World, see Westad, *Global Cold War*, 66–72.

34. Joseph Satterthwaite, William Attwood, Richard Freund, Philip Kaiser, and Leon Poullada to G. Mennen Williams, [Aug. 1961?], box 2, NSF, JFKL; statement by

Ambassador Poullada at the Lagos Regional African Conference, revised, [Aug. 1961?], box 2, NSF, JFKL.

35. Satterthwaite, Attwood, Freund, Kaiser, and Poullada to Williams, [Aug. 1961?], box 2, NSF, JFKL; statement by Ambassador Poullada at the Lagos Regional African Conference, revised, [Aug. 1961?], box 2, NSF, JFKL.

36. Macmillan, "The Wind of Change," 17. For more on the speech and its significance, see Butler and Stockwell, *Wind of Change*.

37. Irwin, "A Wind of Change?," quote on 903.

38. Telegram from Rusk to American Embassy Pretoria, 25 Aug. 1961, box 2, NSF, JFKL.

39. Telegram from Rusk to American Embassy Pretoria, 25 Aug. 1961, box 2, NSF, JFKL.

40. Telegram from Satterthwaite to Rusk, 7 Sept. 1961, box 2, NSF, JFKL.

41. "Guidelines for Policy and Operations: Republic of South Africa," Department of State, May 1962, box 2, NSF, JFKL.

42. Telegram from Rusk to American Embassy Pretoria, 25 Aug. 1961, box 2, NSF, JFKL.

43. Memorandum from Bowles to Bundy, 21 Sept. 1961, box 2, NSF, JFKL; memorandum from Jerome "Jerry" Weisner to Bundy, 18 Oct. 1961, box 2, NSF, JFKL.

44. Muehlenbeck, *Betting on the Africans*, 190.

45. Zeiler, *Dean Rusk*, 86.

46. Zeiler, 92.

47. Zeiler, 93.

48. Noer, *Cold War and Black Liberation*, 5–6.

49. Brinkley, *Dean Acheson*, quote on 307.

50. Rodrigues, "About Face," quote on 5.

51. Mahoney, *JFK*, 188; Schneidman, *Engaging Africa*, 14–15.

52. Schneidman, 15–16, quote on 15.

53. Noer, *Soapy*, quote on 257.

54. Schmidt, *Foreign Intervention in Africa*, 85; Schneidman, *Engaging Africa*, 24–28.

55. Mennen Williams to John Kennedy, "Report of Second Trip to Africa," 9 Sept. 1961, box 2, NSF, JFKL.

56. Williams to Kennedy, "Report of Second Trip to Africa," 9 Sept. 1961, box 2, NSF, JFKL.

57. Rodrigues, "About Face," 6–7.

58. Schneidman, *Engaging Africa*, 9, 30.

59. Schneidman, quote on 5. For more on Acheson and Portugal, see Brinkley, *Dean Acheson*, 303–15.

60. Heiss, "Whistling in the Dark," 128–29.

61. Noer, *Soapy*, 260; Muehlenbeck, *Betting on the Africans*, 106–11; Schneidman, *Engaging Africa*, 36; Rodrigues, "About Face," 9.

62. Noer, *Soapy*, quote on 253.

63. Noer, quote on 259.

64. Scholars continue to wrestle with the extent to which Kennedy changed U.S. policy. Philip Muehlenbeck has written extensively about Kennedy's break with the past and his "four-pronged" approach to courting Africa, while acknowledging that in critical areas such as Portuguese colonies and South Africa, Kennedy was not as bold. Thomas Noer, Jason Parker, and others see less of a break and less fundamental change. "For all the emphasis on change that Kennedy's election purportedly represented," writes Parker, "it is easy to overstate his differences with his predecessor. The continuities in his diplomacy are at least as striking in retrospect." Kennedy cared about Africa, yet as has been the case before and since for those who have entered the White House, new initiatives and bold changes gave way to striking continuities. Parker, *Hearts, Minds, Voices*, 116; Muehlenbeck, *Betting on the Africans*; Noer, *Cold War and Black Liberation*.

65. Memorandum from Schlesinger to Kennedy, "Our Policy in Africa," 1 July 1963, in *FRUS, 1961–1963*, 21:497, https://history.state.gov/historicaldocuments/frus1961-63v21/d315.

66. Mennen Williams to John Kennedy, "Report of Second Trip to Africa," 9 Sept. 1961, box 2, NSF, JFKL.

67. Telegram from Arthur Beach to Department of State, "Movement of American Refugees from the Congo through Johannesburg," 1 Aug. 1960, box 2311, 811.411/8-160, CDF, 1960–63, RG 59, NARA.

68. Telegram from Beach to Department of State, "Movement of American Refugees from the Congo through Johannesburg," 1 Aug. 1960; Dow, "Accidental Diplomats."

69. McAlister, "Guess Who's Coming to Dinner," 37.

70. A. J. Dens to Lyndon Johnson, 22 Nov. 1961, folder "Foreign Relations—Africa," box 79, Subject File—1961, Vice Presidential Papers, 1961–1963, LBJL.

71. J. C. Phillips to Johnson, 5 Dec. 1961, folder "Foreign Relations—Africa," box 79, Subject File—1961, Vice Presidential Papers, 1961–1963, LBJL.

72. Mennen Williams to John Kennedy, "Report of Second Trip to Africa," 9 Sept. 1961, box 2, NSF, JFKL.

73. Bennie Nix to Lyndon Johnson, 8 Jan. 1963, folder "Foreign Relations—Africa," box 195, Subject File—1963, Vice Presidential Papers, 1961–1963, LBJL.

74. James Del Rio to Hobart Taylor, 23 July 1962, folder "Foreign Relations—Africa," box 134, Subject File—1962, Vice Presidential Papers, 1961–1963, LBJL.

75. "Remarks of Senator John F. Kennedy, Elks Auditorium, Los Angeles, Calif., November 1, 1960," in U.S. Congress, Senate, Committee on Commerce, *Freedom of Communications*, pt. 1, 846; Davis, "Black Americans and United States Policy," 243; Krenn, *Black Diplomacy*.

76. For more on Springer, see Richards, *Maida Springer*.

77. George McCray to A. Philip Randolph, 3 July 1958, A. Philip Randolph Papers, reel 2, frame 89; Randolph to McCray, 10 July 1958, A. Philip Randolph Papers, reel 2, frames 90–92.

78. Representative citations for these projects include Randolph to George Meany, 8 June 1956, A. Philip Randolph Papers, reel 3, frame 303; Randolph to

Arthur A. Ochwada, Assistant General Secretary of the Kenya Federation of Labour, 15 Aug. 1957, Brotherhood of Sleeping Car Porters Records, box 95, folder "Africa," LOC; Randolph to Tom Mboya, 25 Aug. 1958, Brotherhood of Sleeping Car Porters Records, box 95, folder "Africa," LOC; Randolph to Sascha Voliman, Institute of International Labor Research, 29 Apr. 1958, Brotherhood of Sleeping Car Porters Records, box 95, folder "Africa," LOC; Mary-Louise Hooper, West Coast Representative of the South African Defense Fund, to Randolph, 27 Jan. 1959, Brotherhood of Sleeping Car Porters Records, box 95, folder "Africa," LOC.

79. A. Philip Randolph to "Dear Friend," 15 Dec. 1959, A. Philip Randolph Papers, reel 3, frame 593; James Farmer to Roy Wilkins, John Morsell, Henry Lee Moon, and Gloster Current, 28 Dec. 1959, box 34, folder, "Africa, General, 1956–59," Series A, NAACP Papers, III, LOC.

80. For more on the Council on African Affairs, see the authoritative Von Eschen, *Race against Empire*.

81. Call letter for the ANLCA, [Aug. 1962?], folder "ANLCA 1962," box 2, National Urban League Papers, II, 1, LOC.

82. T. J. Sellers, the Bronx, to Roy Wilkins, 25 Nov. 1962, folder "ANLCA, 1962," box 199, Series A, NAACP Papers, III, LOC; John Morsell to Sellers, 5 Dec. 1962, box 199, Series A, NAACP Papers, III, LOC.

83. Martin Luther King Jr., "The Negro Looks at America," *New York Amsterdam News*, 8 Dec. 1962, 13. For more on the Arden House conference, see Meriwether, "American Negro Leadership Conference on Africa"; Plummer, *In Search of Power*, 122–25.

84. ANLCA to John F. Kennedy, 17 Dec. 1962, folder "ANLCA, 1962," box 198, Series A, NAACP Papers, III, LOC; Irwin, "Imagining Nation, State, and Order," 20.

85. Theodore Brown to Conference Participant, 21 Dec. 1962, folder "ANLCA 1962," box 2, National Urban League Papers, II, 1, LOC.

86. "JFK, 'Big Six' Meet; Discuss Africa and Colored Americans," *Baltimore Afro-American*, 29 Dec. 1962, 14.

87. Selvage and Lee memo, "Ponto de Vista relativo a Portugal," 25 Nov. 1963, Pasta [folder] 40, AOS/NE-21 (caixa 413), Salazar Archives, Arquivo National da Torre do Tombo, Lisbon (with thanks to Joe Parrott for the reference).

88. Roy Wilkins, Chair of the Call Committee, "Letter of Invitation," 28 Feb. 1964, folder "American Negro Leadership Conference on Africa, 1964–65," box 199, Series A, General Office File, 1956–1965, NAACP Papers, III, LOC.

89. Call for the Shoreham Conference, folder "ANLCA 1964," box 2, NUL Papers, II, 1, LOC.

90. ANLCA resolutions, 1964 Second National Conference, n.d., folder "ANLCA, 1964–65," box 199, Series A, NAACP Papers, III, LOC; program for the Second National Conference, 24–27 Sept. 1964, folder "ANLCA 1964—Reports," box 2, NUL Papers, II, 1, LOC; John Morsell to Roy Wilkins, 30 Sept. 1964, folder "American Negro Leadership Conference on Africa, Second National Conference, Sept. 1964," box 199, Series A, NAACP Papers, III, LOC.

91. Program for the Second National Conference, 24–27 Sept. 1964, folder "ANLCA 1964—Reports," box 2, NUL Papers, II, 1, LOC; ANLCA resolutions, 1964 Second

National Conference, n.d., folder "ANLCA, 1964–65," box 199, Series A, NAACP Papers, III, LOC.

92. ANLCA resolutions, 1964 Second National Conference, n.d., folder "ANLCA, 1964–65," box 199, Series A, NAACP Papers, III, LOC.

93. ANLCA resolutions, 1964 Second National Conference.

94. Memo from Komer to Bundy, 6 Jan. 1965, box 76, Country Files, NSF, LBJL.

95. DeRoche, *Black, White, and Chrome*, quote on 104–5. See also Lerner, "Climbing Off the Back Burner," 596–97.

96. Memo from Bill Moyers to President, 14 June 1965, box 6, Subject File—Countries, White House Central File, LBJL; memorandum from Haynes to Bundy, 15 June 1965, in *FRUS, 1964–1968*, 24:305.

97. Memorandum from Haynes to Bundy, 15 June 1965, in *FRUS, 1964–1968*, 24:304–5, quote on 304.

98. Lerner, "Climbing Off the Back Burner," 586. Action memorandum from Williams to Rusk, 17 Sept. 1965, in *FRUS, 1964–1968*, 24:308, http://history.state.gov/historicaldocuments/frus1964-68v24/d200.

99. Action memorandum from Williams to Rusk, 17 Sept. 1965, in *FRUS, 1964–1968*, 24:308.

100. Memorandum from Rusk to LBJ, 14 Oct. 1965, in *FRUS, 1964–1968*, 24:311–12. An ongoing conversation examines whether Lyndon Johnson and his administration paid less attention to Africa than did John Kennedy and his administration. While Noer (*Cold War and Black Liberation*), Lyons ("Keeping Africa off the Agenda"), and Muehlenbeck (*Betting on the Africans*) point to Kennedy as being more engaged with Africa, Lerner ("Climbing Off the Back Burner") argues that LBJ was as much or even more engaged. Some differences are based on whether one is looking at the individual or the broader administrations, others on interpretations about whether there were policy changes from the previous administration. While the differences of opinion are meaningful, in the longer arc of this era of decolonization there was a consistency in approaches toward the continent.

101. Survey, "African Students in the US," [June 1963], R-215, box 18, Office of Research, Special Reports, 1960–1963, RG 306, USIA, NARA.

102. While highlighting numerous efforts toward Africa during the Johnson years, historian Mitch Lerner makes the case that Johnson wanted his concern for Africa to fly under the radar. Casting Johnson as having "regularly refused high-profile meetings with African officials" as a conscious positive strategy, however, does not seem to align with the publicity-laden efforts taken by a man keeping score against his predecessor. Lerner, "Climbing Off the Back-Burner," 583.

103. Memorandum for the record from Rick Haynes to Bundy, Moyers, Komer, and Saunders, 14 Oct. 1965, box 76—Africa, NSF, LBJL.

104. Memo from Hamilton to Johnson, 22 Aug. 1967, folder "Africa, General," box 1, Files of Edward K. Hamilton, NSF, LBJL.

105. After he left the presidency, Teddy Roosevelt journeyed, hunted, and wrote extensively in East Africa. While president, Franklin Roosevelt stopped over in Gambia and Liberia on his journey to the 1943 Casablanca Conference. Prior to his presidency, Dwight D. Eisenhower led troops through North Africa during World War II.

106. Lerner, "'Big Tree of Peace and Justice,'" 360.

107. Lerner, 390.

108. Lerner, 392–93.

109. State Department telegram #2156 to ambassadors or principal officers, 6 May 1965, folder 2/64–6/64, box 76 [1 of 2], Africa—General, memos & misc [2 of 2], vol. 1, Country File, Africa, NSF, LBJL, cited in Lerner, review, 10.

110. Lerner, "Climbing Off the Back Burner," quote on 597.

111. Dudziak, *Cold War Civil Rights*, quotes on 172, 173.

112. "Remarks of the President at White House Reception Celebrating the Third Anniversary of the Organization of African Unity," 26 May 1966, box 14, NSC History, NSF, LBJL.

113. "Remarks of the President at White House Reception," 26 May 1966.

114. "Remarks of the President at White House Reception," 26 May 1966.

115. "Remarks of the President at White House Reception," 26 May 1966.

116. "Remarks of the President at White House Reception," 26 May 1966.

117. "Press and Diplomatic Reactions to the President's May 26 Speech on Africa," box 14, NSC History, NSF, LBJL.

Chapter 4

1. Jomo Kenyatta to Lyndon Johnson, 8 April 1965, box 1, Files of Edward K. Hamilton, NSF, LBJL. For more on links between Kenya and the United States during the 1960s, see Dudziak, *Exporting American Dreams*.

2. Jomo Kenyatta to Lyndon Johnson, 8 April 1965, box 1, Files of Edward K. Hamilton, NSF, LBJL.

3. "The White Redoubt," 28 June 1962, paper prepared in the Department of State, in *FRUS, 1961–1963*, 21:491–92, quotes on 491.

4. "The Liberation Movements of Southern Africa," NIE 70-1-67, 24 Nov. 1967, p. 3, box 8, National Intelligence Estimates, NSF, LBJL.

5. Guinea-Bissau claimed independence from Portugal in September 1973; Portugal recognized the independence in September 1974.

6. "The Place of Africa in US Foreign Policy," p. 7, vol. 1, chap. 5: Africa, State Department Administrative History, 1968, box 2, Administrative Histories, LBJL. Shortly before leaving office, President Johnson mandated that each executive branch area write a history of its work during his presidential years.

7. "The Place of Africa in US Foreign Policy," pp. 1–3, vol. 1, chap. 5: Africa, State Department Administrative History, 1968, box 2, Administrative Histories, LBJL.

8. *Report of the Task Force on the Review of African Development Policies and Programs*, 22 July 1966, in *FRUS, 1964–1968*, 24:334–49, quote on 336.

9. *Report of the Task Force on the Review of African Development Policies and Programs*, 22 July 1966, in *FRUS, 1964–1968*, 24:334–49, quotes on 336, 348.

10. "The Place of Africa in US Foreign Policy," pp. 7, 12, quote on 12, vol. 1, chap. 5: Africa, State Department Administrative History, 1968, box 2, Administrative Histories, LBJL.

11. "President Johnson's New Aid Strategy for Africa," pp. 4–7, quotes on p. 7, vol. 1, chap. 5: Africa, Section B, box 2, State Department Administrative History, 1968, LBJL.

12. "The Liberation Movements of Southern Africa," 24 Nov. 1967, NIE 70-1-67, folder "South and East Africa, box 8, National Intelligence Estimates, NSF, LBJL.

13. "The Place of Africa in US Foreign Policy," p. 21, vol. 1, chap. 5: Africa, State Department Administrative History, 1968, box 2, Administrative Histories, LBJL.

14. "The Liberation Movements of Southern Africa," 24 Nov. 1967, NIE 70-1-67, folder "South and East Africa, box 8, National Intelligence Estimates, NSF, LBJL.

15. Westad, *Global Cold War,* quote on 209–10.

16. Watts, *Rhodesia's Unilateral Declaration of Independence,* 14–16; DeRoche, *Black, White and Chrome,* 98–100.

17. Mungazi, *Last British Liberals in Africa.*

18. Minter, *King Solomon's Mines Revisited,* 203–5.

19. DeRoche, *Black, White and Chrome,* 107, 111.

20. Minter, *King Solomon's Mines Revisited,* Smith quote on 237; Michel, "The Luster of Chrome," *Time* quote on 142.

21. "Repercussions of a Unilateral Declaration of Independence by Southern Rhodesia," 13 Oct. 1965, p. 3, Special NIE 72-65, box 8, National Intelligence Estimates, NSF, LBJL.

22. "Repercussions of a Unilateral Declaration of Independence by Southern Rhodesia," 13 Oct. 1965, pp. 1–2, quote on p. 1, Special NIE 72-65, box 8, National Intelligence Estimates, NSF, LBJL.

23. DeRoche, *Black, White and Chrome,* 108–9, quote on 108.

24. For a comprehensive examination of the UDI, see Watts, *Rhodesia's Unilateral Declaration of Independence.*

25. DeRoche, *Black, White and Chrome,* 106.

26. DeRoche, 116.

27. "Special Problem Areas," vol. 1, chap. 5: Africa, Section C, Subsection 8: Southern Africa, pp. 22–23, State Department Administrative History, 1968, box 2, Administrative Histories, LBJL; DeRoche, *Black, White and Chrome,* 128; Noer, *Cold War and Black Liberation,* 186.

28. Memo from Bundy to Rusk, cc'd to Secretary of Defense, Director of CIA, and Head of AID, [Dec. 1965?], box 97, Africa—Rhodesia, Country Files, NSF, LBJL. See Watts, *Rhodesia's Unilateral Declaration of Independence,* chap. 5.

29. See Memorandum from Haynes to Bundy, 7 Oct. 1965, box 3, Files of Edward K. Hamilton, NSF, LBJL; memorandum from Haynes to Komer on "Rhodesia Working Group Meeting, November 23, 1965," box 1, Files of Ulric Haynes, NSF, LBJL; Haynes to Bundy, "Situation Report: Rhodesian Crisis," 6 Jan. 1966, box 1, Files of Ulric Haynes, NSF, LBJL.

30. DeRoche, *Black, White and Chrome,* quote on 115.

31. Valenti to McGeorge Bundy, 19 Nov. 1965, quoted in Watts, "African Americans and US Foreign Policy," 111.

32. A. Philip Randolph and Donald Harrington to LBJ, 11 Nov. 1965, box 7, Subject File—Countries, White House Central File, LBJL; Snyder, "Rise of Human Rights during the Johnson Years," 46–47.

33. King telegram to LBJ, 11 Nov. 1965, quoted in Watts, "African Americans and US Foreign Policy," 110; Wilkins telegram to LBJ, 12 Nov. 1965, quoted in Watts, "African Americans and US Foreign Policy," 110–11.

34. Watts, "African Americans and US Foreign Policy," 107–18.

35. Snyder, *From Selma to Moscow,* 59. See also DeRoche, *Black, White and Chrome,* 126; Lake, *"Tar Baby" Option,* 89.

36. Letter from LBJ to Jomo Kenyatta, 10 Nov. 1966, CO 250, box 11, Confidential File, White House Central File, LBJL; Snyder, *From Selma to Moscow,* 42–53.

37. Snyder, "Rise of Human Rights during the Johnson Years," quote on 248.

38. Robert Komer to LBJ, 6 Dec. 1965, box 3, Files of Edward K. Hamilton, NSF, LBJL; Mlambo, "'Honoured More in the Breach,'" 372.

39. "Repercussions of a Unilateral Declaration of Independence by Southern Rhodesia," 13 Oct. 1965, p. 1, Special NIE 72-65, box 8, National Intelligence Estimates, NSF, LBJL; "Rhodesia and Zambia: From Voluntary to Mandatory Sanctions," CIA, Jan. 1967, box 11, Confidential File, White House Central File, LBJL.

40. Memorandum from John P. Roche to Moyers, 9 Dec. 1966, CO 250, box 11, Confidential File, White House Central File, LBJL.

41. Minter, *King Solomon's Mines Revisited,* 209; Mlambo, "'Honoured More in the Breach.'"

42. Kaunda quote in Noer, *Cold War and Black Liberation,* 236–37; Minter, *King Solomon's Mines Revisited,* 212.

43. DeRoche, *Black, White and Chrome,* 130.

44. Becnel, *Senator Allen Ellender of Louisiana,* quote on 209.

45. Michel, "Luster of Chrome," quote on 147.

46. Goldwater, letter to his children, 8 Dec. 1967, in Dean and Goldwater, *Pure Goldwater,* 191.

47. Horne, *From the Barrel of a Gun,* 45; "Rhodesia: Kicking the Gong Around."

48. Horne, *From the Barrel of a Gun,* 105.

49. Brinkley, *Dean Acheson,* quote on 303. See also Noer, *Cold War and Black Liberation,* 229–30.

50. Noer, *Cold War and Black Liberation,* quote on 231.

51. Noer, 234.

52. Goldwater, letter to his children, 19 Dec. 1967, in Dean and Goldwater, *Pure Goldwater,* 192; Horne, *From the Barrel of a Gun,* 101.

53. Michel, "Luster of Chrome," 145–46; Noer, *Cold War and Black Liberation,* 231.

54. Noer, *Cold War and Black Liberation,* 234.

55. Lawson, *Running for Freedom,* 72–74; White, *Making of the President,* 203–4.

56. For more on Frances Bolton and her important work, see DeRoche, "Frances Bolton, Margaret Tibbetts, and the US Relations with the Rhodesian Federation."

57. Memorandum of discussion of the NSC, April 14, 1960, in *FRUS, 1958–1960,* 14:126–28.

58. Hersh, *Price of Power,* 141–42.

59. Lerner, "Climbing Off the Back Burner," 590–96, 600.

60. Hersh, *Price of Power,* 111. For more on Nixon's racial views from someone inside the White House, see Morris, *Uncertain Greatness*; O'Reilly, *Nixon's Piano*;

or listen to his tapes: https://millercenter.org/the-presidency/secret-white-house-tapes/research-the-tapes.

61. With appreciation for the reference to Andrew DeRoche, "Attempting to Assert African Agency," 492.

62. Suri, *Henry Kissinger and the American Century*, 236.

63. Memorandum from Kissinger to Nixon, NSC review of policy toward Southern Africa, 3 Apr. 1969, in *FRUS, 1969–1976*, 28:7, http://history.state.gov/historicaldocuments/frus1969-76v28/d5.

64. Memorandum from Kissinger to Nixon, NSC review of policy toward Southern Africa, in *FRUS, 1969–1976*, 28:7–8.

65. National Security Study Memorandum 39, 10 Apr. 1969, in *FRUS, 1969–1976*, 28:9, http://history.state.gov/historicaldocuments/frus1969-76v28/d6.

66. Paper prepared by the NSC Interdepartmental Group for Africa, 9 Dec. 1969, in *FRUS, 1969–1976*, 28:29.

67. Paper prepared by the NSC Interdepartmental Group for Africa, 30–32, quotes on 30, 32.

68. Paper prepared by the NSC Interdepartmental Group for Africa, 34, 39.

69. Paper prepared by the NSC Interdepartmental Group for Africa, 40–41. Anthony Lake writes that there were five options considered, and others have used this number; however, six options were presented. Lake, *"Tar Baby" Option*, 128–29.

70. NSC Interdepartmental Group for Africa, 48–49.

71. NSC Interdepartmental Group for Africa, 43.

72. Minutes of NSC meeting, 17 Dec. 1969, in *FRUS, 1969–1976*, 28:58.

73. NSC Interdepartmental Group for Africa, xx.

74. NSC Interdepartmental Group for Africa, 44–45.

75. Minutes of NSC meeting, 17 Dec. 1969, in *FRUS, 1969–1976*, 28:57–63, quotes on 59.

76. Minutes of NSC meeting, 17 Dec. 1969, in *FRUS, 1969–1976*, 28:57–63, quotes on p. 62.

77. Lake, *"Tar Baby" Option*, 129.

78. For a detailed description of NSSM 39 and the decision, see Michel, *White House and White Africa*, 90–96. On whether Nixon's choice of Option 2 was a reversal of policy from previous administrations, Michel sees a significant change in policy, see as well "Luster of Chrome," 151. On the other hand, two historians steeped in U.S. policy in the region see the adoption of Option 2 as no fundamental shift. See DeRoche, *Black, White and Chrome*, 164; Noer, *Cold War and Black Liberation*, 239.

79. Michel, "Luster of Chrome," 155.

80. Brinkley, *Dean Acheson*, 327. For details of the legislative procession of the Byrd Amendment, see DeRoche, *Black, White and Chrome*, 170–77; Lake, *"Tar Baby" Option*, 198–238. For corporate interests, see Minter, *King Solomon's Mines Revisited*, 238–39.

81. Telegram from mission to UN to Department of State, 24 Sept. 1971, in *FRUS, 1969–1976*, 28:141.

82. Memorandum from Kissinger to Nixon, 28 Sept. 1978, in *FRUS, 1969–1976*, 28:142.

83. Conversation between Nixon and Kissinger, 28 Sept. 1971, in *FRUS, 1969–1976*, 28:143–45.

84. Conversation between Nixon and Kissinger, 28 Sept. 1971, in *FRUS, 1969–1976*, 28:143–45.

85. Conversation among Nixon, Douglas-Home, Kissinger, and Ziegler, 30 Sept. 1971, in *FRUS, 1969–1976*, 28:146.

86. Conversation between Nixon and Kissinger, 6 Oct. 1971, in *FRUS, 1969–1976*, 28:149.

87. Conversation between Nixon and Kissinger, 6 Oct. 1971, in *FRUS, 1969–1976*, 28:149.

88. Conversation between Nixon and Kissinger, 6 Oct. 1971, in *FRUS, 1969–1976*, 28:149.

89. Snyder, *From Selma to Moscow*, 56.

90. Memorandum from Kissinger to Nixon, 17 Jan. 1972, in *FRUS, 1969–1976*, 28:169–70.

91. Mlambo, "'Honoured More in the Breach,'" 384–85.

92. Sithole quote in DeRoche, *Black, White and Chrome*, 177; *Zambia Daily Mail* quote in DeRoche, "Attempting to Assert African Agency," 18–19.

93. Plummer, *In Search of Power*, 287.

94. "U.S. against the Charter," editorial, *New York Times*, 12 Nov. 1971, 46.

95. Morgan, "The World is Watching," 520–47; Plummer, *In Search of Power*, 281–85; Nesbitt, *Race for Sanctions*, 89–96; African Activist Archive, "Polaroid and South Africa," https://africanactivist.msu.edu/document_metadata.php?objectid=210-808-8084.

96. Plummer, *In Search of Power*, 253–59; Nesbitt, *Race for Sanctions*, 74, 94.

97. "Repression in Southern Africa: An Indictment of Harvard University," Pan-African Liberation Committee, Sept. 1971, African Activist Archive, https://africanactivist.msu.edu/document_metadata.php?objectid=210-808-8173.

98. Plummer, *In Search of Power*, 277.

99. Plummer, 277–78.

100. Parrott, "*A Luta Continua*," 20–35; Plummer, *In Search of Power*, 277–80.

101. For an insightful analysis of Arthur Ashe and sporting boycotts, see Morgan, "Black and White at Center Court." See also Nesbitt, *Race for Sanctions*, 82–89.

Chapter 5

1. The UN General Assembly passed Resolution 2372 (XXII) on 12 June 1968, stating that South West Africa would henceforth be known as Namibia, in accordance with the wishes of its people.

2. Gleijeses, *Visions of Freedom*, 26–27, quote on 27; Schneidman, *Engaging Africa*, 16, 50–51; Westad, *Global Cold War*, 210–11.

3. "Sinister Man," editorial, *Washington Star*, 26 Apr. 1964, folder "Angola," box 79, Africa—South Africa, NSF, LBJL.

4. "Sinister Man," editorial, *Washington Star*, 26 Apr. 1964.

5. Schmidt, *Foreign Intervention in Africa*, 91–92; Noer, *Cold War and Black Liberation*, 85.

6. Mondlane, excerpt from *Struggle for Mozambique*, 174.

7. Schneidman, *Engaging Africa*, 127. For more on the struggle in Guinea, see Rodrigues, "'For a Better Guinea.'"

8. Memo from Nixon to Haldeman, Ehrlichman, Kissinger, 2 Mar. 1970, in *FRUS, 1969–1976*, E-5, pt. 1, 1–2.

9. Schneidman, *Engaging Africa*, 128–49.

10. Memo from Kissinger to Nixon, 29 April 1974, in *FRUS, 1969–1976*, 28:227.

11. Schneidman, *Engaging Africa*, 143–45.

12. Schneidman, 145.

13. UN Resolution 3061, https://undocs.org/en/A/RES/3061(XXVIII)&Lang=E&Area=RESOLUTION; Rodrigues, "'For a Better Guinea.'"

14. Memorandum from William Colby to Henry Kissinger, 19 Sept. 1974, in *FRUS, 1969–1976*, 28:233; 40 Committee Memorandum, 23 Jan. 1975, *FRUS, 1969–1976*, 28:235; Westad, *Global Cold War*, 217–22; Schmidt, *Foreign Intervention in Africa*, 92–96.

15. Memorandum of conversation, 19 Apr. 1975, in *FRUS, 1969–1976*, 28:236–43, quotes on 237–38.

16. Memorandum, 40 Committee meeting, 5 June 1975, in *FRUS, 1969–1976*, 28:246–48, quotes on 247.

17. Response to NSSM 224: U.S. Policy toward Angola, 13 June 1975, in *FRUS, 1969–1976*, 28:253–55.

18. Memorandum of conversation, 20 June 1975, in *FRUS, 1969–1976*, 28:257–61, quotes on 259.

19. Memorandum of conversation, 20 June 1975, in *FRUS, 1969–1976*, 28:259.

20. Minutes of NSC meeting, 27 June 1975, in *FRUS, 1969–1976*, 28:265–74, quotes on 269.

21. Memorandum, 40 Committee meeting, 14 July 1975, in *FRUS, 1969–1976*, 28:276–81.

22. Memorandum, 40 Committee meeting, 14 July 1975, in *FRUS, 1969–1976*, 28:279.

23. Telegram from consulate in Luanda to State, 25 Sept. 1975, in *FRUS, 1969–1976*, 28:318–22, quote on 322.

24. Memorandum of conversation, Kissinger and Ford, 18 July 1975, in *FRUS, 1969–1976*, 28:286.

25. Memorandum of conversation, Kissinger et al., 27 June 1975, in *FRUS, 1969–1976*, 28:261–64; Westad, *Global Cold War*, 222–28. For more on Soviet involvement, see Shubin, *Hot "Cold War."*

26. Memorandum, 40 Committee meeting, 13 Sept. 1975, in *FRUS, 1969–1976*, 28:305–14.

27. Miller, *African Volk*, 182–87; Westad, *Global Cold War*, 230–31.

28. Miller, *African Volk*, 167.

29. Historian Piero Gleijeses argues that South Africa was "urged on" by Washington, which aligns with Sue Onslow and Chris Saunders arguing that the South

African government felt "betrayed" by Washington after Kissinger and the CIA had encouraged its intervention. Jamie Miller, on the other hand, argues that the South African government made its own calculation to intervene against the communist MPLA. See Gleijeses, *Conflicting Missions*, 273–99, and *Visions of Freedom*, 28–29; Saunders and Onslow, "Cold War and Southern Africa," 229; Miller, *African Volk*, 165–92, esp. 188, and "Yes, Minister."

30. Gleijeses, *Visions of Freedom*, 28–29; Westad, *Global Cold War*, 231–35. For work that emphasizes the Cuban role in Angola, see Gleijeses, *Conflicting Missions* and *Visions of Freedom*; Waters, *Cuba and Angola*. For work that emphasizes the Soviet role, see Shubin, *Hot "Cold War"*; Filatova and Davidson, *Hidden Thread*.

31. Backchannel message from Kissinger to ambassador to Iran Helms, 20 Dec. 1975, in *FRUS, 1969–1976*, 28:406–7.

32. Miller, *African Volk*, 197–98, 216.

33. Westad, *Global Cold War*, quote on 246.

34. Memorandum of conversation, Ford, Kissinger, and Scowcroft, 15 Mar. 1976, https://nsarchive2.gwu.edu//NSAEBB/NSAEBB487/docs/02%20-%20Memorandum%20of%20Conversation,%20March%2015,%201976,%20Ford%20Library.pdf; Washington Special Actions Group meeting, 24 Mar. 1976, https://nsarchive2.gwu.edu//NSAEBB/NSAEBB487/docs/03%20-%20Washington%20Special%20Actions%20Group%20Meeting,%20Cuba,%20March%2024,%201976.pdf.

35. Michel, *White House, White Africa*, 170.

36. DeRoche, *Kenneth Kaunda*, 27–28.

37. Memorandum of conversation, 25 Apr. 1976, in *FRUS, 1969–1976*, 28:484–94, quote on 485.

38. Memorandum of conversation, 27 Apr. 1976, in *FRUS, 1969–1976*, 28:494–97, quote on 496. The reference to four Frontline States reflects Angola not yet having formally joined the Frontline States. For more on Kissinger's trip and speech, see DeRoche, *Kenneth Kaunda*, 67–83.

39. Henry Kissinger, "United States Policy in Southern Africa," 27 Apr. 1976, in *Department of State Bulletin* 74, no. 127 (31 May 1976): 672–73.

40. Kissinger, "United States Policy in Southern Africa," 672–79, quotes on 673, 674, 678.

41. Memorandum of conversation, 27 Apr. 1976, in *FRUS, 1969–1976*, 28:494–97, 496.

42. Kissinger, "United States Policy in Southern Africa," 675; Michel, *White House, White Africa*, 142.

43. Memorandum of conversation, 27 Apr. 1976, in *FRUS, 1969–1976*, 28:494–97, quote on 496.

44. Kissinger, "United States Policy in Southern Africa," 677.

45. Saunders and Onslow, "Cold War and Southern Africa," 230–31; Miller, *African Volk*, chaps. 2–4, 7, esp. 220–21.

46. Westad, *Global Cold War*, 246; Miller, *African Volk*, 220–21.

47. Miller, *African Volk*, 226–32.

48. Miller, 232–38.

49. Memorandum of conversation, 19 Jan. 1977, in *FRUS, 1969–1976*, 28:717. For more on the September negotiations, see Michel, *White House, White Africa*, 155–66; Onslow, "'We Must Gain Time'"; Miller, *African Volk*, 242–59; DeRoche, *Black, White, and Chrome*, 218–22.

50. DeRoche, *Black, White, and Chrome*, quote on 214. See also Watts, "'Dropping the F-Bomb.'"

51. Pallotti, "Tanzania and the 1976 Anglo-American Initiative for Rhodesia," quote on 809; Mitchell, *Jimmy Carter in Africa*, 104–8, 131–32; DeRoche, *Kenneth Kaunda*, 112–13.

52. Telegram from the embassy in Tanzania to Kissinger, 9 Dec. 1976, in *FRUS, 1969–1976*, 28:643–50, quote on 645.

53. Conversation between Nixon and Kissinger, 28 Sept. 1971, in *FRUS, 1969–1976*, 28:143–45, quotes on 144, 145.

54. Jimmy Carter to P. W. Botha, 31 Mar. 1979, box 18, Collection 3: "President's Correspondence with Foreign Leaders File," NSA, Brzezinski Material, JCL.

55. Mitchell, "Tropes of the Cold War," 264.

56. Miller, *African Volk*, 283–90, quotes on 287, 290.

57. NSC Meeting on Southern Africa, 3 Mar. 1977, NLC 28-21-6-2-0, RAC Project, JCL; "Four-Year Foreign Policy Objectives," 29 Apr. 1977, box 23, "Four Year Goals through Meetings," Subject File, Donated Historical Materials, Zbigniew Brzezinski Collection, JCL.

58. "Four-Year Foreign Policy Objectives," 29 Apr. 1977, box 23, "Four Year Goals through Meetings," Subject File, Donated Historical Materials, Zbigniew Brzezinski Collection, JCL.

59. Minter, *King Solomon's Mines Revisited*, 277; Nesbitt, *Race for Sanctions*, 98.

60. Thompson, *History of South Africa*, 212–13.

61. Stevens, "'From the Viewpoint of a Southern Governor,'" 866; Mitchell, *Jimmy Carter in Africa*, 328–37; Nesbitt, *Race for Sanctions*, 98.

62. Congressional Black Caucus, "African-American Manifesto," 27–28.

63. Congressional Black Caucus, 28, 31.

64. Congressional Black Caucus, 30.

65. Congressional Black Caucus, 32.

66. Memorandum for Brzezinski from David Anderson for Peter Tarnoff (State Dept), "The President's Meeting with the Black Caucus," 29 Oct. 1977, folder "CBC: 10/77–12/79," box 15, Collection 7—Subject File, NSA, Brzezinski Material, JCL.

67. Brzezinski to Cong. Parren Mitchell, 27 Dec. 1977, folder "CBC: 10/77–12/79," box 15, Collection 7—Subject File, NSA, Brzezinski Material, JCL; DeRoche, *Black, White and Chrome*, 256.

68. "Press Briefing July 29, 1976," in U.S. Congress, House of Representatives, Committee on House Administration, *Presidential Campaign 1976*, vol. 1, pt. 1, 372.

69. "Position Paper on Foreign Policy and U.S. Security: Policy on Africa," n.d., in U.S. Congress, House of Representatives, Committee on House Administration, *Presidential Campaign 1976*, vol. 1, pt. 1, 686.

70. "Position Paper on Foreign Policy and U.S. Security: Policy on Africa"; "Press Conference with the Black Press October 2, 1976," in U.S. Congress, House

of Representatives, Committee on House Administration, *Presidential Campaign 1976*, vol. 1, pt. 2, 891.

71. Carter, "Address at Commencement Exercises of the University of Notre Dame."

72. Carter.

73. Mitchell, *Jimmy Carter in Africa*, 158–65, quote on 159; Michel, "Luster of Chrome," 160.

74. Stevens, "'From the Viewpoint of a Southern Governor,'" 859–60, 873–75, quote on 860.

75. Kaufman, *Plans Unraveled*, quote on 64.

76. Van Wyk, "USA and Apartheid South Africa's Nuclear Aspirations"; Mitchell, *Jimmy Carter in Africa*, 325–28.

77. "Press Briefing July 29, 1976," in U.S. Congress, House of Representatives, Committee on House Administration, *Presidential Campaign 1976*, vol. 1, pt. 1, 375.

78. Carter, *White House Diary*, 56 (24 May 1977 entry).

79. Sullivan, *Moving Mountains*, 52.

80. Nesbitt, *Race for Sanctions*, 96.

81. Stevens, "'From the Viewpoint of a Southern Governor,'" quote on 875. Returning from South Africa the following year, Jesse Jackson concluded that adopting the Sullivan Principles would create "an illusion that something fundamental is happening where something superficial is happening." Stevens, "'From the Viewpoint of a Southern Governor,'" 875.

82. Larson, "Sullivan Principles," 490.

83. Onslow and Plaut, *Robert Mugabe*, chap. 2.

84. Minter, *King Solomon's Mines Revisited*, 240, 298.

85. Mitchell, *Jimmy Carter in Africa*, quote on 331.

86. Zbigniew Brzezinski to Jimmy Carter, [Mar. 1978?], folder "President, Latin America and Africa, 3/28/78–4/3/78: Overview I," box 9, Collection 4, NSA, Brzezinski Material, JCL.

87. Mitchell, *Jimmy Carter in Africa*; DeRoche, *Black, White and Chrome*, 248–85.

88. Mitchell, *Jimmy Carter in Africa*, 158–64.

89. Reagan, *Reagan: In His Own Hand*, 180.

90. Mitchell, *Jimmy Carter in Africa*, 355–60; White, *Unpopular Sovereignty*, chap. 9.

91. Mitchell, *Jimmy Carter in Africa*, 401–4; DeRoche, *Black, White and Chrome*, 260–81.

92. Albright quote in DeRoche, *Black, White and Chrome*, 267; Brzezinski quote in Mitchell, *Jimmy Carter in Africa*, 407.

93. Congressional Black Caucus, "African-American Manifesto," 32.

94. Richard Gordon Hatcher and Randall Robinson to Jimmy Carter, 22 Sept. 1978, folder "Smith, Ian," box 92, Louis Martin Papers, JCL. For more background on forming TransAfrica, see Nesbitt, *Race for Sanctions*, 97–105.

95. Telegrams from the National Conference of Black Lawyers, 26 Sept. 1978, folder "Smith, Ian," box 92, Louis Martin Papers, JCL; Maynard Jackson, 22 Sept.

1978, folder "Smith, Ian," box 92, Louis Martin Papers, JCL; Carlton Goodlett, 5 Oct. 1978, folder "Smith, Ian," box 92, Louis Martin Papers, JCL; Louis Martin to Members of CBC, 25 Sept. 1978, folder "CBC," box 22, Louis Martin Papers, JCL; Nesbitt, *Race for Sanctions*, 108–9.

96. Mitchell, *Jimmy Carter in Africa*, OAU quote on 565; Nesbitt, *Race for Sanctions*, TransAfrica quote on 109; DeRoche, *Black, White and Chrome*, 274.

97. Memo from Anne Wexler and Louis Martin to Jimmy Carter, 13 June 1979, folder "Zimbabwe-Rhodesia," box 109, Louis Martin Papers, JCL; George Meany to Jimmy Carter, 7 June 1979, Folder "Zimbabwe (Rhodesia), 6/79," box 89, Collection 6, NSA, Brzezinski Material, JCL.

98. Samuel Jackson, chairman of the Council of 100, to various senators, governors, and ambassadors, 1 June 1979, folder "Zimbabwe-Rhodesia," box 109, Louis Martin Papers, JCL; Memo from Anne Wexler and Louis Martin to Jimmy Carter, 13 June 1979, folder "Zimbabwe-Rhodesia," box 109, Louis Martin Papers, JCL; Jesse Jackson, Operation PUSH, to Jimmy Carter, 6 June 1979, folder "Zimbabwe-Rhodesia," box 109, Louis Martin Papers, JCL.

99. Mitchell, *Jimmy Carter in Africa*, 608–9, quotes on 609; DeRoche, *Kenneth Kaunda*, chaps. 5–6.

100. Carter, "Trade Sanctions against Rhodesia."

101. Carter.

102. Mitchell, "Tropes of the Cold War," 264.

103. Hodding Carter to Secretary of State Vance, 9 July 1979, folder "Zimbabwe (Rhodesia), 6/79," box 89, Collection 6, NSA, Brzezinski Materials, JCL.

104. Mitchell, "Tropes of the Cold War," quote on 273.

105. Mitchell, *Jimmy Carter in Africa*, chap. 15, quote on 651–52. See also Michel, *White House, White Africa*, chap. 4; White, *Unpopular Sovereignty*, chap. 10; DeRoche, *Black, White and Chrome*, 283–85.

106. White, *Unpopular Sovereignty*, chaps. 10–11.

Chapter 6

1. "Selma Violence likened to that in South Africa," *Washington Post*, 22 Mar. 1965; memo from Haynes to Bundy, 4 Mar. 1965, folder "Africa—General, Memos and Misc, 7/64–6/65," box 76, Africa, Country File, NSF, LBJL; memo from Haynes to Bundy, 23 Mar. 1965, folder "Africa—General, Memos and Misc, 7/64–6/65," box 76, Africa, Country File, NSF, LBJL; Lerner, "Climbing Off the Back Burner," 582.

2. The territories: Ruanda-Urundi (Belgium); British Cameroons, British Togoland, Tanganyika (Britain); French Camerouns, French Togoland (France); South West Africa (South Africa).

3. Irwin, *Gordian Knot*; United Nations Transition Assistance Group (UNTAG): Background, https://peacekeeping.un.org/sites/default/files/past/untagFT.htm#Background.

4. Gleijeses *Conflicting Missions*, 273; Minter, *King Solomon's Mines Revisited*, 194.

5. Minter, *King Solomon's Mines Revisited*, 241–44.

6. Gleijeses, *Visions of Freedom*, quote on 33.

7. Miller, *African Volk*, 229–31; UN General Assembly Resolution 31/146, December 1976.

8. Gleijeses *Conflicting Missions*, quote on 345; Miller, *African Volk*, 239–41, 246–51.

9. Gleijeses, *Visions of Freedom*, 92–96; Vance, *Hard Choices*, 277.

10. Gleijeses, *Visions of Freedom*, 60–62, 146–50, quote on 61; Minter, *King Solomon's Mines Revisited*, 294–97; Saunders and Onslow, "Cold War and Southern Africa," 232; Vance, *Hard Choices*, 277–83, 310–13. For more on Cassinga, see also Miller, *African Volk*, 309–19.

11. Gleijeses, *Visions of Freedom*, 157.

12. Gleijeses, quote on 149; Vance, *Hard Choices*, 307–8.

13. NSC meeting on Africa, 6 Oct. 1978, NLC-17-2-4-12-4, RAC Project, JCL.

14. For more on the crisis in the Horn of Africa, see Woodroofe, *Buried in the Sands of the Ogaden*; Mitchell, *Jimmy Carter in Africa*, esp. chaps. 4, 6, 8, 9.

15. Mitchell, *Jimmy Carter in Africa*, Church quote on 526; Vance, *Hard Choices*, 308–9.

16. Vance, *Hard Choices*, 308–10.

17. Jimmy Carter to P. W. Botha, 31 Mar. 1979, box 18, Collection 3—"President's Correspondence with Foreign Leaders File," NSA, Brzezinski Material, JCL.

18. Saunders and Onslow, "Cold War and Southern Africa," 235.

19. Naftali, "Ronald Reagan's Long-Hidden Racist Conversation with Richard Nixon."

20. Kyle Longley, "Why Donald Trump Is Just Following in Ronald Reagan's Footsteps on Race," 4 Aug. 2019, *Washington Post*, www.washingtonpost.com/outlook/2019/08/04/why-donald-trump-is-just-following-ronald-reagans-footsteps-race.

21. Ronald Reagan, "Cuba and Africa," 4 Mar. 1977, in Reagan, *Reagan: In His Own Hand*, 184.

22. Shultz, *Turmoil and Triumph*, 1115.

23. Ronald Reagan, "Namibia I," 9 July 1979, in Reagan, *Reagan: In His Own Hand*, 190–91.

24. Ronald Reagan, "South Africa," 6 July 1977, in Reagan, *Reagan: In His Own Hand*, 185–86.

25. Ronald Reagan, "South Africa," 6 July 1977, in Reagan, *Reagan: In His Own Hand*, 185–86.

26. Gleijeses, *Visions of Freedom*, quote on 179.

27. H. W. Brands provides a single brief paragraph on apartheid and South Africa in his over seven-hundred-page *Reagan: The Life*; Sean Wilentz writes slightly further in his *Age of Reagan: A History, 1974–2008*; Richard Reeves barely mentions Africa at all in his *President Reagan: The Triumph of Imagination*. The silences offer an opportunity for historians to expand their approach to the exploration of, and scholarship about, this era.

28. Chester Crocker, "South Africa: Strategy for Change."

29. "A South African Partner," editorial, *Washington Post*, 22 Mar. 1981, quoted in Nesbitt, *Race for Sanctions*, 114.

30. Editorial, *Washington Post*, 18 May 1981, quoted in Nesbitt, *Race for Sanctions*, 115.

31. Nesbitt, *Race for Sanctions*, 117–21.

32. Massie, *Loosing the Bonds*, 524–25, quote on 524.

33. Massie, 550–51.

34. Hall, "Mozambican National Resistance Movement."

35. Minter, Hovey, and Cobb, *No Easy Victories*, 160; Massie, *Loosing the Bonds*, 558–60.

36. Reagan to Joan Joyce Sellers, 28 Jan. 1985, in Reagan, *Reagan: A Life in Letters*, 518.

37. Brinkley, *The Reagan Diaries*, 285.

38. Thomson, "Incomplete Engagement," 88.

39. "Reagan Apologizes for Asserting That Pretoria Segregation Is Over," *New York Times*, 7 Sept. 1985.

40. Brinkley, *The Reagan Diaries*, 299, 428.

41. Tutu, "Sanctions vs. Apartheid," op-ed, *New York Times*, 16 June 1986, A19.

42. Clark and Worger, *South Africa*, 98.

43. Massie, *Loosing the Bonds*, 552–53, 580–82.

44. State Department background paper, "Southern Africa Status Report," July 1985, folder "South Africa," box 92295, Herman J. Cohen Files, RRL; McFarlane to Reagan, "NSDD on U.S. Policy toward South Africa," 3 Sept. 1985, folder "South Africa," box 92295, Herman J. Cohen Files, RRL; Massie, *Loosing the Bonds*, 584–84.

45. Massie, *Loosing the Bonds*, 527–41.

46. Massie, quote on 541.

47. Massie, chaps. 13, 14, esp. 575; Nesbitt, *Race for Sanctions*, 133. For a growing literature on the U.S. anti-apartheid movement, see the richly detailed Massie; the indispensable Nesbitt; the unique source on relatively unsung grassroots efforts in Minter, Hovey, and Cobb, *No Easy Victories*; and important recent work including Grant, *Winning Our Freedoms Together*; Hostetter, *Movement Matters*; Culverson, *Contesting Apartheid*.

48. Nesbitt, *Race for Sanctions*, 133–36.

49. Massie, *Loosing the Bonds*, Dellums quote on 608; Nesbitt, *Race for Sanctions*, 138–42.

50. Talton, *In This Land of Plenty*, 2. For more on the CBC and southern Africa, see Talton, *In This Land of Plenty*, chap. 4.

51. Gleijeses, *Visions of Freedom*, quotes on 280, 282–83.

52. Shultz, *Turmoil and Triumph*, 1122.

53. Memo for Chief of Staff (Regan) from Pat Buchanan (Director of Communications), 14 July 1986, folder 400583–400949, CO 141, WHORM: Subject File, RRL.

54. "Transcript of Talk by Reagan on South Africa and Apartheid," 23 July 1986, *New York Times*, A12.

55. "Transcript of Talk by Reagan on South Africa and Apartheid," A12.

56. Massie, *Loosing the Bonds*, quote on 616.

57. Nesbitt, *Race for Sanctions*, 141–42.

58. Thomson, "Incomplete Engagement," quote on 89; Shultz, *Turmoil and Triumph*, 122–23.

59. Gleijeses, *Visions of Freedom*, 180–85; Gleijeses, "From Cassinga to New York," quote on 207.

60. Gleijeses, *Visions of Freedom*, 180–85, quote on 183.

61. Saunders, "Angola/Namibia Crisis of 1988 and Its Resolution"; Gleijeses, "Moscow's Proxy?"; Gleijeses, "Cuba and the Independence of Namibia."

62. Gleijeses, *Visions of Freedom*, quote on 262.

63. Gleijeses, "From Cassinga to New York," 210; Gleijeses, *Visions of Freedom*, chaps. 15–16.

64. Gleijeses, "From Cassinga to New York," quote on 209. See Gleijeses, *Visions of Freedom*, 393–430.

65. Gleijeses, *Visions of Freedom*, 453–59.

66. Saunders and Onslow, "Cold War and Southern Africa," 238–41; Saunders, "Angola/Namibia Crisis of 1988 and Its Resolution," 229–35. For more on Soviet perspectives, see Shubin, *Hot "Cold War,"* pt. 4.

67. Gleijeses, *Visions of Freedom*, 450–92.

68. Saunders, "Angola/Namibia Crisis of 1988 and Its Resolution," 227–29; Gleijeses, *Visions of Freedom*, 474–81.

69. Reagan officials such as Crocker, *High Noon in Southern Africa*, and Shultz, *Turmoil and Triumph*, understandably argue that it was their policy, but there is little to support their claims. Historians including Gleijeses, *Visions of Freedom*, and Saunders, "Angola/Namibia Crisis of 1988 and Its Resolution," attribute change to forces beyond U.S. control, including Cuban moves and changed thinking in Pretoria.

70. Gleijeses, *Visions of Freedom*, 499.

71. Note that the enclaves of Ceuta and Melilla and three smaller territories remain in dispute between Spain and Morocco. Separately, the area of Western Sahara continues to be in dispute between Morocco and the Polisario Front since Spain's colonial withdrawal in 1975, while Eritrea gained formal independence from Ethiopia in 1993, and South Sudan from Sudan in 2011.

72. Saunders, "Angola/Namibia Crisis of 1988 and Its Resolution," 235.

73. Massie, *Loosing the Bonds*, 626.

74. Mandela, "Address to the U.S. Congress."

75. Nesbitt, *Race for Sanctions*, 167–69; Massie, *Loosing the Bonds*, 672–84.

76. Mandela, "Inaugural Address."

Epilogue

1. Mimi Hall, "U.S. Has Mandela on Terrorist List," *USA Today*, 30 Apr. 2008, http://usatoday30.usatoday.com/news/world/2008-04-30-watchlist_N.htm.

2. Obama, "Remarks by President Obama to the People of Africa."

3. Lutuli, "Nobel Lecture."

4. Kennedy, "Day of Affirmation Address."

Bibliography

Archives and Manuscript Collections

Dwight D. Eisenhower Presidential Library (DDEL), Abilene, KS
- Ann Whitman File
- Christian A. Herter Papers
- John Foster Dulles Papers
- Office of the Staff Secretary Records
- OSANSA Records
- U.S. Council on Foreign Economic Policy, Office of the Chairman: Records, 1954–1961
- White House Office, National Security Council Staff

Harry S. Truman Presidential Library (HSTL), Independence, MO
- Dean G. Acheson Papers
- General Historical Documents Collection
- George C. McGhee Papers
- Intelligence File
- President's Secretary's File (PSF)

Jimmy Carter Presidential Library (JCL), Atlanta, GA
- Louis Martin Records
- Records of the Office of the National Security Advisor
- Remote Archives Capture (RAC) Project
- Zbigniew Brzezinski Collection

John F. Kennedy Presidential Library (JFKL), Boston, MA
- National Security File (NSF)
- Pre-Presidential Papers

Lyndon B. Johnson Presidential Library (LBJL), Austin, TX
- Administrative Histories
- National Security File
  - Country Files
  - Files of Edward K. Hamilton
  - Files of Ulric Haynes
  - Name File
  - National Intelligence Estimates
- Vice Presidential Papers
- White House Central File, Confidential File
- White House Central File, Subject File

Manuscript Division, Library of Congress (LOC), Washington, DC
Brotherhood of Sleeping Car Porters Records
Jackie Robinson Papers
National Association for the Advancement of Colored People Papers
National Urban League Papers
Mugar Memorial Library, Boston University, Boston
Martin Luther King Jr. Papers
National Archives and Records Administration (NARA), College Park, MD
United States Information Agency, RG 306, Office of Research, Special Reports, 1953–1963
U.S. Department of State Records, RG 59, Central Decimal File (CDF), 1930–1963
U.S. Department of State Records, RG 59, Lot and Office Files, Bureau of African Affairs
Richard Nixon Presidential Library (RNL), Yorba Linda, CA
Pre-Presidential Papers (formerly at National Archives–Laguna Niguel)
Ronald Reagan Presidential Library (RRL), Simi Valley, CA
White House Staff and Office Files
Herman J. Cohen File
White House Office of Records Management (WHORM) Subject File
Young Research Library, University of California, Los Angeles
Ralph J. Bunche Papers

Published Archives, Manuscript Collections, and Primary Sources

African Activist Archive. Michigan State University. http://africanactivist.msu.edu.

A. Philip Randolph Papers. Bethesda, MD: University Publications of America, 1990.

Carter, Jimmy. "Address at Commencement Exercises of the University of Notre Dame." 22 May 1977. www.presidency.ucsb.edu/documents/address-commencement-exercises-the-university-notre-dame.

———. "Trade Sanctions against Rhodesia, Remarks Announcing Continuation of U.S. Sanctions." 7 June 1979. www.presidency.ucsb.edu/documents/trade-sanctions-against-rhodesia-remarks-announcing-continuation-the-us-sanctions.

Department of State Bulletin. U.S. Department of State. 89 vols. 1939–1989. www.state.gov.

Foreign Relations of the United States. Office of the Historian. Department of State. https://history.state.gov/historicaldocuments.

Foreign Relations of the United States, 1934. Vol. 2, *Europe, Near East and Africa*, edited by Newton O. Sappington, Kieran J. Carroll, and Francis C. Prescott. Washington: United States Government Printing Office, 1951.

Foreign Relations of the United States, 1935. Vol. 1, *General, the Near East and Africa*, edited by Rogers P. Churchill, Matilda F. Axton, Shirley F. Landau, and Francis C. Prescott. Washington: United States Government Printing Office, 1953.

Foreign Relations of the United States, 1948. Vol. 5, pt. 1, *The Near East, South Asia, and Africa*, edited by Herbert A. Fine and David H. Stauffer. Washington: United States Government Printing Office, 1975.

Foreign Relations of the United States, 1950. Vol. 5, *The Near East, South Asia, and Africa*, Herbert A. Fine, Lisle A. Rose, Joan M. Lee, John A. Bernbaum, Charles S. Sampson, Evans Gerakas, David H. Stauffer, Paul Claussen, and William Z. Slany. Washington: United States Government Printing Office, 1978.

Foreign Relations of the United States, 1951. Vol. 5, *The Near East and Africa*, edited by John A. Bernbaum, Paul Claussen, Joan M. Lee, Carl N. Raether, Lisle A. Rose, Charles S. Sampson, and David H. Stauffer. Washington: United States Government Printing Office, 1982.

Foreign Relations of the United States, 1952–1954. Vol. 3, *United Nations Affairs*, edited by Ralph R. Goodwin. Washington: United States Government Printing Office, 1979.

Foreign Relations of the United States, 1952–1954. Vol. 11, pt. 1, *Africa and South Asia*, edited by Paul Claussen, Joan M. Lee, David W. Mabon, Nina J. Noring, Carl N. Raether, William F. Sanford, Stanley Shaloff, William Z. Slany, and Louis J. Smith. Washington: United States Government Printing Office, 1983.

Foreign Relations of the United States, 1955–1957. Vol. 18, *Africa*, edited by Stanley Shaloff. Washington: United States Government Printing Office, 1989.

Foreign Relations of the United States, 1958–1960. Vol. 14, *Africa*, edited by Harriet Dashiell Schwar and Stanley Shaloff. Washington: United States Government Printing Office, 1992.

Foreign Relations of the United States, 1961–1963. Vol. 21, *Africa*, edited by Nina Davis Howland. Washington: United States Government Printing Office, 1995.

Foreign Relations of the United States, 1961–1963. Vol. 20, *Congo Crisis*, edited by Harriet Dashiell Schwar. Washington: United States Government Printing Office, 1994.

Foreign Relations of the United States, 1964–1968. Vol. 24, *Africa*, edited by Nina Davis Howland. Washington: United States Government Printing Office, 1999.

Foreign Relations of the United States, 1969–1976. Vol. E-5, pt. 1, *Documents on Sub-Saharan Africa, 1969–1972*, edited by Joseph Hilts and David C. Humphrey. Washington: United States Government Printing Office, 2005.

Foreign Relations of the United States, 1969–1976. Vol. E-6, *Documents on Africa, 1973–1976*, edited by Peter Sampson and Laurie Van Hook. Washington: United States Government Printing Office, 2005.

Foreign Relations of the United States, 1969–1976. Vol. 28, *Southern Africa*, edited by Myra F. Burton. Washington: United States Government Printing Office, 2011.

Foreign Relations of the United States, 1977–1980. Vol. 16, *Southern Africa*, edited by Myra F. Burton. Washington: United States Government Printing Office, 2016.

Kennedy, John F. *"Let the Word Go Forth": The Speeches, Statements, and Writings of John F. Kennedy, 1947 to 1963*. Edited by Theodore Sorensen. New York: Delacorte, 1988.

Kennedy, Robert F. "Day of Affirmation Address. " 6 June 1966. https://www.jfklibrary.org/learn/about-jfk/the-kennedy-family/robert-f-kennedy/robert-f-kennedy-speeches/day-of-affirmation-address-university-of-capetown-capetown-south-africa-june-6-1966.

Lutuli, Albert. "Nobel Lecture: Africa and Freedom. " 11 December 1961. http://www.nobelprize.org/nobel_prizes/peace/laureates/1960/lutuli-lecture.html.

Macmillan, Harold. "The Wind of Change." 3 February 1960. http://www.africanrhetoric.org/pdf/ayor%206.2%205%20Harold%20MacMillan%20-%20The%20wind%20of%20change.pdf.

Mandela, Nelson. "Address to the U.S. Congress." 26 June 1990. http://africanactivist.msu.edu/document_metadata.php?objectid=32-130-2D2.

Mandela, Nelson. "Inaugural Address." 10 May 1994. www.africa.upenn.edu/Articles_Gen/Inaugural_Speech_17984.html.

National Association for the Advancement of Colored People (NAACP) Papers. Bethesda, MD: University Publications of America, 1981–1995.

Part 1: Meetings of the Board of Directors, Records of Annual Conferences, Major Speeches, and Special Reports, 1909–1950

Supplement to Part 1, 1951–1955

Supplement to Part 1, 1956–60

Part 11: Special Subject Files, 1912–1939

Part 14: Race Relations in the International Arena, 1940–1955

Obama, Barack. "Remarks by President Obama to the Kenyan People." 26 July 2015. www.whitehouse.gov/the-press-office/2015/07/26/remarks-president-obama-kenyan-people.

——. "Remarks by President Obama to the People of Africa." 28 July 2015. www.whitehouse.gov/the-press-office/2015/07/28/remarks-president-obama-people-africa.

Prospects of Mankind with Eleanor Roosevelt. Episode 106, "Africa: Revolution in Haste." 6 March 1960. https://americanarchive.org/catalog/cpb-aacip_15-09wow2sd.

Reagan, Ronald. *Reagan: A Life in Letters*. Edited by Kiron K. Skinner, Annelise Anderson, and Martin Anderson. New York: Free Press, 2003.

Reagan, Ronald. *Reagan: In His Own Hand; The Writings of Ronald Reagan That Reveal His Revolutionary Vision for America*. Edited by Kiron K. Skinner, Annelise Anderson, and Martin Anderson. New York: Free Press, 2001.

Rosenman, Samuel I., comp. *Public Papers and Addresses of Franklin D. Roosevelt*. 13 vols. New York: Macmillan, 1938–50.

Truman, Harry S. "Truman's Inaugural Address to the Nation." *Tru Blog*. 20 January 1949. www.trumanlibraryinstitute.org/historic-speeches-trumans-inaugural-address.

U.S. Congress. House of Representatives. Committee on House Administration. *The Presidential Campaign 1976*. Vol. 1, pts. 1 and 2, *Jimmy Carter*. Washington DC: Government Printing Office, 1978.

U.S. Congress. Senate. Committee on Commerce. *Freedom of Communications*. Pt. 1, *The Speeches, Remarks, Press Conferences, and Statements of Senator John F. Kennedy, August 1 through November 7, 1960*, 87th Cong., 1st Sess. Washington, DC: Government Printing Office, 1961.

U.S. Congress. Senate. Committee on Commerce. *Freedom of Communications*. Pt. 2, *The Speeches, Remarks, Press Conferences, and Study Papers of Vice President Richard M. Nixon, August 1 through November 7, 1960*, 87th Cong., 1st Sess. Washington, DC: Government Printing Office, 1961.

W. E. B. Du Bois Papers. Sanford, NC: Microfilming Corporation of America, 1980.

Newspapers

Atlanta Daily World
Baltimore Afro-American
Chicago Defender
The Crisis (Baltimore, MD)
New York Amsterdam News
New York Times
Pittsburgh Courier
USA Today (Tysons, VA)
Washington Post
Washington Star

Books

Acheson, Dean. *Present at the Creation: My Years in the State Department*. New York: W. W. Norton, 1969.

Adi, Hakim, and Marika Sherwood. *The 1945 Manchester Pan-African Congress Revisited*. London: New Beacon Books, 1995.

Ahlman, Jeffrey S. *Living with Nkrumahism: Nation, State, and Pan-Africanism in Ghana*. Athens, OH: Ohio University Press, 2017.

Anderson, Carol. *Bourgeois Radicals: The NAACP and the Struggle for Colonial Liberation, 1941–1960*. New York: Cambridge University Press, 2015.

Anderson, David. *Histories of the Hanged: Britain's Dirty War in Kenya and the End of Empire*. New York: W. W. Norton, 2005.

Barnes, Kenneth C. *Journey of Hope: The Back-to-Africa Movement in Arkansas in the Late 1800s*. Chapel Hill: University of North Carolina Press, 2004.

Becnel, Thomas. *Senator Allen Ellender of Louisiana: A Biography*. Baton Rouge: Louisiana State University Press, 1993.

Borstelmann, Thomas. *Apartheid's Reluctant Uncle: The United States and Southern Africa in the Early Cold War*. New York: Oxford University Press, 1993.

———. *The Cold War and the Color Line: American Race Relations in the Global Arena*. Cambridge, MA: Harvard University Press, 2001.

Brands, H. W. *Reagan: The Life*. New York: Doubleday, 2015.

Brinkley, Douglas, ed. *Dean Acheson: The Cold War Years, 1953–1971*. New Haven, CT: Yale University Press, 1992.

———. *The Reagan Diaries*. New York: HarperCollins, 2007.

Brzezinski, Zbigniew. *Power and Principle: Memoirs of the National Security Advisor, 1977–1981*. New York: Farrar, Straus, Giroux, 1983.

Butler, Larry, and Sarah Stockwell, eds. *The Wind of Change: Harold Macmillan and British Decolonization*. New York: Palgrave Macmillan, 2013.
Byrne, Jeffrey. *Mecca of Revolution: Algeria, Decolonization, and the Third World Order*. New York: Oxford University Press, 2016.
Campbell, James T. *Middle Passages: African American Journeys to Africa, 1787–2005*. New York: Penguin Books, 2006.
——. *Songs of Zion: The African Methodist Episcopal Church in the United States and South Africa*. New York: Oxford University Press, 1995.
Carter, Jimmy. *White House Diary*. New York: Farrar, Straus and Giroux, 2010.
Chafer, Tony. *The End of Empire in French West Africa: France's Successful Decolonisation?* Oxford: Berg, 2002.
Clark, Nancy L., and William H. Worger. *South Africa: The Rise and Fall of Apartheid*. New York: Routledge, 2016.
Clendenen, Clarence, Robert Collins, and Peter Duignan. *Americans in Africa, 1865–1900*. Hoover Institution Studies 17. Stanford, CA: Hoover Institution Press, 1966.
Clendenen, Clarence, and Peter Duignan. *Americans in Black Africa up to 1865*. Hoover Institution Studies 5. Stanford, CA: Hoover Institution Press, 1964.
Colman, Jonathan. *The Foreign Policy of Lyndon B. Johnson: The United States and the World, 1963–1969*. Edinburgh: Edinburgh University Press, 2010.
Connelly, Matthew. *A Diplomatic Revolution: Algeria's Fight for Independence and the Origins of the Post-Cold War Era*. New York: Oxford University Press, 2003.
Cooper, Frederick. *Citizenship between Empire and Nation: Remaking France and French Africa, 1945–1960*. Princeton, NJ: Princeton University Press, 2014.
Cowans, Jon. *Empire Films and the Crisis of Colonialism, 1946–1959*. Baltimore: Johns Hopkins University Press, 2015.
Crocker, Chester. *High Noon in Southern Africa: Making Peace in a Rough Neighborhood*. New York: W. W. Norton, 1993.
Cullather, Nick. *The Hungry World: America's Cold War Battle Against Poverty in Asia*. Cambridge, MA: Harvard University Press, 2010.
Culverson, Donald. *Contesting Apartheid: U.S. Activism, 1960–1987*. New York: Westview Press, 1999.
Dallek, Robert. *Franklin D. Roosevelt and American Foreign Policy, 1932–1945*. Oxford: Oxford University Press, 1979.
Davies, J. E. *Constructive Engagement? Chester Crocker and American Policy in South Africa, Namibia and Angola*. Athens: Ohio University Press, 2007.
Dean, John W., and Barry M. Goldwater Jr. *Pure Goldwater*. New York: Palgrave Macmillan, 2008.
DeRoche, Andrew. *Black, White and Chrome: The United States and Zimbabwe, 1953–1998*. Trenton, NJ: Africa World Press, 2001.
——. *Kenneth Kaunda, the United States, and Southern Africa*. London: Bloomsbury, 2016.
De Witte, Ludo. *The Assassination of Lumumba*. Translated by Ann Wright and Renée Fenby. London: Verso, 2001.

Dudziak, Mary. *Cold War Civil Rights: Race and the Image of American Democracy.* Princeton, NJ: Princeton University Press, 2002.

——. *Exporting American Dreams: Thurgood Marshall's African Journey.* New York: Oxford University Press, 2008.

Eisenhower, Dwight D. *Waging Peace, 1956–1961.* Garden City, NY: Doubleday, 1965.

Elkins, Caroline. *Imperial Reckoning: The Untold Story of Britain's Gulag in Kenya.* Henry Holt, 2005.

Ellison, Ralph. *Invisible Man.* 1947. Reprint, New York: Vintage Books, 1989.

Filatova, Irian, and Apollon Davidson. *The Hidden Thread: Russia and South Africa in the Soviet Era.* Johannesburg: Jonathan Ball, 2013.

Fischer, Fritz. *Making Them Like Us: Peace Corps Volunteers in the 1960s.* Washington DC: Smithsonian Institution Press, 1998.

Fredrickson, George. *Black Liberation: A Comparative History of Black Ideologies in the United States and South Africa.* Oxford: Oxford University Press, 1995.

Gaines, Kevin. *American Africans in Ghana: Black Expatriates and the Civil Rights Era.* Chapel Hill: University of North Carolina Press, 2007.

Gatheru, R. Mugo. *Child of Two Worlds.* London: Routledge & Kegan Paul, 1964.

Gerard, Emmanuel, and Bruce Kuklick. *Death in the Congo: Murdering Patrice Lumumba.* Cambridge, MA: Harvard University Press, 2015.

Getachew, Adom. *Worldmaking After Empire: The Rise and Fall of Self-Determination.* Princeton, NJ: Princeton University Press, 2019.

Gleijeses, Piero. *Conflicting Missions: Havana, Washington, and Africa, 1959–1976.* Chapel Hill: University of North Carolina Press, 2002.

——. *Visions of Freedom: Havana, Washington, Pretoria, and the Struggle for Southern Africa, 1976–1991.* Chapel Hill: University of North Carolina Press, 2013.

Goldsworthy, David. *Tom Mboya: The Man Kenya Wanted to Forget.* London: Heinemann, 1982.

Grant, Nicholas. *Winning Our Freedoms Together: African Americans and Apartheid, 1945–1960.* Chapel Hill: University of North Carolina Press, 2017.

Grubbs, Larry. *Secular Missionaries: Americans and African Development in the 1960s.* Amherst: University of Massachusetts Press, 2009.Hersh, Seymour. *The Price of Power: Kissinger in the Nixon White House.* New York: Summit Books, 1983.

Hitchcock, William I. *The Age of Eisenhower: America and the World in the 1950s.* New York: Simon & Schuster, 2018.

Hoffman, Elizabeth Cobbs. *All You Need Is Love: The Peace Corps and the Spirit of the 1960s.* Cambridge, MA: Harvard University Press, 1998.

Horne, Gerald. *Black and Red: W. E. B. Du Bois and the Afro-American Response to the Cold War, 1944–1963.* Albany: State University of New York Press, 1986.

——. *From the Barrel of a Gun: The United States and the War against Zimbabwe, 1965–1980.* Chapel Hill: University of North Carolina Press, 2001.

Hostetter, David. *Movement Matters: American Anti-apartheid Activists and the Rise of Multicultural Politics.* New York: Routledge, 2006.

Houser, George. *No One Can Stop the Rain: Glimpses of Africa's Liberation Struggle.* New York: Pilgrim Press, 1989.

Hull, Cordell. *The Memoirs of Cordell Hull*. 2 vols. New York: Macmillan, 1948.
Hunt, Michael. *Ideology and U.S. Foreign Policy*. New Haven, CT: Yale University Press, 1977.
Immerwahr, Daniel. *Thinking Small: The United States and the Lure of Community Development*. Cambridge, MA: Harvard University Press, 2015.
Irwin, Ryan. *Gordian Knot: Apartheid and the Unmaking of the Liberal World Order*. New York: Oxford University Press, 2012.
Jackson, Henry F. *From the Congo to Soweto: U.S. Foreign Policy toward Africa since 1960*. New York: William Morrow, 1982.
Jeal, Tim. *Stanley: The Impossible Life of Africa's Greatest Explorer*. New Haven, CT: Yale University Press, 2007.
Kalb, Madeleine G. *The Congo Cables: The Cold War in Africa—from Eisenhower to Kennedy*. New York: Macmillan, 1982.
Kapur, Sudarshan. *Raising Up a Prophet: The African-American Encounter with Gandhi*. Boston: Beacon Press, 1992.
Karp, Matthew. *This Vast Southern Empire: Slaveholders at the Helm of American Foreign Policy*. Cambridge, MA: Harvard University Press, 2016.
Kaufman, Scott. *Plans Unraveled: The Foreign Policy of the Carter Administration*. DeKalb: Northern Illinois Press, 2008.
Kissinger, Henry. *Diplomacy*. New York: Simon & Schuster, 1994.
Krenn, Michael. *Black Diplomacy: African Americans and the State Department, 1945–1969*. M.E. Sharpe, 1999.
Lake, Anthony. *The "Tar Baby" Option: American Policy toward Southern Rhodesia*. New York: Columbia University Press, 1976.
Latham, Michael. *Modernization as Ideology: Social Science and "Nation Building" in the Kennedy Era*. Chapel Hill: University of North Carolina Press, 2000.
Lauren, Paul G. *Power and Prejudice: The Politics and Diplomacy of Racial Discrimination*. Boulder, CO: Westview Press, 1988.
Lawson, Steven. *Running for Freedom: Civil Rights and Black Politics in America since 1941*. Philadelphia: Temple University Press, 1991.
Lee, Christopher J., ed. *Making a World After Empire: The Bandung Moment and Its Political Afterlives*. Athens: Ohio University Press, 2010.
Leffler, Melvyn. *A Preponderance of Power: National Security, the Truman Administration, and the Cold War*. Stanford, CA: Stanford University Press, 1992.
Lewis, David Levering. *W. E. B. Du Bois: Biography of a Race, 1868–1919*. New York: Henry Holt, 1993.
Lodge, Tom. *Black Politics in South Africa since 1945*. New York: Longman, 1983.
Logevall, Fredrik, and Andrew Preston, eds. *Nixon in the World: American Foreign Relations, 1969–1977*. New York: Oxford University Press, 2008.
Louis, Wm. Roger. *Imperialism at Bay: The United States and the Decolonization of the British Empire, 1941–1945*. New York: Oxford University Press, 1978.
Macekura, Stephen J., and Erez Manela, eds. *The Development Century: A Global History*. Cambridge: Cambridge University Press, 2018.
Mahoney, Richard. *JFK: Ordeal in Africa*. New York: Oxford University Press, 1983.

Manela, Erez. *The Wilsonian Moment: Self-Determination and the International Origins of Anticolonial Nationalism*. New York: Oxford University Press, 2007.
Massie, Robert Kinloch. *Loosing the Bonds: The United States and South Africa in the Apartheid Years*. New York: Doubleday, 1997.
Mazov, Sergey. *A Distant Front in the Cold War: The USSR in West Africa and the Congo, 1956–1964*. Stanford, CA: Stanford University Press, 2010.
McGhee, George. *Envoy to the Middle World: Adventures in Diplomacy*. New York: Harper & Row, 1983.
McMahon, Robert J. *Colonialism and Cold War: The United States and the Struggle for Indonesian Independence, 1945–1949*. Ithaca, NY: Cornell University Press, 1981.
McVety, Amanda Kay. *Enlightened Aid: US Development as Foreign Policy in Ethiopia*. New York: Oxford University Press, 2012.
Meriwether, James H. *Proudly We Can Be African: Black Americans and Africa, 1935–1961*. Chapel Hill: University of North Carolina Press, 2002.
Merriam, Alan P. *Congo: Background of Conflict*. Chicago: Northwestern University Press, 1961.
Michel, Eddie. *White House, White Africa: Presidential Policy toward Rhodesia during the UDI Period, 1965–1979*. New York: Routledge, 2019.
Miller, Jamie. *An African Volk: The Apartheid Regime and Its Struggle for Survival*. New York: Oxford University Press, 2016.
Minter, William. *King Solomon's Mines Revisited: Western Interests and the Burdened History of Southern Africa*. New York: Basic Books, 1986.
Minter, William, Gail Hovey, and Charles Cobb Jr., eds. *No Easy Victories: African Liberation and American Activists over a Half Century, 1950–2000*. Trenton, NJ: Africa World Press, 2008.
Mitchell, Nancy. *Jimmy Carter in Africa: Race and the Cold War*. Washington, DC: Woodrow Wilson Center Press; Stanford, CA: Stanford University Press, 2016.
Morris, Roger. *Uncertain Greatness: Henry Kissinger and American Foreign Policy*. New York: Harper & Row, 1977.
Moses, Wilson. *The Wings of Ethiopia: Studies in African-American Life and Letters*. Ames: Iowa State University Press, 1990.
Muehlenbeck, Philip. *Betting on the Africans: John F. Kennedy's Courting of African Nationalist Leaders*. New York: Oxford University Press, 2012.
Munene, Macharia. *The Truman Administration and the Decolonisation of Sub-Saharan Africa*. Nairobi: Nairobi University Press, 1995.
Mungazi, Dickson. *The Last British Liberals in Africa: Michael Blundell and Garfield Todd*. Westport, CT: Praeger, 1999.
Munro, John. *The Anticolonial Front: The African American Freedom Struggle and Global Decolonisation, 1945–1960*. New York: Cambridge University Press, 2017.
Namikas, Lise. *Battleground Africa: Cold War in the Congo*. Stanford, CA: Stanford University Press, 2013.
Nesbitt, Francis Njubi. *Race for Sanctions: African Americans against Apartheid, 1946–1994*. Bloomington: Indiana University Press, 2004.
Nielsen, Waldemar. *The Great Powers and Africa*. New York: Praeger, 1969.

Noer, Thomas J. *Cold War and Black Liberation: The United States and White Rule in Africa, 1948–1968*. Columbia: University of Missouri Press, 1985.

——. *Soapy: A Biography of G. Mennen Williams*. Ann Arbor: University of Michigan Press, 2005.

Nwaubani, Ebere. *The United States and Decolonization in West Africa, 1950–1960*. Rochester, NY: University of Rochester Press, 2001.

Obama, Barack. *Dreams from My Father: A Story of Race and Inheritance*. 1995. Reprint, New York: Three Rivers Press, 2004.

O'Malley, Alanna. *The Diplomacy of Decolonisation: America, Britain, and the United Nations during the Congo Crisis, 1960–1964*. Manchester: Manchester University Press, 2018.

Onslow, Sue, and Martin Plaut. *Robert Mugabe*. Athens: Ohio University Press, 2018.

O'Reilly, Kenneth. *Nixon's Piano: Presidents and Racial Politics from Washington to Clinton*. New York: Free Press, 1995.

Parker, Jason. *Hearts, Minds, Voices: US Cold War Public Diplomacy and the Formation of the Third World*. New York: Oxford University Press, 2016.

Plummer, Brenda Gayle. *In Search of Power: African Americans in the Era of Decolonization, 1956–1974*. New York: Cambridge University Press, 2013.

——. *Rising Wind: Black Americans and U.S. Foreign Affairs, 1935–1960*. Chapel Hill: University of North Carolina Press, 1996.

Reeves, Richard. *President Reagan: The Triumph of Imagination*. New York: Simon & Schuster, 2005.

Richards, Yevette. *Maida Springer: Pan-Africanist and International Labor Leader*. University of Pittsburgh Press, 2000.

Rivlin, Benjamin. *The United Nations and the Italian Colonies*. New York: Carnegie Endowment for International Peace, 1950.

Rostow, W. W. *The Stages of Economic Growth: A Non-Communist Manifesto*. New York: Cambridge University Press, 1960.

Saigbe Boley, G. E. *Liberia: The Rise and Fall of the First Republic*. New York: Macmillan, 1983.

Schlesinger, Arthur. *A Thousand Days: John F. Kennedy in the White House*. Boston: Houghton Mifflin, 1965.

Schmidt, Elizabeth. *Cold War and Decolonization in Guinea, 1946–1958*. Athens: Ohio University Press, 2007.

——. *Foreign Intervention in Africa: From the Cold War to the War on Terror*. New York: Cambridge University Press, 2013.

Schmitz, David F. *The United States and Right-Wing Dictatorships, 1965–1989*. New York: Cambridge University Press, 2006.

Schneidman, Witney W. *Engaging Africa: Washington and the Fall of Portugal's Colonial Empire*. Lanham, MD: University Press of America, 2004.

Schraeder, Peter. *United States Foreign Policy toward Africa: Incrementalism, Crisis and Change*. New York: Cambridge University Press, 1994.

Schuyler, George. *Slaves Today: A Story of Liberia*. New York: Brewer, Warren, and Putnam, 1931.

Schwarz, Karen. *What You Can Do for Your Country: An Oral History of the Peace Corps*. New York: William Morrow, 1991.

Scott, Michael. *A Time to Speak*. New York: Doubleday, 1958.

Selassie, Haile. *My Life and Ethiopia's Progress*. Vol. 2, *Addis Ababa 1966*. 4th ed. Barnsley, UK: Frontline Books, 1999.

Shachtman, Tom. *Airlift to America: How Barack Obama, Sr., John F. Kennedy, Tom Mboya, and 800 East African Students Changed Their World and Ours*. New York: St. Martin's Press, 2009.

Shubin, Vladimir. *The Hot "Cold War": The USSR in Southern Africa*. London: Pluto Press, 2008.

Shultz, George P. *Turmoil and Triumph: My Years as Secretary of State*. New York: Charles Scribner's Sons, 1993.

Smith, Ian. *The Great Betrayal: The Memoirs of Ian Douglas Smith*. London: Blake, 1997.

Snyder, Sarah. *From Selma to Moscow: How Human Rights Activists Transformed U.S. Foreign Policy*. New York: Columbia University Press, 2018.

Sullivan, Leon H. *Moving Mountains: The Principles and Purposes of Leon Sullivan*. Valley Forge, PA: Judson Press, 1998.

Sundiata, Ibrahim. *Brothers and Strangers: Black Zion, Black Slavery, 1914–1940*. Durham, NC: Duke University Press, 2003.

Suri, Jeremy. *Henry Kissinger and the American Century*. Cambridge, MA: Harvard University Press, 2007.

Swindall, Lindsey R. *The Path to the Greater, Freer, Truer World: Southern Civil Rights and Anticolonialism*. Gainesville: University Press of Florida, 2014.

Talton, Benjamin. *In This Land of Plenty: Mickey Leland and Africa in American Politics*. Philadelphia: University of Pennsylvania Press, 2019.

Thompson, Leonard. *A History of South Africa*. 3rd ed. New Haven, CT: Yale University Press, 2001.

Vance, Cyrus. *Hard Choices: Critical Years in America's Foreign Policy*. New York: Simon & Schuster, 1983.

Von Eschen, Penny. *Race against Empire: Black Americans and Anticolonialism, 1937–1957*. Ithaca, NY: Cornell University Press, 1997.

———. *Satchmo Blows Up the World: Jazz Ambassadors Play the Cold War*. Cambridge, MA: Harvard University Press, 2006.

Waters, Mary-Alice. *Cuba and Angola: Fighting for Africa's Freedom and Our Own*. New York: Pathfinder Press, 2013.

Watts, Carl P. *Rhodesia's Unilateral Declaration of Independence: An International History*. Palgrave Macmillan, 2012.

Weissman, Stephen R. *American Foreign Policy in the Congo, 1960–1964*. Ithaca, NY: Cornell University Press, 1974.

Westad, Odd Arne. *The Global Cold War: Third World Interventions and the Making of Our Times*. New York: Cambridge University Press, 2005.

White, Luise. *Unpopular Sovereignty: Rhodesian Independence and African Decolonization*. Chicago: University of Chicago Press, 2015.

White, Theodore E. *The Making of the President, 1960*. New York: Atheneum House, 1961.
Wilder, Gary. *Freedom Time: Negritude, Decolonization, and the Future of the World*. Durham, NC: Duke University Press, 2015.
Wilentz, Sean. *The Age of Reagan: A History, 1974–2008*. New York: HarperCollins, 2008.
Williams, Susan. *Colour Bar: The Triumph of Seretse Khama and His Nation*. New York: Penguin, 2006.
Williams, Walter L. *Black Americans and the Evangelization of Africa, 1877–1900*. Madison: University of Wisconsin Press, 1982.
Woodroofe, Louise. *Buried in the Sands of the Ogaden: The United States, the Horn of Africa, and the Demise of Detente*. Kent, OH: Kent State University Press, 2013.
Worger, William H., Nancy L. Clark, and Edward A. Alpers. *Africa and the West: A Documentary History*. Vol. 2, *From Colonialism to Independence, 1875 to the Present*. 2nd ed. New York: Oxford University Press, 2010.
Young, Robert C. *Postcolonialism: An Historical Introduction*. Oxford: Blackwell, 2001.
Zeiler, Thomas W. *Dean Rusk: Defending the American Mission Abroad*. Wilmington, DE: Scholarly Resources, 2000.

Articles, Book Chapters, and Dissertations

"Americans and Africa." In "Africa: A Continent in Ferment." Special issue, *Life*, 4 May 1953, 178.
Anderson, Carol. "The Histories of African Americans' Anticolonialism during the Cold War." In *The Cold War in the Third World*, edited by Robert J. McMahon, 178–91. New York: Oxford University Press, 2013.
———. "International Conscience, the Cold War, and Apartheid: The NAACP's Alliance with the Reverend Michael Scott for South West Africa's Liberation, 1946–1951." *Journal of World History* 19, no. 3 (September 2008): 297–325.
———. "Rethinking Radicalism: African Americans and the Liberation Struggles in Somalia, Libya, and Eritrea, 1945–1949." *Journal of the Historical Society* 11, no. 4 (December 2011): 385–423.
Babou, Cheikh Anta. "Decolonization or National Liberation: Debating the End of British Colonial Rule in Africa." *Annals of the American Academy of Political and Social Sciences* 632, no. 1 (November 2010): 41–54.
Bamba, Abou. "'Mightier Than Marx': Hassoldt Davis and American Cold War Politics in Postwar Ivory Coast." *International History Review* 41, no. 6 (2019): 1123–44.
———. "Transnationalising Decolonization: The Print Media, American Public Spheres and France's Imperial Exit in West Africa." *Journal of Transatlantic Studies* 11, no. 4 (2013): 327–39.
"Black Africa: Primitive Society Holds Out South of the Sahara." In "Africa: A Continent in Ferment." Special issue, *Life*, 4 May 1953, 91–100.

Bradley, Mark Philip. "Decolonization, the Global South, and the Cold War, 1919–1962." In *The Cambridge History of the Cold War.* Vol. 1, *Origins*, edited by Melvyn P. Leffler and Odd Arne Westad, 464–85. New York: Cambridge University Press, 2010.

Branch, Daniel. "Political Traffic: Kenyan Students in Eastern and Central Europe, 1958–1969." *Journal of Contemporary History* 53, no. 4 (2018): 811–31.

Cloete, Stuart. "'I Speak for the African': One Drum Pulse from Savagery, He Is Lost in Strange New World." In "Africa: A Continent in Ferment." Special issue, *Life*, 4 May 1953, 111–26.

Congressional Black Caucus. "The African-American Manifesto on Southern Africa." *Black Scholar* 8, no. 4 (January/February 1977): 27–32.

Crocker, Chester. "South Africa: Strategy for Change." *Foreign Affairs* 59, no. 2 (Winter 1980/81): 323–51.

——. "Southern Africa: Eight Years Later." *Foreign Affairs* 68, no. 4 (Fall 1989): 144–64.

Davis, John A. "Black Americans and United States Policy toward Africa." *Journal of International Affairs* 23, no. 2 (1969): 236–49.

DeRoche, Andrew. "Attempting to Assert African Agency: Kenneth Kaunda, the Nixon Administration, and Southern Africa, 1969–1973." *South African Historical Journal* 71 no. 3 (2019): 466–94.

——. "Frances Bolton, Margaret Tibbetts, and the US Relations with the Rhodesian Federation, 1950–1960." In *Living the End of Empire: Politics and Society in Late Colonial Zambia*, edited by Jan-Bart Gewald, Marja Hinfelaar, and Giacomo Macola, 299–325. Leiden: Brill, 2011.

Dow, Philip. "Accidental Diplomats: The Influence of American Evangelical Missionaries on US Relations with the Congo during the Early Cold War Period, 1959–1963." In *Foreign Policy at the Periphery: The Shifting Margins of US International Relations since World War II*, edited by Bevan Sewell and Maria Ryan, 172–205. Lexington: University Press of Kentucky, 2017.

Duara, Prasenjit. Introduction to *Decolonization: Perspectives from Now and Then.* Edited by Prasenjit Duara, 1–20. London: Routledge, 2003.

Du Bois, W. E. B. "A Chronicle of Race Relations." *Phylon* 5, no. 1 (1944): 68–89.

Dudziak, Mary. "Desegregation as a Cold War Imperative." *Stanford Law Review* 41 (November 1988): 61–120.

Fraser, Cary. "An American Dilemma: Race and Realpolitik in the American Response to the Bandung Conference, 1955." In *Window on Freedom: Race, Civil Rights, and Foreign Affairs, 1945–1988*, edited by Brenda Gayle Plummer, 115–40. Chapel Hill: University of North Carolina Press, 2003.

Gaines, Kevin. "Black Americans' Racial Uplift Ideology as 'Civilizing Mission.'" In *Cultures of United States Imperialism*, edited by Amy Kaplan and Donald Pease, 433–55. Durham, NC: Duke University Press, 1993.

Gerhart, Gail. "The Eve of Sharpeville and Afterwards." In *Challenge and Violence, 1953–1964*, edited by Thomas Karis and Gail M. Gerhart, 332–34. Vol. 3 of *From Protest to Challenge: A Documentary History of African Politics in South*

Africa, 1882–1964, edited by Thomas Karis and Gwendolyn M. Carter. Stanford, CA: Hoover Institution Press, 1987.

Gerits, Frank. "Hungry Minds: Eisenhower's Cultural Assistance to Sub-Saharan Africa, 1953–1961." *Diplomatic History* 41, no. 3 (June 2017): 439–59.

Getachew, Adom. "Kwame Nkrumah and the Quest for Independence." *Dissent* 66, no. 3 (Summer 2019): 33–40.

Gleijeses, Piero. "Cuba and the Independence of Namibia." *Cold War History* 7, no. 2 (May 2007): 285–303.

——. "From Cassinga to New York: The Struggle for the Independence of Namibia." In *Cold War in Southern Africa: White Power, Black Liberation*, edited by Sue Onslow, 201–24. New York: Routledge, 2009.

——. "Moscow's Proxy? Cuba and Africa, 1975–1988." *Journal of Cold War Studies* 8, no. 2 (Spring 2006): 3–51.

Guillory, Sean. "Culture Clash in the Socialist Paradise: Soviet Patronage and African Students' Urbanity in the Soviet Union, 1960–1963." *Diplomatic History* 38, no. 2 (April 2014): 271–81.

Hall, Margaret. "The Mozambican National Resistance Movement (Renamo): A Study in the Destruction of an African Country." *Africa: Journal of the International African Institute* 60, no. 1 (1990): 39–68.

Harris, Robert L. "Racial Equality and the United Nations Charter." In *New Directions in Civil Rights Studies*, edited by Armstead Robinson and Patricia Sullivan, 126–48. Charlottesville: University of Virginia Press, 1991.

Heiss, Mary Ann. "Whistling in the Dark: US Efforts to Navigate UN Policy toward Decolonization, 1945–1963." In *Foreign Policy at the Periphery: The Shifting Margins of US International Relations since World War II*, edited by Bevan Sewell and Maria Ryan, 125–51. Lexington: University Press of Kentucky, 2017.

Høgsbjerg, Christian. "Remembering the Fifth Pan-African Congress." *Leeds African Studies Bulletin* 77 (Winter 2015/16): 119–39, https://lucas.leeds.ac.uk/article/remembering-the-fifth-pan-african-congress-christian-hogsbjerg.

Iandolo, Alessandro. "Imbalance of Power: The Soviet Union and the Congo Crisis, 1960–61." *Journal of Cold War Studies* 16, no. 2 (Spring 2014): 32–55.

——. "The Rise and Fall of the 'Soviet Model of Development' in West Africa, 1957–1964." *Cold War History* 12, no. 4 (November 2012): 683–704.

Immerwahr, Daniel. "Modernization and Development in U.S. Foreign Relations." *Passport*, September 2012, 22–25.

Irwin, Ryan. "Imagining Nation, State, and Order in the Mid-Twentieth Century." *Kronos* 37 (November 2011): 12–22.

——. "A Wind of Change? White Redoubt and the Postcolonial Moment, 1960–1963." *Diplomatic History* 33, no. 5 (November 2009): 897–925.

Itote, Waruhiu. Excerpt from *"Mau Mau" General*. In *Africa and the West: A Documentary History*, edited by William H. Worger, Nancy L. Clark, and Edward A. Alpers, 75–82. New York: Oxford University Press, 2010.

Kalu, Kenneth. "The Postcolonial African State and Its Citizens." In *Africa's Big Men: Predatory State-Society Relations in Africa*, edited by Olajumoki Yakob-Haliso, Toyin Falola, and Kenneth Kalu, 21–35. New York: Routledge, 2018.

Kent, John. "British Policy and the Origins of the Cold War." In *Origins of the Cold War: An International History*, edited by Melvyn Leffler and David Painter, 155–66. 2nd ed. New York: Routledge, 2005.

———. "United States Reactions to Empire, Colonialism, and Cold War in Black Africa, 1949–57." *Journal of Imperial and Commonwealth History* 33, no. 2 (May 2005): 195–220.

Kirby, James. "'Our Bantustans are Better than Yours': Botswana, the United States, and Human Rights in the 1970s." *International History Review* 39, no. 5 (2017): 860–84.

Larson, Zeb. "The Sullivan Principles: South Africa, Apartheid, and Globalization." *Diplomatic History* 44, no. 3 (June 2020): 479–503.

Lerner, Mitch. "'A Big Tree of Peace and Justice': The Vice Presidential Travels of Lyndon Johnson." *Diplomatic History* 34, no. 2 (April 2010): 357–93.

———. "Climbing Off the Back Burner: Lyndon Johnson's Soft Power Approach to Africa." *Diplomacy and Statecraft* 22, no. 4 (2011): 578–607.

———. Review of *Kennedy, Johnson, and the Nonaligned World*, by Robert B. Rakove. *H-Diplo Roundtable Review* 14, no. 39 (2013), 8–11, https://issforum.org/roundtables/PDF/Roundtable-XIV-39.pdf.

Little, Douglas. "Cold War and Colonialism in Africa: The United States, France, and the Madagascar Revolt of 1947. " *Pacific Historical Review* 59, no. 4 (November 1990): 527–52.

Louis, Wm. Roger. "Libyan Independence, 1951: The Creation of a Client State." In *The Transfer of Power in Africa: Decolonization, 1940–1960*, edited by Prosser Gifford and Wm. Roger Louis, 159–84. New Haven, CT: Yale University Press, 1988.

Louis, Wm. Roger, and Ronald Robinson. "The United States and the Liquidation of the British Empire in Tropical Africa." In *The Transfer of Power in Africa: Decolonization, 1940–1960*, edited by Prosser Gifford and Wm. Roger Louis, 31–56. New Haven, CT: Yale University Press, 1988.

Lyons, Terrence. "Keeping Africa off the Agenda." In *Lyndon Johnson Confronts the World: American Foreign Policy, 1963–1968*, edited by Warren I. Cohen and Nancy Bernkopf Tucker, 245–78. New York: Cambridge University Press, 1994.

Marable, Manning. "The Pan-Africanism of W. E. B. Du Bois." In *W. E. B. Du Bois on Race and Culture*, edited by Bernard Bell, Emily Grosholz, and James Stewart, 193–218. New York: Routledge, 1996.

McAlister, Melani. "Guess Who's Coming to Dinner: American Missionaries, Racism, and Decolonization in the Congo," *OAH Magazine of History* 26, no. 4 (2012): 33–37.

McMahon, Robert J. "How the Periphery Became the Center: The Cold War, the Third World, and the Transformation in US Strategic Thinking." In *Foreign Policy at the Periphery: The Shifting Margins of US International Relations since*

World War II, edited by Bevan Sewell and Maria Ryan, 19–35. Lexington: University Press of Kentucky, 2017.

———. Introduction to *The Cold War in the Third World*, edited by Robert J. McMahon, 1–10. New York: Oxford University Press, 2013.

McVety, Amanda Kay. "Wealth and Nations: The Origins of International Development Assistance." In *The Development Century: A Global History*, edited by Stephen J. Macekura and Erez Manela, 21–39. Cambridge: Cambridge University Press, 2018.

Meriwether, James H. "The American Negro Leadership Conference on Africa and Its Arden House Conference: Politicizing and Institutionalizing the Relationship with Africa." *Afro-Americans in New York Life and History* 21, no. 2 (July 1997): 39–63.

———. "Reagan and Africa." In *A Companion to Ronald Reagan*, edited by Andrew Johns, 378–92. Malden, MA: John Wiley & Sons, 2015.

———. "'A Torrent Overrunning Everything': Africa and the Eisenhower Administration." In *The Eisenhower Administration, the Third World, and the Globalization of the Cold War*, edited by Andrew L. Johns and Kathryn Statler, 175–96. Lanham, MD: Rowman & Littlefield, 2006.

———. "'Worth a Lot of Negro Votes': Black Voters, Africa, and the 1960 Presidential Campaign." *Journal of American History* 95, no. 3 (December 2008): 737–63.

Michel, Eddie. "The Luster of Chrome: Nixon, Rhodesia, and the Defiance of UN Sanctions." *Diplomatic History* 42, no. 1 (January 2018): 138–61.

Miller, Jamie. "Things Fall Apart: South Africa and the Collapse of the Portuguese Empire, 1973–74." *Cold War History* 12, no. 2 (May 2012): 183–204.

———. "Yes, Minister: Reassessing South Africa's Intervention in the Angolan Civil War, 1975–1976." *Journal of Cold War Studies* 15, no. 3 (Summer 2013): 4–33.

Mir, Farina. "Roundtable: Archives of Decolonization." *American Historical Review* 120, no. 3 (June 2015): 844–51.

Mitchell, Nancy. "Tropes of the Cold War: Jimmy Carter and Rhodesia." *Cold War History* 7, no. 2 (May 2007): 263–83.

Mlambo, Alois S. "'Honoured More in the Breach Than in the Observance': Economic Sanctions on Rhodesia and International Response, 1965 to 1979." *South African Historical Journal* 71, no. 3 (2019): 371–93.

Mondlane, Eduardo. Excerpt from *The Struggle for Mozambique*. In *Africa and the West: A Documentary History*, edited by William H. Worger, Nancy L. Clark, and Edward A. Alpers, 174. New York: Oxford University Press, 2010.

Morgan, Eric J. "Black and White at Center Court: Arthur Ashe and the Confrontation of Apartheid in South Africa." *Diplomatic History* 36, no. 5 (November 2012): 815–41.

———. "The World is Watching: Polaroid and South Africa." *Enterprise and Society* 7, no. 3 (September 2006): 520–49. Naftali, Tim. "Ronald Reagan's Long-Hidden Racist Conversation with Richard Nixon." *Atlantic*, 30 July 2019, www.theatlantic.com/ideas/archive/2019/07/ronald-reagans-racist-conversation-richard-nixon/595102.

Namikas, Lise. Review of *FRUS, 1964–1968*. Vol. 23, *Congo, 1960–1968*, edited by Nina D. Howland, David C. Humphrey, and Harriet D. Schwar. *FRUS* Review No. 33, 19 Oct. 2017. www.tiny.cc/FRUS33.

Noer, Thomas, J. "'Non-Benign Neglect': The United States and Black Africa in the Twentieth Century." In *American Foreign Relations: A Historiographical Review*, edited by Gerald Haines and J. Samuel Walker, 271–92. Westport, CT: Greenwood Press, 1981.

———. "Truman, Eisenhower, and South Africa: The 'Middle Road' and Apartheid." *Journal of Ethnic Studies* 11 (Spring 1983): 75–104.

Nyerere, Julius K. "The African and Democracy." In *Africa and the West: A Documentary History*, edited by William H. Worger, Nancy L. Clark, and Edward A. Alpers, 158–63. New York: Oxford University Press, 2010.

Onslow, Sue. "'We Must Gain Time': South Africa, Rhodesia, and the Kissinger Initiative of 1976." *South African Historical Journal* 56, no. 1 (2006): 123–53.

Pallotti, Arrigo. "Tanzania and the 1976 Anglo-American Initiative for Rhodesia." *Journal of Imperial and Commonwealth History* 45, no. 5 (2017): 800–822.

Parker, Jason C. "Cold War II: The Eisenhower Administration, the Bandung Conference, and the Reperiodization of the Postwar Era." *Diplomatic History* 30, no. 5 (November 2006): 867–92.

———. "'Made-in-America Revolutions'? The 'Black University' and the American Role in the Decolonization of the Black Atlantic." *Journal of American History* 96, no. 3 (December 2009): 727–50.

Parrott, R. Joseph. "*A Luta Continua*: Radical Filmmaking, Pan-African Liberation and Communal Empowerment." *Race and Class* 57, no. 1 (2015): 20–38.

Paterson, Thomas G. "Foreign Aid Under Wrap: The Point Four Program." *Wisconsin Magazine of History* 56, no. 2 (Winter 1972–73): 119–26.

Redkey, Edwin S. "The Meaning of Africa to Afro-Americans, 1890–1914." Paper presented at a conference sponsored by the Council on International Studies, SUNY Buffalo, April 20–23, 1969.

"Rhodesia: Kicking the Gong Around." *Time*, 18 Nov. 1966, http://content.time.com/time/subscriber/article/0,33009,828407,00.html.

Rich, Evelyn Jones. "United States Government Sponsored Higher Educational Programs for Africans: 1957–1970, with Special Attention to the Role of the African-American Institute." PhD diss., Columbia University, 1978.

Rodrigues, Luís Nuno. "About Face: The United States and Portuguese Colonialism in 1961." *E-Journal of Portuguese History* 2, no. 1 (Summer 2004): 1–10.

———. "'For a Better Guinea': Winning Hearts and Minds in Portuguese Guinea." In *Race, Ethnicity, and the Cold War: A Global Perspective*, edited by Philip Muehlenbeck, 118–41. Nashville: Vanderbilt University Press, 2012.

Rosen, Seymour M. *Soviet Training Programs for Africa*. U.S. Department of Health, Education, and Welfare, Bulletin 1963, no. 9. Washington, DC: U.S. Government Printing Office.

Saunders, Chris. "The Angola/Namibia Crisis of 1988 and Its Resolution." In *Cold War in Southern Africa: White Power, Black Liberation*, edited by Sue Onslow, 225–40. New York: Routledge, 2009.

Saunders, Chris, and Sue Onslow. "The Cold War and Southern Africa, 1976–1990." In *The Cambridge History of the Cold War*, Vol. 3, *Endings*, edited by Melvyn P. Leffler and Odd Arne Westad, 222–43. New York: Cambridge University Press, 2010.

Smith, Mansfield Irving. "The East African Airlifts of 1959, 1960, and 1961." PhD diss., Syracuse University, 1966.

Snyder, Sarah. "The Rise of Human Rights during the Johnson Years." In *Beyond the Cold War: Lyndon Johnson and the New Global Challenges of the 1960s*, edited by Francis J. Gavin and Mark Atwood Lawrence, 237–60. New York: Oxford University Press, 2014.

Stephanson, Anders. "Senator John F. Kennedy: Anti-imperialism and Utopian Deficit." *Journal of American Studies* 48, no. 1 (February 2014): 1–24.

Stevens, Simon. "'From the Viewpoint of a Southern Governor': The Carter Administration and Apartheid, 1977–81." *Diplomatic History* 36, no. 5 (November 2012): 843–80.

Stith, Charles. Epilogue to *African Americans in U.S. Foreign Policy: From the Era of Frederick Douglass to the Age of Obama*, 213–23. Edited by Linda Heywood, Allison Blakely, Charles Stith, and Joshua Yesnowitz. Urbana: University of Illinois Press, 2015.

Thomas, Martin C. "Innocent Abroad? Decolonisation and US Engagement with French West Africa, 1945–56." *Journal of Imperial and Commonwealth History* 36, no. 1 (March 2008): 47–73.

Thomson, Alex. "Incomplete Engagement: Reagan's South Africa Policy Revisited." *Journal of Modern African Studies* 33, no. 1 (March 1995): 83–101.

Van Wyk, Anna-Mart. "The USA and Apartheid South Africa's Nuclear Aspirations, 1949–1980." In *Cold War in Southern Africa: White Power, Black Liberation*, edited by Sue Onslow, 55–83. New York: Routledge, 2009.

Watts, Carl P. "African Americans and US Foreign Policy: The American Negro Leadership Conference on Africa and the Rhodesian Crisis." In *The US Public and American Foreign Policy*, edited by Andrew Johnstone and Helen Laville, 107–22. New York: Routledge, 2010.

———. "'Dropping the F-Bomb': President Ford, the Rhodesian Crisis, and the 1976 Election." Paper delivered at the SHAFR Annual Conference, Lexington, KY, 2014.

Weissman, Stephen. "What Really Happened in Congo: The CIA, the Murder of Lumumba, and the Rise of Mobutu." *Foreign Affairs* 93, no. 4 (July/August 2014): 14–24.

Wood, Robert E. "From the Marshall Plan to the Third World." In *Origins of the Cold War: An International History*, edited by Melvyn Leffler and David Painter, 239–50. 2nd ed. New York: Routledge, 2005.

Index

MIX
Paper from
responsible sources
FSC® C008955
FSC
www.fsc.org